The Pi
Operat

The Pick Operating System

Malcom Bull
Northgate Computer Services
London

LONDON   NEW YORK
Chapman and Hall

First published in 1987 by
Chapman and Hall Ltd
11 New Fetter Lane, London EC4P 4EE
Published in the USA by
Chapman and Hall
29 West 35th Street, New York NY 10001

© *1987 M. Bull*

Printed in Great Britain at the
University Press, Cambridge

ISBN 0 412 28040 X (hardback)
ISBN 0 412 28050 7 (paperback)

005.43
Bul

British Library Cataloguing in Publication Data

Bull, Malcolm
    The Pick operating system. — (Chapman
    and Hall computing)
    1. Pick (Computer operating system)
    I. Title
    005.4'3   QA76.7

    ISBN 0-412-28040-X
    ISBN 0-412-28050-7 Pbk

Library of Congress Cataloging in Publication Data

Bull, Malcolm, 1941–
    The Pick Operating System

    Bibliography:p.
    Includes index
    1. Pick (Computer operating system)
    I. Title
QA76.76.063B85   1987   005.4'3   88-41608
ISBN 0-412-28040-X
ISBN 0-412-28050-7 (pbk.)

Contents

Preface

This book is intended for those programmers and analysts who are using or who are about to use the Pick* operating system. It presents all the essential features of Pick in a manner which, it is hoped, is more readable and more accessible than the reference manuals which are provided with the equipment, but it is not intended to replace those reference manuals.

In addition to the purely factual content, the book also summarizes the advantages and the disadvantages of the various aspects of the Pick operating system and contains a number of practical tips and techniques for using the features of the system to advantage. These are based upon my own experience of using the Pick operating system over a number of years.

The book is suitable for those technical managers who are to work with Pick-based application systems, and wish to gain an appreciation of how the facilities offered can be used within their own organization, and of how the operating system will affect the design and use of proposed systems. The material is presented in a general way, to suit the managers, and then in a more technical way to suit the analysts and programmers. For this reason, it is also hoped that instructors might find the book useful in the teaching environment.

An extensive index is provided, and it is hoped that this will be a useful reference tool and that the reader will use this to establish a link between the various aspects of Pick.

Since the Pick operating system was originally developed, it has been implemented on many machines and in many versions. The material in the present book is based upon a composite superset which is essentially that of the larger implementations offered by Microdata – now McDonnell Douglas Information Systems – and is arranged such that it covers the major versions, although, at the moment, there is no single machine which offers all the facilities described here. However, at the time of writing, discussions are in progress between the larger suppliers and other interested parties with a view to standardizing the various systems which they offer.

MALCOLM BULL
Tianjin, People's Republic of China
1986

* Pick is a trademark of Pick Systems, Irvine, California.

Acknowledgements

A number of people have contributed directly or indirectly to the conception and the final presentation of this book. It is impossible to mention them all, but I am particularly indebted to the directors and staff of Northgate Computer Services and Northgate China Computer Services; to Jerry Lees for his encouragement and the resources which he made available, and to Richard Bassett, Tony Schmitt, Balbir Thind and Mark Wheeler, for their help and suggestions.

I should also like to thank Peter Bowen and Simon Buck of Northgate-Haven Training for their valuable comments and suggestions, and Alan Pritchard of ALLM Books for information supplied.

Credit is also due to the various students and teachers, be they British, Arabic or Chinese, who, over the years, have helped me develop the contents of the lecture material upon which the present book is based.

Finally, I should like to thank Paul Anstee for his tireless reading, re-reading and proof-reading of the text in its various manifestations.

If, after all this support, there are any omissions or any errors remaining in the book, then the responsibility and blame for these can only be laid at my own door.

M.B.

1
The Pick operating system – overview

How long is it since you heard about the Pick operating system? Two years? Possibly five years?

It was back in the mid 1960s when Richard – Dick – Pick and his colleagues conceived a new, end-user oriented, operating system, one in which there was less need for the users to concern themselves with the physical details and constraints of a real computer. The new operating system would let the users do what they wanted to do, and not only what the machine made them do. Indeed, the first ideas evolved *in vacuo* without any machine at all. After the concepts had been developed, the system was implemented on an IBM System/360 under the name Generalized Information Retrieval Language System – GIRLS – and was later delivered to the US Army.

In 1971 Dick Pick signed an agreement with the Microdata Corporation to implement his system on their model 800 computer which, until that time, had been marketed without an operating system. The Microdata version was enhanced to include a Data/Basic compiler, and by the time that Microdata launched their Reality computer in 1974, the Pick operating system had most of the features which we know today.

When Dick Pick left Microdata, in order to establish Pick and Associates, he began to produce a whole range of new implementations of the operating system on other machines. In 1982 Pick and Associates changed their name to Pick Systems, although the operating system still remained essentially as it had been in 1965. The ideas behind Pick were revolutionary in 1965, but newer computers and newer operating systems had overtaken it in certain areas – notably graphics and communications.

The year 1984 saw the announcement of the Open Architecture version of the operating system with enhancements which would remove many of the restrictions of earlier versions and bring Pick up to date and into the 1990s.

So let us take a look at Pick.

In this first chapter we shall introduce the general features of the Pick operating system, including:

(a) The fundamental file-oriented nature of the operating system.
(b) The database retrieval language which is used to make inquiries about the data held on your files.
(c) The languages available for you to write your own programs.
(d) The terminal control language – TCL – the set of primitive commands which are used to control the computer.
(e) The system software – the standard programs and utilities, such as the Editor and the Runoff word-processing features.
(f) The security aspects which enable you to restrict or authorize access to your data.

Subsequent chapters will look more closely at these features of the Pick operating system, and discuss them both in a general manner and also with specific reference to the interesting or attractive aspects.

1.1 THE LOGICAL STRUCTURE

The Pick operating system is available on a wide range of equipment from a wide range of manufacturers. Some systems support only a few users, whilst others will handle several hundred terminals. Whatever its size, every Pick system is made up of the same basic components, as shown in Fig. 1.1.

(a) The central processor unit and the operating system.
(b) The memory – this holds all the data and programs which are being processed by the users at any moment.
(c) The user terminals – Pick is designed to be used from a VDU keyboard terminal. The actual number of terminals which may be used depends upon the configuration. Pick will support the familiar keyboard terminals, including VDU and printers, but many features of the operating system are designed specifically for VDU terminals and screen displays.
(d) The printer – this may be a simple serial printer or a full-size line printer. A part of the operating system, known as the *spooler*, enables two or more users to produce printed reports at the same time.
(e) The off-line storage – this may be a standard reel-to-reel magnetic-tape deck, a streamer or a diskette, and is used to pass data from one system to another and to produce back-up copies of the system and its files for security purposes.
(f) The fixed disk which holds all the programs and the data files, including those created and processed by the individual users and those used by the operating system. Disk storage space is shared by all users of the system, and the number of disks and the size of the

available disk space depends upon the configuration of the equipment. The larger installations may have several thousand megabytes of storage at their disposal. We shall see how the *virtual memory* feature of Pick means that this disk space can also be regarded as an extension of the memory space.

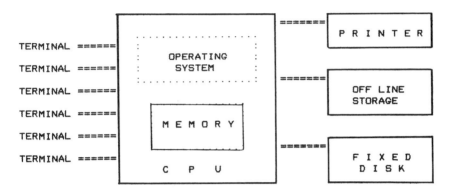

Figure 1.1

Based around this fundamental configuration, it is perfectly feasible to attach analog equipment and devices such as bar-code readers and encoders, plotters and telex machines. Such devices are linked to Pick via a terminal or a printer channel.

Networking between Pick systems is also possible with products such as those described in Section 1.13 below.

1.2 FILE MANAGEMENT

The Pick system is designed for ease of storage, maintenance and retrieval of data files, and it is essentially a file-oriented system. Indeed, many sales brochures for equipment which support the operating system use phrases such as 'a data management system' or 'a business system', to indicate this important end-user orientation of the system.

Each file is identified by name, and you will identify and access a record by specifying the name of the file on which it can be found and the record key which identifies the record within that file. This organization is the same, whether the item of information is a Basic program or a simple data record.

You will identify the individual fields by their sequential position within the record. In this manner, the field may be accessed by either of the programming languages, Basic or Proc, by the system utilities, or by Access, the database retrieval language.

Other fundamental principles of Pick eliminate many of the more troublesome areas for the systems analyst:

(a) A file may hold as many records as you need. Once you have established your file, you may add any number of new records to the file without causing any overflow problems. The operating system will automatically tack on disk space to your file in order to accommodate the new records.

  This may eventually result in slow access times, but the operating system has facilities for correcting this by allowing you to re-allocate the shape and size of your files at any time.

(b) A record may have as many fields as you need. The record layout may be changed at any time, adding new fields, changing fields and deleting old fields.

(c) A record field may be as long as you need. Each field is terminated by a field separator, thus allowing null fields or fields of up to 32 000 characters!

We shall look at file structure in Chapter 2.

1.3   ACCESS – DATABASE RETRIEVAL LANGUAGE

A powerful inquiry language is available to allow you to interrogate your files simply by typing sentences such as:

```
SORT NAME AGE ADDRESS OF PERSONNEL BY START-DATE

LIST NAME BALANCE OF ACCOUNTS '1000' '2000'

LIST INVOICES WITH NAME = "JOHN BROWN & CO" LPTR

LIST PAYROLL WITH DEPARTMENT "PACKING" AND AGE
    GREATER THAN "60"

SORT STOCK DESCRIPTION STOCK PRICE TOTAL VALUE

SORT EMPLOYEES BY DEPT NAME AGE BREAK-ON DEPT
```

This means that, with absolutely no programming whatsoever, you can produce displayed or printed reports of the data on your files, allowing you to:

(a) Indicate which fields you want to display – as in the first example where we ask for the NAME, AGE and ADDRESS of the personnel to be shown on the report.

(b) Specify any order in which the report is to be sorted – the first example sorts the report into ascending order of starting date.

(c) Choose specific items from the file – the second example includes account 1000 and account 2000 only.

(d) Select specific records only – the third example processes only the invoices relating to Messrs John Brown & Company.

(e) Display the report on the terminal screen or specify LPTR to print the report on the printer, as in the third example.

(f) Specify several selection criteria – the fourth example selects only those personnel records relating to employees who work in the Packing Department and who are over 60 years old.

(g) Produce sub-totals and grand totals – the fifth example displays and accumulates the value of all the items on the stock records file.

(h) Sort the report into ascending or descending order using a number of key fields.

(i) Make control breaks in the report – the last example produces a listing of the employee details, sorted by department, and produces a control break on the change of department.

Throughout this book, we shall use the name Access for the database retrieval language, although it may be known by other names such as Query, English or Recall on your implementation.

The format of the report is controlled by Access dictionary definitions, for data elements such as NAME, AGE and START-DATE, which you – as analyst – will establish. These allow you to specify how the data will appear on the printed report: any identifying text heading; the width of the printed field; whether it is to be printed left- or right-justified; any arithmetic or re-formatting which is to be performed on the raw data.

The Access language makes an excellent tool for non-specialist staff, such as sales clerks, stock-control staff, sales personnel and others, enabling them to interrogate the files with ease. In addition to its use for producing *ad hoc* reports and inquiries, Access also reduces the work of the programmer who will find that program-generated reports are rarely necessary, and efficient systems can be easily designed to incorporate extensive Access reporting and inquiry facilities.

We shall look at Access in Chapter 4.

1.4   TCL – TERMINAL CONTROL LANGUAGE

The Pick operating system is designed to be used from keyboard terminals, and TCL, the terminal control language, is the fundamental operating medium. By means of the commands which you type in at your terminal keyboard, TCL offers extensive facilities to:

(a) Create, copy and delete files and records.
(b) Display and print the contents of files and records.
(c) Inspect any area of virtual memory.
(d) Perform magnetic-tape operations: read and display the contents of a magnetic tape, rewind and manipulate the tape, read or write labels.
(e) Create, maintain and compile a Basic program.
(f) Execute a standard Basic program or a user-written Basic program.
(g) Create and maintain a Proc – a procedure written in the Pick Proc language.
(h) Invoke a standard utility Proc or a user-written Proc.
(i) Interrogate the system status, current activities, available file space, the time, the date and so on.
(j) Pass messages to other users.
(k) Perform simple decimal and hexadecimal arithmetic.

Furthermore, almost all of these facilities can be invoked by programmers within their Basic or Proc programs.

Three of the standard TCL commands are EDIT, BASIC and RUN. To illustrate the use of the TCL, let us see how these commands are used in conjunction with the file organization mentioned above.

The Pick Editor will allow you to create, change or delete a record, and is invoked by typing in a command of the form:

`EDIT MYPROGS PAY1`

This command will allow you to create and change the program which is held on the file MYPROGS with the name PAY1. To compile this program we should use the command:

`BASIC MYPROGS PAY1`

and to execute the program we should use the command:

`RUN MYPROGS PAY1`

The 'vocabulary' of available commands is held on a master dictionary for each account, and can be extended, if required, by adding your own commands. This is particularly convenient in situations where non-specialist users are required to perform a long or complex sequence of tasks, and they may then achieve this by typing in a simple TCL-like command which you have constructed for them.

On the other hand, you may remove any of the standard vocabulary from the master dictionary, if you feel that the powerful ones – like the Editor – are likely to be mis-used.

We shall look at TCL in Chapter 5.

1.5 BASIC PROGRAMMING LANGUAGE

Access allows you to produce reports and analyses based upon the data which are held on your files, but it does not allow you to create or change information which is held on those files. Such data processing is done by traditional programming means.

An extended version of the Dartmouth Basic language is offered in a form which makes it suitable for processing Pick file data – opening files, reading or writing records according to the record key, extracting or replacing data fields within the record, converting the format of the data fields and deleting records. Most of the other features of the language will be completely familiar to anyone who has used Basic on other computers.

We shall look at the Basic language in Chapter 6.

1.6 PROC – PROCEDURAL LANGUAGE

The Proc language was initially designed to allow you to store a single command or a sequence of several TCL or Access commands, and invoke these by means of a single keyword when required. For example, if you wished to issue the following Access sentence frequently:

```
LIST PAYROLL WITH DEPARTMENT "PACKING" AND AGE
    GREATER THAN "60"
```

then Pick will allow you to save this sentence under any name you choose – let us say MYPROC – and then next time you need to produce this report, you will simply type in

```
MYPROC
```

When you save such a sentence or a sequence of sentences, it is known as a Proc – a procedure – in much the same way as a sequence of Basic statements is called a program.

Since its conception, Proc has extended into a more flexible programming language offering facilities for program control, data input, data output, calculation and, on some implementations, file handling. So, with a little modification, your original Proc could produce a report for any department or for any age limit by entering the required parameters:

```
MYPROC PACKING 60
```

to produce the above report, or

```
MYPROC WAGES 25
```

to report on all employees of the wages department aged more than 25.

We shall look at the Proc language in Chapter 7.

1.7   RUNOFF – WORD-PROCESSING PACKAGE

A word-processing package called Runoff is standard on Pick, and enables you to assemble, edit and correct the text for documents, letters or specifications. When you print these documents, Runoff offers such features as line formatting, page numbering, page headings, page footings, underlining, bold printing, chapter and section heading and numbering. The present book was prepared with the help of Runoff.

Many systems also support packages such as Jet, Superjet and Text-pro, which offer more user-friendly word-processing facilities than Runoff.

We shall look at Runoff and Jet in Chapter 8.

1.8   DATA AND SYSTEM SECURITY

Although, in the simplest situation each user only has access to his/her own data files, there are occasions when one user needs to access files which belong to another user. For example, a *sales analysis* program used by the Sales Department may need to access the names of salesmen held on the Personnel file which belongs to the Payroll Department. This inter-user access can be prohibited or permitted by the owner of the file, and, if permitted, the owner may restrict the others' access to:

(a) Permit READ from the file and permit WRITE to the file.
(b) Permit READ from the file and prohibit WRITE to the file – this would probably be the sort of security which you would need in this example.
(c) Permit WRITE to the file and prohibit READ from the file.
(d) Prohibit READ from the file and prohibit WRITE to the file.

Such security is available by using a set of lock codes which you can place on any or all of your files.

The operating system can support many simultaneous users, and these users may use the same programs and data files with no contention problems. Each user is serviced on a first come, first served basis. But if two or more users are attempting to change the same record at the same time, then there may be problems. For example, let us suppose that we have written an airline reservation system and at this very moment there are passengers at three different booking-offices inquiring about the one remaining seat on flight ABC123 to New York. If the programmer has not taken due care, it is possible for all three passengers to have a confirmed reservation for that one seat! The simple Pick solution of locking is available to prohibit this situation. With locking, the very first inquiry will lock the booking record, and the other inquiries will have to wait until the first passenger has accepted or rejected the booking.

Another security feature is afforded by the fact that all files are updated immediately. This means that:

(a) The data on the files are always up to date.
(b) There is minimal loss of data in the event of a mechanical failure.

We shall look at the security aspects of Pick in Chapter 9.

1.9   VIRTUAL MEMORY

Earlier, we saw that the fixed disks and the memory are two important components of any Pick system. All the users' data and programs – and parts of the operating system – are stored on fixed disks. All information is brought into memory for processing, be it a program which you are executing or a data record which you are updating.

If you need to process a large program, then the operating system will load as much as possible into memory, and then keep swapping further parts of your program in and out – between disk and memory – as you need them. This means, irrespective of the size of the memory of the machine, the Pick operating system gives you as much space as you need for your programs and data, allowing you to utilize the entire disk storage space as if it were true memory. The system will automatically handle job-scheduling and the management and movement of your data between memory and disk backing storage.

Most of these processes are performed by software, but on some implementations, those parts of the operating system which are used frequently – such as the memory-to-disk data handler, the Basic compiler and the Access processor – are held on separate chips or separate boards within the Pick processor. Such items of firmware are much faster than would be the equivalent object program.

We look at some of the Pick system features in Chapter 12.

1.10   THE SPOOLER

The user terminal is important for both the input and the output of information: you establish your identity by typing in your log-on code; you initiate your processing by typing your instructions; all your output – such as an Access report or the results of your Basic program – can be displayed on the terminal screen.

Pick has very simple facilities to direct any output to the printer, but with only one printer and with several users at any one time – and each one may be producing a printed report – there could be considerable confusion. But all output to the printer is handled by the *spooler* to avoid such confusion. As each line of a user's report is sent to the *printer* it is intercepted by the spooler and placed in a queue on disk until the report is completed. When the report has been completed, the spooler sends the report to the printer when the printer is next free.

The ordinary user works quite unaware of the work performed by the spooler. To such users, it appears that their jobs are sent straight to the printer and appear there in due course.

For more sophisticated users, a comprehensive set of commands is available to allow them to perform operations on the reports which are held by the spooler, enabling them to change the number of copies of a report, re-route reports to alternative output devices, delete reports, hold reports for overnight printing, change the stationery or check the form-alignment.

We shall look at the spooler in Chapter 10.

1.11   USER ACCOUNTS AND LOGGING

In order to use the Pick operating system, users will log on to an account. An account is a working environment based upon a set of files which are available to users of that account. There may be any number of accounts. A small installation may have only one or two accounts; a large company may have one account for each project and for each department. For example, there may be a PERSONNEL account to process the information relating to the work force, their names, addresses and their rates of pay. There may be a SALES account whose users will process the information relating to customers, invoices and sales figures.

You may log on to – and use – any account from any terminal, and there may be any number of people using an account at any time. To log on to the computer, you will type in the account name – PERSONNEL or SALES – to tell the operating system which account you want to use, and you may also have to type in a password if the owner of the account demands it.

A history file is automatically maintained to record the usage of the system. Whenever you log on to the PERSONNEL account, for example, then the operating system will record the date and time when you logged on. When you log off, the system will also record how long you were logged on, how much computer time you used and how much disk activity your processing demanded. This logging information can be used as a basis for departmental charging for computer time.

Obviously, there are security implications in what we have said here, and in the later chapters we shall see how these are handled and overcome.

We shall look at the concept of Pick accounts in Chapter 3.

1.12 WHICH HARDWARE?

You should remember that the various implementations of the Pick operating system on an increasing range of hardware, and their subsequent updates, differ slightly in the extent and versatility of the features mentioned above – chiefly in what their TCL, Proc and spoolers offer.

The Pick operating system is available on a number of machines, from microcomputers and minicomputers through to mainframe computers, and currently include:

Adds Mentor	Datamedia	Prime
Altos	Fujitsu	Sabre
CIE Systems	General Automation	SMI
Clan	IBM	Sperry
Climax	In Informatique	TDI Pinnacle
Columbia	McDonnell Douglas	Ultimate
Cosmos	Nixdorf	Wicat
Crystal	Pertec	Zebra

The Revelation software offers many of the features of Pick and will run within other standard operating systems.

Because of this diversity of equipment and the range of user-terminals which are available, the present book does not discuss hardware. Nor shall we discuss the detail of using the hardware – which switch to press, which knob to turn and so on. Full details of these topics are given in the user manuals for the specific equipment and the implementation which you are using.

1.13 WHICH SOFTWARE?

To keep their product up to date and to make their Pick systems attractive to the users, the various manufacturers and suppliers provide a wide range of software, packages, programs and other utilities. Typical of these are:

(a) Viewdata systems, such as Viewbase.
(b) Financial and business packages, such as Compu-Sheet, Supercalc and Wizard.
(c) Graphics software, such as Superplot, Supergraph and UltiPlot.

(d) Fourth-generation languages, program generators and system development software, such as System Builder, Easy Screen and A*L*L – the Application Language Liberator – a version of the PRO IV fourth-generation language, is available on McDonnell Douglas and other versions of Pick.
(e) Extended precision and floating-point arithmetic software.
(f) Screen painters.
(g) Proc and Basic program-development utilities.
(h) Communications software, such as Comsys, Picknet and UltiNet.
(i) Word-processing software, such as Jet, Superjet, Textpro and UltiWord.

The discussion of such proprietary software is outside the scope of this book, but your Pick user-group and application software directories offer an excellent way of interchanging ideas and news about the latest developments in this area.

The material concerning the Pick operating system and the software which is presented in the present book is based upon a composite superset – essentially that of the larger McDonnell Douglas implementations – and is arranged such that it covers the major versions, although, at the moment, there is no single implementation which offers all the facilities described here. At the time of writing, discussions are in progress between the larger suppliers and other interested parties with a view to standardizing the various systems which they offer.

1.14   WHY CHOOSE PICK?

We can summarize the advantages of Pick as follows:

- It offers easy conversational computing via a VDU keyboard terminal.
- It allows a large number of users to work simultaneously. This is a standard feature of Pick and does not demand any additional networking facilities.
- It offers automatic logging of the usage made of the system.
- It can be used for small or very large application systems.
- It allows the user to have any number of files.
- It relieves the systems analyst of file-size problems – you may have any number of records on your files.
- It relieves the systems analyst of record-layout problems – you may have any number of fields on your records, and you can add to these at any time.
- It relieves the systems analyst of record-size problems – the record fields may be of any length.
- It allows you to impose security locks on your files.

- It has a ready-made database retrieval language to produce reports and analyses – you do not have to write programs either for a standard report or for an *ad hoc* inquiry.
- It offers the Basic programming language for bespoke user programs.
- All files are updated immediately – the user does not have to wait until the end of the day's business to learn the latest situation.
- It is portable between the various implementations, such that an application developed on one Pick system can be implemented on another Pick system with few – if any – modifications.
- It offers a comprehensive command language for the user.
- You may augment this command language with your own vocabulary, or you may remove any elements of the command language to restrict the activities which your users may perform.
- The commands for any sequence of operations can be established and saved for use later.
- The virtual memory feature removes program-size restrictions.

Pick offers the ideal business and data management system. One which is flexible enough to adapt to the high-level needs of the end-user, and one which is detailed enough to satisfy the technical needs of the systems programmer and the applications programmer.

2
Storage and files

All Pick files – whether they contain data records, Basic programs, Runoff text or Procs – are held on disk storage. The disk – or disks – are permanently mounted, and the actual physical location of any file is allocated by the operating system. At any moment, it is almost impossible to say which disk holds any particular file. Indeed, the data may be spread out over several disks, and the files will almost certainly be moved around each time you dump a copy of the system to magnetic tape and then restore and re-organize the disks from this copy. This is no disadvantage, since you identify each file by name, and your *master dictionary* directs you via this name to the true physical disk location of your data.

So let us see how this physical and logical organization works in practice.

2.1 DISK STORAGE

The operating system accesses the physical disk storage in units called frames. Each frame is 512 bytes in size, of which 500 bytes are reserved for storage of data, and the remaining 12 bytes are reserved for control information, showing the logical linkage between the frames. On Open Architecture Pick, the frame is 1048 bytes of which 1000 bytes are available for user data, and on other implementations it is 2048 bytes of which 2000 bytes are available for user data.

Each frame is identified by its unique FID, the frame identifier. This is a sequential number – starting at 0 and going up to the maximum FID for your particular system – and shows the position of that frame on disk.

For most practical purposes, the end-user may remain ignorant of the physical nature and structure of his or her data.

2.2 FILE STRUCTURE

The file organization is one of the idiosyncratic features of the Pick operating system. Is is also one of the features which make Pick attractive to analysts and programmers alike.

When we look at the subject of file layout, we shall see that a file comprises one or more linked frames of storage space. Within this file space, the records are held one behind the other *in the sequence in which they were originally added to the file.*

As the file expands, whether by an increase in the size of the records or by an increase in the number of records, the operating system will automatically link in more frames at the end of the file to accommodate the records.

2.3 ACCOUNTS

A Pick account is a collection of files which are available to users of that account. For example, there may be a *personnel* account to hold and to process the information relating to the work force, their names and addresses, their rates of pay and so on. There may also be a *sales* account whose users will process the information relating to customers, invoices, sales figures and so on.

You may log on to – and use – any account from any terminal, and there may be any number of people using an account at any time. In order to be able to log on to an account, a user must enter a valid account name – PERSONNEL or SALES – and possibly a password for that account. Details of the accounts on your system are held on a file called *SYSTEM*, and accounts may be added to your system or deleted as required.

2.4 *SYSTEM*; MD; DICT; DATA-FILE LINKAGE

The *file hierarchy* diagram shown in Fig. 2.1 is of fundamental importance in understanding the logical structure of the Pick system. Each box represents a *file* and each dotted line represents the pointer-linkage by which a record on one file enables us to find the location of a file lower down the diagram.

Let us have a look at the various components.

The file called *SYSTEM* is the most important file on any Pick system, and holds one record for every account on the system. The information in this record points to the disk location of the *master dictionary* for that account. The master dictionary is known variously as M/DICT and MD, and is a file containing definitions relating to all the files which you have created on that account, and definitions and pointers relating to all the standard system files. The MD also holds:

(a) Definitions for all the standard TCL verbs.
(b) Definitions for all the standard Access verbs and connectives.
(c) Catalogued program pointers for all the standard system programs.

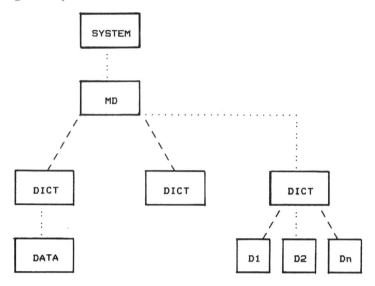

Figure 2.1

(d) Catalogued program pointers for all those programs which you have created and catalogued.
(e) Pointers to all standard Procs.
(f) Pointers to all the Procs which you have created.

On the MD there is a record relating to each data file, and this points to the dictionary section of that file, DICT, which holds the dictionary definitions which will allow you to use the Access language to interpret your data records.

In addition to the Access definitions, the DICT of the file also contains a record called the *data-level identifier* which points to the data section of that file. According to the particular implementation which you are using there may be only one data-level identifier and one data section – as shown by the file on the left of the diagram – or there may be several different data-level identifiers on the DICT of the file, each referring to one of a number of files which share the same dictionary – as shown by the file on the right of the diagram. This latter structure allows several data files – sometimes called sub-files – to share a common dictionary, and is a very powerful Pick feature. It will be used in situations where several files – for example, four separate data files *NORTH.SALES*, *SOUTH.SALES*, *EAST.SALES* and *WEST.SALES* – hold the sales figures for our four regions and have the same record format. These can, therefore, use the same Access dictionary definitions.

The data-level identifier may have the same name as the file to which it refers, or on those implementations which only allow one data section, the data-level identifier may have the item-id DL/ID.

The data section of the file contains the true data records – our sales data, the personnel records or the invoice information. If the file has no data section – as with the file in the centre of the diagram – then the data-level identifier on the DICT section points back to the DICT section. This probably means that you do not want to use Access with the data which are held on this file. It may be a file used for holding programs or Runoff documents, for example.

The file definition records which relate to other files contain the following information about the file:

(a) The *base FID* = the frame identifier of the first frame in the file.
(b) The *MOD* = the modulo of the file.
(c) The *SEP* = the separation of the file; we shall see more about MOD and SEP in Section 2.6.
(d) The *L/RET* security = the lock code to retrieve, or read from, the file; we shall see more about lock codes in Section 3.2.
(e) The *L/UPD* security = the lock code to update, or write to, the file.

Let us look at this with some (hypothetical) numbers in it, as in Fig. 2.2. If you look through the records on the *SYSTEM* file for the one which points to your account *SALES*, you will find that it points to the MD for the *SALES* account, like this:

```
record key:  SALES
    field 1:  D        ⇐ this defines a DICT or a data section
    field 2:  12007    ⇐ this is the base FID for the MD
    field 3:  15       ⇐ this is the MOD for the MD
    field 4:  3        ⇐ this is the SEP for the MD
```

telling us the *MOD*, the *SEP* and the base FID. This means that the SALES MD file starts at frame 12007, and occupies the next 45 (= 15 × 3) frames, that is, frames 12007–12051, inclusive.

Now we know that the *SALES* account has two files, *INVOICE* and *MYPROG*. If you look at the record on the MD which identifies the *INVOICE* file, we will find that it points to the DICT section of *INVOICE*:

```
record key:  INVOICE
    field 1:  D
    field 2:  28123
    field 3:  1
    field 4:  1
```

telling us that this starts at frame 28123, and occupies just one frame.

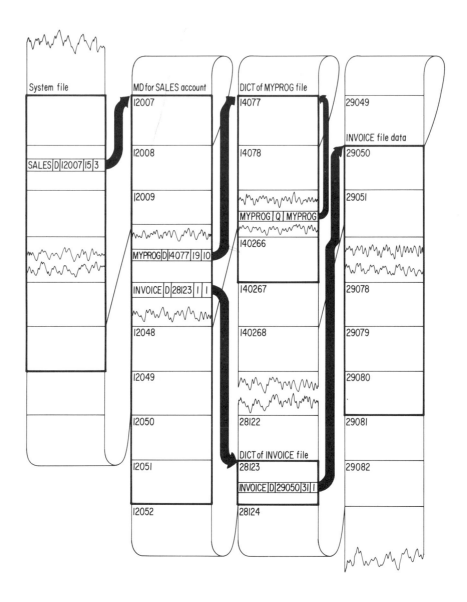

System file

MD for SALES account

DICT of MYPROG file

INVOICE file data

SALES D 12007 15 3

12007

12008

12009

MYPROG D 4077 19 10

INVOICE D 28123 1 1

12048

12049

12050

12051

12052

14077

14078

MYPROG Q MYPROG

140266

140267

140268

28122

DICT of INVOICE file

28123

INVOICE D 29050 31 1

28124

29049

29050

29051

29078

29079

29080

29081

29082

Figure 2.2

Finally, the data-level identifier record on the DICT section of the *INVOICE* file points to the actual invoice data:

        record key: dl/id
            field 1:   D
            field 2:   29050
            field 3:   31
            field 4:   1

telling you that the data on your *INVOICE* file occupies frames 29050–29080, inclusive.

If you do the same for the file *MYPROG*, then you will find that the *MYPROG* record on the MD:

        record key: MYPROG
            field 1:   D
            field 2:   14077
            field 3:   19
            field 4:   10

tells us that the DICT section of *MYPROG* occupies frames 14077–14266, inclusive.

If you look at the data-level identifier record on the DICT section on the *MYPROG* file, then you will see that this points to the same frame (14077) or it may simply be a pointer back to itself:

        record key: DL/ID   or   MYPROG
            field 1:   D   Q
            field 2:   14077   MYPROG
            field 3:   19
            field 4:   10

telling us that this is the same as the DICT.

Now let us look at Fig. 2.3. This shows a system with two accounts – *SALES* and *WAGES*. We have just given them two files each for the sake of simplicity. There are a couple of more esoteric points which you can appreciate from these diagrams:

(a) An account is any file for which there is a pointer on the *system* file.
(b) A master dictionary is any file for which there is a pointer on the *system* file. We shall utilize this fact in Section 3.7.1, when we see how to create empty accounts.
(c) An account and its master dictionary are synonymous.
(d) A file always has a pointer on the master dictionary of the account to which it belongs.

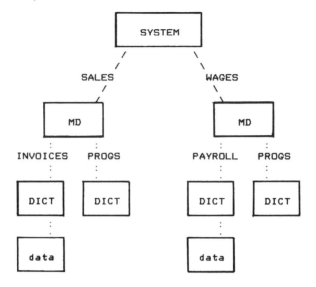

Figure 2.3

(e) A file called *PROGS* held on the *SALES* account is quite separate from a file called *PROGS* held on the *WAGES* account.

We leave you to justify these comments for yourself.

2.5 FILE; ITEM; ITEM-ID; DATA FIELDS

The logical storage is accessed in terms of records on files.

(a) A file is a collection of records holding data of a similar nature. The records on the *INVOICE* file would hold information about invoices, the records on the *PERSONNEL* file would hold information about the staff and personnel, and so on. This is identical to the standard use of the term *file* within data processing.
(b) *Item* is the Pick terminology for *record*.
(c) *Item-id* is the Pick terminology for *record key*.
(d) *Attribute* is the Pick terminology for *field*.
(e) Each item may comprise one or more attributes separated by *attribute marks*.
(f) Each attribute may comprise one or more *values* separated by *value marks*.

(g) Each value may comprise one or more *secondary values* separated by *secondary-value marks*.

(h) Attributes, values and secondary values are of variable length, each being terminated by the appropriate field separator.

(i) The various fields – attributes, values and secondary values – are identified by their sequential position within the item.

(j) Data fields – attributes, values and secondary values – are held in variable-length format, each taking up as much space as necessary.

(k) Null (empty) fields are represented only by the associated (following) field separator – attribute mark, value mark or secondary-value mark.

To illustrate these points, let us suppose that we have a file which holds details of the salesmen working for the company, and the number of orders which each salesman has taken. The record for salesman number *1283, John Smith*, might look like this:

```
1283^J. SMITH^45082
```

showing that he took 45 082 orders during the year. The record contains the record key – 1283 – and two data fields – J. SMITH and 45082 – separated by the attribute mark ^.

However, we may wish to break down the sales figures, showing how many orders were from the north of his region and how many from the south. So we could re-organize the second data field:

```
1283^J. SMITH^26615]18467
```

arranging the sales figures as two values, showing that he took 26 615 orders from the north of the region and 18 467 orders from the south. The individual values are separated by the value mark].

We may wish to re-organize the sales figures further, to show the sales for each quarter of the year:

```
1283^J. SMITH^5022\5300\8203\8090]
    4530\4504\4903\4030
```

showing that he took 5022 orders in the north in the first quarter, 5300 in the north in the second quarter, 8203 in the north in the third quarter, 8090 in the north in the fourth quarter, 4530 in the south in the first quarter, 4504 in the south in the second quarter, and so on. Within each value, the various secondary values are separated by the secondary-value mark \.

Data investigation and record layout is as important in Pick as in any other operating system, and the structure of the data records would normally be decided by the analyst when the system was designed. The sort of re-organization which we have considered here can, however, be

implemented at any time, provided that the necessary changes are made
to the Basic programs and Access dictionary definitions which process
the file.

From now on we shall use the terms item, item-id and attribute
instead of record, record key and field.

2.6 FILE LAYOUT

When you create a file, you specify the size of the space to be allocated
for the DICT section, and, if there's going to be one, for the data section
of the file.

As we saw in the earlier diagrams, for most purposes, the DICT and
data section are separate parts of the file; the DICT is found by means of
information contained on the MD entry for the file; the data section is
found by means of information contained in the data-level identifier
item on the DICT section of the file.

The way in which items are held on a file is the same whether the
items are on the DICT section or on the data section.

To illustrate how the items are held on a file, let us consider the case of
a simple file which has been created such that it occupies a single frame
of disk space.

When first created, the frame (the primary file space) is empty:

```
. . . . . . . . . . . . . . . . . . . . . . . . . . . . . . . . . . . . . . . . . . . . . . . . . . . . . . .
 : ~???????????????????????????????????????????????????????????:
 : ~???????????????????????????????????????????????????????????:
```

with only the *end-of-data* indicator ~ set in the first character position to
indicate the end of the physical data in that frame.

As we start adding items to the file, they are placed in this primary
area in the order in which they are added. Let us first add an item with
item-id 6:

```
. . . . . . . . . . . . . . . . . . . . . . . . . . . . . . . . . . . . . . . . . . . . . . . . . . . . . . .
 :  6  : ~????????????????????????????????????????????????????:
 : . . . . : ~????????????????????????????????????????????????????:
```

In these diagrams, only the item-ids will be shown inside a box representing the item – a larger box for a longer item. Unused space in the
frame is shown by question marks, and the end-of-data indicator is
represented by the character ~.

Adding an item with item-id 11, we get:

```
. . . . . . . . . . . . . . . . . . . . . . . . . . . . . . . . . . . . . . . . . . . . . . . .
:  6  :  11   : ~???????????????????????????????????????????????:
:. . . .:. . . . . : ~???????????????????????????????????????????????:
```

and adding an item with item-id UK gives us:

```
. . . . . . . . . . . . . . . . . . . . . . . . . . . . . . . . . . . . . . . . . . . . . . . .
:  6  :  11   :  UK   : ~???????????????????????????????????????????:
:. . . .:. . . . . :. . . . . : ~???????????????????????????????????????????:
```

Adding a further item with item-id 4 gives us

```
. . . . . . . . . . . . . . . . . . . . . . . . . . . . . . . . . . . . . . . . . . . . . . . .
:  6  :  11   :  UK   :  4 :~???????????????????????????????????????:
:. . . .:. . . . . :. . . . . :. . . . : ~???????????????????????????????????:
```

and so on.

If we add another item with the same item-id, say item UK, then this will overwrite the previous item UK. This implies, quite correctly, that all item-ids are unique and no two items on a file may have the same item-id.

```
. . . . . . . . . . . . . . . . . . . . . . . . . . . . . . . . . . . . . . . . . . . . . . . .
:  6  :  11   :  UK      :  4 :~???????????????????????????????????:
:. . . .:. . . . . :. . . . . . . . . . :. . . . : ~???????????????????????????????:
```

Adding further items, we get:

```
. . . . . . . . . . . . . . . . . . . . . . . . . . . . . . . . . . . . . . . . . . . . . . . .
:  6  :  11   :  UK      :  4 :  54        :  GB      :  3     :~??????:
:. . . .:. . . . . :. . . . . . . . . . :. . . . :. . . . . . . . . :. . . . . . . . :. . . . . . . :~??????:
```

If we update an item, say item 4, and this becomes larger, then all the trailing items are moved towards the end of the frame:

```
. . . . . . . . . . . . . . . . . . . . . . . . . . . . . . . . . . . . . . . . . . . . . . . .
:  6  :  11   :  UK      :  4        :  54      :  GB      :  3     :~?:
:. . . .:. . . . . :. . . . . . . . . . :. . . . . . . . . :. . . . . . . . :. . . . . . . . :. . . . . . . :~?:
```

On some Pick implementations, an updated item is retained *in situ*, and on others an updated item is placed at the end of the group. So item 4 may have been updated like this:

```
. . . . . . . . . . . . . . . . . . . . . . . . . . . . . . . . . . . . . . . . . . . . . . .
 :  6  :  11  :  UK      :  54         :  GB      :  3      :  4           :~?:
 :. . .:. . . . .:. . . . . . . .:. . . . . . . . .:. . . . . . . . . .:. . . . . . . . . .:. . . . . :~?:
```

If we update an item, say item UK, and this becomes smaller, then all the trailing items are moved towards the front of the frame:

```
. . . . . . . . . . . . . . . . . . . . . . . . . . . . . . . . . . . . . . . . . . . . . . .
 :  6  :  11  :  UK  :  4        :  54        :  GB      :  3      :~?????:
 :. . .:. . . . .:. . . . .:. . . . . .:. . . . . . . .:. . . . . . . .:. . . . . . . :~?????:
```

If we delete an item, say item 54, then we get:

```
. . . . . . . . . . . . . . . . . . . . . . . . . . . . . . . . . . . . . . . . . . .
 :  6  :  11  :  UK  :  4          :  GB      :  3      :~??????????????:
 :. . .:. . . . .:. . . . .:. . . . . . . . .:. . . . . . . . .:. . . . . :~??????????????:
```

If we subsequently re-create a previously deleted item, it is, of course, added to the end of the file:

```
. . . . . . . . . . . . . . . . . . . . . . . . . . . . . . . . . . . . . . . . . . . . . . .
 :  6  :  11  :  UK      :  4        :  GB      :  3      :  54  :~?????:
 :. . .:. . . . .:. . . . . . . .:. . . . . . . .:. . . . . . . .:. . . . . . . . .:. . . . . :~?????:
```

If we now wish to add further items, say item 56 and then item 2, we may find that there is insufficient space, so the system will automatically find another unused frame and link this overflow space to our primary space:

```
. . . . . . . . . . . . . . . . . . . . . . . . . . . . . . . . . . . . . . . . . . . . . . .
P  :  6  :  11  :  UK      :  4        :  GB      :  3      :  54  :  56  :
   :. . .:. . . . .:. . . . . . . .:. . . . . . .:. . . . . . . .:. . . . . . .:. . . . . :

. . . . . . . . . . . . . . . . . . . . . . . . . . . . . . . . . . . . . . . . . . . . . . .
O  :      :  2  :~???????????????????????????????????????????????????????:
   :. . . . :. . . . :~???????????????????????????????????????????????????????:
```

Rest of item 56.

and this overflow frame (labelled O) is now linked to our primary space (labelled P) by means of the control information held within each frame.

In this example, the data held in item 56 are spread across the two frames. If, in turn, this space becomes insufficient, then further extra frames will be linked to provide more space as required.

However, the larger the number of items in our file, and the more linked frames we have, the longer the system will take to retrieve an item. Let us imagine that we want to process item 2, then the operating system will first read in our primary frame, and scan this to see if item 2 is there. If it cannot find the item, it will read in the first overflow frame and look for it there. If it is not there it will read the next overflow frame, and so on until it finds the item we need, or until it reaches the end-of-data marker showing that the item cannot be found on the file.

Before we see how to overcome this time-consuming process, let us have a look at what this means in physical terms.

2.6.1 Records – physical structure

Let us look at the actual disk-storage frame in which some of our items might be held. We have seen that our master dictionary tells us the frame at which a file starts. Let us suppose that we have found that our *ADDRESSES* file starts at frame number 9876, that is FID 9876.

We could then use the TCL DUMP verb to look at this frame:

```
DUMP 9876
```

which will display the contents of frame number 9876 as shown in Fig. 2.4. The first 12 bytes, shown here as dots, are the control and linkage information which tells us if this frame is linked to any other frames. The byte references 000–500 are also shown on this display.

```
FRAME:  9876

000  ............0029S100^MICHAEL SMITH^34 HIGH ST^ANYT
050  ON^0026B100^MARY BROWN^12 MAIN RD^BEATON^~????????
100  ??????????????????????????????????????????????????
150  ??????????????????????????????????????????????????
200  ??????????????????????????????????????????????????
250  ??????????????????????????????????????????????????
300  ??????????????????????????????????????????????????
350  ??????????????????????????????????????????????????
400  ??????????????????????????????????????????????????
450  ??????????????????????????????????????????????????
500  ??????????????
```

Figure 2.4

The actual data items consist of:

(a) A 4 byte item-length count showing the length of the item in hexadecimal – the item lengths are 0029 (= 41 decimal) and 0026 (= 38 decimal), respectively, for these two items.

(b) The item-id followed by an attribute mark. The item-ids are S100 and B100, respectively, for these two items. The attribute mark is shown here as ^.

(c) The attributes separated by attribute marks.

(d) A final attribute mark after the last attribute.

There is also the final end-of-data marker, shown as ~ in this illustration, which indicates 'there are no more data in this frame relating to this file'. Some systems use the attribute mark as this end-of-data indicator without any ambiguity.

The rest of the frame is unused and is shown here as full of question marks. The actual contents of this space will depend upon what happened to be in frame 9876 when the frame was allocated to this file. The original data which were held in that frame are left intact, and are only overwritten when required.

The frame shown here would represent the following two items:

item-id:	S100	B100
attribute 1:	MICHAEL SMITH	MARY BROWN
attribute 2:	34 HIGH ST	12 MAIN RD
attribute 3:	ANYTON	BEATON

This example illustrates the following points concerning physical item layout:

(a) The items are not held in any specific order. They are held in the order in which they were added to the file.

(b) The item-length count is always 4 bytes long: 0029 (= 41 decimal) and 0026 (= 38 decimal) for the two items on our file.

(c) The item-id immediately follows the item-length count: *S100* and *B100*.

(d) An attribute mark follows the item-id.

(e) The item-length count informs the system how much disk space 'belongs' to this item.

(f) The item-length count shows the length of the current item, including the item-length count itself and all field-separator characters.

(g) When the item-length count has been satisfied, the next character must be either the start of another item-length count, if another item follows, or the end-of-data indicator.

(h) The end-of-data marker comes after the last item in the frame.

To remind ourselves how multi-values are held, let us look at the frame belonging to another file. In these items, attribute 1 is the name, attribute 2 is the address line, comprising four multi-values representing street, town, county and postcode, respectively, and attribute 3 is the telephone number. The display is shown in Fig. 2.5. The value mark – shown here as] – separates the various values of attribute 2.

```
FRAME: 12345

000 . . . . . . . . . . . .0026J001^JOHN JONES^11 MAIN ST]ANYTON]
050 ANYSHIRE]AN1 1NA^ANYTON 1324^0041G007^ANNE GREEN^1
100 7 ASHE RD]BEATON]BEASHIRE]BE1 1EB^0222-2222^^?????
150 ????????????????????????????????????????????????
200 ????????????????????????????????????????????????
250 ????????????????????????????????????????????????
300 ????????????????????????????????????????????????
350 ????????????????????????????????????????????????
400 ????????????????????????????????????????????????
450 ????????????????????????????????????????????????
500 ?????????????
```

Figure 2.5

The frame shown here would represent the following two items:

item-id:	J001	G007
attribute 1:	JOHN JONES	ANNE GREEN
attribute 2:	11 MAIN ST	17 ASHE RD
	ANYTON	BEATON
	ANYSHIRE	BEASHIRE
	AN1 1NA	BE1 1EB
attribute 3:	ANYTON 1324	0222-2222

The same argument may be used if we were to introduce secondary values and secondary-value marks into our data.

2.6.2 Records – overflow

Now let us see what happens if we add some items to our file and the original frame 12345 overflows. To simplify the picture, we shall first add an item with an item-id *AAAA* and containing a single attribute consisting of 200 A's. The contents of the frame are shown in Fig. 2.6.

The data in the frame tell us that the length of our new item is 00D2 (= 210 decimal); that is 4 (for the 4-byte count) + 4 (for the item-id

```
FRAME:  12345

000 ............0026J001^JOHN JONES^11 MAIN ST]ANYTON]
050 ANYSHIRE]AN1 1NA^ANYTON 1324^0041G007^ANNE GREEN^1
100 7 ASHE RD]BEATON]BEASHIRE]BE1 1EB^0222-2222^00D2AA
150 AA^AAAAAAAAAAAAAAAAAAAAAAAAAAAAAAAAAAAAAAAAAAAAAAAA
200 AAAAAAAAAAAAAAAAAAAAAAAAAAAAAAAAAAAAAAAAAAAAAAAAAAAA
250 AAAAAAAAAAAAAAAAAAAAAAAAAAAAAAAAAAAAAAAAAAAAAAAAAAAA
300 AAAAAAAAAAAAAAAAAAAAAAAAAAAAAAAAAAAAAAAAAAAAAAAAAAAA
350 AAA^^????????????????????????????????????????????????
400 ??????????????????????????????????????????????????????
450 ??????????????????????????????????????????????????????
500 ????????????
```

Figure 2.6

$AAAA$) + 1 (for the attribute mark after the item-id) + 200 (for the data) + 1 (for the attribute mark at the end of the item).

But if we add a further item *BBBB* consisting of 250 B's, there is not sufficient space in frame 12345. In this case, the Pick operating system looks around for an unused frame – let us suppose that frame 34567 is available – and then writes the information away, overflowing into frame 34567. We can use the command:

`DUMP 12345 (G)`

to display the contents of frame 12345 and then go on to display the linked frames in this group, as shown in Fig. 2.7. You see how the data just flow into the next frame.

The linkage information shown in the first 12 bytes of each frame has been changed, as you can see by the *FROM:* and *TO:* values displayed. The linkage information in frame 12345 shows that this frame is followed by frame 34567, and the linkage information in frame 34567 shows that this frame comes from frame 12345 and goes no further.

If we were now to delete item *AAAA*, the contents of the frames would be as shown in Fig. 2.8. If you look carefully, you will see that item *BBBB* has been moved up into the space previously occupied by item *AAAA*, and the end-of-data marker now appears immediately after the final attribute mark in item *BBBB*. The remnants of the old item *BBBB* can still be seen in its old position, although the new end-of-data marker at byte number 404 of frame 12345 makes the old item *BBBB* data inaccessible. Frame 34567 is still linked to frame 12345 although it is not needed.

```
FRAME: 12345      TO: 34567         FROM: 0

000 ............0026J001^JOHN JONES^11 MAIN STJANYTONJ
050 ANYSHIREJAN1 1NA^ANYTON 1324^0041G007^ANNE GREEN^1
100 7 ASHE RDJBEATONJBEASHIREJBE1 1EB^0222-2222^00D2AA
150 AA^AAAAAAAAAAAAAAAAAAAAAAAAAAAAAAAAAAAAAAAAAAAAAAAA
200 AAAAAAAAAAAAAAAAAAAAAAAAAAAAAAAAAAAAAAAAAAAAAAAAAAAA
250 AAAAAAAAAAAAAAAAAAAAAAAAAAAAAAAAAAAAAAAAAAAAAAAAAAAA
300 AAAAAAAAAAAAAAAAAAAAAAAAAAAAAAAAAAAAAAAAAAAAAAAAAAAA
350 AAA^0104BBBB^BBBBBBBBBBBBBBBBBBBBBBBBBBBBBBBBBBBBBB
400 BBBBBBBBBBBBBBBBBBBBBBBBBBBBBBBBBBBBBBBBBBBBBBBBBBBB
450 BBBBBBBBBBBBBBBBBBBBBBBBBBBBBBBBBBBBBBBBBBBBBBBBBBBB
500 BBBBBBBBBBBB

FRAME: 34567      TO: 0             FROM: 12345

000 ...........BBBBBBBBBBBBBBBBBBBBBBBBBBBBBBBBBBBBBBBB
050 BBBBBBBBBBBBBBBBBBBBBBBBBBBBBBBBBBBBBBBBBBBBBBBBBBBB
100 BBBBBBBBBBBBB^^????????????????????????????????????
150 ??????????????????????????????????????????????????
200 ??????????????????????????????????????????????????
250 ??????????????????????????????????????????????????
300 ??????????????????????????????????????????????????
350 ??????????????????????????????????????????????????
400 ??????????????????????????????????????????????????
450 ??????????????????????????????????????????????????
500 ????????????
```

Figure 2.7

```
FRAME: 12345      TO: 34567         FROM: 0

000 ............0026J001^JOHN JONES^11 MAIN STJANYTONJ
050 ANYSHIREJAN1 1NA^ANYTON 1324^0041G007^ANNE GREEN^1
100 7 ASHE RDJBEATONJBEASHIREJBE1 1EB^0222-2222^0104BB
150 BB^BBBBBBBBBBBBBBBBBBBBBBBBBBBBBBBBBBBBBBBBBBBBBBBB
200 BBBBBBBBBBBBBBBBBBBBBBBBBBBBBBBBBBBBBBBBBBBBBBBBBBBB
250 BBBBBBBBBBBBBBBBBBBBBBBBBBBBBBBBBBBBBBBBBBBBBBBBBBBB
300 BBBBBBBBBBBBBBBBBBBBBBBBBBBBBBBBBBBBBBBBBBBBBBBBBBBB
350 BBBBBBBBBBBBBBBBBBBBBBBBBBBBBBBBBBBBBBBBBBBBBBBBBBBB
400 BBB^^BBBBBBBBBBBBBBBBBBBBBBBBBBBBBBBBBBBBBBBBBBBBBBB
450 BBBBBBBBBBBBBBBBBBBBBBBBBBBBBBBBBBBBBBBBBBBBBBBBBBBB
500 BBBBBBBBBBBB

FRAME: 34567      TO: 0             FROM: 12345

000 ............BBBBBBBBBBBBBBBBBBBBBBBBBBBBBBBBBBBBBBBB
050 BBBBBBBBBBBBB^^??????????????????????????????????
100 ??????????????????????????????????????????????????
150 ??????????????????????????????????????????????????
200 ??????????????????????????????????????????????????
250 ??????????????????????????????????????????????????
300 ??????????????????????????????????????????????????
350 ??????????????????????????????????????????????????
400 ??????????????????????????????????????????????????
450 ??????????????????????????????????????????????????
500 ????????????
```

Figure 2.8

All this implies that:

(a) When you read an existing record, the following operations take place:
  (i) The operating system reads through all the records in the file space until it finds the record which is to be read.
  (ii) It returns the record to you for processing.
(b) When you add a new record to the file, the following operations take place:
  (i) The operating system reads through all the records in the file space until it finds the end-of-data marker.
  (ii) The new record is written at the (physical) end of the file.
  (iii) The end of data marker is re-set.
(c) When you update an existing record, the following operations take place:
  (i) The operating system reads through all the records in the file space until it finds the record which is to be updated.
  (ii) The old data are overwritten by the new data.
  (iii) All following records are moved in or out, depending upon whether the new updated record is shorter or longer than the old predecessor.
(d) When you delete an existing record, the following operations take place:
  (i) The operating system reads through all the records in the file space until it finds the record to be deleted.
  (ii) All following records are moved up into the space previously occupied by the deleted record.
(e) *There is no absolute sequence for the records on the file* – the records are held in the order in which they were added to the file.
(f) *There is no index kept of the records on a file* – the only way that Pick knows if a record exists is if it can find that record by searching through the file.

Now let us see how to cope with these implications in practice.

2.6.3   File separation

From what we said earlier, you will have realized that the larger the number of items in a file, and the more linked frames we have, the longer the system will take to retrieve an item.

Pick allows us to overcome this time-consuming task in the first instance by asking that our primary space has not just one frame, but several contiguous frames.

In this case, when we want to look for an item, the operating system will read in the whole group of frames at once. This group of frames – and you may have up to 127 frames in each group – can then be scanned in memory without the system having to read in any further frames. Some implementations only read in one frame at a time, but arrange the frames in their group in such a manner that the disk read-head is in the correct position if further frames in the group have to be read in.

The number of such contiguous frames is called the *separation* of the file. The separation will be in the range 1–127. A large separation is particularly important if your items are themselves greater than 500 bytes (= one frame) in size, as this would require several frames to be read for each record.

If a group of frames overflows, then additional frames will be linked on the end – one at a time – exactly as we saw earlier.

2.6.4 File groups

Let us have another look at the simple file we had earlier:

```
. . . . . . . . . . . . . . . . . . . . . . . . . . . . . . . . . . . . . . . . . . . . . . . . . . . . . .
: 6 : 11 : UK    : 54       : GB      : 3    : 4       : ~?:
: . . . : . . . . . . . . : . . . . . . . . . . : . . . . . . . . . . . : . . . . . . . . . . . : . . . . . . . . . : . . . . . . . . : ~?:
```

Since the items are held in the order in which they are added to the file, the entire file has to be scanned if we wish to find, say, item 11. The system reads the first item (item-id = 6) and checks if this is the item we want, if not, it reads the second item (item-id = 11) and, since this is the item we want, passes this to our program.

Clearly, the more items we have on the file, the longer it will take to retrieve any one item. Even if we have a very large separation this could take quite some time.

To overcome this situation we can (conceptually) split our file into several primary spaces, instead of just one. Each such space is called a *group*, and each group may consist of one or more frames, just as with the simple primary space described above. The number of groups in our file is called the *modulo* of the file.

Let us look at an example of a file with three groups, schematically called G0, G1 and G2:

```
. . . . . . . . . . . . . . . . . . . . . . . . . . . . . . . . . . . . . . . . . . . . . . . . . . . . . .
G0 : 6 : 3    : 54       : ABC   : ~???????????????????????????:
   : . . . : . . . . . . . : . . . . . . . . . . : . . . . . . : ~???????????????????????????:
```

```
. . . . . . . . . . . . . . . . . . . . . . . . . . . . . . . . . . . . . . . .

G1 : 4 : UK      : ~???????????????????????????????????????????:

  :....:.......: ~???????????????????????????????????????????:



. . . . . . . . . . . . . . . . . . . . . . . . . . . . . . . . . . . . . . . .

G2 : GB : 11    : 56   : ~??????????????????????????????????????:

  :......:..........:.......: ~??????????????????????????????????:
```

The items are scattered across the three groups according to the *hashing algorithm*. Thus, if we want to find a particular item, say the item with item-id *GB*, the individual characters of the item-id are converted to their decimal equivalents, weighted according to their position within the item-id, and then their sum is divided by the modulo for the file. The remainder indicates the required group. Let us take the item-id *GB* as an example. The decimal value of the character G is 71, and that of the character B is 66. So the algorithm gives us:

$$G \times 10 + B \Rightarrow 71 \times 10 + 66 \Rightarrow 776$$

$$776/3 = 258 \text{ remainder } 2$$

So the item with item-id *GB* should occur in group G2. The operating system then scans all the items in this group. But since we have three groups, the system only has to scan one-third of the items on our file, not all of them, as will be the case if the file has a modulo of 1.

Let us apply this hashing algorithm to some of the other item-ids in this diagram:

(a) Item-id = 3: decimal equivalent of character 3 = 51. Dividing this by 3 gives a remainder directing us to group 0.
(b) Item-id = 56: 53 (decimal equivalent of character 5) $\times$ 10 + 54 (character 6) gives a total of 584. Dividing this by 3 gives a remainder directing us to group 2.
(c) Item-id = ABC: [65 (decimal equivalent of character A) $\times$ 100] + [66 (character B) $\times$ 10] + 67 (character C) gives a total of 7227. Dividing this by 3 gives a remainder directing us to group 0.
(d) Item-id = UK: 85 (decimal equivalent of character U) $\times$ 10 + 75 (character K) gives a total of 925. Dividing this by 3 gives a remainder directing us to group 1.

If we have a longer item-id, the same principle applies:

Item-id = ABCDEFG: [65 (character A) $\times$ 1000000] + [66 (character B)

× 100000] + [67 (character C) × 10000] + [68 (character D) × 1000] + [69 (character E) × 100] + [70 (character F) × 10] + 71 (character G) gives a total of 72345671. Dividing this by 3 gives a remainder directing us to group 2.

Ideally, it may seem that it is a good idea to have as many groups as we have items on the file, but this is not realistic, since, even with a large modulo, you may still find that the items bunch into certain groups, according to the nature of the item-ids. For example, if you have one hundred items with item-ids (101–200 on a file with a modulo of 7, then these will be distributed reasonably uniformly through the seven groups, like this:

```
Group #0: *************
Group #1: *************
Group #2: *************
Group #3: *************
Group #4: **************
Group #5: **************
Group #6: *************
```

each asterisk representing one item in the group.

But if the one hundred items have non-sequential item-ids, such as *ABC88*, *X43AA* and so on, then we might find the distribution to be something like this:

```
Group #0: ***********
Group #1:
Group #2: ******************
Group #3: *********************************
Group #4: ***********
Group #5: **********
Group #6: *************
```

with some groups empty and other groups full to overflowing. This can be particularly wasteful of space if the file has a large separation.

The choice of modulo and separation for a file depends upon the size of the items and upon the number of items on the file, as we shall see in Section 2.14.2.

2.7 SUMMARY

Some important points to remember about the file and record structure on the Pick operating system are:

• The modulo – *MOD* – is the number of groups in the file.

- You may have any number of groups, although some will give a better distribution of the items than others. Choose a prime number, if possible, and do not use a *MOD* which is a multiple of 2, 5 or 10.
- The separation – *SEP* – is the number of frames in each, and every, group of the file.
- Every group in a file has the same separation.
- Some implementations place limits on the *MOD* and *SEP*. Typically these are 8,388,607 and 127, respectively.
- The items on the file are distributed between the groups according to the standard Pick hashing algorithm.
- The hashing algorithm is standard throughout the Pick system, and *cannot be modified or re-specified by the user*.
- You will specify the *MOD* and *SEP* for the DICT section of the file, and the *MOD* and *SEP* for the data section of the file when you create the file.
- The *MOD* and *SEP* for the DICT section of a file will not normally be the same as the *MOD* and the *SEP* for the data section of the file.
- The DICT section and the data section of a file are essentially separate and distinct areas.
- The actual location of the DICT section of a file and its data section will be decided by the operating system, and these will not necessarily be adjacent on disk.
- The number of frames in the primary file space which is allocated to the file is equal to the *MOD* multiplied by the *SEP*.
- When a new file is created, the operating system looks around for any suitable disk space which will accommodate the file.
- The primary file space is always a block of contiguous frames.
- Any overflow of space for a group is handled automatically by the operating system.
- Whenever a group overflows, the system will automatically link in one more frame to that group. This overflow frame is taken from the system's pool of unused frames.
- If a group overflows too much, this will degrade the access time for items in the overflow group.
- The *MOD* and *SEP* may be changed, and your file re-organized if you find that the current size and shape of the file is inefficient.
- All item-ids are unique within the file and you cannot have two or more items with the same item-id on a file.
- If you re-write an item which already exists, then the new item will overwrite the old item.
- The items are held in the sequence in which they were added to the file.

- There is no index of items. The item only exists if it can be found in the file.
- The maximum size of an item is 32 768 bytes, although this limitation is removed in Open Architecture Pick. The length of the item includes the data fields themselves, the attribute marks and other field separators, the item-id and the item-length indicator.
- There is no limit on the number of attributes in an item.
- There is no limit on the size of an attribute.
- Attributes are held as variable-length fields terminated by a single attribute mark.
- Trailing spaces need not be held.
- Leading zeros need not be held. A null (empty) attribute is interpreted as 0 by the arithmetic features of Access.
- There is no limit on the number of values in an attribute.
- There is no limit on the size of a value.
- Values are held as variable-length fields terminated by a single value mark.
- There is no limit of the number of secondary values in a value.
- There is no limit on the size of a secondary value.
- Secondary values are held as variable-length fields terminated by a single secondary-value mark.
- Any field, attribute, value, secondary value or item-id may consist of any characters except the four ASCII characters: 252, 253, 254 and 255.
- The segment mark – character 255 – is used for many purposes by the operating system and should not be used within strings or data values.
- The item-id may be up to fifty characters in length.
- There is no other restriction on the format of the item-id. However, if an item-id contains apostrophes, brackets, parentheses, quotation marks, spaces or commas, then it may be ambiguous in certain contexts.

The TCL verbs ISTAT, HASH-TEST, GROUP, ITEM, I-DUMP and S-DUMP, which are used in connection with the structure of your files, are discussed in Section 5.3, which deals with file layout verbs. The verbs CREATE-FILE, CLEAR-FILE, DELETE-FILE and COPY are discussed in Section 5.4, which deals with file processing verbs.

2.8 FILE-DESIGN CONSIDERATIONS

If you are designing files for use on the Pick system, you will go through the same systems investigation process as for any other system, interviewing your users and their staff, determining what data elements are used by whom, and so on. But the actual task of deciding how to hold the data and where to hold the data can be approached slightly differently.

If you are familiar with database normalization techniques, then you will realize that the Pick file structure fits in well with the various normalized forms which are developed there. The concept of values and secondary values, however, will probably cause you restless nights. We discuss the normalization of databases in Section 2.9.

The Pick database retrieval language – Access – offers a most efficient and powerful way of producing reports and inquiries on your files. Therefore, unless some other consideration prevents it, files should be designed so that reports can be produced from the file by the use of Access. By doing this your system benefits in that retrieval is faster and less coding is required for the output processes. When we discuss Access, we shall see that the language has extensive facilities for:

(a) Report output formatting – you can easily change the content of a report.
(b) Extraction of data from the attributes of an item – the data can be picked up from anywhere within a record either as a simple attribute or as a sub-string of an attribute. For example, we could pick up the employees' initials from within the attribute holding their full names.
(c) Translation of values via reference and cross-reference files – your *INVOICE* file need only hold the customer number, and this will allow you to refer across to your CUSTOMER file for the name and address or for the credit limit.
(d) Conversion of numerical values of attributes – you can hold numbers without decimal points, and dates and times may be held in a compressed form.
(e) Arithmetic and logical computations on the attributes of an item – the *cost* can be derived from the PRICE and QUANTITY fields held on the record.

The Access format of data is completely compatible with other Pick processors, such as the Basic and Proc languages, and does not demand that the data on the records be held in any special format. Let us now consider the problems of designing the DICT section of a file, the item-ids of the items on the file and the data items themselves. We shall also take a brief look at database normalization procedures.

2.8.1 File-dictionary design

The efficiency and speed with which your Access statements are processed is affected by the ease with which the definitions can be located on the DICT section of your files.

You should ensure that the dictionaries of your files are efficient by observing the following points:

(a) Only have those definitions which are necessary. The database administrator – or his or her equivalent – should keep a careful record of what definitions exist and where they are used.
(b) Do not store large items – such as programs and Procs – amongst the definitions. Store these on a separate file.
(c) Within the dictionary definitions themselves, remember that attribute 3 need only contain a text heading when this differs from the attribute definition name; attributes 4, 5 and 6 will normally be blank, and attributes 11 and upwards can be omitted.
(d) Use default outlist definitions – 1, 2, 3 and so on – only where necessary.
(e) Carefully selected values for the MOD and SEP of the dictionary can improve its efficiency.

Some of these points will become clearer when you have looked at Access and the dictionary definitions which it uses.

2.8.2 Item-id design

There are a few points to bear in mind when you are designing the item-ids for the items on your files. We have already touched upon some of them in the earlier sections:

(a) If it proves to be a problem, undesirable bunching of the items within the groups of a file can be minimized if the item-ids are sequential. For example, items with item-ids 100, 101, 102 and so on, will be distributed more evenly through the groups than will those with item-ids SMITH, JONES, JENKINS and so on.
(b) You can hold meaningful data within your item-id. This has two advantages: firstly, the information need not be held within the record, and, secondly, you can determine the item-id more easily. Thus, if we have an item keyed on account and month, then we can immediately read the item 1234*12 to retrieve the information relating to account 1234 in December.

Let us suppose that you have a system recording transactions on accounts, for example. Then it is perfectly feasible to design the item-id so that it incorporates the time and the account number.

4046011 will be the item-id of the item holding, say, the details of the transaction on account number 11 at 11 : 14 : 20 (= internal clock time 40460),

4158424 will be for account number 24 at 11 : 33 : 04,

4229887 for account number 87 at 11 : 44 : 58,

5241271 for account number 71 at 14 : 33 : 32,

3533043 for account number 43 at 09 : 48 : 50,

4166013 for account number 13 at 11 : 34 : 20

and so on.

If the two fields are not of fixed length, then you could use a separator character, like this:

460*11 will be the item-id of the item holding, say, details of transaction 460 on account number 11,

4184*123 will be for transaction 4184 on account number 123,

422298*8 for transaction 422298 on account number 8,

577412*7741 for transaction 577412 on account number 7741

and so on. The asterisk seems to be the *de facto* standard delimiter amongst Pick programmers, but you may use any character to separate the fields.

In either case, the separate pieces of information can be extracted from the item-id quite simply in Access, Proc or Basic. Notice, also, how this method uses the uniqueness of the item-id to advantage.

2.8.3 Data-record design and layout

The main criterion in the design points laid out here is that the items on the file should be as small as possible. In this way, you will have the benefit of improved file-access time as well as the reduced file space.

The points to observe are:

- Try to keep your records as small as possible, and below 500 bytes in length if this is feasible.
- Fields which are most often empty, null or omitted, should be placed at the end of the item. As a general rule, the fields should be included in the order in which they are most likely to have actual values. Thus, the arrangement

```
NAME
BIRTH DATE
ADDRESS
MARITAL STATUS
NUMBER OF CHILDREN
```

is preferable to

```
NUMBER OF CHILDREN
MARITAL STATUS
ADDRESS
BIRTH DATE
NAME
```

since many employees will have no children, but all employees will have a name. This is because the system does not hold trailing null fields nor does it hold the associated attribute mark.

The sharp-eyed reader will notice that the Pick system items, such as dictionary definitions, Q-pointers and file definition items, do not use this principle. In these items there is invariably a large (wasteful) gap between attributes 4 and 9.

- For numeric fields, values of zero should be represented by null wherever possible.

For Access, Basic and Proc purposes, this will have the same interpretation as zero.

- Fields which can have a default – or most likely – value should represent this default value by null. Thus, if an indicator represents MALE or FEMALE, then the most frequent (or likely) indicator, let us suppose this is male, should be represented by null, the other by 1 or F (but never by the word FEMALE).

This point also applies to YES/NO indicators and flags, and may even be used in situations where an attribute may have one of a range of values. For example, let us suppose that a code may take any one of the values 0, 1, 2 or 3, and that the value 2 is the most common; then the actual values held on file should be 0, 1, null and 3, respectively, with the associated program, and Access conversions and correlatives, using logic such as:

```
IF CODE = " " THEN CODE = "2"
```

- If a field can have one of several known values, it is more efficient to hold a code which cross-refers to a file containing the table of possible values. Thus, if a file is to hold attributes representing:

Name of client
Goods purchased

it is more efficient to hold the information

```
J. SMITH^102]483]293
```

rather than

```
J. SMITH^SETTEE]TABLE]DINING SUITE
```

where the codes 102, 483 and 293 refer to a reference file of goods. Or, even better,

```
4055^102]483]293
```

where the code 4055 refers to a reference file of clients.

This principle could be used even more widely. A local government system might hold the addresses:

```
34 HIGH ST
76 HIGH ST
42 FLORAL AVE
9 FLORAL AVE
```

as:

```
34 H001
76 H001
42 F910
9 F910
```

and use a separate cross-reference file which has records:

```
H001 = HIGH ST
F910 = FLORAL AVE
```

and so on. This offers advantages of less space and consistency, in return for relatively small overheads on file-access times.

• Numeric fields should be held without a decimal point.

Thus, prices and sums of money should be held in pence, and converted to pounds by a simple conversion code in Access and within Basic programs.

You may also use packed decimal for numeric fields.

• Dates and times should be held in internal format. Thus, the internal date 1234 takes up less space than any of the external formats *18 MAY 1971* or *18/05/71* or *18/5/71*. With the conversion codes of Access, Basic and Proc, all of these forms are equally accessible.
• Remember that meaningful data can be held in the item-id – as discussed in Section 2.8.2 where we consider item-id design.
• Information held in the item-id should not be repeated within the body of the item.

- If the items comprise data which are truly static, or rarely changed, together with data which are very volatile, it is more efficient to hold the two parts on separate files, as is mentioned when we discuss normalization of files in Section 2.9. For example, if it is required to hold the following pieces of information:

Name   ← static data
Address   ← static data
Telephone number   ← static data
Order number
Date of order(s)
Item(s) on order(s)
Price(s)
Total value of order(s)

then the static data – name, address and telephone number – should be held on one file, with the remaining variable data on a second file. Note that, since the information is being held on two separate files, the same item-id could be used for both items.
- In Sections 3.2 and 9.5, where we deal with file security, we see how you can allow or prevent other users from accessing your files. Pick, however, does not allow you to prohibit access to only a *part* of a file.

To illustrate this, let us suppose that your *PERSONNEL* file contains the employees' names and their salaries. It is not possible to allow your users to look at an employee's name but prevent them from looking at the employee's salary held on the same item. To achieve this, you would have to hold the name on one file with read-access, and hold the salary on another file without read-access. In such situations, the corresponding items could have the same item-ids on the two files.

The database normalization procedures, which we discuss in Section 2.9, are also relevant here.

2.8.4 Other considerations

In the discussion of file layout, we saw how items are added to the file, and how the items in a group may overflow from the primary file space. This has important implications in the efficiency of updating items. When an item near the front of a group is updated, all trailing items in that group will be moved if the updated item is longer or shorter than before. If it is known that certain items are more likely to be updated than others, then these should be placed at the end of the group. Indeed, some Pick implementations move any updated item to the end of its group. The following illustration shows how the item *ITEMB* can be placed at the end of its group:

```
COPY FILEA ITEMB (D)
TO: *DUMMY*ITEM*
```

```
COPY FILEA *DUMMY*ITEM* (D)
TO: ITEMB
```

The first COPY creates a dummy item and deletes the existing *ITEMB*, and the second COPY creates a new item *ITEMB* – this will be added at the end of its group – and then deletes the dummy item. This technique is particularly useful if you are developing a large Basic program, and will save you much time when the Editor has to retrieve and file the item.

The number of frame faults – the occasions on which the operating system needs to read in a frame of data from disk – is the factor that causes the most degradation of overall system response. This number increases dramatically as the number of frames per group increases, due to the fact that, on average, one-half of the frames in a group have to be read in order to find an item, and these have to be re-written when the item has been updated.

The ideal configuration for a file would be one in which every item could be accessed with, at most, only one frame fault. To make full use of storage capacity, the groups in the file would have to be one frame long and completely full. File design should aim for the closest possible approximation to this ideal.

The higher the proportion of groups which consist of a single frame, the faster the average access time for the file. If a single item must be retrieved from a second frame, the access time for that item will be about twice the access time for an item which is completely contained in one frame. Longer groups are correspondingly slower. The number of items per group is generally unimportant compared with the number of frame accesses needed for an average item in the group.

This applies only if the typical item size is less than 500 bytes. Runoff text files, Proc files and Basic program files, however, normally consist of items larger than this. In such cases it would be desirable to specify a separation greater than one.

It might seem possible to speed up access by attempting to obtain a situation where your file has a single item per group. But unless the item size was consistently close to 500 bytes, this would mean that a significant part of the frame would normally represent wasted space. This might not be a drawback if the file were only to be accessed randomly, but some of the most powerful features of Access scan the file sequentially, and these would not work efficiently with such a sparse data structure. A search through a file, for example, as specified by a LIST statement with selection criteria, causes sequential access of the entire file, and the most significant factor affecting the speed of such a process is the density with which the items are packed onto the frames – the more items per group, the more efficient the Access processing.

A similar consideration argues against the placing of all data into one huge file. Whether access is random or sequential, the skipping of attributes whose values are not regularly required for processing will cause a loss of efficiency. A better organization is to store dynamic information in one file, and relatively static data in another. A good structure is a master item, which is seldom updated, linked to a number of detail items which are constantly being modified.

2.9 DATABASE NORMALIZATION TECHNIQUES

The process of database normalization is not peculiar to Pick, and most analysts will be familiar with the processes involved. This section is included to show how the Pick file structure is reconciled to the current techniques.

The process of normalizing a database involves arranging the data which your company needs in such a way that they are readily accessible to all the systems which you develop. There are three standard steps which are followed in the process to normalize a database. We might summarize these by saying that the data in an item should depend upon 'the item-id, the whole item-id and nothing but the item-id'.

(a) *First normal form.* The first step in the normalization of a database is to *remove any repeating groups*. It is at this stage that all the multi-values and secondary values of Pick are rejected.
(b) *Second normal form.* The second step is to ensure that, if the item has a composite item-id then any single attribute in the item should be dependent upon the whole item-id and not just a part of the item-id.
(c) *Third normal form.* The third step is to ensure that you remove any attributes which are dependent upon other attributes and put these in a separate item.

Let us illustrate these steps by considering the Sales Order shown in Fig. 2.9.

We could assemble this information on an item such as:

```
111111: 02/02/86: 33333: JOHN SMITH AND CO LTD:
34 HIGH STREET, YORK: 44444: WOODEN
CHAIRS: 5: 66. 00: 330. 00: 77777: STEEL TABLES: 8:
99. 00: 792. 00: 1122. 00
```

where the entire item of information is held on our *order* file and is
identified by the item-id 111111 which is the ORDER NUMBER.

```
***** ANSTEE FURNITURE COMPANY LIMITED *****

***** SALES ORDER *****

ORDER:  111111                              DATE: 02/02/86

        CUSTOMER : 33333
                 :
                 : JOHN SMITH AND CO LTD
                 : 34 HIGH STREET,  YORK
.........................................................
: ITEM : PRODUCT : DESCRIPTION  :QTY  :  UNIT :   COST   :
:      :         :              :     :  PRICE :         :
.........................................................
: 1    : 44444   : WOODEN CHAIRS :  5  : 66.00 : 330.00  :
: 2    : 77777   : STEEL TABLES  :  8  : 99.00 : 792.00  :
:      :         :               :     :       :         :
:      :         :               :     :       :         :
:      :         :               :     :       :         :
:      :         :               :     :       :         :
:      :         :               :     :       :         :
.........................................................
                                        TOTAL    1122. 00 :
                                        ..................
```

Figure 2.9

2.9.1   First normal form

The first step in the normalization of a database is to *remove any repeating
groups*. In this case, we remove the repeated order detail information.
After this step, we have two files:

(a) A modified *ORDER* file with items consisting of:

ORDER NUMBER (the item-id), ORDER DATE, CUSTOMER
NUMBER, CUSTOMER NAME, CUSTOMER ADDRESS and
ORDER TOTAL.

In this case, the item would contain:

```
111111^02/02/86^33333^JOHN SMITH AND CO LTD
34 HIGH STREET, YORK^1122. 00
```

(b) An *ORDER DETAIL* file, with a composite item-id comprising the ORDER NUMBER and the LINE-SEQUENCE NUMBER with items consisting of:

ORDER NUMBER (part of the item-id), LINE-SEQUENCE NUMBER (part of the item-id), PRODUCT NUMBER, PRODUCT NAME, QUANTITY ORDERED, PRODUCT PRICE and PRODUCT TOTAL.

In this case, the items would contain:

111111/1^44444^WOODEN CHAIRS^5^66. 00^330. 00

111111/2^77777^STEEL TABLES^8^99. 00^792. 00

2.9.2 Second normal form

The second step is to ensure that, if an item has a composite item-id then every attribute in the item should be dependent upon the whole item-id and not just a part of the item-id. In our example, the PRODUCT NAME and PRODUCT PRICE on the *ORDER DETAIL* file are dependent upon only the line-sequence-number part of the item-id. So we remove this to a third file.

After this step, we have the same *ORDER* file, and a modified *ORDER DETAIL* file with items containing:

ORDER NUMBER (part of the item-id), LINE-SEQUENCE NUMBER (part of the item-id), PRODUCT NUMBER, QUANTITY ORDERED and PRODUCT TOTAL.

In this case, the items would contain:

111111/1^44444^5^330. 00

111111/2^77777^8^792. 00

We would have a new *PRODUCT* file with items containing:

PRODUCT NUMBER (the item-id), PRODUCT NAME and PRODUCT PRICE.

In this case, the items would contain:

44444^WOODEN CHAIRS^66. 00

77777^STEEL TABLES^99. 00

We do this because the PRODUCT NAME and the PRODUCT PRICE are not specific to this line (01, 02 and so on) of this order (11111), but they are specific to this line only. The PRODUCT NUMBER, QUANTITY ORDERED and PRODUCT TOTAL are specific to this line of this order.

2.9.3   Third normal form

The third and final step is to ensure that you remove any attributes which are dependent upon other attributes and put these in a separate item. After this has been done, we should have the following files:

(a) A modified *ORDER* file. In practice, the *ORDER* file item could also contain a count of the number of lines on each order:

ORDER NUMBER (the item-id), ORDER DATE, CUSTOMER NUMBER, ORDER TOTAL and NUMBER-OF-ORDER LINES.

In this case, the item would contain:

`111111^02/02/86^33333^1122. 00^2`

(b) The *ORDER PRODUCT* file containing:

ORDER NUMBER (part of the item-id), LINE-SEQUENCE NUMBER (part of the item-id), PRODUCT NUMBER and QUAN TITY ORDERED.

In this case, the items would contain:

`111111/1^44444^5`

`111111/2^77777^8`

We also remove the PRODUCT TOTAL from this file, since the PRODUCT TOTAL depends upon the QUANTITY ORDERED.

(c) The *PRODUCT* file has an item containing:

PRODUCT NUMBER (the item-id) PRODUCT NAME and PRO-DUCT PRICE.

In this case, the item would contain:

`44444^WOODEN CHAIRS^66. 00`

`77777^STEEL TABLES^99. 00`

(d) A *CUSTOMER* file containing:

CUSTOMER NUMBER (the item-id), CUSTOMER NAME and CUS-TOMER ADDRESS.

In this case, the item would contain:

`33333^JOHN SMITH AND CO LTD^34 HIGH STREET, YORK`

Just as we have held the various lines of the order as separate items on our *ORDER* file, we could hold the various lines of the customer's name and address as separate items on a *CUSTOMER-ADDRESS* file: with the items on the *CUSTOMER* file containing:

CUSTOMER NUMBER (the item-id), CUSTOMER NAME and NUMBER-OF-ADDRESS LINES.

In this case, the item would contain:

```
33333^JOHN SMITH AND CO LTD^4
```

and there would also be a *CUSTOMER-ADDRESS* file containing:

CUSTOMER NUMBER (part of the item-id), SEQUENCE NUMBER (part of the item-id) and CUSTOMER-ADDRESS lines.

In this case, the item would contain:

```
33333/1^34 HIGH ST
33333/2^YORK
33333/3^EAST YORKSHIRE
33333/4^YO5 6AA
```

You may possibly feel that much of this would be obvious to most analysts and programmers. The justification for including this section is that the nature of Pick means that some users may be new to data processing and not yet exposed to formal systems analysis training.

2.10 OTHER FILE STRUCTURES

On the physical level, all Pick files consist of a set of items, each of which is uniquely identified by its item-id, and, as we have also seen, the data within the item may consist of one or more attributes. But on the logical level, this structure can, and does, have many interpretations. We have already met some of them earlier in this chapter, but now let us look at some further interpretations of Pick files.

Much of what we present here follows from the discussion of database normalization, and all the file structures discussed are completely compatible with Access and the other features of Pick.

2.10.1 Reference files

A reference file is one which holds information and codes to be used by other processes, and generally reduces file space and improves other aspects of processing. For example, we may have a STOCK file which contains the type, material and colour of a product. If we hold the item relating to product 1334 as:

```
1334^CHAIR^RED^STEEL^35^20^5600
```

then our system will work quite adequately. But if we use a reference file to hold the product type (CHAIR), the colour (RED) and the material (STEEL) then we can condense this – and every – STOCK item to represent it as:

1334^2^R^ST^35^20^5600

and have reference files. The reference file for product type might contain an item:

2^CHAIR

and the reference file for colour might contain an item:

R^RED

and the reference file for material might contain an item:

ST^STEEL

We might also need a reference file to encode the information the other way – an inverted material file – which would have an item:

STEEL^ST

and so on.

Such files could also be used for the entry and validation of data. The keyboard operator could enter ST or STEEL or any other agreed code, and the program could easily derive the correct contraction and full form of the material indicator from the inverted file. For this reason, such files are often called translation files.

2.10.2   Inverted files

We can illustrate a more powerful use of inverted files by a *PERSONNEL* file which contains items such as those shown in Fig. 2.10.

```
1000^ALDERTON, A^LAB^3456^2837^5744
2000^WATSON, J. A^ADMIN^1928^4933^1928
2030^ALLINSON, B^LAB^1928^8443^2332
2040^WHEELER, M^LAB^3744^8876^4633
2050^DENTON, M^ADMIN^3222^8766^2344
```

Figure 2.10

The second attribute – the department – might be one which we need to use frequently in reports and searches. We could, therefore, simplify such processes by having an inverted *DEPT.PERSONNEL* file with items such as:

```
LAB^1000^2030^2040^
ADMIN^2000^2050
```

the items on the *DEPT.PERSONNEL* file showing the item-ids of the items on the *PERSONNEL* file for each of the various departments.

Such inverted files can be used for any of the fields in the master-file items. For example, we might have an inverted *INITIAL.PERSONNEL* file with items:

```
A^1000^2030
D^2050
W^2000^2040
```

enabling us to find all employees whose surnames begin with A, and so on.

Such a system obviously needs care when items on the *PERSONNEL* file are added, changed or deleted, since the inverted files must also be changed, but the general principle greatly reduces processing time for other operations, such as the production of Access reports which require a search for a specific criterion, where the sequence:

```
FORM-LIST DEPT.PERSONNEL ADMIN
LIST PERSONNEL NAME SALARY
```

would be very much quicker than would the equivalent Access sentence with selection criteria:

```
LIST PERSONNEL NAME SALARY WITH DEPT = "ADMIN"
```

We mention this again when we consider the processing of select lists and saved lists.

2.10.3 BOMP files

Another file structure is that associated with bill of materials processing, and might be used in such situations as a parts file in which certain items on the file imply the use and supply of other parts on the file. As a simple example, let us consider an office-supply company's catalogue which contains the following items, some of which imply other items from the catalogue:

- Item no. 800A is a Teaching kit A, and comprises three student's units and one teacher's unit.
- Item no. 800B is a Teaching kit B, and comprises five student's units and two teacher's units.
- Item no. SU01 is a Student's unit, and comprises one desk, one chair, one student literature pack and one cassette player.

- Item no. TU01 is a Teacher's unit, and comprises one teacher's desk, one chair, one teacher literature pack and one student literature pack.
- Item no. TD01 is a teacher's desk, and comprises one cassette player and one desk.
- Item no. D001 is a desk.
- Item no. CH01 is a chair.
- Item no. SL01 is a student literature pack.
- Item no. TL01 is a teacher literature pack.
- Item no. CP01 is a cassette player.

```
800A^Teaching kit A^^SU01]SU01]SU01]TU01
800B^Teaching kit B^^SU01]SU01]SU01]SU01]SU01]TU01]TU01
SU01^Student's unit^^D001]CH01]SL01]CP01
TU01^Teacher's unit^^TD01]CH01]TL01]SL01
TD01^Teacher's desk^^CP01]D001
D001^Desk^34^^5600
CH01^Chair^23^^3700
SL01^Student literature pack^56^^1200
TL01^Teacher literature pack^67^^2500
CP01^Cassette player^7^^2600
```

Figure 2.11

Then we would create items on our file CATALOGUE with the content shown in Fig. 2.11, where the attributes represent:

item-id:	item no.
attribute 1:	description
attribute 2:	quantity in stock, for a primitive component
attribute 3:	item-ids of subordinate components, if any
attribute 4:	price, for a primitive component

Pick has a special facility to handle such a file structure. By setting attribute 8 of the data-level identifier for our file to

`V;;3`

we indicate that attribute 3 of the items on this data file contains a list of other item-ids from the same file. We can then use the special WITHIN modifier in an Access sentence such as

`LIST WITHIN CATALOGUE '800B' DESCR QTY TOTAL PRICE`

to produce a report like that in Listing 2.1. This shows the nature, the stock level and the price of all the stock items which are needed to supply one item *800B*.

The dictionary definitions for DESCR and QTY are perfectly standard,

```
LIST WITHIN CATALOGUE '800B' DESCR QTY TOTAL PRICE

PAGE    1

LEVEL CATALOGUE. DESCR.................... QTY.. PRICE

  1   800B        Teaching kit B
  2   SU01        Student's unit
  3   D001        Desk                       34 56.00
  3   CH01        Chair                      23 37.00
  3   SL01        Student literature pack    56 12.00
  3   CP01        Cassette player             7 26.00
  2   SU01        Student's unit
  3   D001        Desk                       34 56.00
  3   CH01        Chair                      23 37.00
  3   SL01        Student literature pack    56 12.00
  3   CP01        Cassette player             7 26.00
  2   SU01        Student's unit
  3   D001        Desk                       34 56.00
  3   CH01        Chair                      23 37.00
  3   SL01        Student literature pack    56 12.00
  3   CP01        Cassette player             7 26.00
  2   SU01        Student's unit
  3   D001        Desk                       34 56.00
  3   CH01        Chair                      23 37.00
  3   SL01        Student literature pack    56 12.00
  3   CP01        Cassette player             7 26.00
  2   SU01        Student's unit
  3   D001        Desk                       34 56.00
  3   CH01        Chair                      23 37.00
  3   SL01        Student literature pack    56 12.00
  3   CP01        Cassette player             7 26.00
  2   TU01        Teacher's unit
  3   TD01        Teacher's desk
  4   CP01        Cassette player             7 26.00
  4   D001        Desk                       34 56.00
  3   CH01        Chair                      23 37.00
  3   TL01        Teacher literature pack    67 25.00
  3   SL01        Student literature pack    56 12.00
  2   TU01        Teacher's unit
  3   TD01        Teacher's desk
  4   CP01        Cassette player             7 26.00
  4   D001        Desk                       34 56.00
  3   CH01        Chair                      23 37.00
  3   TL01        Teacher literature pack    67 25.00
  3   SL01        Student literature pack    56 12.00

  0   ***                                      967.00

40 ITEMS LISTED.
```

Listing 2.1

as described in Section 4.1. The column headed LEVEL is produced by the LIST WITHIN processor. You may only use the WITHIN modifier in LIST and COUNT sentences.

2.10.4 Header and detail files

We have already met these during our discussion of database normaliz- ation. We saw that it is better to hold the simple account information – the order number, date, customer number, total cost of order – on one file, called the header file, and the individual line records showing the order line number, the product number and the quantity ordered – on another file, called the detail file.

This same structure can be used in any situation where a repeating group, such as the order details in this example, can occur an unlimited number of times. This is particularly appropriate to files which record historical information which grows with time or circumstances. Other examples are bank accounts, with the individual transactions held on a detail file; wages files, with the salary history – dates and new salary – held on a detail file; telephone directory information, with the various addresses and telephone numbers for a large subscriber held on a detail file.

2.11 STANDARD FILES

Pick has several files holding information which is necessary to all users. When a new account is created, pointers to these files are established on the new master dictionary.

The most important of these standard files are:

ACC
BLOCK-CONVERT
ERRMSG
NEWAC
PROCLIB
SYSTEM
POINTER-FILE

As with many features of Pick, the ordinary end-user is quite unaware of these files, and most end-users lead full and happy lives without ever concerning themselves with such matters!

2.11.1 ACC file

This file holds the accounting information for all users who have been, or currently are, logged on to the system, showing:

(a) The account name – this is the item-id.
(b) The time at which the user logged on.
(c) The time at which the user logged off.
(d) The time for which the user was connected.
(e) The amount of CPU time used.
(f) The number of disk accesses made.

The file also holds information about the current users of the system showing:

(a) The FID of the workspace used by this port. This is the item-id of the ACC item.
(b) The account name.
(c) The date when the port logged on.
(d) The time when the port logged on.

At this point we could formalize the use of the terms *port*, *terminal* and *line*. Each Pick system has a number of physical connections, known as ports. Each port enables a terminal to link up to the CPU. Each port is uniquely identified by a port number: 0 for the first port, 1 for the next and so on. For most practical purposes the terms port, terminal and line are synonymous.

Reports can be produced by means of Access sentences such as

LIST ACC LPTR

The DICT of the *ACC* file holds an item for each port which contains a single attribute giving a description of the location or the usage of this terminal as displayed by the LISTU verb. This is only used for information purposes. For example:

> item-id: 15
> attribute 1:   J.JONES – NORTH END OF FACTORY

would indicate that terminal number 15 was used by J. Jones who worked at the north end of the factory.

2.11.2   BLOCK CONVERT file

The file holds information about the large block characters which you may display on your terminal – with the BLOCK-TERM command – or on the printer – with the BLOCK-PRINT command. These characters are used for printing identification messages, and so on, as described in Section 5.8.2, where we disuss the BLOCK-TERM and BLOCK-PRINT verbs.

The format of the items on the *BLOCK-CONVERT* file is illustrated in

```
          item-id:  A
attribute   1:  12
attribute   2:  B4]4]4
attribute   3:  B3]6]3
attribute   4:  B2]8]2
attribute   5:  B1]4]2]4]1
attribute   6:  C4]4]4
attribute   7:  C12
attribute   8:  C12
attribute   9:  C4]4]4
attribute  10:  C4]4]4
```

Figure 2.12

Fig. 2.12, which shows the item holding the pattern for the letter A. The item-id is the character which is to be printed.

Attribute 1 specifies the width (in characters) of the block letter. Attributes 2–10 specify the pattern for each line which makes up the block letter. If the attribute starts with a B, then this means start with a blank. If the attribute starts with a C, then this means start with the character – that is the letter A. Then, working along the attribute, a number tells how many blanks or characters are to be printed, and a value mark tells to switch from a blank to a character, or from a character to a blank. The above pattern will generate the letter shown in Fig. 2.13.

```
    AAAA
   AAAAAA
  AAAAAAAA
 AAAA    AAAA
 AAAA      AAAA
 AAAAAAAAAAAA
 AAAAAAAAAAAA
 AAAA      AAAA
 AAAA      AAAA
```

Figure 2.13

2.11.3   ERRMSG file

This file contains the text for all the standard error messages, compiler diagnostics messages and informative messages put out by the system.

You may amend the standard error messages, if you wish, in order to make them more user-friendly. You may also establish your own messages to this file and use them within your system for such purposes as the Basic STOP statement. Since the actual system error messages may change between implementations and between releases, you are advised to take care when using the standard messages within your own systems.

Each message is held as a separate item on the *ERRMSG* file, and each item is identified by a message-id. The items comprise a series of attributes which are used to construct a string of data. This string is then displayed at the terminal. The attributes in the message have the following format:

Hxxxxxxx output the literal-string 'xxxxxxx'. The string may contain any characters, including the special screen effects, such as clear the screen, flashing letters and so on.

L output a line-feed/carriage-return character.

L(n) output 'n' line-feed/carriage-return characters.

A output the next parameter – this is illustrated below.

A(n) output the next parameter left-justified in a field of length 'n' characters.

R(n) output the next parameter right-justified in a field of length 'n' characters.

E output the message-id, enclosed in square brackets [ ].

Exxxxxx output the message-id, enclosed in square brackets [ ] and followed by the string xxxxxx.

S(n) shift the subsequent output to position 'n' of the line – this is rather like a tab-stop position.

T output the current time in the format hh : mm : ss.

D output the current date in the format dd mmm yyyy.

In each case, the alphabetic code letter must appear in the first position of the attribute.

When the message is interpreted, the above controls are used to produce a string of characters which is then displayed at the terminal. Listing 2.2 shows that the contents of an item on the *ERRMSG* file in the

```
H   ***************************************************
L
H  *        WELCOME TO THE PICK OPERATING SYSTEM        *
L
H  *
S(9)
T
S(34)
D
S(53)
H*
H   ***************************************************
```

Listing 2.2

item '335' and Fig. 2.14 shows the appearance of this message as it will be displayed when a user logs on to the Pick system.

```
******************************************************
*       WELCOME TO THE PICK OPERATING SYSTEM         *
*          10: 30: 00                    31 DEC 1985  *
******************************************************
```

Figure 2.14

When an error message is invoked from a Basic program, parameters may be passed across for inclusion in the message by means of a statement of the form:

```
STOP "MYERRO02", ITEMA, FILE32
```

where *MYERR002* is the message-id, and the values of the variables 'ITEMA' and 'FILE32' are to be the parameters.

If the message *MYERR001* has the following format:

```
HCANNOT OPEN FILE '
A
H'
```

and message *MYERR002* has the following format:

```
HCANNOT FIND ITEM '
A
H' ON FILE '
A
H'
```

then a program sequence such as:

```
ITEMA='AB/123'
FILE='UPDATE-MASTER'
OPEN FILE ELSE STOP 'MYERRO01', FILE
READ RECORD FROM ITEMA ELSE STOP 'MYERRO02', ITEMA,
    FILE
```

might terminate the execution with one of the messages:

```
CANNOT OPEN FILE 'UPDATE-MASTER'
```

```
CANNOT FIND ITEM 'AB/123' ON FILE 'UPDATE-MASTER'
```

if the file could not be opened (error message *MYERR001*) or if the item could not be found on the file (error message *MYERR002*).

A full list of the error messages for your system is given at the back of most reference manuals, but the following messages are frequently encountered:

Bnnn the Basic compilation error messages.

LOGON is used for you to supply your own messages which are to be displayed immediately before the standard log-on message (335) at log on.

3	VERB?
86	FILE REFERENCE ATTEMPTED ON FILE NOT PREVIOUSLY OPENED
201	pp IS NOT A FILE NAME
202	'pp' NOT ON FILE.
221	'pp' FILED.
222	'pp' DELETED.
223	'pp' EXISTS ON FILE
335	the welcome message at log on, as shown above.
336	the log-off message showing time and date.
340	the port connect time, connect duration, CPU usage and disk usage.
401	NO ITEMS PRESENT
415	'pp' EXISTS ON FILE.
552	ITEM 'pp' HAS INVALID FORMAT
611	TYPE Y (YES) OR N (NO)+
680	SYNTAX ERROR
781	'pp' ADDED
782	'pp' UPDATED
783	'pp' DELETED
1004	ITEM 'pp' IS NOT ON FILE.
1006	ITEM 'pp' EXISTS ON FILE

In each case, pp is a parameter supplied as shown above.

Remember that the item-ids and the text of these error messages may be different on your implementation.

2.11.4 NEWAC file

This file holds all the basic verbs and other necessary items common to all users. A copy of this file is made when an account is created, and becomes the MD, the master dictionary, of the new account.

When an account has been created, *NEWAC* is no longer available to the account.

2.11.5 PROCLIB file

This file holds the standard general purpose routines and procedures provided for all users, including those shown in Section 5.9, and is a good place to add any utility Procs which you may wish to make available to your users.

2.11.6   SYSTEM file

This file holds the account definition items for all the accounts on your system, as we have seen.

2.11.7   POINTER-FILE file

This file holds pointers to all saved lists. These items have the format:

item-id:	RETIRERS	
attribute 1:	C	
attribute 2:	128854	⇐ the frame where the list is stored
attribute 3:	1	⇐ the number of frames used
attribute 4:	12	⇐ the number of entries in the saved list
attribute 5:	10 : 30 : 00 31/12/85	⇐ when saved

which would refer to the list saved by means of the command:

`SAVE-LIST RETIRERS`

On some implementations, the account name is included in the item-id, for example:

`MYACC*L*RETIRERS`

which would refer to the list *RETIRERS* saved on the *MYACC* account. On some implementations, information relating to catalogued programs is also held on *POINTER-FILE*. Such items have the format:

item-id:	MYACC*C*ADDRECS	
attribute 1:	C	
attribute 2:	150033	⇐ the frame where the object program is stored
attribute 3:	2	⇐ the number of frames used
attribute 4:		
attribute 5:	10 : 11 : 12 31/12/85	⇐ when catalogued

which will refer to the program catalogued on the *MYACC* account by means of a command of the form:

`CATALOG MYPROGS ADDRECS`

Since *POINTER-FILE* is a standard Pick file, it can be interrogated by means of such Access sentences as:

```
LIST POINTER-FILE

LIST POINTER-FILE = "[RETIRERS]"
```

and so on.

Catalogued programs are discussed in Section 6.19, and saved lists in Section 4.7.

2.12   ADVANTAGES OF PICK FILE STRUCTURE

The summary in Section 2.7 discusses many features of the Pick file structure, and the following points should be borne in mind when you are designing files and records for use on Pick systems:

(a) There is no limit on the size of a file.
(b) Once a file has been created, its physical extent will change as necessary to accommodate the new items added to the file.
(c) There is no limit on the number of items in a file.
(d) There is no limit on the number of attributes in an item.
(e) There is no limit on the size of an attribute.
(f) Attributes, values and secondary values are held as variable-length fields terminated by a field separator.
(g) Trailing spaces need not be held.
(h) Leading zeros need not be held because a null (empty) field is interpreted as 0 by the arithmetic features of Access.
(i) Any field, attribute, value, secondary value or item-id may consist of any characters except the four ASCII characters: 252, 253, 254, 255.
(j) The item-id may be up to fifty characters in length.
(k) There is no other restriction on the format of the item-id. However, if an item-id contains apostrophes, brackets, parentheses, quotation marks, spaces or commas, then it may be ambiguous in certain contexts.

2.13   DISADVANTAGES OF PICK FILE STRUCTURE

The chief disadvantages of the file structure – some real and some psychological – are:

(a) There is no true sequential access.
(b) There is no direct access to a specific record. The entire group must be searched.
(c) No index is kept of the records on a file.
(d) On average, in order to find a specific record, the system will have to scan half the records in the group:

$$\frac{\text{total number of records in the file}}{2 \times \text{the modulo of the file}}$$

(e) To add a new record to a file, the system will have to scan all the records in the group in order to ensure that it does not exist.

(f) Disks are not interchangeable, thus it is not possible to have a specific file/files on a specific disk.

2.14 TIPS AND TECHNIQUES – FILE STRUCTURE

Now let us see how this information is utilized when designing a file structure.

2.14.1 To keep your MD clean

The MD is the most important – and possibly the most inefficient – file on any account. The items on the MD comprise Access verbs, TCL verbs, Procs and many other bits of rubbish. And the more rubbish there is on the MD, the longer it takes to find and process any particular verb.

You can improve the performance of your MD by a number of simple measures:

(a) The MD should contain only TCL verbs, Access verbs, file definition items, Proc pointers and items used by the operating system.

(b) Do not hold programs or Runoff text on the MD.

(c) Do not hold the text of Procs on the MD – instead, use a 'pointer' to pass control to the true text which is held on a separate file. We shall read more about this in Chapter 7 when we deal with Procs.

(d) Try to keep all important verbs – LIST, SORT and so on – near the front of their groups.

(e) Delete all unnecessary verbs from the MD.

You should maintain a regular check on the items held on the MD. The author has done this by maintaining a list of item-ids which are *acceptable* and then periodically deleting all *non-acceptable* items from the MD.

2.14.2 To decide the file modulo and separation

In Section 5.3 we look at the file layout verbs:

```
GROUP
ITEM
ISTAT
STAT
HASH-TEST
```

together with the other verbs which you can use to investigate the structure of a file which already exists. But what can you do in this respect when you are designing a new file?

In general terms, a large item size implies a large separation, and a large number of items implies a large modulo.

There are algorithms for determining the optimum modulo and separation when creating a file, and these suggest that:

(a) The optimum separation is an integer equal to the number of frames required to hold a single typical item.
(b) Using this separation, we can calculate the packing factor, that is the number of typical items which can be held in one group.
(c) The optimum modulo is calculated by dividing the total number of items on the file by this packing factor.

Since the Pick hashing algorithm uses 10 as a weighting factor, any modulo which is a multiple of 10 or 5 or 2 would produce noticeable bunching of the items. To avoid this, the modulo is usually chosen to be the nearest prime number.

To illustrate this, let us imagine a file which is expected to hold up to 3000 items each up to 60 bytes long. Following the above algorithm, we get:

Separation = 1 frame per group.
Packing factor = $1 \times 500/60 = 8.33$ items per group.
Modulo = $3000/8.33 = 360$ to which the nearest prime number is 367.

So we should use a modulo of 367 and a separation of 1.

This does assume an ideal situation in which all items are the same length and in which the item-ids are sequential or uniformly distributed. Items which are longer than the average may cause overflow problems, and if the items have diverse item-ids then this may cause bunching problems in which the groups are not evenly filled.

On most implementations, the operating system accesses the frames one at a time. Therefore, in a multi-user environment, there is no great advantage in having a separation greater than 1 since, by the time the system needs to access the next frame in a group – whether it is in the primary file space or in the overflow area – the disk read–write head will almost certainly have moved to some other position and will have to be re-set to get this next frame. For this reason, a separation of 1 is generally used *after* the modulo has been calculated as above.

The simple sequence shown in Listing 2.3 performs this calculation, and can be easily incorporated into a more sophisticated program for general use. If your implementation uses a frame of other than 512 bytes, then you should amend the value held in *UNIT* accordingly.

```
*  NUMBER = NUMBER OF ITEMS ON FILE
*  LENGTH = AVERAGE LENGTH OF AN ITEM
*
     UNIT=500
*
*       GET NUMBER AND LENGTH
*
     PRINT 'HOW MANY ITEMS':
     INPUT NUMBER
     PRINT 'WHAT IS THE AVERAGE LENGTH OF ITEMS':
     INPUT LENGTH
*
*       CALCULATE SEPARATION
*
     SEP=INT((LENGTH+UNIT-1)/UNIT)
     IF SEP<1 THEN SEP=1
*
*       CALCULATE PACKING FACTOR
*
     PACKFACT=UNIT*SEP/LENGTH
*
*       CALCULATE MOD
*
     MOD=INT(NUMBER/PACKFACT)
*
*       FIND NEAREST PRIME NUMBER TO MOD
*
     IF MOD<4 THEN MOD=3; GO 30
10   XX=SQRT(MOD)
     FOR I=2 TO 19
         IF INT(XX)=MOD THEN GO 20
         ZZ=INT(XX)
         TEST=MOD/ZZ
         IF TEST=INT(TEST) THEN MOD=MOD+1; GO 10
20       XX=I
     NEXT I
*
*       DISPLAY RESULTS
*
30   PRINT 'MODULO=':MOD
     PRINT 'SEPARATION=':SEP:' ... BUT YOU MAY USE 1'
     END
```

Listing 2.3

2.14.3 To change the shape of a file – 1

The modulo and separation of a file can be changed in either of two ways. With one method, the file is re-shaped when the files on the account are next dumped to magnetic tape and then restored; with the second method, the file is re-shaped directly. In these illustrations, we assume that the file to be re-shaped is called ORIGFILE.

The first method causes the shape – that is, the modulo and the separation – of the file to be changed when the files on the account are next dumped to magnetic tape and then restored. This process is described in Chapter 11 when we discuss the file-save and account-save operations.

(a) To change the shape of the DICT section of the file – amend attribute 13 of the MD entry for the file to show the modulo and separation required for the DICT section, by means of the following sequence of commands to the Editor:

```
EDIT MD ORIGFILE
G13
R
(13,1)
FI
```

This requests that the DICT section of the file should have a modulo of 3 and a separation of 1.

(b) To change the shape of the data section of the file – amend attribute 13 of the data-level identifier on the DICT of the file to show the modulo and separation required for the data section:

```
EDIT DICT ORIGFILE dl/id
G13
R
(67,3)
FI
```

This requests that the data section of the file has a modulo of 67 and a separation of 3. *dl/id* is the item-id of the data-level identifier; on most Pick implementations this will be the same as the file name *ORIGFILE*, and on other implementations it will be *DL/ID*. So the EDIT command will be either

```
EDIT DICT ORIGFILE ORIGFILE
```

or

```
EDIT DICT ORIGFILE DL/ID
```

If you only want to re-shape the data section of the file, then you will only perform step (b).

The next file-save and file-restore, or account-save and account-restore, operations will take care of the actual changes in the shape of your file.

2.14.4   To change the shape of a file – 2

There are two ways of changing the file shape immediately. *This is the safest method for most users.*

(a) Dump all the items on the DICT section and the data section of your file to magnetic tape:

```
T-DUMP DICT ORIGFILE
```

```
T-DUMP ORIGFILE
```

(b) Delete the original file:

```
DELETE-FILE (ORIGFILE
```

and then re-create it with the required modulo and separation:

```
CREATE-FILE (ORIGFILE b,c d,e
```

where *ORIGFILE* is the name of your original file; *b* and *c* are the *MOD* and *SEP* which you require for the DICT section of your file; *d* and *e* are the *MOD* and *SEP* of the data section of your file.

(c) Load all the items back to the DICT section and the data section of your file from magnetic tape:

```
T-LOAD DICT ORIGFILE
```

```
T-LOAD ORIGFILE
```

(d) If – *and this is most unusual* – the MD entry for your file, or the data-level identifier on the file dictionary, have any special values in attributes 5, 6, 7, 8, 9 or 10, then be sure to re-set these correctly now by means of the Editor.

If it is inconvenient to use your magnetic-tape device, then the items from the DICT and the data sections of your file can be saved on the DICT and data section of a temporary file which you create and delete just for this exercise. The shape and size of this temporary file is quite arbitrary.

2.14.5   To change the shape of a file – 3

This is an alternative method of changing the shape of a file immediately, but, since it requires you to edit the master dictionary, we emphasize that *this should not be attempted by the inexperienced user.*

(a) Take a hard copy of the MD entry for your original file, in case anything goes wrong:

```
COPY MD ORIGFILE (P)
```

(b) Create a new file with the required modulo and separation:

```
CREATE-FILE (TEMPFILE b,c d,e
```

where *TEMPFILE* is any name you choose, it must not exist on your MD when you start; *b* and *c* are the *MOD* and *SEP* which you require for the DICT section of your file; *d* and *e* are the *MOD* and *SEP* of the data section of your file.

(c) Copy all the items from the original file to the new file:

```
COPY DICT ORIGFILE *
TO:(DICT TEMPFILE

COPY ORIGFILE *
TO:(TEMPFILE
```

(d) Interchange the MD entries for the two files by typing the sequence exactly as shown in Fig. 2.15. *WORKB* is any name you choose, it must not exist on your MD.

```
EDIT MD WORKB TEMPFILE ORIGFILE WORKB
ME999/TEMPFILE/
FI            ... store the definition for TEMPFILE in WORKB
DE999
F
ME999/ORIGFILE/
FI        .... store the definition for ORIGFILE in TEMPFILE
DE999
F
ME999/WORKB/
FI          ... store the definition for TEMPFILE in ORIGFILE
FD                    ... delete the temporary item WORKB
```

Figure 2.15

(e) Delete the temporary file:

```
DELETE-FILE (TEMPFILE
```

(f) If – *and this is most unusual* – the MD entry for your file, or the data-level identifier on the file dictionary, have any special values in attributes 5, 6, 7, 8, 9 or 10, then be sure to re-set these correctly now by means of the Editor.

2.14.6 To organize the attributes within the item

An attribute, or field, of a Pick item can be of any length from 0, that is a null field, up to 32K, each attribute being terminated by an attribute mark. This means that a null attribute is represented only by the trailing attribute mark. Furthermore, null fields at the end of an item are not represented.

Thus, if a typical payroll item looked like this:

```
1111^SMITH, J^D001^9500^64L^17^Y^N
```

then a payroll item with null values for the final three attributes will look like this:

```
2222^JENKINSON, A.W^M02^15000
```

The implication here is that, to conserve file space, any fields which are likely to be null, such as NUMBER OF CHILDREN, HOURS LATE, DAYS OF UNEXPLAINED   ⌐ENCE or SPECIAL PRICE CODE, should be placed at the end of the physical item.

2.14.7   To change a file name

You may wish to change the name of a file in order to make it more user-friendly. Thus, a file which, during development, was known as *MB0043* might be more intelligible to your users if it were to be called *STOCK* or *PARTS* or *INVENTORY*. If the file is to be known as any or all of these, then the simplest way to achieve this 're-naming' is by setting Q-pointers, as described in Section 3.6 and leaving the original file *MB0043* on your account.

If you really wish to re-name the file, so that the original name may be deleted from the MD and used for some other purpose, then this should be done by a sequence of commands such as that shown in Fig. 2.16. If required, you could then set Q-pointers to the *STOCK* file in the manner mentioned above.

```
ED MD STOCK MB0043
NEW ITEM
TOP
.ME999/MB0043/
EOF 10
.FI
'STOCK' FILED

TOP
.FD
'MB0043' DELETED
```

Figure 2.16

2.14.8   To change an item-id

This sounds much more complex than it is. But if you will consider the structure of Pick files and Pick items – particularly when you have looked at the COPY verb – you will see that the simplest way to 'change' an item-id is by a sequence of the form:

```
COPY MYFILE ORIG (D)
TO:NEW
```

which will take the item with the item-id *ORIG* on the file *MYFILE*, save it with the item-id *NEW*, and finally delete the original item.

2.14.9 To simulate sequential access

Items are held on a Pick file in the same order as that in which they were added to the file – *not in ascending order of item-id*. This means that there is no absolute sequence to the records.

Access will easily produce reports sorted according to one or more of the fields in the items. For example:

```
SORT PAYROLL BY DEPT BY GRADE BY NAME
```

or

```
SORT PAYROLL BY GRADE BY AGE BY DEPT
```

If you want to process the records on a file in order of their keys, then you must devise some way to achieve this.

3
Accounts

We have already seen that a Pick account is a user, or group of users, who has access to a common set of files. We have also seen that details of all the accounts on your machine are held as account definition items on the file called *SYSTEM*.

A typical commercial Pick system might have separate accounts for *PERSONNEL, SALES, ADMIN* and so on. At any one time there may be any number of people logged on to an account, and each of these will be processing quite independently of the others. Thus, at 10:30 there may be two people using the *PERSONNEL* account, three people using the *SALES* account and one person using the *ADMIN* account. Each of these people may be working quite independently of the others, or they may be processing data on the same files.

We have seen that each account – *PERSONNEL, SALES, ADMIN* – has its own files, and – in the simplest case – these are inaccessible to other accounts. For example, a user who is logged on to the *PERSONNEL* account cannot look at the contents of the *INVOICES* file held on the *SALES* account.

However, life is not quite so simple. There are many occasions on which two or more accounts might wish to share information. The *ADMIN* account might want to use the *NAME. ADDRESS* file which belongs to *PERSONNEL*. The *SALES* account might need to pass budgeting information to the *ADMIN* account. Now we are faced with two problems:

(a) How can you allow your files to be accessed by another account?
(b) How can you restrict that access? For example, how can you stop people amending files which they are only supposed to look at?

The Pick solutions to these problems are *Q-pointers* and *Lock codes*. In the rest of this chapter, we look at these solutions and we see how to live with your account.

3.1 AN ACCOUNT

Each user of an account has access to the same *master dictionary*, because each account is identified by its master dictionary, and, in many contexts, the term *account* is synonymous with the *master dictionary of that account*.

The details about each account – essentially the definition for its master dictionary – are held in the account definition items on the *SYSTEM* file. A typical account definition item might look like this:

```
        item-id:   PERSONNEL
attribute   1:   D
attribute   2:   87111
attribute   3:   37
attribute   4:   1
attribute   5:   ABC
attribute   6:   XYZ
attribute   7:   MARY
attribute   8:   SYS2(20)
attribute   9:   L
attribute  10:   10
```

the fields representing the following information:

(a) item-id: PERSONNEL – this is the account name which will be used to log on to the system. Since this is the item-id for the account definition item on the SYSTEM file, it may (like any other item-id) be up to fifty characters in length, and may contain any characters except field separators, as described in Section 2.12.

(b) Attribute 1: this is a D indicating that this is a data-file definition. In this case, the file which we are defining is the MD of the *PERSONNEL* account.

(c) Attribute 2: 87111 – this is the base FID, that is, the identity number of the first frame of the MD of this account and is allocated by the operating system when the account is created. Thereafter, it is maintained by the file-save and file-restore routines.

(d) Attribute 3: 37 – this is the modulo of the MD and is specified when the account is created.

(e) Attribute 4: 1 – this is the separation of the MD and is specified when the account is created.

(f) Attribute 5: ABC – this is the *L/RET* lock code or codes necessary to read from any locked files on this account.

(g) Attribute 6: XYZ – this is the *L/UPD* lock code or codes necessary to write to any locked files on this account. As we see below, the lock-code fields may be null if you do not want to have any lock codes on your files.

(h) Attribute 7: MARY – this is the password which is necessary to log on to this account. This field will be null if there is not to be a password on the account. On some implementations, the password is held in a coded form, and can only be changed by a special utility program.

(i) Attribute 8: SYS2(20) – this is the system privileges and additional workspace assignment for this account. We discuss these below.

(j) Attribute 9: L – this is the logging indicator, and will be either U, indicating that the usage is to be recorded on the *ACC* file whenever this account logs on and off; or it may be L, as in this case, indicating that the usage is not to be recorded.

(k) Attribute 10: this contains the value 10 in the present context, but is redundant on most implementations and may be omitted.

Attributes 5, 6, 7, 8, 9 and 10 may be changed as required, as we shall see in Section 3.4.3.

3.2 LOCK CODES

The Pick operating system allows you to restrict access to your files by imposing a lock code, so that you can stop other people looking at your files or changing them. These lock codes are held in attributes 5 and 6 of:

(a) Your entry on the *SYSTEM* file.
(b) The file definition item on the master dictionary which identifies the file which is to be locked – this will lock the DICT section of the file.
(c) The data-level identifier item on the dictionary of the file – this will lock the data section of the file.

This is shown in Fig. 3.1.

If you are only imposing read-restrict access, then the simplest solution is to lock the DICT section – by putting lock codes on the file definition item on the MD – and this prevents access to the data section, since the data-level identifier must be read from the DICT section of the file.

These lock codes are known symbolically as *L/RET* and *L/UPD*:

L/RET is held in attribute 5 of the definition item and will restrict access for retrieving data from the file; this includes such activities as using Access, reading, printing or copying from the file.

L/UPD is held in attribute 6 of the definition item and will restrict access for writing data to the file; this includes such activities as writing, updating or editing the file.

The lock codes on the account definition item may be multi-valued, as

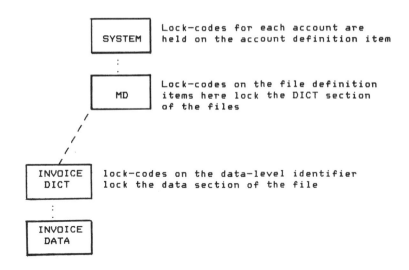

Figure 3.1

shown in the examples below. The lock codes on the file definition items are not multi-valued.

Whenever you attempt to access a file, whether your own or one belonging to another user, the lock codes on the file definition item on the owner's MD and those on the data-level identifier on the file dictionary are checked against those on the account definition item for your account which is held on the SYSTEM file. If no match is found, then the process will be terminated with a message:

`FILE 'INVOICE' IS ACCESS PROTECTED`

Table 3.1 shows how the comparison is made. It is carried out from left to right, and stops when the code on the *file* has been exhausted. Note that if a synonym of an account has different lock codes from the main account, then it may be prevented from accessing the files belonging to the main account.

In many installations it is the responsibility of the SYSPROG account to assign lock codes to accounts, and they may be assigned when the account is created. Account lock codes may be changed by editing the account entry on the SYSTEM file, and file lock codes may subsequently be changed by editing the file definition item on the MD and/or the data-level identifier item on the file dictionary.

Table 3.1

Code on file	User's code on SYSTEM	Result
ABC	ABC	Match – access allowed
AB	ABC	Match – access allowed
ABC	AB	No match – access prohibited
ABC	ABC]XYZ	Match – access allowed
ABC	XYZ]ABC	Match – access allowed
null	ABC	Match – access allowed
ABC	null	No match – access prohibited
null	null	Match – access allowed

3.3 SYSTEM PRIVILEGES

The system-privilege code which is held in attribute 8 of the account definition items in the SYSTEM file will be one of:

SYS2 offering all Pick facilities, including file-save and file-restore operations, use of the DUMP processor and use of any debug command.
SYS1 allowing the account to edit the master dictionary, and to perform magnetic-tape operations and any other features except those specific to SYS2.
SYS0 allowing the account to use only the P, G, END and OFF debug commands and any other features except those specific to SYS1 or SYS2.

The code allows you to restrict the general level of activity which users of that account may perform. The message:

`YOUR SYSTEM PRIVILEGE LEVEL IS NOT SUFFICIENT`

is displayed if you attempt to perform an action for which your privilege level is inadequate.

3.3.1 Additional workspace

When you log on to the Pick operating system, you will have three work spaces allocated to you. These are areas which your processes will use to:

(a) Read in data records.
(b) Hold your program frames.
(c) Perform your processing.
(d) Generate your output records.
(e) Generally keep a copy of the areas of 'memory' which relate to you.

Each user has eighteen frames in all, each workspace being six frames in extent. If you wish to edit large items or process large programs, you may find that this workspace is inadequate, and the process will terminate with the message:

`INSUFFICIENT WORKSPACE`

In such cases, you may obtain a larger workspace when you log on by specifying the required number of frames on your account definition item on the SYSTEM file. In the above example, we saw that the *PERSONNEL* account had

`SYS2(20)`

in attribute 8 of the account definition item. The (20) parameter requests twenty frames for each of the three workspaces. Thus, users of the *PERSONNEL* account will have a total of sixty frames of workspace, instead of the standard eighteen frames. If there are not sixty contiguous frames of space available when such a user logs on, then he or she will be allocated only the basic eighteen frames, and a warning message will inform him or her of this. This is discussed further in Section 12.2, when we deal with primary workspace.

The command WORKSPACE will display the workspace currently allocated to your users.

3.4 CREATING A NEW ACCOUNT

A new account is established by means of the

`CREATE-ACCOUNT`

process on the *SYSPROG* account. This asks you to supply the information which is to be used in the account definition item for the new account, as described in Section 5.4.1.

After an account has been created in this way, the data held in attributes 5–10 of the account definition item may be changed at any time by means of the Editor, as we shall see.

3.4.1 Account synonyms – Q-pointer

This should only be done by an authorized user, and preferably when no other users are logged on to the system.

If you had an account called *WAGES*, and wished to establish a synonym account called *TIMEKEEPER*, then you would use the Editor to create the following item on the SYSTEM file:

item-id:	TIMEKEEPER
attribute 1:	Q
attribute 2:	WAGES
attribute 3:	
attribute 4:	
attribute 5:	
attribute 6:	
attribute 7:	
attribute 8:	
attribute 9:	L
attribute 10:	10

Having established this synonym definition item, you can change the information – such as the password or the system privileges – at any time as shown below.

3.4.2   Changing an account name

If – and this is most unusual – you want to change the name of the account permanently, then this can be done by re-naming the file definition item for the account concerned. Let us suppose that you wish to change the name of the account *STANLEY* to *MARJORIE*. The sequence will be:

```
COPY SYSTEM STANLEY (D)
TO:MARJORIE
```

If your implementation does not allow you to copy file definition items, then use the technique of changing the D to X which we used when creating the empty account in Section 3.7.1.

  This should only be done by an authorized user, and preferably when no other users are logged on to the system.

3.4.3   Changing the account information

This should only be done by an authorized user, and preferably when no other users are logged on to the system.

  The account information can be changed quite effectively by editing the item on the SYSTEM file which identifies the account:

```
EDIT SYSTEM HOLDINGALL
```

In this manner, you can change any or all of the lock codes, the password, the system privileges, the additional workspace and the logging indicator. When you edit this item, you must remember the meaning and format of the account definition item on the SYSTEM file:

(a) Item-id = the account name.
(b) Attribute 1 = a D indicating that this is a data-file definition.
(c) Attribute 2 = the base FID for the MD. You must not change this field.
(d) Attribute 3 = the modulo of the MD. You must not change this field.
(e) Attribute 4: = the separation of the MD. You must not change this field.
(f) Attribute 5 = the *L/RET* lock code. There may be any number of these, separated by the value mark, or the field may be null if you do not want any lock codes on your files.
(g) Attribute 6 = the *L/UPD* lock code. There may be any number of these, separated by the value mark, or the field may be null if you do not want any lock codes on your files.
(h) Attribute 7 = the password. This field will be null if there is not to be a password on the account. On some implementations the password is held in a coded form, and can only be changed by a special utility program.
(i) Attribute 8 = the system privileges and additional workspace in the form:

SYSn(f)

(j) Attribute 9 = the logging indicator. This may be either U or L.

There are a couple of important points to bear in mind when you are amending the entries on the *SYSTEM* file in this manner: firstly, the amended parameters will only be effective when you *next* log on to the account, and, secondly, a word of warning:

If someone amends an item of the SYSTEM file,
and if that item is not the last item in its group,
and if the following items in the group represent accounts,
and if you are already logged on to one of these accounts,
then you may find that the system has forgotten your lock codes and will not allow you to access your own files.

However:

If no one else is logged on to the system,
or if the amended item on the SYSTEM file is the only item in its group,
or if no one is logged on to an item in the same group,
then there will be no problems.

The safest rule is *only amend the SYSTEM file when all other users are logged off* – and then log off yourself.

3.5   DELETING AN ACCOUNT

An account is removed from the system by means of the

DELETE-ACCOUNT

process on the *SYSPROG* account.

Account deletion involves several tasks, including that of deleting all the files relating to that account, and its master dictionary. The final task of removing the account definition item from the SYSTEM dictionary may disturb the log-on information for active users, and consequently it is usually recommended that account deletion only takes place when all other users are logged off.

An account may be deleted quickly and easily by removing the account definition item from the *SYSTEM* file. This can be done quite simply by means of the Editor or the DELETE Proc:

DELETE SYSTEM OLDACC

The obvious weakness in this solution lies in the fact that it does not immediately release the file space used by the account and its files. But if a file-save and file-restore operation is done soon afterwards, then the space previously occupied by the account and its files will be returned to the common pool.

3.6   FILE SYNONYMS – Q-POINTERS

A Q-pointer is an item on your MD which allows you to access a file on another account.

For the purposes of this explanation, we shall use the following terms:

(a) The *local account* is the name of the account – your account – which is attempting to access the other person's files.
(b) The *remote account* is the name of the account which you are trying to access.
(c) The *remote file* is the name of the file which you are trying to access on the remote account.

The format of the Q-pointer is:

(a) Item-id: pointer name. This is any name by which you wish to identify the remote file.
(b) Attribute 1: Q. This identifies the definition as that for a Q-pointer.
(c) Attribute 2: remote-account name. This is the name of the remote account.
   In some implementations of Pick, this field may be empty (null) in which case the name of the local account will be assumed.

(d) Attribute 3: remote-file name. This is the name of the remote file to be accessed.

According to the Pick implementation, a null field has one of the following interpretations:

(i) The master dictionary of the remote account will be assumed – this is the general case.

(ii) The name of the file on which the pointer is held will be assumed; this is on those implementations where Q-pointers may appear on files other than the MD.

(e) Attribute 4: null.

On some implementations the remaining attributes may be omitted.

(a) Attribute   5: null.
(b) Attribute   6: null.
(c) Attribute   7: null.
(d) Attribute   8: null.
(e) Attribute   9: L.
(f) Attribute 10: 10.

To illustrate this, let us suppose that you are using the *ADMIN* account and have this Q-pointer on your MD:

item-id:	MYOWN
attribute 1:	Q
attribute 2:	SALES
attribute 3:	INVOICE
attribute 4:	
attribute 5:	
attribute 6:	
attribute 7:	
attribute 8:	
attribute 9:	L
attribute 10:	10

You can use the file as if it were your own, issuing Access sentences such as:

`LIST MYOWN CUSTOMER AMOUNT DATE. DUE`

or TCL verbs, such as

`EDIT MYOWN 1022`

Any such references to MYOWN will – via the Q-pointer – refer to the INVOICE file owned by the *SALES* account. The Access definitions –

such as CUSTOMER, AMOUNT, and DATE. DUE – will be held on the DICT section of the INVOICES file.

If there are any lock codes on the INVOICE file, then you must have matching lock codes on your own account definition item, in order to access the file.

Incidentally, some implementations do not allow you to have a Q-pointer pointing to a Q-pointer. That is, you could not have a further Q-pointer item referring to the file *MYOWN* in the above example:

item-id:		MYOTHER1
attribute	1:	Q
attribute	2:	ADMIN
attribute	3:	MYOWN
attribute	4:	
attribute	5:	
attribute	6:	
attribute	7:	
attribute	8:	
attribute	9:	L
attribute	10:	10

Notice that, although this last example may be invalid on some implementations, you may still have a Q-pointer to your own files. This is a useful way of having file synonyms, that is, calling one file by several names. So, if we – on the *ADMIN* account – have a file called *STOCK*, then we could create a Q-pointer like this:

item-id:		INVENTORY
attribute	1:	Q
attribute	2:	ADMIN
attribute	3:	STOCK
attribute	4:	
attribute	5:	
attribute	6:	
attribute	7:	
attribute	8:	
attribute	9:	L
attribute	10:	10

and then issue sentences such as:

`LIST INVENTORY DESCR VALUE LOCATION`

or

`LIST STOCK DESCR VALUE LOCATION`

Both sentences will have the same effect.

3.6.1 Creating a Q-pointer

There is a standard Proc which will allow you to set up a simple Q-pointer. This is used by entering a command of the form:

```
SET-FILE WAGES RATES
```

and will set up a Q-pointer called QFILE on your MD, and this points to the file *RATES* owned by the *WAGES* account, thus:

item-id:		QFILE
attribute	1:	Q
attribute	2:	WAGES
attribute	3:	RATES
attribute	4:	
attribute	5:	
attribute	6:	
attribute	7:	
attribute	8:	
attribute	9:	L
attribute	10:	10

Subsequently, by using the name *QFILE*, in such commands as:

```
LIST QFILE
EDIT QFILE *
COUNT QFILE
```

you will be accessing the file RATES held on the *WAGES* account, just as we saw in our general discussion of Q-pointers.

Each time you – or anyone else on your account – uses the SET-FILE Proc, the previous *QFILE* item will be overwritten. Therefore, you will only use this method for those Q-pointers which you want to use as a one-off. If you wish to use the Q-pointer for a longer time, then you should copy the QFILE item to a more permanent place on your MD, like this:

```
COPY MD QFILE
TO:WAGES*RATES
```

It is good practice to use meaningful names for your Q-pointers, as in this example.

You might also be interested in Section 2.14.7 where we see how to change the name of a file.

3.7   ACCOUNT PROCESSING

The following tips may be of interest when creating or deleting accounts. Some of them are quite technical and utilize the fact that an account is simply a dictionary file (the master dictionary of that account) to which a D-pointer is held on the *SYSTEM* file, and is thus interpreted as an account definition item.

3.7.1   Creating empty accounts

The simplest way to create a new account is by means of the

```
CREATE-ACCOUNT
```

facility on the *SYSPROG* account, as described above. There is, however, frequently a need to have an account for holding files which are accessed by Q-pointers from other accounts. On this *HOLDING* account, there is no need to have a complete master dictionary with all its verbs and Procs, as this would take up unnecessary space.

An empty holding account may be established by the following sequence of operations:

(a) Log on to any account.
(b) Create a DICT level file which is to become the MD of the new account:

```
CREATE-FILE (DICT HOLDINGALL 13,1
```

(c) Create a definition for the name 'MD' on the file:

```
COPY MD HOLDINGALL
TO: (DICT HOLDINGALL
```

or, on McDonnell Douglas implementations:

```
COPY MD HOLDINGALL
TO: (DICT HOLDINGALL DL/ID
```

This will allow you to set Q-pointers to the MD of the account-to-be, as we shall see in the next section.

(d) At this stage, you can also copy items, such as verbs, from your own MD to the MD-to-be of *HOLDINGALL*:

```
COPY MD SORT LIST CREATE-FILE DELETE-FILE OFF
TO: (DICT HOLDINGALL
```

Remember that, if you do not do this, the MD of *HOLDINGALL* will be empty, and you will not be able to do any work when you log on. The verbs which you should have are:

```
CREATE-FILE
DELETE-FILE
EDIT
LIST
SORT
OFF
```

The verb OFF is very important, since, if you do log on to *HOLD-INGALL* at any time, you will not be able to log off, except by means of the break key and OFF!

(e) Copy the file definition for this new file to the *SYSTEM* file:

```
COPY MD HOLDINGALL (D)
  TO: (SYSTEM
```

thereby establishing the new account definition item. It is this step which changes your DICT file into the master dictionary of the *HOLDINGALL* account.

Some implementations will not allow you to copy a D-item from one file to another. You can get around this problem by using the Editor to change the D in attribute 1 to some other character, and then change it back to a D after copying. Then copy this item, as in these two steps:

```
COPY MD HOLDINGALL
TO: (DICT HOLDINGALL

COPY MD HOLDINGALL (D)
TO: (SYSTEM
```

and, if necessary, re-set the D on both items, by means of the Editor:

```
EDIT SYSTEM HOLDINGALL
```

and

```
EDIT DICT HOLDINGALL MD
```

(f) Set the password, system privileges and logging indicator as described in Section 3.4.3.

You should only change the *SYSTEM* file when there are no other users logged on to the system.

Now let us see how to push files from one account to another, so that we can get files onto this holding account.

3.7.2 Pushing a file to another account

Since a file is *owned* by the account on whose MD the file definition item appears, the act of *pushing* or *pulling* a file from one account to another is a simple matter of moving the file definition to another master dictionary. Thus, to move the file *MOVING1* from your own account to another remote account, *HOLDINGALL*, the sequence of operations would be:

(a) Establish a Q-pointer to the master dictionary of the remote account:

```
SET-FILE HOLDINGALL MD
```

(b) Copy the file definition from your MD to that of the account called *HOLDINGALL*:

```
COPY MD MOVING1 (D)
TO: (QFILE
```

If your implementation does not allow you to copy file definition items, then use the technique of changing the D to X which we used when creating the empty account in the previous section.

(c) You may then wish to set a Q-pointer to the file *MOVING1* which is now *owned* by the *HOLDINGALL* account.

When moving files between accounts, as described in this and the following section, you should consider any Q-pointers which pointed to the original file, and remember that some implementations do not allow you to have a Q-pointer to a Q-pointer.

If you are likely to have to *push* files across in this manner, then you could establish a Proc, as shown in Listing 3.1.

3.7.3 Pulling a file from another account

This is the reverse of the previous technique. Now, you will have to copy the file definition item *from* the remote account *to* your own account. Thus, to move the file *MOVING1* from the remote account *HOLDINGALL* to your own account, the sequence of operations would be:

(a) Establish a Q-pointer to the master dictionary of the remote account:

```
SET-FILE HOLDINGALL MD
```

(b) Copy the file definition from the MD of *HOLDINGALL* to your own MD:

```
COPY QFILE MOVING1 (D)
TO: (MD
```

If your implementation does not allow you to copy file definition items,

```
PQ
OPUSH TO WHICH ACCOUNT+
IP?
HED MD QFILE
STON
HDE999<
HF<
HI Q<
C NEXT LINE HAS A SPACE AT THE END .
HI
A1
H<
HI MD<
HI ,<
HI ,<
HI ,<
HI ,<
HI ,<
HI L<
HI 10<
HF<
HR999/,//<
HFI
P
O
OQFILE RESET
OPUSH WHICH FILE+
IP?
HED MD
A2
STON
HR/D/X<
HFI
P
HCOPY MD
A2
H(D)
STON
H(QFILE
P
HED QFILE
A2
STON
HR/X/D/<
HFI
P
```

Listing 3.1

then use the technique of changing the D to some other character which we used when creating the empty account in Section 3.7.1.

If you are likely to have to *pull* files across in this manner, then you could establish a Proc, as shown in Listing 3.2.

```
PQ
OPULL FROM WHICH ACCOUNT+
IP?
HED MD QFILE
STON
HDE999<
HF<
HI Q<
C NEXT LINE HAS A SPACE AT THE END
HI
A1
H<
HI MD<
HI , <
HI , <
HI , <
HI , <
HI , <
HI L<
HI 10<
HF<
HR999/, //<
HFI
P
O
OQFILE RESET
OPULL WHICH FILE+
IP?
HED QFILE
A2
STON
HR/D/X/<
HFI
P
HCOPY QFILE
A2
H(D)
STON
H(MD
P
HED MD
A2
STON
HR/X/D<
HFI
P
```

Listing 3.2

4

Access – database retrieval language

Interrogation of files and report production is greatly simplified on the Pick operating system by the concept of the database retrieval language. According to the implementation, the database retrieval language is known variously as Access, English, Query or Recall. In this book, we shall use the name Access.

Let us begin by looking at a few Access statements, and see how they are constructed.

```
LIST STOCK FILE WITH STOCK-ON-HAND LESS THAN "100"
SORT PERSONNEL BY NAME WITH AGE < "21" TOTAL SALARY
SORT NAME AGE ADDRESS OF PERSONNEL BY START-DATE
LIST NAME ADDRESS SEX OF PERSONNEL WITH SURNAME =
   "JONES"
SORT INVOICES BALANCE BY DATE BREAK-ON DATE LPTR
```

The sort of output which these sentences might produce is shown in the examples in Section 4.1 entitled Looking at Access.

We can see that an Access sentence comprises a number of syntax elements:

(a) LIST or SORT is the instruction to produce a report.
(b) INVOICES to list the records on the file called *INVOICES*. We also use the *STOCK* file and the *PERSONNEL* file.
(c) NAME to print the contents of the field called NAME – this element may be repeated as required.
(d) BY NAME to sort the report in ascending order of the field called NAME – this element may be repeated as required to sort one field within another – see Section 4.4.4 which deals with sort criteria.
(e) WITH AGE < "21" to include only those records for which the field called AGE satisfies the condition shown – this element may be repeated as required joined with OR and/or AND operators – see Section 4.4.5 which deals with selection criteria.
(f) BREAK-ON DATE to produce a control break when the field called DATE changes – this element may be repeated as required – see Section 4.4.7 which deals with control breaks.

(g) TOTAL SALARY to accumulate the field called SALARY and print this at each control break and at the end of the report – this element may be repeated as required – see Section 4.4.6 which deals with field totals.

(h) LPTR to direct the report to the line printer, rather than the screen.

For each field which is to be used in the Access sentence, you must create a *dictionary definition* which specifies:

(a) The name by which that field is to be known in the Access sentence – we used NAME, AGE, DATE and BALANCE in the above examples.

(b) A text heading which is to be used when printing that field.

(c) The maximum column width which is to be allowed for that field on the printed report.

(d) The justification of the field – left or right – within the column width. Columns of numbers look neater if they are right-justified.

(e) Any output conversion which is to be performed on the data in that field – such as inserting a decimal point, preceding a pound sign, converting to day–month–year format and so on.

(f) Whether the data are to be taken from a single field, or whether they are the result of calculations involving one or more other fields on this record – for example, we might request Access to calculate the value of our stock by multiplying the quantity-on-hand by the unit-cost.

As the analyst, you will be responsible for creating these definitions. There may be as many dictionary definitions as you like.

4.1 LOOKING AT ACCESS

Before we take a detailed look at Access, let us consider a few of the items on our *STOCK* file, and see how Access will allow us to produce reports on these items. The raw data are shown in Table 4.1.

Table 4.1

1479^LADDERS, STEEL, RED^UK2/965^6^10^6096^6850
1005^STOOLS, SPECIAL, BLUE^UK2/75^52^50^5997^3750
1000^CHAIRS, WOODEN, RED^UK/614^64^50^6125^5875
0567^STOOLS, STEEL, BLUE^MN/206^4^^5967^5677
0372^DESKS, STEEL, VIOLET^MN/384^22^10^6104^4222

The significance of the various fields is:

(a) The item-id, sometimes called attribute 0, is the stock number. This is four digits and is 1479 on the first item.
(b) Attribute 1 is the product description – item, material, colour – LADDERS, STEEL, RED on the first item.
(c) Attribute 2 is the location, showing the depot code and the shelf number – UK2/965 on the first item.
(d) Attribute 3 is the quantity in stock – 6 on the first item.
(e) Attribute 4 is the minimum level – 10 on the first item.
(f) Attribute 5 is the date last ordered in the internal date format – 6096 on the first item.
(g) Attribute 6 is the unit price in pence – 6850 on the first item.

Before we create any dictionary definition items on the DICT of the *STOCK* file, we have only limited use of Access:

`LIST STOCK`

will display the report shown in Fig. 4.1 and

`SORT STOCK = "1]"`

will display the report shown in Fig. 4.2 showing only the name of the file, and the item-ids of the items on the file.

```
STOCK. . . . .

1479
1005
1000
0567
0372
```

Figure 4.1

```
STOCK. . . . .

1000
1005
1479
```

Figure 4.2

4.1.1 Creating dictionary definitions

All Access dictionary definitions are held on the DICT section of the file
– *STOCK* in our case – and you will create and maintain these by means
of the ordinary Editor.

```
        item-id:  DESCR      LOCN       QTY
    attribute   1:  A          A          A
    attribute   2:  1          2          3
    attribute   3:
    attribute   4:
    attribute   5:
    attribute   6:
    attribute   7:
    attribute   8:
    attribute   9:  L          L          L
    attribute  10:  22         7          5

        item-id:  MINIMUM    DATE       PRICE
    attribute   1:  A          A          A
    attribute   2:  4          5          6
    attribute   3:
    attribute   4:
    attribute   5:
    attribute   6:
    attribute   7:
    attribute   8:
    attribute   9:  L          L          L
    attribute  10:  7          4          5
```

Figure 4.3

We establish six dictionary definition items, one for each of the
attributes in the item, as shown in Fig. 4.3. In these definitions:

(a) The item-id is the name which we shall use in our Access sentences
to identify the field – this is DESCR in the first definition.

(b) Attribute 1 is a letter A, meaning that this is a definition for an
attribute.

(c) Attribute 2 is a number which tells Access which field of our data
records we are going to call DESCR.

(d) Attributes 3–8 are blank here – we shall see some of the information
which goes there later.

(e) Attribute 9 is a letter L, meaning that DESCR and the other values
are to be shown left-justified on the report.

(f) Attribute 10 is a number which tells Access how wide the column is
to be when the field is printed.

We can now use these definitions in an Access sentence such as

`SORT STOCK DESCR LOCN QTY MINIMUM DATE PRICE`

to produce the report shown in Listing 4.1, or we could type the sentence:

`LIST STOCK PRICE QTY QTY`

to produce the report shown in Listing 4.2. You will see how the 'vocabulary' of the Access sentence includes our own definitions DESCR, LOCN and QTY, and these may be used in any order and in any combination in our Access sentences.

Incidentally, it is easy to get confused when we talk about the attributes of our data items and the attributes of our dictionary definition

STOCK.....	DESCR...................	LOCN...	QTY..	MINIMUM	DATE	PRICE
0372	DESKS, STEEL, VIOLET	MN/384	22	10	6104	4222
0567	STOOLS, STEEL, BLUE	MN/206	4		5967	5677
1000	CHAIRS, WOODEN, RED	UK/614	64	50	6125	5875
1005	STOOLS, SPECIAL, BLUE	UK2/75	52	50	5997	3750
1479	LADDERS, STEEL, RED	UK2/965	6	10	6096	6850

Listing 4.1

STOCK.....	PRICE	QTY..	QTY..
1479	6850	6	6
1005	3750	52	52
1000	5875	64	64
0567	5677	4	4
0372	4222	22	22

Listing 4.2

items. This is because Pick itself does not distinguish between the two sorts of item. It is only Access which uses the information held in the dictionary definition items to interpret the data items on our files. Take it slowly, and make sure you understand each of these sections before going on to the next.

4.1.2 Changing the heading

As you can see, the names which we gave the definition – DESCR, LOCN and QTY – were used as the column headings. We could change the definition for the name DESCR so that it displays the full word DESCRIPTION, like this:

         item-id: DESCR
    attribute 1: A
    attribute 2: 1
    attribute 3: DESCRIPTION
    attribute 4:
    attribute 5:
    attribute 6:
    attribute 7:
    attribute 8:
    attribute 9: L
    attribute 10: 22

So that the Access sentence:

`SORT STOCK DESCR QTY`

will produce the report shown in Listing 4.3.

```
STOCK.....    DESCRIPTION...........  QTY..

0372          DESKS, STEEL, VIOLET     22
0567          STOOLS, STEEL, BLUE       4
1000          CHAIRS, WOODEN, RED      64
1005          STOOLS, SPECIAL, BLUE    52
1479          LADDERS, STEEL, RED       6
```

Listing 4.3

If we type the Access sentence:

`SORT STOCK DESCR QTY BY DESCR`

then we should get the report shown in Listing 4.4, with the report sorted in ascending order of description.

```
STOCK.....    DESCRIPTION...........  QTY..

1000          CHAIRS, WOODEN, RED      64
0372          DESKS, STEEL, VIOLET     22
1479          LADDERS, STEEL, RED       6
1005          STOOLS, SPECIAL, BLUE    52
0567          STOOLS, STEEL, BLUE       4
```

Listing 4.4

Attribute 3 is particularly useful when the heading which you want to appear on the report is:

(a) Long – DESCR is much easier to type than DESCRIPTION.
(b) To consist of several words – we could have had NAME OF PRODUCT at the head of the column by having

```
NAME OF PRODUCT
```

in attribute 3 of the dictionary definition.
(c) To be more than one line – if attribute 3 of the dictionary definition contained

```
NAME]OF]PRODUCT
```

with the value mark to separate the lines, then the heading line on the above report would have been:

```
STOCK . . . . . . . . NAME . . . . . . . . . . . . . QTY . .
                      OF
                      PRODUCT
```

4.1.3 Changing the justification – left or right

You can see that all the fields are left-justified – even the numbers. We have seen what happened when we typed the sentence:

```
SORT STOCK DESCR QTY BY DESCR
```

and got the report sorted in order of description, but if we typed the sentence:

```
SORT STOCK DESCR QTY BY QTY
```

to sort the report in order of quantity, we should get the report shown in Listing 4.5. Not quite what we wanted. Do you see why? It is because our definition for QTY says that the field is *left-justified*.

```
STOCK. . . . .   DESCRIPTION. . . . . . . . . .   QTY. .

0372             DESKS, STEEL, VIOLET             22
0567             STOOLS, STEEL, BLUE              4
1005             STOOLS, SPECIAL, BLUE            52
1479             LADDERS, STEEL, RED              6
1000             CHAIRS, WOODEN, RED              64
```

Listing 4.5

We could change this by using the definition:

```
        item-id:  QTY
attribute  1:  A
attribute  2:  3
attribute  3:
attribute  4:
attribute  5:
attribute  6:
attribute  7:
attribute  8:
attribute  9:  R
attribute 10:  5
```

the R in attribute 9 specifying that the field is right-justified.

It is particularly important to get the justification right when you are sorting. If we now type the sentence:

`SORT STOCK DESCR QTY BY QTY`

we should get it right, as shown in Listing 4.6, and if we type the sentence:

`SORT STOCK DESCR TOTAL QTY`

we should get the report shown in Listing 4.7, with the numbers right-justified, and the total neatly underneath.

```
STOCK.....   DESCRIPTION..........   QTY..

0567         STOOLS, STEEL, BLUE          4
1479         LADDERS, STEEL, RED          6
0372         DESKS, STEEL, VIOLET        22
1005         STOOLS, SPECIAL, BLUE       52
1000         CHAIRS, WOODEN, RED         64
```

Listing 4.6

```
STOCK.....   DESCRIPTION..........   QTY..

0372         DESKS, STEEL, VIOLET        22
0567         STOOLS, STEEL, BLUE          4
1000         CHAIRS, WOODEN, RED         64
1005         STOOLS, SPECIAL, BLUE       52
1479         LADDERS, STEEL, RED          6

***                                    148
```

Listing 4.7

4.1.4 Changing the column width

Attribute 10 of the dictionary definition tells the Access processor how wide the displayed column is to be. We might feel that the QTY column is too wide, so we could change it:

```
       item-id:  QTY
attribute  1:  A
attribute  2:  3
attribute  3:
attribute  4:
attribute  5:
attribute  6:
attribute  7:
attribute  8:
attribute  9:  R
attribute 10:  3
```

so that the Access sentence:

`SORT STOCK DESCR TOTAL QTY`

will now produce the report shown in Listing 4.8.

```
STOCK.....  DESCRIPTION...........  QTY

0372        DESKS, STEEL, VIOLET    22
0567        STOOLS, STEEL, BLUE      4
1000        CHAIRS, WOODEN, RED     64
1005        STOOLS, SPECIAL, BLUE   52
1479        LADDERS, STEEL, RED      6

***                                148
```

Listing 4.8

```
STOCK.....  DESCRIPTION....  QTY

0372        DESKS, STEEL, V  22
            IOLET
0567        STOOLS, STEEL,    4
            BLUE
1000        CHAIRS, WOODEN,  64
            RED
1005        STOOLS, SPECIAL  52
            , BLUE
1479        LADDERS, STEEL,   6
            RED
```

Listing 4.9

If the column is not wide enough – let us suppose that our DESCR definition only gave a width of 15 – then you might get something like the report shown in Listing 4.9, with the text just being broken down into fifteen-character wide chunks.

The columns can be as wide as you like. But if they are too wide, you may find that the neat tabular form is upset, and the Access processor might display the report like the report shown in Listing 4.10, going 'down the page' instead of across in neat columns, because the Access processor cannot fit the required report within the width of the screen or the printed page.

```
STOCK : 0372
DESCRIPTION    DESKS, STEEL, VIOLET
LOCN    MN/384
QTY    22
MINIMUM    10
DATE    6104
PRICE    4222

STOCK : 0567
DESCRIPTION    STOOLS, STEEL, BLUE
LOCN    MN/206
QTY    4
DATE    5967
PRICE    5677
```

Listing 4.10

4.1.5 Converting numbers

Let us go back to the PRICE field. At the beginning we said that the price in attribute 6 is in pence. Why do we hold it this way? Why not hold it with a decimal point? How can we show a decimal point on our reports?

Well, we hold the number without a decimal point for two reasons: firstly, it takes less space on our file; secondly, so that we can total the figures in Access (we'll see more about this later).

We can always put the decimal point back in by using a *conversion* code in attribute 7 of the dictionary definition:

```
        item-id:  PRICE
    attribute  1:  A
    attribute  2:  6
    attribute  3:
    attribute  4:
    attribute  5:
    attribute  6:
```

```
        attribute  7:   MD2
        attribute  8:
        attribute  9:   R
        attribute 10:   5
```

The MD2 means that the value is to be shown with a decimal mask (or pattern) of *two* places of decimals. We can now issue the Access sentence:

`SORT STOCK DESCR LOCN QTY DATE PRICE`

to produce the report shown in Listing 4.11.

```
STOCK.....   DESCRIPTION..........   LOCN...   QTY DATE PRICE

0372         DESKS, STEEL, VIOLET    MN/384     22 6104 42.22
0567         STOOLS, STEEL, BLUE     MN/206      4 5967 56.77
1000         CHAIRS, WOODEN, RED     UK/614     64 6125 58.75
1005         STOOLS, SPECIAL, BLUE   UK2/75     52 5997 37.50
1479         LADDERS, STEEL, RED     UK2/965     6 6096 68.50
```

Listing 4.11

4.1.6   Converting dates

The DATE in attribute 5 is held in the internal format, but we can make it meaningful by putting a *conversion* code in attribute 7 of the dictionary definition:

```
          item-id:  DATE
        attribute  1:  A
        attribute  2:  5
        attribute  3:
        attribute  4:
        attribute  5:
        attribute  6:
        attribute  7:  D
        attribute  8:
        attribute  9:  L
        attribute 10:  11
```

The D means that this is to be converted to *date* format. Notice that we have also changed the column width (attribute 10). We can now issue the Access sentence:

`SORT STOCK DESCR LOCN DATE PRICE BY DATE`

to produce the report shown in Listing 4.12.

```
STOCK.....   DESCRIPTION..........   LOCN...  DATE.......  PRICE

0567         STOOLS,  STEEL,  BLUE    MN/206    2 MAY 1984 56.77
1005         STOOLS,  SPECIAL,  BLUE  UK2/75    1 JUN 1984 37.50
1479         LADDERS,  STEEL,  RED    UK2/965   8 SEP 1984 68.50
0372         DESKS,  STEEL,  VIOLET   MN/384   16 SEP 1984 42.22
1000         CHAIRS,  WOODEN,  RED    UK/614    7 OCT 1984 58.75
```

Listing 4.12

As we shall see later, we could also have requested the date to be shown in other forms, for example:

```
16/09/84
16/09/1984
16.09.84
09/16/84
```

4.1.7 Picking parts of a field

So far we have seen how to process an entire field. But can we pick out a part of a field – just the DEPOT CODE from attribute 2, for example? Or the COLOUR from attribute 1? The answer to both these is *yes*. Like this:

	DEPOT	COLOUR
item-id:		
attribute 1:	A	A
attribute 2:	2	1
attribute 3:		
attribute 4:		
attribute 5:		
attribute 6:		
attribute 7:		
attribute 8:	G0/1	G2 1
attribute 9:	L	L
attribute 10:	5	10

In this definition for DEPOT, the code G0/1 means *regard this field as being made up of groups separated by / and skip 0, such groups then display the next 1* so that UK2/965 will be interpreted as two groups UK2 and 965, then no groups will be skipped, and UK2 will be displayed.

In our definition for COLOUR, G2 1 will interpret DESKS, STEEL, VIOLET as three groups separated by spaces, skip 2 (DESKS and STEEL), and display the next 1 (VIOLET).

So the Access sentence:

```
SORT STOCK BY COLOUR BREAK-ON COLOUR DESCR DEPOT
    DATE
```

will produce the report shown in Listing 4.13.

```
STOCK.....   COLOUR....   DESCRIPTION...........   DEPOT DATE......

0567         BLUE         STOOLS, STEEL, BLUE      MN     2 MAY 1984
1005         BLUE         STOOLS, SPECIAL, BLUE    UK2    1 JUN 1984

             ***

1000         RED          CHAIRS, WOODEN, RED      UK     7 OCT 1984
1479         RED          LADDERS, STEEL, RED      UK2    8 SEP 1984

             ***

0372         VIOLET       DESKS, STEEL, VIOLET     MN    16 SEP 1984

             ***

***
```

Listing 4.13

4.1.8 Performing arithmetic

Our data records hold the price of each item (in attribute 6) and the number of items in stock (in attribute 3). If we want to know the value of the stock – that is, the PRICE multiplied by the QTY – then we could use a dictionary definition to perform this calculation for us:

```
      item-id:  VALUE
  attribute  1:  A
  attribute  2:  0
  attribute  3:
  attribute  4:
  attribute  5:
  attribute  6:
  attribute  7:  MD2
  attribute  8:  F;3;6;*
  attribute  9:  R
  attribute 10:  10
```

The code F;3;6;* in attribute 8 of this definition means 'take attribute 3 of our data items, and attribute 6, and multiply them together' and then after this calculation has been done the MD2 code inserts the decimal point for us, as before.

Notice that it doesn't matter what number we write in attribute 2 of this definition, since attribute 8 only concerns attributes 3 and 6 of our data items. It is, however, good practice to use 0.

Now the sentence:

```
SORT STOCK DESCRIPTION QTY PRICE TOTAL VALUE
```

will produce the report shown in Listing 4.14.

```
STOCK.....  DESCR.................  QTY PRICE VALUE.....

0372        DESKS, STEEL, VIOLET    22 42.22    928.84
0567        STOOLS, STEEL, BLUE      4 56.77    227.08
1000        CHAIRS, WOODEN, RED     64 58.75   3760.00
1005        STOOLS, SPECIAL, BLUE   52 37.50   1950.00
1479        LADDERS, STEEL, RED      6 68.50    411.00

***                                           7276.92
```

Listing 4.14

These, then, are some of the features of Access. They are all produced simply by creating a dictionary definition item on the DICT of the file. When you have established your definitions – and you may have as many as you want – you can use them in a variety of Access sentences to produce reports on the contents of your files.

4.2 SUMMARY OF ACCESS FEATURES

The application of Access is in those areas which demand:

- Displayed or printed reports.
- *Ad hoc* reports.
- File interrogation by non-technical users.
- Standard reports sorted according to specific criteria – produce a list of all employees sorted by salary within age within department.
- Standard reports of records selected according to specific criteria – produce a list of all employees with age greater than 21 and with salary less than £6500.
- Searches of files for specific records – display records for MARY SMITH and PETER MILES.
- Searches of files for specific strings in specific fields – display the personnel records for everyone called SMITH.
- The reports may be sorted into ascending or descending sequence on any numbers of sort keys.
- Any data field may be held in packed decimal, or in internal date or internal time format.
- Format conversion may be performed on the raw data, inserting decimal points, pound sign and commas.
- Calculations may be performed on the raw data held on the file.
- Control breaks may be produced as required.
- Totals and sub-totals may be produced for any data fields.
- Page headings and page footings may be generated and, at control breaks, the break field may be displayed within these headings or footings.

The beauty of Access lies in its flexibility. Once the analyst has established a set of dictionary definitions for the data fields on the records of a file, then these may be used in any way and in any combination to produce the required reports.

It might be argued that Access becomes unwieldy when the non-technical user has to type in complex sentences to get a standard report. In such situations, the combination of Access and Proc enables such sentences to be retained and invoked by means of a single command. This is a particularly valuable feature if the sentence – or sequence of sentences – is to be used over and over again.

The advantages of Access – particularly over certain other database retrieval systems – include:

(a) The files do not have to be specially constructed – Access will work with any Pick data.
(b) The raw data can be converted as they are output – a date may be held in the internal form and displayed as:

```
01 JAN 1986
01/01/86
01.01.1986
```

This is a valuable feature, since it allows a report to be sorted by the internal date and then output in external format, as shown above.
(c) Calculations can be performed on the raw data – the value of the stock items may be obtained by multiplying the unit-price field by the quantity in stock, as shown above.
(d) Strings can be extracted from within data fields – the depot code can be extracted from the location field.
(e) The raw data can be interpreted as keys pointing to other files – the customer number on the *INVOICE* file can point directly to the *CLIENTS* file. In this way you can show the client's name on the *INVOICE* report, even though the name is not held on the *INVOICE* file.
(f) You may have any number of definitions for a field. Thus, attribute 1 of our *STOCK* file might be known variously as DESCR, D, DESCRIPTION, NAME, TITLE, PRODUCT, D50, D30 and so on. Each such definition may have different output characteristics, different field width, different heading or different justification, but all will refer to the data held in attribute 1.

The rest of this chapter is aimed at a fairly technical level, so if you begin to feel that you are getting out of your depth, leave it for now and come back to it again later when you need to.

4.3 ACCESS – DATABASE RETRIEVAL LANGUAGE VERBS

Table 4.2 shows the verbs which are available for use with the Pick database inquiry language. Each of these verbs may be used in the same context as LIST and SORT. So that:

```
LIST PERSONNEL NAME DEPARTMENT SALARY WITH AGE <
   "21"
```

is parallel to:

```
COUNT PERSONNEL NAME DEPARTMENT SALARY WITH AGE <
   "21"
```

The LIST sentence will display the fields of the appropriate records, whereas the COUNT sentence will ignore the output list – NAME, DEPARTMENT and SALARY – and simply print a message such as:

```
25 ITEMS COUNTED
```

and could have been typed as:

```
COUNT PERSONNEL WITH AGE < "21"
```

Table 4.2

CHECK-SUM	LIST	SORT	STAT
COUNT	LIST-LABEL	SORT-LABEL	SUM
HASH-TEST	REFORMAT	SREFORMAT	T-DUMP
I-DUMP	S-DUMP	SSELECT	T-LOAD
ISTAT	SELECT	ST-DUMP	

4.4 SENTENCE FORMAT

Let us look at the structure of an Access sentence a little more thoroughly. The format of the Access sentences is as follows:

verb, file name, item list, selection criteria,
sort criteria, field totals, break criteria, output list,
heading details, device specification,

where:

(a) Verb is any of the Access verbs shown in Table 4.2. For example,

```
SORT . . .
```

This verb must be the first element of the Access sentence. The remaining elements may appear in any order.

(b) File name is the name of the file which is to be processed. For example:

`SORT STOCK . . .`

The file name may be a Q-pointer to another file. In such a case, the attribute definitions will be on the dictionary of the remote file at which the Q-pointer is directed.

If you are using Access to process the items on the DICT section of a file, then you will use the form:

`LIST DICT STOCK . . .`

If you are using Access with sub-files which share a common DICT section, then you will use the form:

`LIST DSTOCK,SFILE . . .`

where *DSTOCK* is the name of the dictionary, and *SFILE* is the name of the data file.

The remaining elements of the sentence are optional, and may be omitted, or they may be included in any logical sequence.

(c) Item list is any list of item-ids for items which are to be submitted for processing.The item-ids are enclosed in apostrophes. For example:

`SORT STOCK '1000' '2000' '3000' . . .`

The list of item-ids may be as long as required.

(d) Selection criteria specify the criteria which each item must satisfy in order to be acceptable for processing by the Access command. For example:

`SORT STOCK . . . WITH ON-HAND > "10" . . .`

will display only those items for which the field defined as ON-HAND contains a value greater than 10.

(e) Sort criteria specify the sequence in which the items are to be sorted. For example:

`SORT INVOICES . . . BY DATE . . .`

Descending sequence is obtained by the operator BY-DSND. Several such sorting specifications may be given:

`. . . BY NAME BY-DSND AGE BY DEPT . . .`

(f) Break criteria specify the control breaks which are to be made. For example:

`SORT PERSONNEL . . . BY DEPT . . . BREAK-ON DEPT . .`

(g) Output list specifies the names of the attributes which are to appear in the printed output, if any. For example:

`LIST PERSONNEL . . . NAME AGE TELEPHONE AGE . . .`

If you are using Access to process items held on the DICT section of a file, then the names in the output list will be held on the MD. Thus:

`LIST DICT MD *A1 *A2`

assumes that the dictionary definitions for *A1 and *A2 are held on your MD.

(h) Heading details specifies the page heading which is to be given to the report. For example:

`SORT STATEMENTS . . . HEADING "STATEMENT LISTING"`

Footing details may also be specified.

(i) Device specification is the destination of the printed output, if any. For example:

`SORT INVOICES . . . LPTR`

If no device specification is given, then the report will be displayed at the terminal.

Other elements which are commonly encountered in an Access statement include:

(a) ID-SUPP which will suppress the automatic printing of the item-ids of the items listed.

(b) HDR-SUPP which will suppress the standard page heading showing the date, time and page number.

(c) COL-HDR-SUPP which will suppress the column header titles.

(d) When an Access report is being displayed on the terminal screen, the system will pause at the end of each page, and you must then press <RETURN> to continue with the next page. If required, the report can be abandoned at this stage by pressing the <CONTROL> X character, or the <CONTROL> E character on some implementations, instead of <RETURN>.

If you do not want the report to halt at the foot of each page – you may only be interested in the final totals, for example – then you may use the NOPAGE modifier. Some implementations assume NOPAGE as the default, and on these you would have to use the PAGE modifier to pause at the foot of each page.

(e) TOTAL BALANCE which will be included within the output-list element, and will cause the attribute BALANCE to be accumulated and printed at control breaks and at end-of-report.

These elements of an Access sentence are discussed below.

Table 4.3 shows a group of words which are known as *throwaway connectives* and you may include them anywhere within an Access sentence in order to render it intelligible. The words are ignored by the processor.

Table 4.3

!	CALLED	NOW	PLEASE
*	FILE	OF	THAN
A	FOR	ON	THE
ALL	FROM	OR	THEN
AN	IN	PAGE	THOSE
ANY	IS	PAY	UNDER
ARE	ITEMS	PG	YOU

Thus, the following three sentences are equivalent:

```
LIST THE INVENTORY FILE OF ITEMS WITH A STOCK < "100"
    PLEASE
LIST INVENTORY WITH STOCK < "100"
LIST ANY ITEMS ON THE INVENTORY FILE WITH THE STOCK
    LESS THAN "100"
```

Note that A is a throwaway connective and will therefore be ignored if it is used as a data name in an output list. This is a frequent source of confusion when you create dictionary definition items A, B, C and so on, as you will find that only B, C and D are output from a sentence such as:

```
LIST STATISTICS A B C D
```

4.4.1 Item list

The item list is any list of item-ids for items which are to be submitted for processing. All other items in the file will be ignored.

The item-ids are enclosed in apostrophes, and may be expressed explicitly:

```
SORT STOCK '1000' '2000' '3000'
```

The list of item-ids may be as long as required, and may include relational and logical operators:

```
LIST PROGFILE > '£'
SORT STOCK <= '4000' AND >= '1000'
LIST ACCOUNTS # '1000' AND # '2000' AND # '3000'
SORT INVOICES BEFORE '0100'
SORT DETAILS 'A0001' OR >= 'B0100' AND < 'C0000'
```

Note that no identifier precedes the relational operator.

The following points may apply, according to implementation:

(a) Quotation marks may be used instead of apostrophes:

```
SORT STOCK "1000" "2000" "3000"
```

(b) Square brackets may be used to restrict the value search, although the following should be noted:

```
SORT STOCK = '1]'
```

will list all items with item-ids starting with a 1, whereas

```
SORT STOCK '1]'
```

will expect to find an item with an item-id consisting of the two characters 1].

(c) Spaces may be omitted between item-ids:

```
SORT STOCK '1000''2000''3000'
```

4.4.2 Output list

The output list specifies the definition names of the attributes which are to appear in the printed output. For example:

```
LIST PERSONNEL NAME AGE TELEPHONE AGE
```

This assumes that there are definitions on the dictionary of the file *PERSONNEL* for NAME, AGE, TELEPHONE and AGE. If any of these definitions is missing, then the sentence will not be processed, and an error message will be displayed.

```
THE WORD "AGE" CANNOT BE IDENTIFIED
```

4.4.3 Default output list

There is a useful Access facility which allows you to produce a report without specifying any display field names in the sentence.

If you use the form:

```
LIST PERSONNEL
```

then the processor will look to the dictionary of the *PERSONNEL* file for a definition with the name '1'. If this exists the processor will assume that you have entered:

`LIST PERSONNEL 1`

It will then look for a definition with the name '2'. If this exists the processor will assume that you have entered:

`LIST PERSONNEL 1 2`

It will then look for definitions with the names '3', '4' and so on, until the sequence breaks.

If definition '1' is missing, then the sentence:

`SORT PERSONNEL`

will simply display a list of all the items on the file sorted in ascending item-id sequence.

Note that an explicit output list which is specified in a sentence such as:

`LIST PERSONNEL NAME AGE TELEPHONE AGE`

will override any default names 1, 2, 3 and so on.

If the Access sentence includes either of the modifiers:

`BREAK-ON . . .`
`TOTAL . . .`

then the associated attributes will be displayed and these too will suppress the default output list 1, 2, 3 and so on.

There are default definitions on your MD. That is the reason why a sentence such as:

`LIST DICT PERSONNEL`

displays the attributes of the items on your dictionary. The form:

`LIST ONLY DICT PERSONNEL`
`LIST ONLY STOCK`

should be used if you want to suppress such a default output list.

You will construct the definition items 1, 2, 3 and so on, in exactly the same way as other dictionary definition items, but using the numbers as the definition name, instead of words such as DESCR, DEPT or NAME. For example, if we wished to display the name (attribute 1) and the department (attribute 7) of the records on the *PERSONNEL* file, we might do this with two definitions such as:

```
            item-id:  1              2
   attribute   1:  A              A
   attribute   2:  1              7
   attribute   3:  A              A
   attribute   4:  NAME           DEPT
   attribute   5:
   attribute   6:
   attribute   7:
   attribute   8:
   attribute   9:  T              R
   attribute  10:  10             5
```

and with such definitions, we may use the Access sentence:

LIST PERSONNEL

to produce a report showing the item-id, the name and the department for all the records on the file. These default definitions may be used in the usual explicit manner:

LIST PERSONNEL 2 1
LIST PERSONNEL 1 AGE

If you have such a range of numeric definition, and you wish to suppress one, you should change the A to X in attribute 1 of that definition.

4.4.4 Sort criteria

In an Access sentence, the sort criteria specify the sequence in which the entries in the report are to be sorted. For example:

SORT INVOICES BY DATE

will produce a listing of the *INVOICES* file with the entries sorted in ascending order of DATE. The field mentioned in the sort criteria will not be displayed unless it is included in the output list or included in a BREAK-ON or TOTAL clause.

Descending sequence is obtained by the modifier BY-DSND:

SORT INVOICES BY-DSND AMOUNT

Several such sorting specifications may be given:

SORT INVOICES BY CLIENT BY-DSND DATE BY AMOUNT

in which case the major sort key will be CLIENT, then within CLIENT the items will be sorted in descending order of DATE, then within DATE the items will be sorted in ascending order of AMOUNT, and then finally in ascending order of item-id.

If no sort criteria are specified, the SORT verb will sort in ascending order of item-id.

In the simple examples shown above, any multi-valued attribute which is used as a sort field will be regarded as a single string.

Thus, if an attribute, say the AMOUNT, consists of several values separated by value marks, like this:

```
1200]1000]1400
```

then, in a sentence such as:

```
SORT INVOICES BY AMOUNT AMOUNT
```

this field will be sorted as if it were a fourteen-character string and would appear on the listing between items whose corresponding attributes were 1100 and 1300, the values 1000 and 1400 here being ignored as individual elements, like this:

```
INVOICES. .    AMOUNT

124/44            997
5/66              999
495/6            1000
98/77            1105
3/55             1200
                 1000
                 1400
56/77            1250
11/622           1300
3/511            1350
9/88             1400
```

Notice the way in which the multi-values are shown, each one on a separate line, the first (physical) multi-value being shown alongside the item-id.

If it is required to include each of the multi-values in the sort, then the by-exploded modifier, BY-EXP, may be used, in which case the sort criteria might be:

```
SORT INVOICES BY-EXP AMOUNT AMOUNT
```

to produce a report like this with separate lines for each of the three values:

```
INVOICES. .    AMOUNT

124/44            997
5/66              999
3/55             1000
495/6            1000
98/77            1105
```

```
3/55            1200
56/77           1250
11/622          1300
3/511           1350
3/55            1400
9/88            1400
```

The modifier BY-EXP-DSND is also available.

4.4.5 Selection criteria

In an Access sentence, the selection criteria specify the criteria which each item must satisfy in order to be acceptable for processing by the sentence. For example, the report produced by the sentence:

```
SORT STOCK WITH ON-HAND > "10"
```

will only show those items for which the ON-HAND field has a value greater than 10. If the ON-HAND field is multi-valued, then all the multi-values will be scanned to see if any one meets the required criterion.

A selection criterion starts with the word

```
WITH
```

or

```
IF
```

followed by a field name, followed by an *operator*, followed by a control value enclosed in quotation marks. The following are all valid:

```
. . . WITH AGE > "32" . . .
. . . WITH BALANCE NOT < "0" . . .
. . . IF BALANCE LESS THAN "0" . . .
. . . WITH DATE BEFORE "01 JAN 1985" . . .
```

The following are invalid:

WITH AGE < **65** . . .   the control value is not enclosed in quotes
IF STOCK – MINIMUM < "0" . . .   only one field name must be used
WITH QUANTITY < **MINIMUM** . . .   the control value is not enclosed in quotes.

You can use any of the operators shown in Table 4.4.

Any number of conditions may be included and linked by the operators AND and OR:

```
. . . WITH PRICE > "100" AND WITH QTY < "10" . . .

. . . IF AGE > "65" OR AGE < "18" . . .
```

Table 4.4

#	>	GT
<	>=	LE
<=	AFTER	LT
=	BEFORE	NE
=<	EQ	NO
=>	GE	NOT

If you are interested in a part of the field, instead of the entire contents, then you may use the following forms:

`. . . WITH NAME = "CH]" . . .`

this will select all items of which the NAME field begins with the letters CH and might include names such as CHARLESWORTH, CHADWICK and CHIVERS. The form:

`. . . WITH NAME = "[SON" . . .`

will select all items of which the NAME field ends with the letters SON and might include names such as WILSON, JOHNSON and MICHAEL-SON. The form:

`. . . WITH NAME = "[ST]" . . .`

will select all items of which the NAME field contains the string ST in any position, and might include names such as STEVENS, ANSTEE and WEST. The form:

`. . . WITH NAME = "^A]"`

will select all items of which the NAME field has the letter A in the second position. The character ^ indicates 'any character'. This might include names such as WATSON and CASTLE, but would not include ANSTEE or BEATTY. In all these forms, the ^ and [and] are the normal keyboard characters and *not* the Pick field separators.

Since the second operand must be a literal value enclosed in quotation marks, forms such as:

`LIST STOCK WITH QUANTITY < MINIMUM`

are invalid. Such a situation can be handled with Access by means of a definition, DIFF:

item-id:		DIFF
attribute	1:	A
attribute	2:	0
attribute	3:	
attribute	4:	

```
attribute  5:
attribute  6:
attribute  7:
attribute  8:    F;4;3;–
attribute  9:    R
attribute 10:    4
```

which represents the difference between QUANTITY (in attribute 3) and MINIMUM (in attribute 4), and might be used in a sentence such as:

`LIST STOCK WITH DIFF < "0"`

to produce the desired effect.

   The following are useful variations on the general form shown above:

LIST STOCK WITH NO QTY which will display those items for which the QTY field is zero or null.
LIST STOCK WITHOUT QTY which is identical in effect to the previous sentence.
LIST STOCK WITH QTY "50" is identical to the sentence:

`LIST STOCK WITH QTY = "50".`

Selection criteria based upon the item-id were discussed in Section 4.4.1 when we discussed item lists.

   If the relational operator is omitted, as in the sentence:

`LIST STOCK WITH QTY "50"`

then the Access processor will assume the sentence:

`LIST STOCK WITH QTY = "50"`

If the WITH or IF modifier is omitted, as in the sentence:

`LIST STOCK QTY "50"`

or

`LIST STOCK QTY = "50"`

then all items on the file will be listed with two columns, one for the item-id and one for the field QTY, but the QTY will only be shown for those items which have a QTY of 50. Similarly, the sentence:

`LIST STOCK QTY ≠ "50"`

will display the item-id of all items on the file, but it will only show the QTY for those items which have a QTY of other than 50. The sentence:

`LIST STOCK WITH QTY = "50" OR = "55"`

is interpreted as:

```
LIST STOCK WITH QTY = "50" OR WITH QTY = "55"
```

4.4.6 Field totals

Any field may be totalled by means of the TOTAL modifier:

```
SORT INVOICES BY DATE TOTAL AMOUNT NAME
```

which will produce the report shown in Listing 4.15.

```
INVOICES. .  AMOUNT. . . .  NAME. . . . . . . . . . . . . . .

1933              36. 75 JOHN WATLING AND CO
2733           1, 000. 50 ACME CREDIT SUPPLIES
4633           4, 321. 87 BORROWTON ORDER CO

***            5, 358. 62
```

Listing 4.15

Any number of TOTAL clauses may be used, and you should note that the inclusion of a TOTAL field automatically implies that this field is to be displayed. The reason for this is that the Access processor must have a column space in which to display the total.

The TOTAL processor assumes that the data which are to be totalled comprise only numeric digits. If any non-numeric character is encountered, it will be interpreted as the end of the field. For example:

123 will be interpreted as 123
12.3 will be interpreted as 12
.123 will be interpreted as 0
1,230 will be interpreted as 1
12AB34 will be interpreted as 12

For this reason, any conversion, such as MD2, in the above example, which inserts a decimal point or other non-numeric characters into the data, should be applied as a *conversion* (in attribute 7 of the dictionary definition), that is, after the totalling has taken place. Notice, also, that the conversion MD2 is also applied to the final total.

4.4.7 Control breaks

The break criteria specify the control breaks which are to be made in the report. For example:

```
SORT PERSONNEL BY DEPT AGE BREAK-ON DEPT NAME
```

will sort the entries into ascending order of DEPT and produce a control break when the DEPT field changes, as shown in Listing 4.16.

Notice the following about this report:

(a) The BREAK-ON field, DEPT, will appear in the report in the position in which it appears within the output-list names.

(b) The control break is highlighted by the characters

    ***

```
PERSONNEL. AGE DEPT........  NAME...............

1000        34 A009         SMITH, J. A
9871        45 A009         WATKINS, R
8122        29 A009         WATSON, B

            ***

7322        23 B010         BIGGLES, W. C
8744        22 B010         DAYTON, R

            ***

***
```

Listing 4.16

This may be changed to any message by a specification of the form:

    ... BREAK-ON DEPT "   " ...

which will print spaces instead of the asterisks, or

    ... BREAK-ON DEPT "DEPT" ...

which will print the word DEPT instead of the three asterisks, or

    ... BREAK-ON DEPT "END OF 'V'" ...

which will produce a control-break indicator of the form END OF A009 which includes the break value, as shown below.

(c) The end of the report is also a control break and is signalled by the characters:

    ***

This may be changed to any output string by a specification of the form:

    GRAND-TOTAL "FINISH"

as shown below.

(d) Several BREAK-ON modifiers may be used in a context such as:

```
. . . BREAK-ON DEPT BREAK-ON SALARY . . .
```

We might illustrate some of these features in the sentence:

```
SORT PERSONNEL BY DEPT AGE BREAK-ON DEPT
   "END OF 'V'" WITH ANNUAL > "10000" NAME
   GRAND-TOTAL "END"
```

to produce the report shown in Listing 4.17.

```
PERSONNEL.  AGE DEPT. . . . . . .  NAME. . . . . . . . . . . . . . .

1000         34 A009             SMITH,  J. A
9871         45 A009             WATKINS,  R
8122         29 A009             WATSON,  B

             END OF A009

7322         23 B010             BIGGLES,  W. C
8744         22 B010             DAYTON,  R

             END OF B010

FINISH
```

Listing 4.17

The following options are enclosed in apostrophes and may be used within the text string following a BREAK-ON modifier, as shown by the example above which uses the 'V' option:

B ties up with the B option of an associated HEADING or FOOTING, and will cause the break value to be displayed in that HEADING or FOOTING.

D suppresses the control-break indicator if there was only one detail line.

L suppresses the blank line before the control-break indicator.

P will cause a skip to a new page.

R causes two or more simultaneous control breaks to be output on the same page.

U causes any TOTAL fields to be underlined at the control break.

V will display the break value, as in the above illustration.

4.4.8 Headings and footings

The heading details specify the page heading or page footing which is to be shown in the report. For example:

```
. . . HEADING "PAGE 'P' *** STATEMENT
  LISTING'L'===='LL'" . . .
```

will replace the standard two-line page heading:

```
...........................................................................
:                                                                         :
PAGE p                                        hh:mm:ss dd mmm yyy
blank line
PERSONNEL. NAME ...........DEPT........ AGE
```

showing the page number, time and date, by the four-line heading:

```
PAGE n *** STATEMENT LISTING

blank line
blank line
PERSONNEL. NAME ...........DEPT........ AGE
```

The entire heading is specified within quotation marks, and within this heading there may be options enclosed in apostrophes, as in the above example which uses the options P and L.

The options are:

B indicates the position at which a break value is to be printed – as described in Section 4.4.7 which deals with control breaks.

D the current date is printed in the format:

```
01 JAN 1900
```

F the file name is printed.

L a new line is started – as in the above example.

N causes the end-of-page pause to be cancelled on terminal output.

P prints the current page number – as in the above example. Of course, it is not necessary to include the word PAGE in the heading or footing when displaying the page number.

PP prints the current page number right-justified within a field of four blanks.

T prints the current time and date in the format:

```
10 : 30 : 59  01 JAN 1900
```

The HEADING command does not affect the standard column headings. If these are not required, they may be suppressed by means of:

```
COL-HDR-SUPP
```

If no page heading whatsoever is required, the standard heading may be suppressed by means of:

```
HDR-SUPP
```

Footing details may be declared by means of the

```
FOOTING
```

specification, and may be used with or instead of HEADING specifications. This has exactly the same format and options as the HEADING, for example:

```
FOOTING "'L'----------'L'PAGE 'PP'"
```

We shall see later that some of these option codes are used in headings and footings in other areas of Pick, such as Basic and Runoff.

4.5   DICTIONARY DEFINITION ITEMS

When we were looking at Access, we met some dictionary definition items. It was clear that before an attribute name may be used in an Access sentence, a definition with that name must be created on the DICT section of the file where it is to be used. Now let us look at these items rather more formally.

The format of the dictionary definition item is:

(a) Item-id: this is any alphanumeric name which is to be used in Access sentences.
(b) Attribute 1: this tells you what sort of definition this is, and will be one of:

  A indicating that this is an attribute definition.
  S indicating that this is a synonym definition.
    For most purposes there is no difference between the action of an A item and an S item.
  X indicating that this attribute is not to be printed. This was   discussed further in Section 4.4.3 when we dealt with default   output list.

  This field is often referred to by the name D/CODE.
(c) Attribute 2: this is a number specifying which attribute in the data item is described by this definition item, and will be 0 if you are producing a dictionary definition item referring to the item-id of your data items. This field is often referred to by the name AMC – attribute-mark count.
(d) Attribute 3: this is the actual text which is to be printed as the column heading when this attribute is printed.
    If this text contains the value mark] this will be interpreted as a 'new line' indicator allowing the text to be spread over more than one line of the column heading. If this is null and attribute 1 is A, then the item-id of this definition will be used as a column heading.
(e) Attributes 4, 5 and 6 are null.

(f) Attribute 7: this code specifies the output *conversion* which is to be used by the Access processor to convert data immediately before output. This field is often referred to by the name V/CONV.

(g) Attribute 8: this code specifies the *correlative* which is to be used by the Access processor to convert data immediately after they are taken from the record on disk. This field is often referred to by the name V/CORR.

(h) Attribute 9: this specifies the type and justification of the output data, and will be one of:

L indicating that the data are to be printed left-justified.
R indicating that the data are to be printed right-justified.
T indicating that the data are to be printed left-justified and folded at blanks.
U indicating that the data are to be printed left-justified and may overflow into the field(s) to the right. This field is often referred to by the name V/TYPE.

(i) Attribute 10: this is a number specifying the maximum width of the print column to be allowed for this field. This field is often referred to by the name V/MAX.

(j) Attribute 11: this field is redundant on most implementations and specifies the minimum width of the print column to be allowed for this field. This field is often referred to by the name V/MIN.

If any attributes of the dictionary definition item are unused, then they must be null and not a blank space.

4.6 CONVERSIONS AND CORRELATIVES

The *conversion* and *correlative* codes in dictionary definition items allow you to specify:

(a) Any re-formatting of the raw data which is to be performed when displaying or printing those data by means of an Access sentence. This re-formatting may include:
   (i) Extracting a part of a data field.
   (ii) Inserting decimal points, commas, floating pound sign or filling with asterisks.
   (iii) Converting internal date format to external format.
   (iv) Converting internal time format to external format.
   (v) Converting packed decimal to external format.
   (vi) Converting hexdecimal to external format.
(b) The relationship between one piece of data and another.

  (i) Concatenating data fields and/or literals.
  (ii) Performing arithmetic calculations involving one or more attributes from the data file. For example, if you hold the PRICE and QUANTITY of a product on the file, then this facility will allow you to define VALUE as the result of multiplying PRICE by QUANTITY.

(c) Using the raw data as an item-id to pick up data from another file.

In general, the forms of these codes are acceptable either as conversions (in attribute 7) or as correlatives (in attribute 8), provided that you remember that the *correlative* is applied *before Access* processing is performed, whereas the *conversion* is applied *after Access* processing – such as totalling and sorting – has been performed and *before* output. When selecting by means of the WITH modifier, both correlative and conversion codes will be applied before the WITH condition is tested. This is shown in Fig. 4.4.

```
             RAW DATA ON THE FILE
                      :
         correlatives applied to data
                      :
     sort BY and TOTAL modifiers processed
                      :
         conversions applied to data
                      :
 WITH conditions of selection criteria tested
                      :
            data sent to report
```

Figure 4.4

We have already met some of the conversions and correlatives which you can use in Access dictionary definitions. Let us look at these in rather more detail, but remember that some of these may differ slightly on your implementation.

When an Access sentence is processed, the following sequence is followed:

(a) If an item-list is specified, then these items will be selected for processing, otherwise all the items on the file will be selected.
(b) Any *correlatives* specified in attribute 8 of dictionary definition items will be applied to the input data and the modified input used for subsequent processing.
(c) If any sort criteria are specified, then the selected items will be sorted in the required sequence and carried forward for subsequent processes.
(d) If any sub-totals are required, then these will be formed.

(e) If an output list is specified, then any *conversions* specified in attribute 7 of dictionary definition items for the elements in the output list will be applied, and the output produced as appropriate.

Conversions in attribute 7 are processed *before* selection if the definition appears in a

```
. . . WITH . . .
```

selection criterion.

4.6.1   A correlative

The A correlative allows you to perform arithmetic and other processing on attributes, and offers greater flexibility than does the F; conversion/ correlative described below. It must appear as a correlative, that is, in attribute 8 of the dictionary definition item.

Reference may be made to the results of evaluating other dictionary definitions in statements such as:

```
A;N(QTY)*N(PRICE)
```

which will evaluate the definitions for QTY and PRICE, then multiply the results together and return the product:

```
A; (N(FLD1)+(N(FLD2))*N(PRICE)+5
```

which will evaluate the definitions for FLD1, FLD2 and PRICE and perform the calculation shown, and then add the contents of attribute number 5:

```
A; ((N(QTY)—N(ALLOWANCE))/"1000")*"20"
```

which will perform the calculation using the results of evaluating the definitions for QTY and ALLOWANCE, together with the constants 1000 and 20. Note that constants are enclosed in quotation marks.

If the attributes defined by definitions QTY, PRICE and so on are multi-valued, then this will give a separate result for each multi-valued QTY multiplied by its corresponding multi-valued PRICE.

The following operands may be used in expressions in the A; conversion:

N(d) where *d* is the name – that is, the item-id – of any dictionary definition item. This uses the result of processing the *d* definition in the expression.

n this uses the current value of attribute *n* in the data item.

"**n**" this uses the constant *n* in the expression.

D indicating the system date.

NI indicating the current item counter – this is effectively the *line number* on the output report.

ND indicating the number of detail lines since the last BREAK – this is most often used when the definition is used in a TOTAL clause. On a detail line it has a value of 1, on a break line it has a value equal to the number of the detail line, and on a grand total line it has a value equal to the number of items in the report.

NV indicating the current multi-value counter – this is 1 unless a BY-EXP sort has been specified.

NS indicating the current secondary-value counter – this is 1 unless a BY-EXP sort has been specified.

The following operators may be used:

+   addition
−   subtraction
/   division
*   multiplication
:   concatenation
( )   parentheses may be used to specify the processing hierarchy

On some Pick implementations, the form:

```
A; N(QTY)*N(PRICE)
```

will give incorrect results if one attribute is single-valued and the other is multi-valued. A set of multi-values may be repeatedly matched against a single-valued attribute by a correlative such as:

```
A; N(QTY)*N(PRICE)R
```

where the letter R indicates that the single value of PRICE is to be used repeatedly with each of the successive multi-values of QTY.

Output conversions may be specified on the result of any arithmetic calculation by a correlative such as:

```
A; (N(QTY)*N(PRICE))(MD2)
```

```
A; (N(QTY)*N(PRICE)R)(MD2)
```

If two attributes are multi-valued, the S(operator allows corresponding values in the two attributes to be used. For example:

```
A; (S(N(QTY)*N(PRICE)))(MD2)
```

will process multi-valued QTY and multi-valued PRICE fields.

On some implementations there is a further logical element in the A correlative, such that:

```
A; 4=5
```

would return a value of 1 (true) if attribute 4 of a date item were equal to attribute 5, otherwise a value of 0 (false) would be returned. This element could be used in a context such as:

```
A; (N(QTY)>"0")*N(QTY)*N(PRICE)
```

of which the element

```
N(QTY)>"0"
```

would return a value of 0 or 1, and then this value would be used in the arithmetic computation to return either the value of the stock (QTY times PRICE) or 0.

The operators =, > and < may be used in this form of the A correlative.

4.6.2 A; IF correlative

This allows you to make logical tests within a definition, and tailor the output data accordingly. For example:

```
A; IF 7 < "0" THEN "DEBIT" ELSE "CREDIT"
```

will test the value of attribute 7 of each data item, and if the value is less than 0, then the word DEBIT will be output, otherwise the word CREDIT will be output. Further examples are shown in Fig. 4.5.

```
A; IF 1 AND 2 THEN 1+2 ELSE "0"
A; IF 2+4 > 7 THEN 2+4 ELSE 7
A; IF 1 OR 7 THEN "OK" ELSE "ERROR"
A; IF 1 AND 7 THEN IF 1 > 7 THEN 1 ELSE 7 ELSE "0"
A; IF N(VALUE) > "1000" THEN "REVIEW" ELSE N(VALUE)/100
A; IF 1 THEN IF 2 THEN 3 ELSE 4 ELSE 5
A; IF N(S0) < "100" THEN N(S1) ELSE N(S2)
A; S(IF 2+4 > 7 THEN 2+4 ELSE 7)

A; IF N(CODE)R = "2" THEN (N(QTY)*N(PRICE2)R)(MD2) ELSE
IF N(CODE)R = "3" THEN (N(QTY)*N(PRICE3)R)(MD2) ELSE
(N(QTY)*N(PRICE1)R)(MD2)

A; S(IF 1 = "" OR 1 = "*CANCELLED" THEN "" ELSE
N(PRICE1))
```

Figure 4.5

The following points are illustrated by these examples:

(a) Many of the parameters and other features are similar to those of the simple A correlative.
(b) The A; IF statement must appear as a correlative, that is, in attribute 8, and the last two examples in Fig. 4.5 will appear in attribute 8 of their respective definition items.
(c) AND and OR operators may be included.
(d) Constants are enclosed in quotation marks.
(e) Simple numbers represent attributes.
(f) N(d) refers to the result of processing dictionary definition d.
(g) There must be at least one space between the operators and the operands.
(h) Nested clauses may be used.
(i) There must be an ELSE clause for each THEN.
(j) For multi-valued attributes, the S(element should be used.
(k) The)R element is used to indicate that a single-valued attribute is to be used repeatedly with multi-valued attributes.

See also the extended form of the A correlative:

```
A; 4=5
```

which is described in the previous section.

4.6.3   C conversion/correlative

You will use this code to concatenate attributes and/or literals. It has the general form:

```
C x s x s x s x
```

where x is a literal (enclosed in single apostrophes) or an attribute-mark count, and s is any separator character which is to be inserted between the concatenated values of x. There may be any number of attributes and/or literals. If the semicolon is used as a separator character, then this means that no separator character will be displayed in the output string. This output string overrides the actual output value of the attribute concerned.

Let us assume that in one of our data items attribute 1 contains the value 111, and attribute 2 contains 222. Table 4.5 shows the effect of the various codes.

4.6.4   C; a; b; c; d and Dx correlative

These are used in some implementations in attribute 4 of dictionary definitions and have the effect described below for D1 and D2.

Table 4.5

Code	Output
C'TOTAL=';1	TOTAL=111
C1*2	111*222
C1; 2	111222
C'QTY=';1;' UNITS'	QTY=111 UNITS
C1;' '; 2	111 222
C'====='	=====
C' '	

4.6.5   D conversion/correlative

This code allows you to convert internal dates to external format, as we have already seen. The general format of the code is:

`D{y}{dn}{s}`

where

y is 0, 1, 2, 3 or 4 and indicates the number of digits to be printed in the year field. If y is omitted, then 4 is assumed.

d is a non-numeric separator dividing the field such that *n* divisions are to be skipped before the date portion of the attribute is to be retrieved. This feature is not offered on all implementations.

s is a non-numeric separator which is to separate the day, month and year fields on output. If s is omitted, then a space is assumed.

Note that the braces – or curly brackets – are used in the above model to indicate optional parameters, and are not themselves a part of the code. Table 4.6 illustrates this.

Table 4.6

Data value	Code	Output
1234	D	18 MAY 1871
1234	D2	18 MAY 71
1234	D2/	05/18/71
1234	D2–	05–18–71
1234*ABCD	D2*1/	05/18/71

4.6.6 D1 and D2 correlative

This feature allows two or more attributes of an item to be associated with each other on the output report. These are called associative attributes.

The main (primary) attribute has a correlative:

```
D1; a; b; c; d . . .
```

where *a*, *b* and so on are the attribute-mark counts of the secondary attributes. The secondary attributes will have correlatives:

```
D2; x
```

where *x* is the attribute-mark count of the primary attribute. For example, if we consider the *PERSONNEL* file, then the three definitions:

attribute		NAME	ADDRESS	TELEPHONE
0	:	NAME	ADDRESS	TELEPHONE
1	:	A	A	A
2	:	1	4	7
3	:			
4	:			
5	:			
6	:			
7	:			
8	:	D1; 4; 7	D2; 1	D2; 1
9	:	T	T	R
10	:	20	20	15

will declare NAME as the primary associative attribute, and ADDRESS and TELEPHONE as the secondary associative attributes.

The following points relate to the use of these names in Access sentences:

(a) The D1 and D2 codes must be specified as correlatives, that is, in attribute 8.

(b) A sentence such as:

```
LIST PERSONNEL NAME ADDRESS TELEPHONE
```

will produce the standard output but with the following heading:

```
PERSONNEL. NAME....... ADDRESS....... TELEPHONE....
                  *                 *
```

the asterisk showing that this is a secondary attribute.

(c) names may be entered in any order, and the format of the report will be the same. Thus, the above report will be produced by sentences such as:

`LIST PERSONNEL NAME TELEPHONE ADDRESS`

`LIST PERSONNEL TELEPHONE ADDRESS NAME`

(d) The primary attribute definition must be included in the Access sentence. Therefore, a statement such as:

`LIST PERSONNEL ADDRESS`

will only produce a list of item-ids.

(e) The primary attribute definition alone will be processed as a normal definition. The sentence:

`LIST PERSONNEL NAME`

will produce

`PERSONNEL. NAME. . . . . . . . . . . .`

(f) Any or all secondary definitions may be used in conjunction with the primary definition:

`LIST PERSONNEL ADDRESS NAME`

`LIST PERSONNEL NAME ADDRESS`

will produce a report showing:

`PERSONNEL. NAME. . . . . . . . ADDRESS. . . . . . ADDR. . . . . .`

(g) Other definitions may be included in the Access sentence with the primary and secondary definitions:

`LIST PERSONNEL NAME ADDRESS BALANCE`

If the Access sentence contains dictionary names for attributes which are included on the D1 correlative, but which definitions do not themselves contain the D1 correlative, then a sentence such as:

`LIST PERSONNEL NAME ADDR`

where ADDR is an alternative definition for attribute 4 and does not have the D1 correlative, will produce a report showing:

`PERSONNEL. NAME. . . . . . . . ADDRESS. . . . . . ADDR. . . . . .`

the actual value being shown twice, once with an asterisk.

On some implementations this facility is offered by the C; a; b; c; d and Dx codes.

4.6.7 F; conversion/correlative

This allows you to perform arithmetic and other processing based upon the value of attributes:

`F;{op1}{;op2}{;op3} . . . {;opn}`

where *op1* to *opn* are the attribute numbers, constants and arithmetic operators. For example,

`F;1;2;+;C100;*`

will add the contents of attribute 1 and attribute 2 and multiply the result by 100.

The syntax of this code is a little complicated at first sight. When it is processed, the code is processed from left to right, and when a numeric operand is encountered that value is placed at the top of a stack. When an operator is encountered that operation is performed, as described below, the operands are deleted from the stack and the result is placed at the top of the stack. When all the operators and operands have been processed, then the value at the top of the stack will be retained for processing by the Access processor. Like the A correlative, which has replaced the F; code on some implementations, all arithmetic is done in integers.

The operands are any of:

(a) Attribute numbers.
(b) Constants enclosed in quotation marks or written as C followed by an integer. For example "100" or C100.
(c) D indicating the system date.
(d) T indicating the system time.
(e) NI indicating the current item counter – this is effectively the *line number* on the output report.
(f) ND indicating the number of detail lines since the last BREAK – this is most often used when the definition is used in a TOTAL clause, and is 1 for the detail lines and the total line shows the number of detail lines.
(g) NV indicating the current multi-value counter – this is 1 unless a BY-EXP sort has been specified.
(h) NS indicating the current secondary-value counter – this is 1 unless a BY-EXP sort has been specified.
(i) Attribute numbers of the form:

`n{R}{(c)}`

where *n* is the attribute number; the letter *R* indicating that this is to be repeated for each of the multi-values of attribute *n* (see the note on multi-values below), and *c* enclosed in parentheses is any valid Access conversion to be applied to the data as it is moved into the stack.

The operators are any of:

+   adds stack #1 and stack #2.
−   subtracts stack #2 from stack #1. Subtraction and division operate differently from those of Proc.
*   multiplies stack #1 by stack #2.
/   divides stack #1 by stack #2, leaving the integer quotient in stack #1.
R   divides stack #1 by stack #2, leaving the remainder in stack #1.
S   places the sum of all the multi-values in stack #1 at the top of the stack.
_   exchanges stack #1 and stack #2.
:   concatenates stack #2 with stack #1.
^   deletes stack #1, that is, 'pops' the stack.
"   duplicates stack #1 at the top of stack.
[ ] takes the *substring* of the contents of stack #3; stack #2 specifies the starting position, and stack #1 specifies the number of characters to be taken.
=   places a value of 1 into stack #1 if stack #1 is *equal to* stack #2, otherwise places a value 0 into stack #1.
<   places a value of 1 into stack #1 if stack #1 is *less than* stack #2, otherwise places a value 0 into stack #1.
>   places a value of 1 into stack #1 if stack #1 is *greater than* stack #2, otherwise places a value 0 into stack #1.
places a value of 1 into stack #1 if stack #1 is *not equal to* stack #2, otherwise places a value 0 into stack #1.
[places a value of 1 into stack #1 if stack #1 is *less than or equal to* stack #2, otherwise places a value 0 into stack #1.
]   places a value of 1 into stack #1 if stack #1 is *greater than or equal to* stack #2, otherwise places a value 0 into stack #1.

Stack #1 is the top element in the stack, *stack #2* is the next, and so on.
    The above F; statements will work accurately if all attributes are single valued, or if all values are multi-valued. If it is required to process each of a set of multi-values against a single-valued attribute, then the form:

`F;1;2R;+;C100;*`

will add the contents of each multi-value of attribute 1 and the single value in attribute 2 and multiply the result by 100.

4.6.8 G conversion/correlative

This code is used for extracting a part of an attribute, as we saw in an earlier example. The general format of the code is:

Gnsm

using the character *s* as a group separator, skip *n* groups and extract the next *m* groups. Table 4.7 illustrates this:

Table 4.7

Data value	Code	Output
12/34/56/78	G1/2	34/56
12/34/56/78	G0/1	12
12*34*56*78	G*2	12*34
12 34 56 78	G2 99	56 78
11/22*33/44	G1*1]G1/1	44

4.6.9 L conversion/correlative

This code tests the length of the data field and takes appropriate action. For example:

L0

will display the length of the data field. A non-zero parameter, such as:

L6

will display the data if the field is six characters or less in length, otherwise it will display null. The form:

L6,10

will display the data if the field is six, seven, eight, nine or ten characters in length, otherwise it will display null.

4.6.10 MD conversion/correlative

You will use this code for scaling and converting decimal numbers, as we saw earlier. It has the general form:

MDn{m}{Z}{,}{£}{i x}{c}

where:

n specifies the number of decimal places which are to be printed.

m indicates that the input value is to be scaled down (that is, divided by 10 to the power *m*).

Z indicates that leading zeros are to be suppressed.

, indicates that commas are to be inserted between thousands.

£ indicates that a floating pound sign is to precede the output value.

ix indicates that the output field is to be overlaid on a field of *x* characters of length *i*.

c is a code specifying the way in which negative values are to be displayed. The code C will display CR after negative values; the code < will enclose negative values in < and > characters; the default code − will print a minus sign before negative values.

Table 4.8 illustrates this.

Table 4.8

Data value	Code	Output
1234	MD2	12.34
1234	MD0,10*	*****1,234
1234	MD2£	£12.34
−12345	Md2£<	£<123.45>
−12345	MD2£C	£123.45CR
12.345	MD2	12.345

4.6.11   ML and MR conversion/correlative

These allow you to specify a format mask when outputting the data. The mask has the same form as those described in Section 6.13.1 which deals with *printing with a format mask* in Basic.

4.6.12   MP conversion/correlative

You will use this code to convert numbers to or from packed-decimal format. This has advantages of reduced file size, and also of security since the packed numbers are less easily read.

Table 4.9

External decimal value	Length of string	Internal packed value	Internal displayed as	Length of string
22	1 byte	22	"	1 byte
+123	4 bytes	0123	. .	2 bytes
−123	4 bytes	D123	. .	2 bytes

Standard unpacked numbers occupy 1 byte per digit plus 1 byte for a sign. Packed decimal numbers occupy $\frac{1}{2}$ byte per digit plus $\frac{1}{2}$ byte for the sign. Table 4.9 shows some typical values as they would appear in various forms.

4.6.13 MT conversion/correlative

This code is used for time conversion and has the general form:

`MT{H}{S}`

where:

H indicates that the 12-hour clock is to be used and times will be followed by AM or PM. If H is omitted then the 24-hour clock will be used and AM or PM will be omitted.
S indicates that the seconds field is to be output.

Table 4.10 illustrates this.

Table 4.10

Data value	Code	Output
1234	MT	00:20
1234	MTH	12:20AM
1234	MTHS	12:20:34AM
1234	MTS	00:20:34

4.6.14 MX conversion/correlative

You will use this code to display characters in hexadecimal notation. The hexadecimal output string requires two print positions per input character. Table 4.11 illustrates this.

Table 4.11

Data value	Code	Output
1234	MX	31323334
ABC	MX	414243
A B C	MX	4120422043
3233	MX	33323333

4.6.15 P conversion/correlative

You will use this to indicate that the data are only to be output if they match one (or more) of a specific set of patterns. The general form of the code is:

`P(pattern);(pattern) . . . (pattern)`

with any number of format patterns, separated by the semicolon. For example:

```
P(9N);(3A-4N)
```

will test that the data field is either nine digits (9N) or three letters, a hyphen and four digits (3A-4N). If a match is found, then the data will be output, otherwise a null will be output.

4.6.16   R conversion/correlative

You will use this to indicate that the data are only to be output if they fall within one (or more) of a specified range of values. The general format of the code is:

```
R range ; range . . . range
```

with any sets of ranges separated by semicolons. Each individual range has the format:

```
s, e
```

where s and e are integers specifying the start and end of the range. For example:

```
R1,6;8,10
```

will test that the data field is in the range 1–6 (= 1, 2, 3, 4, 5, 6) or in the range 8–10 (= 8, 9, 10). If the value is in either range, then the data will be output, otherwise a null will be output.

4.6.17   S conversion/correlative

This allows you to output a specified string if a given attribute has a value 0. For example:

```
S10; 'ZERO'
```

will output the word ZERO if attribute 10 has a value of 0, otherwise it will output the value held in attribute 10.

4.6.18   T conversion/correlative

This code is used for extracting part of a value. It has the general form:

```
T{n,}m
```

and will extract m characters starting at character number n of the input string. If n, is omitted, then 1 will be assumed. Table 4.12 illustrates this.

Table 4.12

Data value	Code	Output
ABCDEFGH	T2, 3	BCD
1234567	T5	12345
QWERTYUIO	T4, 99	RTYUIO

4.6.19   Tfile conversion/correlative

This is a particularly useful feature of Access which allows you to use a data value as an item-id to pick up a value from another file. This is illustrated below. The Tfile code has the following general form:

T{*}f;{c};a;b

where:

* indicates that the DICT of file *f* is to be used. If * is omitted, then the data section of the file will be used.

f is the name of the file to be used.

c is the translate code and will be one of:

    C indicates that a non-existent value is to return the original value.

    X indicates that a non-existent value is to return null.

    V indicates that a non-existent value is to abort the processing.

    I input verify only, this is equivalent to V on input, C on output.

    O output verify only, this is equivalent to C on input, V on output.

a is the attribute-mark count in the translation file for input translation. After locating the translation item, using the input value as the item-id, the attribute value for this attribute will replace (convert) the original value – if this parameter is null, no input translation will take place.

b is the number of the attribute which is to be returned from the translation file. If this parameter is null, no output translation will take place.

This is best illustrated by an example. Let us suppose that our *ORDER* file has records holding the order number (the item-id), customer number, product number and date, as shown in Fig. 4.6, and the

```
1111^0001^34^5986
2222^0001^7^5987
3333^0002^100^4955
4444^0002^1^6999
5555^0001^2^6004
```

Figure 4.6

```
0001^AB^432^SANDERS AND CO^01-123 4567
0002^WW^9^ATKINSON AND CO^022-333 444
```

Figure 4.7

CUSTOMER file has records holding the customer number (the item-id), the sales area, the discount code, the customer name and the telephone number, as shown in Fig. 4.7, then the definition:

item-id:		CUSNAME
attribute	1:	A
attribute	2:	1
attribute	3:	CUSTOMER NAME
attribute	4:	
attribute	5:	
attribute	6:	
attribute	7:	
attribute	8:	TCUSTOMER;C;2;3
attribute	9:	T
attribute	10:	20

on the dictionary of the *ORDER* file could be used in Access sentences such as:

SORT ORDER BY CUSNAME CUSNAME

to display the report shown in Listing 4.18.

```
ORDER.....  CUSTOMER NAME.......

3333        ATKINSON AND CO
4444        ATKINSON AND CO
1111        SANDERS AND CO
2222        SANDERS AND CO
5555        SANDERS AND CO
```

Listing 4.18

The definition CUSNAME will pick up attribute 2 (the customer number) from the *ORDER* file record, then use this as the item-id of a record on the *CUSTOMER* file, the processor will return attribute 3 (the customer name) from the *CUSTOMER* file record. Similarly, the sentence:

SORT ORDER WITH CUSNAME = "ATKIN]" CUSNAME

will display the report shown in Listing 4.19.

```
ORDER..... CUSTOMER NAME.......

3333        ATKINSON AND CO
4444        ATKINSON AND CO
```

Listing 4.19

4.6.20 U conversion/correlative

You will use this code to do the sort of special processing illustrated by the examples in Table 4.13. The general form of a user exit is:

```
Uefff
```

fff being the FID of the frame containing the instructions, and *e* being the entry point of the specific routine within that frame. These user exits are very much dependent upon the implementation, and care should be taken if these are to be used in transportable applications. The ones shown here are used on the McDonnell Douglas implementation, but they are typical of the function of such user exits.

Table 4.13

Data value	Code	Output	Action
1,2,3,4	U11A9/,	1234	Removes commas
1020304	U11A9/0	1234	Removes zeros
A B 3 C D	U01A9	AB3CD	Removes spaces
A B 3 C D	U01A5	a b 3 c d	Converts to lower case
A,B 3 C,D	U21A9	AB3CD	Removes non-alphanumerics
A, B C, D	U31A9/,*	A*B C*D	Converts commas to asterisks

4.6.21 Multiple conversions/correlatives

It is possible to specify that several conversions are to be performed one after another on data values. In such cases, the codes are held in the required sequence separated by value marks. Each code is processed in turn, and the result of each process is passed on as input for the next code. For example, the conversion:

```
G1*1]MD2
```

will perform the group extraction *G1*1* and then submit the result of this conversion to the conversion *MD2*. Thus, if the data field on the record is:

`111*222*333`

then the above conversion will produce the result:

`2.22`

Similarly, the correlative may also consist of a sequence of codes separated by value marks.

4.6.22   Conversions versus correlatives

We can summarize this to emphasize the main differences between *conversions* which are held in attribute 7 of the dictionary definitions, and *correlatives* which are held in attribute 8:

(a) *Correlatives* are performed on the input data as they come in from the file.
(b) *Conversions* are performed on the output data just before they are printed.

This can be illustrated by an example using data representing the internal date. Let us imagine that we have a file of data of which attribute 1 represents the internal date. If we use the definitions:

item-id:	DATE7	DATE8
attribute 1:	A	A
attribute 2:	1	1
attribute 3:	DATE	DATE
attribute 4		
attribute 5		
attribute 6		
attribute 7:	D	
attribute 8:		D
attribute 9:	R	R
attribute 10:	11	11

in an Access sentence such as:

`SORT DEMOFILE1 BY DATE8 DATE7 DATE8`

the *correlative* code D in attribute 8 will be performed on the *input* data *before* the sort process, therefore we should get the report shown in Listing 4.20. This is sorted by the *external* form of the date, giving an unexpected result in which the dates are sorted as character strings 03 MAY 1983 and so on.

If we issue the Access sentence:

`SORT DEMOFILE1 BY DATE7 DATE7 DATE8`

```
DEMOFILE..  DATE.......  DATE.......

1000        03 MAY 1983 03 MAY 1983
1007        04 APR 1983 04 APR 1983
1014        05 JUN 1983 05 JUN 1983
1008        09 OCT 1982 09 OCT 1982
1009        11 OCT 1981 11 OCT 1981
1004        19 APR 1982 19 APR 1982
1006        22 MAR 1982 22 MAR 1982
1003        24 JAN 1984 24 JAN 1984
1013        25 JUN 1983 25 JUN 1983
1002        26 DEC 1983 26 DEC 1983
1001        29 JUN 1982 29 JUN 1982
1011        29 OCT 1981 29 OCT 1981
1012        30 SEP 1982 30 SEP 1982
1005        31 MAY 1984 31 MAY 1984
```

Listing 4.20

the *conversion* code D in attribute 7 will be performed on the *output* data *after* the sort process, therefore we should get the report shown in Listing 4.21, which is sorted by the *internal* form of the date, giving the expected results.

```
DEMOFILE..  DATE.......  DATE.......

1009        11 OCT 1981 11 OCT 1981
1011        29 OCT 1981 29 OCT 1981
1006        22 MAR 1982 22 MAR 1982
1004        19 APR 1982 19 APR 1982
1001        29 JUN 1982 29 JUN 1982
1012        30 SEP 1982 30 SEP 1982
1008        09 OCT 1982 09 OCT 1982
1007        04 APR 1983 04 APR 1983
1000        03 MAY 1983 03 MAY 1983
1014        05 JUN 1983 05 JUN 1983
1013        25 JUN 1983 25 JUN 1983
1002        26 DEC 1983 26 DEC 1983
1003        24 JAN 1984 24 JAN 1984
1005        31 MAY 1984 31 MAY 1984
```

Listing 4.21

4.7 PROCESSING LISTS

When you issue a sentence such as:

```
SORT PERSONNEL WITH AGE = "65" BY NAME
```

the Access processor will read each record on the file to test whether or not it satisfies the selection criterion:

```
. . . WITH AGE = "65" . . .
```

If you want to perform a series of such sentences:

```
SORT PERSONNEL WITH AGE = "65" AND WITH SEX = "F" BY
  NAME
```

```
SORT PERSONNEL WITH AGE = "65" AND WITH DEPARTMENT =
  "LAB"
```

```
SORT PERSONNEL WITH AGE = "65" AND WITH SALARY =
  "6000"
```

then the entire file will be read three times, that is, once for each sentence.

Access has a feature – often known as *select lists* or *saved lists* – which enables you to perform an initial scan of the entire file to find which items satisfy a criterion, in this case:

```
. . . WITH AGE = "65" . . .
```

and then save this list of item-ids for future use.

Let us see how we could use select lists to simplify and speed up the processing of the above four sentences.

(a) Produce a list of items which satisfy the condition:

```
SELECT PERSONNEL WITH AGE = "65"
```

Notice that there is no displayed output from this command, other than a simple message showing how many items have been found.

(b) Save this list of item-ids:

```
SAVE-LIST RETIRERS
```

The name *RETIRERS* can be any name you choose.

(c) Retrieve the list for re-use:

```
GET-LIST RETIRERS
```

(d) Issue the Access sentence to process this list:

```
SORT PERSONNEL BY NAME
```

This time we need not specify any selection criteria.

You will then repeat steps (c) and (d) for each of the other Access sentences which process this list:

```
GET-LIST RETIRERS
SORT PERSONNEL WITH SEX = "F" BY NAME
```

```
GET-LIST RETIRERS
SORT PERSONNEL WITH DEPARTMENT = "LAB"
```

```
GET-LIST RETIRERS
SORT PERSONNEL WITH SALARY = "6000"
```

Each of these will be much faster than before, because the Access processor only works on the item-ids which are held in the select list and not on the entire file.

There are several Access verbs which are associated with select lists:

(a) SELECT – this produces a list of item-ids and holds it for processing by the very next TCL verb or Access sentence.
(b) SSELECT – this is the same as SELECT except that the item-ids are sorted according to any sort criteria which are specified. For example:

```
SSELECT PERSONNEL BY AGE
```

The parallel between SELECT and SSELECT is similar to that between LIST and SORT.

(c) SAVE-LIST – this saves the list of item-ids for use later, as we have just seen.

(d) GET-LIST – this retrieves a previously saved list, as we have just seen.

(e) FORM-LIST – this is something like GET-LIST except that you will have created your own list of item-ids and hold them on a file. On some implementations this function is performed by the QSELECT verb.

Suppose you had used the Editor to create a list of item-ids and save this as an item *GLADYS* on a file *WORK9* – one item-id per attribute – then you could retrieve this list by means of the statement:

```
FORM-LIST WORK9 GLADYS
```

or

```
QSELECT WORK9 GLADYS
```

according to your implementation. The results will be processed in exactly the same way as the results of the GET-LIST verb we saw earlier.

If we had an inverted file of *AGE. PERSONNEL*, like those discussed in Section 2.10.2, then we could use a sequence such as:

```
FORM-LIST AGE. PERSONNEL 65
SORT PERSONNEL WITH SEX = "F" BY NAME
```

or

```
QSELECT AGE. PERSONNEL 65
SORT PERSONNEL WITH SEX = "F" BY NAME
```

(f) COPY-LIST – this enables you to copy the contents of a saved list to either another saved list or to an ordinary file. For example:

```
COPY-LIST RETIRERS
TO: SENIORS
```

will establish a new saved list with the name *SENIORS*. You could then use *SENIORS* in GET-LIST and other contexts, exactly like *RETIRERS*. Whereas:

```
COPY-LIST RETIRERS
TO: (MYLISTS SENIORS
```

will copy the contents of the saved list and save it as an ordinary item with the item-id *SENIORS* on the file *MYLISTS*.

The COPY-LIST has the same options and features as the standard COPY verb, as described in Section 5.4.4. To display the contents of a saved list, you could use:

```
COPY-LIST RETIRERS (T)
```

and you will get a report something like that shown in Listing 4.22.

```
     RETIRERS
001  100
002  035
003  590
004  098
```

Listing 4.22

(g) DELETE-LIST – this erases a saved list. For example:

```
DELETE-LIST RETIRERS
```

(h) SORT-LIST – this sorts the contents of a saved list into ascending order:

```
SORT-LIST SENIORS
```

(i) EDIT-LIST – this allows you to edit the contents of a saved list, possibly adding further item-ids or deleting item-ids.

```
EDIT-LIST SENIORS
```

The EDIT-LIST has the same commands and features as the standard EDIT verb.

The details of saved lists are held on the *POINTER-FILE*, with item-ids such as:

```
SENIORS
```

or, on some implementations, the name of the account is also used in the item-id:

```
WAGES*L*SENIORS
```

Each time you save a list, the new list overwrites any previous list with that name. So be careful if you use names like X, some other user may be equally unimaginative and overwrite your list with theirs.

Of course, the list stays the same, even if your file changes. So once you have selected all the people

```
. . . WITH AGE = "65" . . .
```

and saved the list, this list will not change with the file, therefore you must perform the SELECT and SAVE-LIST operations again to include any people who have just reached 65 or who have left the company.

Once the list has been generated it is no longer associated with the original file. This is a bit of a mind-blower! But remember that the select list is simply a list of item-ids. There's no flag saying that it belongs to the *PERSONNEL* file. So you could do something like this:

```
SELECT PERSONNEL WITH AGE = "65"
```

will generate a list of all items on the *PERSONNEL* file which satisfy the condition – let us say these are item-ids 100, 035, 590 and 098. The command:

```
SAVE-LIST FREDA
```

then saves the four item-ids under the name *FREDA*. The command:

```
GET-LIST FREDA
```

retrieves the four item-ids *100, 035, 590* and *098*, and the Access sentence:

```
LIST HOLIDAYS NAME DAYS. LEFT
```

takes the four item-ids and picks up those items – *100, 035, 590* and *098* – displaying the NAME and DAYS.LEFT, exactly as if we had specified an item-list in a sentence such as:

```
LIST HOLIDAYS NAME DAYS. LEFT '100' '035' '590' '098'
```

If you were to produce a saved list by means of the BY-EXP modifier, in a sequence such as:

```
SELECT INVOICES BY-EXP VALUE
```

```
SAVE-LIST INVOICES
```

then each entry in the list will contain an item-id followed by the position of the multi-value within the VALUE field. We can illustrate this if we now issue the command:

```
COPY-LIST INVOICES (T)
```

which will produce a report such as that shown in Listing 4.23.

```
        INVOICES
001     4500]2
002     2854]1
003     4500]1
004     0567]1
005     0372]1
006     3488]1
007     2574]1
008     1500]1
009     6314]1
010     5050]4
011     5050]3
012     1000]1
013     6919]1
014     5050]2
015     5050]1
016     2500]1
```

Listing 4.23

When you have generated a select list of item-ids by means of one of the commands:

```
SELECT
SSELECT
FORM-LIST
GET-LIST
QSELECT
```

then the very next action which you perform will use that list – if it is possible. For example, we could use our *RETIRERS* saved list in a sequence such as:

```
GET-LIST RETIRERS
```

```
ED PERSONNEL
```

to edit all the people who are aged 65 on the *PERSONNEL* file, or a sequence such as:

```
GET-LIST RETIRERS
```

```
COPY PERSONNEL (D)
TO:(OLD.EMPLOYEES
```

to copy the items for all the people aged 65 from the *PERSONNEL* file to the *OLD.EMPLOYEES* file. In these situations, we do not specify any item-ids on the Editor or the COPY commands since they are already held in the select list.

Other commands which will process a select list include:

BASIC MYPROGS to compile all the selected items.

RUNOFF MYTEXT to process a document comprising all the selected items.

RUN MYPROGS UPD009 to invoke the program *UPD009* to access the selected items by means of the READNEXT statement.

If you accidentally press <RETURN> when the list is awaiting your next command, then, according to the implementation, you may lose the list and have to start again, or the system will await a valid command. If you give an invalid command, such as:

`ABSIC FILENAME`

then you will lose your list.

4.8   REFORMAT

On many occasions, we have said that, as a database retrieval language, Access is not intended to write to files or to update files. There is, however, one exception to this in the REFORMAT and SREFORMAT verbs which are offered on some implementations.

The sentence:

`REFORMAT STOCK DESCRIPTION ODATE PRICE QTY`

will read the data on the *STOCK* file, re-arrange the data into the order shown, and use them to create new items on a file specified by the user. Only the attributes which are specified in the Access sentence – DESCRIPTION, ODATE, PRICE and QTY in this example – will be written to the destination file. Care should be taken when re-formatting a file back onto itself.

If you specify TAPE as the output file, then the records will be written to magnetic tape. In this case, the processor will pad or fill the fields to produce a fixed length record for each item.

SREFORMAT is also available to produce a sorted output file.

4.9   LABEL PROCESSING

In the simplest case, Access will produce a simple columnar report, listing all the item-ids one beneath another, all the descriptions one beneath another, and so on. But what if we want more than one item per line? Something like that shown in Listing 4.24.

```
0372                      0567
DESKS,  STEEL,  VIOLET    STOOLS,  STEEL,  ORANGE

1000                      1005
CHAIRS,  WOODEN,  RED     STOOLS,  SPECIAL,  PURPLE
```

Listing 4.24

You could use the Access SORT-LABEL and LIST-LABEL verbs to produce such a report. To do this, you have to decide the content and the format of the printout, and then issue a sentence such as:

SORT-LABEL STOCK DESCR

The SORT-LABEL and LIST-LABEL processor requires further information. In this case, you will enter:

2,2,1,0,25,0

meaning that you want:

Two items per line.
Two lines per item.
One blank line between entries.
No indentation (for a header) before each line.
Twenty-five-character width per entry.
No spaces between the columns.

If you specify an indentation of, say twelve characters, then the label processor will proceed to ask you for the twelve characters of text which are to precede each of the two lines on the labels. Thus, if we supplied the parameters:

2,2,1,12,25,0

the system will allow us to enter two heading lines:

PART NUMBER:
DESCRIPTION:

and will produce a report like that shown in Listing 4.25. This is a most useful – and much ignored – feature of Pick.

4.10   BOMP – BILL OF MATERIALS PROCESSING

In Section 2.10.3 we discussed the way in which the items on a file may contain item-ids of other items on the same file, such as is associated

```
PART NUMBER: 0372               0567
DESCRIPTION: DESKS, STEEL, VIOLET   STOOLS, STEEL, ORANGE

PART NUMBER: 1000               1005
DESCRIPTION: CHAIRS, WOODEN, RED    STOOLS, SPECIAL, PURPLE
```

Listing 4.25

with bill of materials – BOMP – processing, and might be used in such situations as a parts file in which certain items on the file imply the use and supply of other parts on the file. In that section we saw a simple file, and used the

```
LIST WITHIN CATALOGUE '800B' DESCR QTY TOTAL PRICE
```

sentence to produce the bill of materials.

The important points to remember in this context are:

(a) The WITHIN modifier can only be used with the LIST and COUNT verbs.
(b) The BY connective cannot be used, since this would imply a SORT verb.
(c) The data-level identifier for the file must have the field:

```
V;;3
```

in attribute 8, to indicate that, in this case, attribute 3 of the data items contains the list of subordinate item-ids.
(d) Any output list may be used, and the dictionary definitions for these are of the usual format.
(e) The column headed LEVEL is produced by the LIST WITHIN processor.

The layout of a typical BOMP file is shown in Fig. 2.11, and a BOMP report is shown in Listing 2.1.

4.11 TIPS AND TECHNIQUES – ACCESS

If any difficulty exists in the use of Access, it is in the construction and use of the conversion and correlative codes. In this chapter we have given examples of most of the codes, and these can be used safely as models. When devising a complex code, such as an F; code or a combination of several codes, then it is best to assemble this gradually, ensuring that each stage works correctly before proceeding to the next.

This can be done quite efficiently by means of a simple Proc such as:

```
PQ
HED DICT STOCK DEF1
P
HLIST STOCK DEF1
P
```

When this Proc is invoked, it will pass to the Editor to allow you to create and amend your dictionary definition DEF1 on the *STOCK* file. When you have filed the amended definition, the Proc will then produce a simple Access report to test the effect of the definition.

4.11.1 To use Access without dictionary definitions

Most of this chapter has been devoted to the construction and use of Access definitions, but any Access verb can be used without the existence of such definitions on the DICT of the file.

Let us suppose that you have a file called HQDATA which does not have any Access dictionary definitions items – it may be a file which holds your Basic programs. You could use any Access verb, such as those shown in the following sentences, without having to create any definitions:

SORT HQDATA = "£]"   this will display all the item-ids starting with a £ character.
LIST HQDATA >= 'A' AND <= 'Z'   this will show all the item-ids which begin with a letter.

```
COUNT HQDATA
SELECT HQDATA
SSELECT HQDATA
STAT HQDATA
SUM HQDATA
```

In such situations, of course, you cannot specify field names, but you can use the Access forms involving the item-id, as shown in the first few examples above.

4.11.2 To use Access efficiently

The use of Access should be a prominent feature of any Pick application system, its flexibility giving many advantages over a user-written report program.

In many situations it is immediately obvious that an Access sentence can do the job, such as:

(a) Inquiries – where a listing is required of the contents of one or more known items from a file.

(b) File listings – where a sorted listing of a whole file is required.
(c) Reports – where file items are selected on certain conditions, sorted and listed.
(d) Analyses – where totals or item counts are required.

However, there are many cases where the user's requirements are not so simple, and it is not immediately obvious that Access can be used.

In such cases, rather than abandoning Access entirely, it is worth trying to incorporate some elements of Access into the system, and use Basic for the detailed areas of processing and updating. In this way we can combine the advantages of both. A few examples will help to illustrate this:

(a) You want a printout of all documents which are rejected by your data entry program.

The first solution that comes to mind is to use 'PRINT' statements in the data entry program wherever a document is rejected. This is just what a mainframe program would do, but with Pick we can do a lot better. The information should be written away to a file, each rejection being a single item with the normal attribute structure. Once this information is filed, it can be listed, sorted or analysed in any way at any time using Access.

The advantages in flexibility and convenience of this approach are tremendous.

(b) It may be a restriction that Access will only produce a report on a single file. If we have a system which requires us to combine reports and produce a single report on the contents of the four files *NORTH.SALES*, *SOUTH.SALES*, *EAST.SALES* and *WEST.SALES*, then a simple solution is to copy all the records from these files to a single work file, and then produce our report from this work file. In this situation the solution might be:

(i)   Establish the work file.
(ii)   Select and copy the records from each of the four files in turn. To avoid duplicate records, the item-ids could be prefixed by an N, S, E or W before the items are copied.
(iii) Establish the dictionary definitions on the work file.
(iv)   Produce the Access report on the work file data.
(v)   Delete the work file.

(c) A *SUPPLIERS* file has one item per supplier. For each supplier there is a list of product types held as multi-values within one attribute. However, for one particular report you want one line per supplier showing number, name and product types.

There are several ways of achieving this, the choice depending on size and frequency of the report, and on the frequency of updating these codes.

One method is to SELECT the required items and run a Basic program which prints the items in the correct format. This is the least flexible solution, but may be favoured if the report is infrequently used or is very large.

Another method is to SELECT the required items and run a Basic program which writes re-formatted items – that is, with spaces between product codes and with superfluous attributes removed – to a work file, then SORT the work file. This is better where multiple copies are required or where the report is small.

Yet another method is to hold the product types in two formats on the *SUPPLIERS* record – one with value marks as separators and one with spaces as separators. The report could then be produced with a single SORT, but updates would be slower and more disk space would be used. This would be appropriate where the report was produced frequently and updates were rare.

4.11.3   To save an Access sentence

You will have realized that it would be convenient to be able to save your Access sentence rather than having to type it in every time. Particularly if it's a long sentence and you're a slow typist!

Let us look at a simple way of setting up a procedure which will allow you to save any Access command on your MD. Once it has been saved, then you may use it simply by typing in the name under which it has been saved. If you already know about Procs and the Editor, then this section will seem elementary to you, and you may wish to skip it. But if the Proc language is a strange, uncharted land, then read on.

You will create a new procedure on your MD by a sequence such as:

```
EDIT MD xxxxxx
```

where *xxxxxx* is the name by which you wish to identify your procedure. The name *xxxxxx* may be any name you choose, but it is a good idea to be consistent and choose a meaningful name such as *P001* or *PROC.LIST.FILES* or *PLF*.

If the system displays the message:

```
NEW ITEM
TOP
```

when you enter the EDIT command then you may proceed. If it displays only:

```
TOP
```

and does not say NEW ITEM, then you should type

EX

and try again with a different name *xxxxxx* otherwise you may destroy someone else's work.

```
:EDIT MD PROCO1
---------------
NEW ITEM
TOP
.I
001 PQ
    ---
002 H LIST STOCK WITH MINIMUM < "100"
    ---------------------------------
003 P
    -
004 <========= press RETURN only here
TOP
.FI
. --
'PROCO1' FILED
```

Figure 4.8

You will then type in your Access sentence so that the whole sequence might look like that shown in Fig. 4.8. Note the following points:

(a) You will type in the information which we have underlined in the above illustration.
(b) You must press the <RETURN> key when you have typed in each line.
(c) You may use any name where we have used *PROC01* but remember the warning if it is not a *new item.*
(d) Your Access sentence will come on the line where we have used:

H LIST STOCK WITH MINIMUM < "100"

(e) You must put an H before your Access sentence when you save it in a procedure. Leave a space between the H and the Access sentence.

When you have created a procedure like this, be sure to make a note of the name of the procedure, and what the procedure does. Look at the examples shown in Fig. 4.9. Notice how a long Access sentence can be entered as several shorter lines each beginning with an H. In this case, the last two procedures have the same effect.

When you have created a procedure in the way described above, then you may use it simply by typing the name of the procedure. This will be

PROC01

in our example. You'll see how to change this procedure when we look at the Editor.

```
PQ
H LIST STOCK DESCRIPTION STOCK MINIMUM
P

PQ
H SORT STOCK BY DESCRIPTION BY STOCK BY MINIMUM LPTR
P

PQ
H SORT STOCK BY DESCRIPTION
H BY STOCK BY MINIMUM
H LPTR
P
```

Figure 4.9

4.11.4   To print larger gaps between columns

If we use a simple Access sentence such as:

`SORT STOCK DESCR LOCN QTY`

we will get a report something like that shown in Listing 4.26, with a single space between the columns of the report. But how could we get a larger gap between the columns, like that shown in Listing 4.27?

STOCK.....	DESCRIPTION..............	LOCATION	QUANTITY
0372	DESKS, STEEL, VIOLET	MN/384	22
0567	STOOLS, STEEL, ORANGE	MN/206	6
1000	CHAIRS, WOODEN, RED	UK/614	64
1005	STOOLS, SPECIAL, PURPLE	UK2/75	50
1479	LADDERS, STEEL, RED	UK2/965	6
1500	DESKS, STEEL, BLUE	MN/600	105

Listing 4.26

STOCK.....	DESCRIPTION..............	LOCATION	QUANTITY
0372	DESKS, STEEL, VIOLET	MN/384	22
0567	STOOLS, STEEL, ORANGE	MN/206	6
1000	CHAIRS, WOODEN, RED	UK/614	64
1005	STOOLS, SPECIAL, PURPLE	UK2/75	50
1479	LADDERS, STEEL, RED	UK2/965	6
1500	DESKS, STEEL, BLUE	MN/600	105

Listing 4.27

This is done quite simply by establishing a dictionary definition called, let us say, GAP, which might look like this:

```
        item-id:  GAP
   attribute   1:  S
   attribute   2:  0
   attribute   3:                  ⇐ there are five spaces
   attribute   4:
   attribute   5:
   attribute   6:
   attribute   7:  C'         '     ⇐ five spaces between the apos-
                                       trophes
   attribute   8:
   attribute   9:  L
   attribute  10:  5
```

We could then issue the Access sentence:

`SORT STOCK GAP DESCR GAP LOCN GAP QTY`

to get the required report.

Incidentally, if you don't put five spaces in attribute 3 of the definition, then you will get dots as a heading. A useful hint is to create definitions with meaningful names such as GAP3, GAP5 and GAP10 for use in your reports. Another useful feature is to create a definition which will produce a report like that shown in Listing 4.28.

```
STOCK CONTROL .......................................... STOCKTAKING

STOCK.....  DESCRIPTION.............. LOCATION QUANTITY ON SHELF.....

0372        DESKS, STEEL, VIOLET      MN/384    .....................
0567        STOOLS, STEEL, ORANGE     MN/206    .....................
1000        CHAIRS, WOODEN, RED       UK/614    .....................
1005        STOOLS, SPECIAL, PURPLE   UK2/75    .....................
1479        LADDERS, STEEL, RED       UK2/965   .....................
1500        DESKS, STEEL, BLUE        MN/600    .....................
```

Listing 4.28

We could create a definition like this:

```
        item-id:  DOTS
   attribute   1:  S
   attribute   2:  0
   attribute   3:  QUANTITY ON SHELF
   attribute   4:
```

```
attribute  5:
attribute  6:
attribute  7:  C'. . . . . . . . . . . . . . . . . .'
attribute  8:
attribute  9:  L
attribute 10:  22
```

and then issue the Access sentence:

```
SORT STOCK DESCR LOCN DOTS
```

to get the required report.

4.11.5 To type in long sentences

Access sentences can get very long, and you may find that you need to enter more than the 140 characters which the terminal buffer can accommodate. This can be resolved by ending each intermediate line with a *continuation sequence* of characters, and the system will respond with the colon prompt for the rest of the sentence.

Thus, you could enter something like this:

```
:LIST ANY ITEMS ON THE INVENTORY <CONTINUATION>
: WITH STOCK <CONTINUATION>
: LESS THAN "100" <RETURN>
```

where <CONTINUATION> is the continuation sequence, and <RETURN> is the normal carriage-return.

According to the implementation, the continuation sequence may be:

```
<SPACE> <CTRL> _<RETURN>
```

or

```
<SPACE> <CTRL> _ <LINE-FEED>
```

or

```
<CTRL> <SHIFT> 0
```

You can, of course, also solve this problem by saving the Access sentence in a Proc, as we described above.

4.11.6 To TOTAL non-integer values

When we looked at field totals in Section 4.4.6, we saw that all totalling is done in integers, and if any non-numeric characters are encountered in a field which is to be totalled, then these will terminate the totalling for that field. Thus, a value such as:

```
25.50
```

will be considered as 25. This is a source of confusion for beginners. For this reason, if a conversion code such as 'MD2', is used, then this should appear in the dictionary definition as a *conversion* in attribute 7. If it is used as a *correlative*, in attribute 8, then the formatting of the data will take place *before* the totalling and when a value such as:

```
4,321.87
```

is encountered, the comma will upset the numeric nature of the field and only the number 4 will be considered.

When a *conversion* is applied, then it will also be applied to the result of the *total*. How could we total the price field if it actually contained a decimal point? How could we total fields such as these?

```
12.34
55.25
123.50
58.41
1234.56
```

Unless we devise a special definition, the TOTAL PRICE clause will total these as 1482, that is, 12 + 55 + 123 + 58 + 1234.

The following definitions offer a solution to this problem:

item-id:	PT1	PT2	PRICE
attribute 1:	A	A	A
attribute 2:	6	6	6
attribute 3:			
attribute 4:			
attribute 5:			
attribute 6:			
attribute 7:			MD2
attribute 8:	G0.1	G1.1	A;N(PT1):N(PT2)
attribute 9:	R	R	R
attribute 10:	10	10	10

We could now use this definition in a sentence such as:

```
LIST STOCK TOTAL PRICE
```

This solution breaks down a field such as 12.34 into PT1 (= 12) and PT2 (= 34), concatenates these in PRICE (= 1234) and then displays this with the MD2 conversion.

Care must be taken if the field is held with other than two decimal places. Thus, 12.0 and 12. will give incorrect results. In such circumstances the correlative for PT2 might be changed to:

```
C6;'000']G1.1]T1,2
```

4.11.7 To display a counter on the report

It is often required to display a line counter on your Access report, like that shown in Listing 4.29.

```
STOCK.....  ITEM DESCRIPTION.............. LOCATION QUANTITY

0372     1     DESKS, STEEL, BLUE          MN/384        22
0567     2     STOOLS, STEEL, ORANGE       MN/206         6
1000     3     CHAIRS, WOODEN, RED         UK/614        64
1005     4     STOOLS, SPECIAL, PURPLE     UK2/75        50
1479     5     LADDERS, STEEL, RED         UK2/965        6
1500     6     DESKS, STEEL, BLUE          MN/600       105
```

Listing 4.29

We can achieve this by means of a definition such as:

item-id:	ITEM
attribute 1:	A
attribute 2:	9998
attribute 3:	
attribute 4:	
attribute 5:	
attribute 6:	
attribute 7:	
attribute 8:	
attribute 9:	L
attribute 10:	4

The above report could be produced by a sentence such as:

```
SORT STOCK ITEM DESCR LOCN QTY
```

The 9998 in attribute 2 means *display the sequence number* and not *display the contents of attribute 9998*.

4.11.8 To display the item length on the report

If you wish, you may include the item length on your Access report or, more usefully, SELECT items according to their length. We could do this with the aid of a definition such as:

```
         item-id:  LENGTH
 attribute   1:  A
 attribute   2:  9999
 attribute   3:
 attribute   4:
 attribute   5:
 attribute   6:
 attribute   7:
 attribute   8:
 attribute   9:  L
 attribute  10:  6
```

We could then issue Access sentences such as:

```
SELECT STOCK WITH LENGTH > "200"
```

or

```
SORT STOCK LENGTH DESCR BY LENGTH
```

This last sentence will produce a report something like that shown in Listing 4.30.

The 9999 in attribute 2 means *display the item length* not *display the contents of attribute 9999*. The value returned is the 4-byte item-length count which we met when we looked at the item layout in Section 2.6.

```
STOCK.....  LENGTH DESCRIPTION.............

1000        191     CHAIRS, WOODEN, RED
1500        198     DESKS, STEEL, BLUE
1479        201     LADDERS, STEEL, RED
1005        207     STOOLS, SPECIAL, PURPLE
0372        213     DESKS, STEEL, BLUE
0567        255     STOOLS, STEEL, ORANGE
```

Listing 4.30

5

TCL – Terminal control language

TCL, the terminal control language, is the lowest level at which the Pick operating system is used. The language comprises a number of commands which are typed in at your keyboard to invoke the primitive operations of the system. You may type in any TCL command when the system displays the prompt

:

Note that on some implementations, the TCL prompt is

>

instead of the colon. We use the colon in the examples in this book.

So let us see what sort of things you have to type in to get the system to work for you:

OFF if you want to log off the system.
WHAT if you want to display the details of your Pick system.

Some TCL commands require a little more information:

DUMP 1234 if you want to display the contents of frame 1234.
T-ATT 1000 if you want to use the magnetic-tape drive and set the record size to 1000 bytes.
BASIC INV.PROGS IVOO33 if you want to invoke the compiler to process one of your Basic language programs.
RUN INV.PROGS IVOO33 if you want to execute one of your Basic programs.

Some commands can get quite complicated:

CREATE-FILE (DICT MRPROCS 19,3

This chapter looks at the general concept of TCL, introducing the more interesting and useful aspects of the language. For full details of the individual commands, you should consult the appropriate reference manuals which are supplied with your system.

For the sake of completeness, we also mention some Access verbs – such as COUNT – in a logical context amongst other purely TCL verbs in this chapter.

5.1 TCL VERBS

For technical reasons, the TCL verbs are divided into two categories: TCL I and TCL II verbs, but the ordinary – or even extraordinary – user will gain no real advantage by learning – or even knowing – the difference between the two. The academic distinction is that TCL I verbs are those which *do not* require a file name amongst their parameters, for example:

`DUMP 12345`

which displays the contents of frame number 12345, and

`ADDD 45 67`

which adds the two decimal numbers 45 and 67.

TCL II verbs are those which *do* require a file name amongst their parameters, for example:

`ISTAT STOCK`

which prints the statistics for the file STOCK.

Strictly speaking, the Access verbs, such as LIST and SORT which were discussed in Chapter 4, are a separate set of operations from the TCL verbs, but this, again, is an academic distinction which need not concern most users.

When moving to another range of equipment, you may find that the effect of TCL verbs on one implementation are achieved by Procs on another.

Table 5.1 shows a list of some of the TCL I verbs and Table 5.2 shows some of the TCL II verbs.

We shall, of course, not look at all these verbs. Some are more useful than others, so we'll concentrate upon the practical and the useful. The verbs for use with magnetic tape are discussed in Section 10.7 and those used with the spooler are discussed in Section 10.8. Your system reference manuals will help you with the details of some of the more unusual verbs.

Table 5.1

ADDD	DIVD	NOHUSH	T-CHK
ADDX	DIVX	P	T-DET
BLOCK-PRINT	DTX	POVF	T-FWD
BLOCK-TERM	ENABLE-BREAK-KEY	PQ-RESELECT	T-RDLBL
BVERIFY	GET-LIST	PQ-SELECT	T-REW
CHARGE-TO	HUSH	SAVE-LIST	T-WEOF
CHARGES	LOADT	SEL-RESTORE	T-WTLBL
COPY-LIST	LOGTO	SLEEP	TERM
DATE-FORMAT	MESSAGE	SORT-LIST	TIME
DELETE-CATALOG	MSG	SUBD	USER
DELETE-FILE	MULD	SUBX	WHO
DELETE-LIST	MULX	T-BCK	XTD

Table 5.2

B/ADD	ECOPY	FORM-LIST	PRINT-HEADER
B/DEL	ED	GROUP	RUN
BASIC	EDIT	ITEM	RUNOFF
CATALOG	EED	LOADF	SET-SYM
COPY	EEDIT	PQ-COMPILE	SHARE
EBASIC	FIX-FILE-ERRORS	PRINT-CATALOG	

5.1.1 Options on TCL verbs

In general, any TCL command may include options to extend the fundamental action of the verb. For example:

```
DUMP 12345
```

will display the contents of frame number 12345 on the terminal screen. But if we specify the P option, like this:

```
DUMP 12345 (P)
```

then the command prints the contents of the frame on the printer. This is rather like the LPTR specification in Access.

The N option is rather like the NOPAGE modifier in Access, and suppresses the normal end-of-page pause when output is sent to the terminal. For example, if you issue the command:

```
RUNOFF MYTEXT CONTRACT32
```

to process the item *CONTRACT32* on the file *MYTEXT* with the Runoff word-processing package, then it will display the document on the screen and halt at the end of every page (screen) until you press <RETURN> to continue. But if you use the N option:

```
RUNOFF MYTEXT CONTRACT32 (N)
```

then the display will continue through to the end without pausing.

The nature and function of the other options are specific to each verb. Some of the more useful options are described in this book, but complete details will be given in your reference manuals.

If you wish to specify several options, then these may be entered in any order but must be separated by commas:

```
DUMP 12345 (G,N,P)
DUMP 12345 (N,G,P)
```

5.1.2 Verbs on the MD

Whenever you are at TCL level – that is when the system displays the colon – the very first word that you type in must be a TCL verb or the name of a Proc. In either case, there must be an item on your MD which has that name. Thus, if you type in

```
OFF
```

then there must be an item on your MD with the item-id OFF. If you type in

```
LIST STOCK
```

then there must be an item on your MD with the item-id LIST. If this item doesn't exist on your dictionary, then the system will not know what to do, and it will display a message. Something like:

```
VERB?
```

So what do these verbs look like on your MD? Let us have a look at a couple. The OFF verb looks like this:

```
      item-id:  OFF
  attribute 1:  PZ
  attribute 2:  32
```

and the LIST verb looks like this:

```
      item-id:  LIST
  attribute 1:  PA
  attribute 2:  35
  attribute 3:  4D
```

So you can see that there is nothing magical about these items. They contain information which directs the operating system to a particular frame which contains the instructions to do the jobs which you request. Incidentally, the above verbs may look different on your implementation, and you can inspect them by means of the CT – copy to terminal – Proc:

`CT MD OFF LIST`

to look at the OFF and LIST verbs.

5.1.3   To create your own verbs

The concept of establishing your own verbs and commands on the MD is an attractive aspect of Pick, and renders the system simpler to use for the non-technical user. Such additions and changes to the standard Pick repertoire include:

(a) Proc procedures – as described in Chapter 7, where we deal with Procs.
(b) Catalogued programs – as described in Section 6.19 of the chapter dealing with Basic.
(c) Re-naming the standard Pick features.

This last sort of change may be made for a couple of reasons.

Firstly, we might wish to remove the more powerful of the standard Pick features and make them available under a less obvious name – thus we might save the EDIT verb under a name such as OP32:

`COPY MD EDIT`
`  TO:OP32`

and then delete the standard MD entries for ED and EDIT:

`DELETE MD EDIT MD`

The new *editor* would then be invoked by TCL commands such as:

`OP32 STOCK '1234'`

to edit item *1234* on the *STOCK* file, and so on.

Secondly, we might wish to make the standard features available under a more obvious name – thus we might re-name the EDIT operation CHANGE or MAINTAIN.

5.2   THE EDITOR

The Editor is a primitive tool for maintaining files and items, allowing you to add new items to a file, change existing items on a file and delete items from a file.

The Editor is normally used when creating and maintaining:

(a) Access dictionary definitions – although some implementations offer utilities to do this.
(b) Basic source programs.
(c) Procs.
(d) Text for Runoff documents.
(e) Test data.

The Editor is invoked at TCL level by a command of the form:

`EDIT PERSONNEL 1022`

which will edit the item with the item-id *1022* on the file called *PERSON-NEL*, or

`EDIT PERSONNEL 101 42 . . . . 909`

which will edit the items *101*, *42* and so on, on the file called *PERSON-NEL*. As you finish changing each item, the Editor will pass the next one to you, until the list is exhausted. The form:

`EDIT PERSONNEL *`

will edit all the items on the file called *PERSONNEL*, passing them to you one by one. When we looked at select lists and saved lists in Section 4.7, we met a further form of the EDIT verb in a context such as:

`SSELECT PERSONNEL WITH AGE > "65"`
`EDIT PERSONNEL`

in which the SSELECT builds a list of all items which satisfy the criterion of AGE being greater than 65, and then passes this list to the Editor for editing one by one.

In any of these commands, the word EDIT may be abbreviated to ED:

`ED PERSONNEL 1022`

`ED PERSONNEL 101 42 . . . . 909`

`ED PERSONNEL *`

The Editor will prompt for a sequence of commands, as shown in the following sections. Whilst you are under the control of the Editor, the prompt is the full stop.

Table 5.3 shows all the commands which are encountered within the various implementations of Pick. You might like to delete those which are not available on your implementation. We shall discuss these commands later.

Table 5.3

?	EXF	L:	RU
?I	F	M	S
?P	FD	ME	T
?S	FI	N	TB
A	FIO	Nn	U
AS	FS	O	W
B	FSO	P	X
C	G	P command	XF
CD	I	PD	Z
DE	I data	PP	n
EX	L	R	

Let us look at the Editor in action, and see how it is used to create a new item, change an existing item and delete an old item. It should be pointed out, however, that in many cases – for the reasons we mention when we deal with security in Section 5.2.10 – these operations are better performed by a user-written program in which the changes to the files and items can be controlled, validated and logged.

5.2.1 Creating a new item

When you use the Editor to create a new item on a file, it will look something like the sequence shown in Fig. 5.1. Note the following points about this example:

```
:EDIT FILEX ITEMG
NEW ITEM
TOP
.I
001 HEGINBOTHAM J E
002 24 THE LARCHES
003 01-999 4766
004 T
005 MANAGER
006 M27
007 1
008 217
009 5123
010 2805
011
TOP
.FI
'ITEMG' FILED.
```

Figure 5.1

(a) The message NEW ITEM is displayed by the Editor to indicate that you are establishing a new item on the file.
(b) The Editor displays the word TOP to show you that it is starting at the top, that is the first line of your item.
(c) Whenever the Editor wants a new command, it displays the full stop as a prompt.
(d) The I command is used to input new data into an item.
(e) When using the I command to input data, the Editor displays the line numbers 001, 002 and so on, and then allows you to input the data for that line.
(f) A null line, that is consisting of only a <RETURN>, will terminate the input activity – as you did at line 011 in this example.
(g) The FI command saves the item on the file.
(h) The Editor confirms that the item has been filed.

So you have now added a new item called *ITEMG* to your file *FILEX*.

5.2.2 Changing an existing item

The process of changing an item is illustrated here. In Fig. 5.2 we list the contents of the item. We then proceed to line 5 where we change

```
:EDIT FILEX ITEMG
TOP
.L999                   <== this lets us look at the item
001 HEGINBOTHAM J E
002 24 THE LARCHES
003 01-999 4766
004 T
005 MANAGER
006 M27
007 1
008 217
009 5123
010 2805
EOF 10
.G5                     <== this takes us to line 5
005 MANAGER
.R/MANAGER/CLERK/        <== this replaces MANAGER by CLERK
005 CLERK
.G9                     <== this takes us to line 9
009 5123
.R/5/9/                  <== this replaces 5 by 9
009 9123
.F                      <== this formats the changes
TOP
```

Figure 5.2

MANAGER to CLERK, and then to line 9 where we change the 5 to 9. We then implement these changes with the F command.

In Fig. 5.3 we list this amended item and then insert new material after line 2. As before, we implement the changes with the F command. In Fig. 5.4 we list this newly amended item and then delete three of the

```
. L999                   <== this lets us look at the item
001 HEGINBOTHAM J E
002 24 THE LARCHES
003 01-999 4766
004 T
005 CLERK
006 M27
007 1
008 217
009 9123
010 2805
EOF 10
. G2                     <== this takes us to line 2
002 24 THE LARCHES
. I                      <== this allows us to insert new lines
002+READING                 after line number 2
002+BERKSHIRE
002+UNITED KINGDOM
. F                      <== this formats the changes
TOP
```

Figure 5.3

```
. L999                   <== this lets us look at the item
001 HEGINBOTHAM J E
002 24 THE LARCHES
003 READING
004 BERKSHIRE
005 UNITED KINGDOM
006 01-999 4766
007 T
008 CLERK
009 M27
010 1
011 217
012 9123
013 2805
EOF 13
. F                      <== this formats the changes
TOP
. G3                     <== this takes us to line 3
003 READING
. DE3                    <== this deletes the next 3 lines
. F                      <== this formats the changes
TOP
```

Figure 5.4

lines. Finally, in Fig. 5.5, we list the amended item and file it back on disk by means of the FI command.

```
. L999                  <== this lets us look at the item
001 HEGINBOTHAM J E
002 24 THE LARCHES
003 01-999 4766
004 T
005 MANAGER
006 M27
007 1
008 217
009 5123
010 2805
. FI                    <== this files the finished item
'ITEMG' FILED.
```

Figure 5.5

Note the following points about this example:

- The Editor did not display NEW ITEM because *ITEMG* already exists on the file *FILEX*.
- The L command displays one or more lines.
- L999 will list all the lines in the file (unless there are more than 999).
- L23 is a convenient number of lines to list, because this is the number of lines which can be held on the screen.
- The EOF – *end of file* – message shows the number of the last line in the file.
- TOP is printed by the Editor to show that it is pointing to the *top* of the item, that is, just before line 001.
- The G command tells the Editor to go to a specific line.
- The R command replaces one character string by another.
- The DE command deletes one or more lines.
- The line numbers are re-organized when an F command is issued. The new numbers start at 1 and go up in steps of one. It is essential that an F command be issued after any changes, such as:
  (i) Insertion of new lines.
  (ii) Deletion of lines.
  (iii) Replacement of lines.
  (iv) Replacement of character strings within lines.
  (v) Merging existing lines from other items.

The changes made will not be shown when an L command is used to list the file, otherwise. Furthermore, a SEQN? error will occur if an attempt is made to modify lines preceding the last change before an F command is issued.

- The I command is used to insert new data into an item.
- When using the I command to insert new lines, the Editor indicates the line number *after* which the lines are to be inserted, 002 in this example, by displaying 002+ when it wants another line.
- A null line, that is a line consisting of only a <RETURN>, will terminate the insert activity – as it did when we were creating the item earlier.
- The FI command saves the item on the file.

We have now changed the item and saved it on the file again.

5.2.3 Deleting an old item

The following sequence of commands will allow the user to delete an item which already exists on the file:

```
:EDIT FILEX ITEMG
TOP
.FD
'ITEMG' DELETED.
```

Note the following points:

(a) TOP is printed by the Editor to show that it is pointing to the *top* of the item, that is, just before line 001.
(b) The FD command is used to delete the item from the file.
(c) The Editor confirms that the item has been deleted.
(d) The Editor terminates when the item has been deleted.
(e) If the item does not exist, then no action will be taken.

Some implementations offer a Proc which will delete an item from a file without using the Editor:

```
:DELETE FILEX ITEMG
'ITEMG' DELETED
```

We have now deleted the item *ITEMG* from the file *FILEX* and there is no longer any record of its existence anywhere on the system.

5.2.4 Editing a Proc or a Basic program

These principles apply, and the same commands will be used, whether the item being edited contains data, as in this example, Proc statements, Basic program statements or a Runoff document.

When you are creating a Proc procedure, remember that each item on the file represents a Proc procedure, and each attribute in the item represents a Proc statement.

When you are creating a Basic program, remember that each item on the file represents a Basic program, and each attribute in the item represents a Basic statement.

When you are creating a Runoff document, remember that each line of the item represents either a Runoff command line or a line of text.

When you are editing an item, the Editor considers this to be a set of lines, or attributes, and moves a pointer up and down to allow you to process each and any line. If you change a line, delete a line or insert any new lines at any point, then the Editor copies all the previous lines across to a new version of your item which it is building up – so there are really two copies of your item, the current one and the newly created one, as shown in Fig. 5.6.

Whenever you look at any lines in the item, you are looking at the current copy. Even if you have made changes to the item these will not be shown until you replace the current copy by the newly created copy. You do this by means of one of the F commands.

If you change the *current line* then it – and all the previous lines – are copied across to the newly created copy. If you delete any lines, then these are *not* copied across to the newly created copy. If you insert any new lines, then the current line and all the preceding lines are copied across, and the new lines which you type in are then added to the newly created copy.

Because the newly created copy in Fig. 5.6 is already larger than the current item, this shows that you have inserted some new lines earlier.

So, essentially, the Editor allows you to:

(a) Inspect a copy of your item (by means of the L command).
(b) Move the pointer up and down the item to *point* to any line = the current line (the G command).

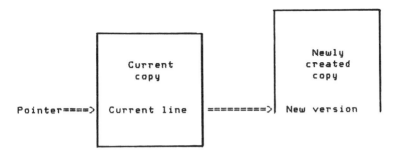

Figure 5.6

(c) Change the current line – and any subsequent lines (the R command).
(d) Delete the current line – and any subsequent lines (the DE command).
(e) Insert new lines immediately after the current line (the I command).
(f) Implement any changes made – replacing the current copy by the newly created copy (the F command).
(g) Delete the item (the FD command).
(h) File the copy of your item on disk (the FI command).

There are many other commands available when you use the Editor.

5.2.5 Some Editor commands

Let us look at some of the Editor commands which you will use most frequently. When we introduce these commands, we shall use braces – curly brackets – to indicate a parameter which may be omitted. The braces themselves are not typed in.

n a simple number moves the pointer to line number 'n' – this is identical to the Gn command.
Null a null line causes the pointer to advance a line at a time.

During a sequence of data lines following an I or R command, a null line indicates the end of the data lines.

A repeats the last L command.
B moves the pointer to the bottom of the item, the EOF.
DE deletes the current line.
DEn deletes n lines starting with the current line. For example:

```
DE7
```

will delete the current line and the next six lines. If you omit the number of lines, then the curernt line only will be deleted.

DE{n}/string/{p{–q}}   deletes all those of the next n lines – including the current line – which contain the string *string* in columns p to q inclusive. For example:

```
DE5/HELP/
```

will delete every one of the next five lines which contains the character string HELP.

```
DE7/GO 2/10—99
```

will delete every one of the next seven lines which contains the character string GO 2 anywhere in columns 10–99 inclusive.

If you omit the number of lines, then the Editor will delete the first line which is found to contain the string. Thus:

```
DE/PRINT/
```

will scan the item from the current line, deleting the first line in which it finds the string PRINT.

EX exits from the Editor and abandons the processing of the current item.

EXK exits from the Editor and then abandons when processing a list of item-ids.

F moves the pointer back to the top of the file and incorporates any amendments made since the last F command.

FD deletes the item from the file.

This command should be treated with respect, because accidental deletion is as permanent as intentional deletion. If an item has been accidentally deleted by means of the Editor FD command, then it may be recovered by using the RECOVER-FD verb immediately after the Editor has terminated. The RECOVER-FD verb requests:

```
INPUT ITEM ID*
```

to which you must enter the item-id of the item which was deleted. The item will then be saved on the original file. The state of the recovered item will be as prior to the last use of the Editor.

RECOVER-FD is a TCL verb and the recovery must be done immediately after the deletion. If any other activity is performed before the RECOVER-FD is issued, then the item may be irretrievable. For this reason, it may not be possible to recover items which have been deleted when the Editor was processing a list of items, as with:

```
EDIT INVOICES *
```

FDK deletes the current item and then abandons the Editor when processing a list of items.

FI implements any changes made to the item, writes the item back to the file, overwriting the original version if there is one, and exits from the Editor. The form:

```
FI(HQDATA MAS044
```

is available to save the item with item-id *MAS044* on the file *HQDATA* leaving the original item unchanged. The form

```
FI(MAS044
```

is available to save the item with item-id *MAS044* on the file which you are editing, leaving the original item unchanged.

FIK files the current item and then abandons the Editor when processing a list of items.

FS implements any changes made to the item, writes the item back to the file, overwriting the original version if there is one, and continues with the editing process – unlike FI which exits from the Editor. The form:

```
FS(ALLPROGS UPDP
```

is available to save the data as item with item-id *UPDP* on the file *ALLPROGS* leaving the original item unchanged. The form:

```
FS(UPDP
```

is available to save the data as item with item-id *UPDP* on the file which you are editing, leaving the original item unchanged.

Gn moves the pointer to line number *n*.
I   allows one or more lines to be inserted after the current line.

The Editor will display a prompt of the form:

```
00n+
```

to show that lines are being inserted after line number *n*. You can then enter the new information, line by line, each line being prompted by the same

```
00n+
```

An input of null will terminate the insert action.

Care must be taken when it is required to insert blank (null) lines. The situation may be solved by inserting lines containing a dummy character string which is then replaced by null. This is illustrated in Fig. 5.7 which has the effect of inserting three blank (null) lines afer line number 5. The same effect can be achieved more simply by typing two attribute marks, that is <CTRL> and the ^ character, as shown in Fig. 5.8.

```
. I
005+; ;
005+; ;
005+; ;
005+              <RETURN> only
. F
. G6
. R3/; ; //
006
007
008
```

Figure 5.7

```
. I
005+  ^^
005+              <RETURN> only
```

Figure 5.8

I data inserts the line of data after the current line. There is a space betwen the I and the data. For example:

```
I PRINT "ENTER NEW ADDRESS"
```

will insert the line

```
PRINT "ENTER NEW ADDRESS"
```

immediately after the current line.

Ln displays *n* lines starting at the line following the current line. For example:

```
L20
```

will display the twenty lines following the current line. If you omit the number of lines, then the Editor will display the next line only.

L{n}/string/{p{−q}} displays all those of the next *n* lines which contain the string *string* in columns *p* to *q* inclusive. For example:

```
L20/AREA/
```

will display those of the next twenty lines which contain the string AREA in any position in the line.

```
L5/AREA/6−12
```

will display those of the next five lines which contain the string AREA within columns 6–12 of the line.

```
L/AREA/
```

will scan the file and display the first line which was found to contain the string AREA in any position in the line.

In these examples, we use the character / to enclose the string, but any non-numeric character may be used. If the colon is used, then this has a special significance:

```
L:AREA
```

will scan the file and display the first line which was found to contain the string AREA in the first four characters of the line.

ME{n}/item/{m} merges, or copies, *n* lines from item *item* on the same file as the current item, starting at line number *m*, and inserts them after the current line in the item being edited. So the command:

`ME5/ANDATA/10`

will copy the five lines from the item *ANDATA,* starting with line 10 (that is, lines 10, 11, 12, 13 and 14) and insert them after the current line in the item which you are editing. The original item *ANDATA* will be unchanged. If you omit the item-id, like this:

`ME5//10`

then this will copy lines 10, 11, 12, 13 and 14 from the current copy of the item which you are editing and insert them after the current line. This duplicates these lines.

Some Pick implementations offer the format:

`ME5/(ALLPROGS UPDP/10`

to copy five lines from the item with item-id *UPDP* on the file *ALLPROGS.*

P this allows you to pre-store and subsequently invoke an Editor command or a series of commands, as described in the next section.

R{n} instructs the Editor to accept *n* lines of information which are to replace the next *n* lines of the item – including the current line.

R{n}/string1/string2/{p{−q}} replaces the string *string1* by the string *string2* for the first (left-most) occurrence in columns *p* to *q* (inclusive) of the next *n* lines starting at the current line.

Note the following points:

(a) If you omit the number of lines, then a value of 1 is assumed. This is standard for the Editor.
(b) The strings may be of different lengths.
(c) In the examples shown below, we use the / character to separate the strings, although any non-numeric character may be used. The separator character must not appear within either string.
(d) Either string may be null.
(e) An asterisk instead of the column range indicates that *all* occurrences are to be replaced.

For example, the command:

`R/WAGE/SALARY/`

will replace the first occurrence of the string WAGE by the string SALARY in the current line.

`R/WAGE/SALARY/*`

will replace *all* occurrences of the string WAGE by the string SALARY in the current line.

R5/WAGE/SALARY/

will replace the first occurrence of the string WAGE by the string SALARY in the next five lines, starting with the current line.

R5/WAGE/SALARY/*

will replace *all* occurrences of the string WAGE by the string SALARY in the next five lines, starting with the current line.

Some implementations offer the RU – *Replace Universal* – command which has forms such as:

RU/WAGE/SALARY/

and

RU5/WAGES/SALARY/

in place of the above two forms which used the asterisk.

R/WAGE/SALARY/30–50

will replace the first occurrence of the string WAGE in columns 30–50 (inclusive) by the string SALARY in the current line.

R5/WAGE/SALARY/30–50

will replace the first occurrence of the string WAGE in columns 30–50 (inclusive) by the string SALARY in the next five lines, starting with the current line.

According to the Pick implementation, the following points may apply:

(a) The same line may be amended once only between F commands.
(b) The same line may be amended several times by issuing the F command after each change.
(c) The character ^ within *string1* represents any character, and the character ^ within *string2* is respected as ^.
(d) An attribute mark within *string2* will terminate the line at that point.

T moves the pointer back to the top of the item – any amendments which have been made will not be effected until an F or FS command is issued.

X cancels the effect of the last ME, R or I command. Some Pick implementations offer extensions of the X command to allow you to cancel the effect of *all* changes made since the last F command or to cancel the effect of *all* changes made in this item – this is similar to the EX command.

5.2.6 Pre-stored commands

If you are using a complicated Editor command over and over again, then you may store the command and recall it when required. Any Editor command can be pre-stored by entering a P, followed by a blank, followed by the command to be stored. For example, if it is required to use the command

    L23

on several occasions, it may be pre-stored by the command

    P L23

and then issued every time the user gives the command

    P

which then has the same effect as issuing the original command L23.

On some implementations, up to ten pre-stored commands may be used, each being identified by its pre-store number: P, P1 through to P9. You should be careful when using these pre-stored commands, because the contents may be carried over from when you last used them. You can use Editor commands of the form ?P3 to display the contents of, in this case, pre-store P3.

All ten pre-stores are used in the same way, and each will generally be used to store a separate command. For example, let us imagine that we wish to change the word WAGE to the word SALARY in attribute 7 of an item, then we might store the commands:

    P1 G7

    P2 R/WAGES/SALARY/

and then every time you give the command, P1 will move the pointer to line (attribute) 7 and P2 will change the word WAGE to the word SALARY.

On some implementations, it is possible to store a sequence of several commands in one pre-store. This is done by separating the individual commands by the escape character:

    [

this is <CTRL>[on some keyboards.

The command separator may be changed to another character by means of the CD command:

    CD /

which will change the command separator to / and is useful when you are generating Editor commands within a Proc when the <CTRL>[character has a special significance.

One feature of such pre-stored commands is that you can construct a *loop* in which the final instruction in the sequence recalls the original pre-stored command. This is particularly useful when a large number of items are to be changed by a complex series of modifications, an effect which might need a complex program to scan and change the items under other circumstances. For example, let us imagine that we have a file of items with the layout:

item-id:	clock-number
attribute 1:	surname, initial
attribute 2:	sex
attribute 3:	department
attribute 4:	telephone number
attribute 5:	age
attribute 6:	address

and the department in attribute 3 is one of:

PERSONNEL
LABORATORY
SALES
ADMINISTRATION

We wish to abbreviate the department, replacing PERSONNEL by P, LABORATORY by L, SALES by S and ADMINISTRATION by A, in every record in the file. The following sequence of commands will allow us to do this easily:

EDIT file * this will cause *all* the items on the file to be submitted to the Editor.

P1 G3[R/PERSONNEL/P[F this will store a set of three commands which will do the following whenever the pre-store command P1 is given:

(a) G3 will move the pointer to attribute 3.
(b) R/PERSONNEL/P will change any occurrence of the word PERSON-NEL to P,if the word does not occur in attribute 3, then no action will be taken.
(c) F will re-format the item, effecting the change.

P2 G3[R/LABORATORY/L[F this will store a similar set of three commands,whereby the P2 command will change each occurrence of the word LABORATORY to L.

P3 G3[R/SALES/S[F this will store a similar set of three commands, whereaby the P3 command will change each occurrence of the word SALES to S.

P4 G3[R/ADMINISTRATION/A[F this will store a similar set of three commands, whereby the P4 command will change each occurrence of the word ADMINISTRATION to A.

P P1[P2[P3[P4[FI[P   this will store a set of six commands, such that when the user issues the command P, all the sequences of commands stored in P1, P2, P3 and P4 will be carried out. Then the first item will be filed by the FI command. The final P will re-invoke the same P command on the second item, and the process will be repeated until all the items on the file have been edited.

Such pre-store commands are a most useful feature of the Editor.

5.2.7 Further Editor commands

The commands shown in the previous section are by far the most frequently used. The following commands are also available, and you may find them useful once you have mastered the elementary set described above.

? displays the current line number.

?I will display, according to the Pick implementation, the name of the file being edited, the name of the item being edited, the size of the item and the current line number.

The contents of these display fields may have been corrupted by long P or R commands.

?S displays a message of the form:

```
ITEM SIZE = n    BYTES AVAILABLE = m
```

showing the current size of the item being edited, and the amount of workspace available for expansion of the item.

AS this is an *on/off* switch used in connection with the Assembler language, and causes the contents of the item to be *displayed* in Assembler columnar format.

C displays the column mask showing the column numbers. This is useful when replacing a specific string in a specific position.

M refers to MACRO facilities which are only used in connection with the Assembler language.

Nn moves the pointer on by *n* lines.

O only used in connection with the Assembler language.

PP causes the contents of all subsequent P and Pn commands to be displayed as they are being processed.

S sets and unsets the switch which indicates whether or not line-number display is to be suppressed.

TB a b c . . . z sets tabulator stops at columns *a*, *b*, *c* and so on, allowing the *TAB* key to be used to shift input text along to the next available tab setting. This is useful when entering Basic programs or tables of information to be processed by Runoff.

Un moves the pointer back *n* lines up the item.

The command U alone has no effect.

Wn displays the twenty-two lines up to and including line number *n* of the item.

Z this is used to re-set the zoning set by a Zp–q command and is equivalent to Z1–999.

Zp–q causes only columns *p* to *q* inclusive to be displayed. For example:

```
Z 1–70
```

will truncate the displayed lines at column 70, although the entire line will be considered when issuing commands such as L and R.

^ sets and unsets the switch which indicates that the character ^ is to be regarded as a character and not as the special character.

Null a null line causes the pointer to advance a line at a time.

During a sequence of data lines following an I or R command, a null line indicates the end of the data lines.

If a full stop precedes any Editor command, the action of that command will be as normal, but there will be no display. For example, the command:

```
R999/abc/def/
```

will normally display all the lines which are changed, but if you precede it by a full stop:

```
.R999/abc/def/
```

the lines will *not* be displayed as they are changed.

On some implementations, a command may be entered in either lower case or capitals. So that:

```
DE999
```

```
de999
```

will both have the same effect.

5.2.8 Error messages

The Editor has a number of possible error messages. This is what they mean:

CMND the Editor is expecting a command and you enter something other than from the list given above.

COL#? you have given an L, R or DE command such as:

R / x x x / y y y / n–m

with invalid values for the column numbers which follow the third separator. This usually arises when you have used a separator character which occurs in one of the strings, for example:

R / 2 6   A U G / 2 6 / 0 8 /

when you wanted to replace 26 AUG by 26/08.

SEQN? you attempt to insert or amend a line which is earlier in sequence than one which has been previously amended. The situation is overcome by issuing an F command, and then repeating the action.

STRNG? you have given an L, R or DE command such as:

R / x x x / y y y / n–m

with inadequate strings and/or delimiters.

5.2.9   Advantages of the Editor

The Editor is used because of the power it affords you:

(a) It is the only way of creating and maintaining Procs, Basic programs and Runoff text items.
(b) It allows you to create and amend data items – this is particularly useful when generating test data for your programs.
(c) It allows you to merge several items into one.
(d) Deleting an item by means of the Editor is quicker and easier than by writing a Basic program to perform the same action.
(e) The pre-store facility offered by the Editor P command offers text-editing capabilities which would only be possible with a complex and time-consuming Basic program – as we saw in Section 5.2.6.

The Editor can be used to advantage in a controlled situation, such as to create, maintain and delete work items used by Basic programs or Procs. In such cases, it is the speed and simplicity of the Editor which makes it preferable to writing a small program or Proc to achieve the same effect.

5.2.10   Disadvantages of the Editor

The powers of TCL which we listed as advantages could also be listed amongst its disadvantages:

(a) If you have access to the Editor and use it to create, amend and delete items, then this could become an auditor's nightmare since there is no check on the activities.
(b) There is no check on the format of the item-id or the nature of the data which are put into the item.
(c) There is no audit trail of the activities at all.
(d) There is no record of who created, changed or deleted an item.

In situations where these factors are important, then the maintenance of files and items should be left to Basic programs, where greater checking and control can be exercised over the action taken.

For this reason, it is customary to limit the user's access to the Editor. This can be done by:

(a) Reducing the user's system privileges, as described in Section 3.3.
(b) Removing the EDIT verbs from his or her MD.
(c) Re-naming the EDIT verbs, as described in Section 5.1.3 of this chapter, where we tell you how to create your own verbs.

So far we've looked at the Editor. Now let us look at some of the other TCL verbs.

5.3   FILE LAYOUT VERBS

Pick has a number of verbs which will allow you to look at the structure of your files:

COUNT an Access verb which displays a count of how many items there are on the file:

```
COUNT INV.PROGS
```

```
COUNT PERSONNEL WITH AGE < "65"
```

GROUP displays a list like that shown in Fig. 5.9 showing, for each group in the file, the FID of the first frame, the item-ids in that group, the length of each item.

```
GROUP PERSONNEL

68918
002B  4877
0027  8923
0031  0677
3 ITEMS 131 BYTES 0/131 FRAMES
68919
0033  9176
0031  2386
```

```
2 ITEMS 100 BYTES 0/100 FRAMES
68920
0038 5642
0035 0021
0036 7749
0038 7644
4 ITEMS 219 BYTES 0/219 FRAMES
68921
0030 9087
0030 9773
2 ITEMS 96 BYTES 0/96 FRAMES
68922
002E 3313
1 ITEMS 46 BYTES 0/46 FRAMES
68923
002A 4280
002E 5435
002D 6471
0035 5148
0030 5085
5 ITEMS 234 BYTES 0/234 FRAMES
68924
0030 4295
002B 2083
002B 6199
3 ITEMS 134 BYTES 0/134 FRAMES
```

Figure 5.9

ITEM displays a listing identical to that for GROUP, but only for the group in which a specific item is (or should be) found, as shown in Fig. 5.10.

```
ITEM PERSONNEL 4280

68923
002A 4280
002E 5435
002D 6471
0035 5148
0030 5085
5 ITEMS 234 BYTES 0/234 FRAMES


ITEM PERSONNEL 0120

ITEM NOT FOUND
68921
0030 9087
0030 9773
2 ITEMS 96 BYTES 0/96 FRAMES
```

Figure 5.10

ISTAT An Access verb which displays the file statistics – modulo, separation, number of items, total length of all items, and the averages –

together with a histogram showing the number of items in each group. Typical output is shown in Fig. 5.11 which specified the H option to display the histogram showing the file structure.

```
ISTAT INVOICES

ISTAT PERSONNEL WITH AGE < "20"


                  ISTAT STOCK (H)


FILE= STOCK MOD= 5 SEP= 1                15:33:09  23 SEP 1985
BYTES    ITMS
00000217 004 *>>>>
00000268 005 *>>>>>
00000322 006 *>>>>>>
00000738 013 *>>>>>>>>>>>>>>
00000000 000 *

ITEM COUNT=          28, BYTE COUNT=       1545, AVG. BYTES/ITEM=     55.1
AVG. ITEMS/GROUP=   5.6, STD. DEVIATION=   4.7, AVG. BYTES/GROUP=   309.0
```

Figure 5.11

HASH-TEST displays file statistics identical to those of ISTAT but for a hypothetical modulo instead of the true modulo of the file. This is useful when testing alternative shapes for your files.

```
HASH-TEST SALARIES
TEST MODULO: 19
```

This will show the distribution of item within the groups *as if* your *SALARIES* file had a modulo of 19.

STAT an Access verb which displays the number of items, the total item length and the average bytes per item for the records on your file:

```
STAT STOCK

STAT PERSONNEL WITH AGE > "60"
```

CHECKSUM an Access verb which displays the file statistics – as with STAT – and also a hash total of all the bytes in the file. By comparing the hash total at one moment with a previous hash total, you can see whether or not your file has been changed. It does not – of course – tell you how the file has changed!

I-DUMP an Access verb which displays the items exactly as they are held on the file – including field separators. This is illustrated in Fig. 5.12.

```
I-DUMP SALES.FIGS

I-DUMP PERSONNEL WITH AGE > "60"
```

```
I-DUMP STOCK
```

```
0567^STOOLS, STEEL, ORANGE^MN/206^6^^5967^5677^
0372^DESKS, STEEL, VIOLET^MN/384^22^10^6104^4222^
9607^LADDERS, PLASTIC, YELLOW^UK2/779^32^40^6081^4555^
4037^TABLES, WOODEN, VIOLET^UK/628^77^60^5924^2177^
9423^DESKS, SPECIAL, GREEN^LS/192^13^10^6173^2655^
5918^TABLES, STEEL, BROWN^GG/810^41^50^6050^4433^
8798^LADDERS, SPECIAL, BLUE^LS/646^7^^6130^6488^
3488^TABLES, PLASTIC, ORANGE^MN/396^32^50^6132^1111^
3333^CHAIRS, WOODEN, RED^UK/6142^41^50^6066^5875^
1479^LADDERS, STEEL, RED^UK2/965^6^10^6096^6850^
2574^DESKS, WOODEN, BLACK^MN/532^22^20^6200^3725^
6084^STOOLS, SPECIAL, YELLOW^GG/676^71^70^6028^6275^
6919^STOOLS, WOODEN, BROWN^UK/641^27^20^6175^2800^
2854^STOOLS, PLASTIC, RED^LS/971^30^30^6176^2100^
6314^CHAIRS, PLASTIC, BLUE^UK/110^19^30^6112^4925^
1500^DESKS, STEEL, BLUE^MN/600^105^90^5627^4825^
3000^LADDERS, WOODEN, ORANGE^LS/814^43^60^5986^3900^
4500^TABLES, SPECIAL, BLACK^MN/145]LS/122^55^40^5597^3525^
4395^CHAIRS, SPECIAL, WHITE^LS/181^62^50^6240^6275^
2625^CHAIRS, WOODEN, GREEN^GG/316^105^90^5978^5525^
1000^CHAIRS, WOODEN, RED^UK/614^64^50^6125^5875^
2500^STOOLS, SPECIAL, VIOLET^UK2/750^100^90^5994^3750^
4000^DESKS, PLASTIC, WHITE^UK/200^68^80^5726^3475^
3010^LADDERS, WOODEN, WHITE^LS/081^101^90^6004^5925^
2000^TABLES, PLASTIC, GREEN^UK/238^15^^6143^2325^
3500^CHAIRS, STEEL, YELLOW^GG/837^78^90^6220^3700^
1005^STOOLS, SPECIAL, PURPLE^UK2/75^50^50^5997^3750^
5050^CHAIRS, WOODEN, RED^UK2/614]UK2/6122]UK/400]UK/32^37^50^6157^5875^
28 ITEMS DUMPED.
```

```
I-DUMP STOCK WITH COLOUR = "RED"
```

```
3333^CHAIRS, WOODEN, RED^UK/6142^41^50^6066^5875^
1479^LADDERS, STEEL, RED^UK2/965^6^10^6096^6850^
2854^STOOLS, PLASTIC, RED^LS/971^30^30^6176^2100^
1000^CHAIRS, WOODEN, RED^UK/614^64^50^6125^5875^
5050^CHAIRS, WOODEN, RED^UK2/614]UK2/6122]UK/400]UK/32^37^50^6157^5875^
5 ITEMS DUMPED.
```

Figure 5.12

S-DUMP identical to I-DUMP except that sort criteria are provided:

```
S-DUMP STATISTICS
```

```
S-DUMP A99DATA WITH MAX > "80" BY MAX
```

Try these now, if you have a Pick terminal. Use the MD if you don't have any files like PERSONNEL or INVOICES.

The P option can be used to direct the output of any of these verbs to the printer. For example:

```
ISTAT STOCK (H,P)
```

5.4 THE FILE PROCESSING VERBS

In Chapter 2 we saw how a file is laid out: the DICT section, the data section, modulo, separation and so on. Now let us see how we use all this to establish the file.

The following verbs are available for file maintenance:

CREATE-FILE to establish the primary space for the file.
CLEAR-FILE to clear the contents of either the DICT section or the data section of the file.
DELETE-FILE to delete the file and its contents and return the space to the pool of available frames.
COPY to copy one or more items from one file to another (or the same) file.

Here we look at the most commonly encountered forms. Full details may be found in the reference literature for your implementation.

5.4.1 CREATE-FILE verb

This command establishes the (empty) primary file space for a file. The format of the command may be:

```
CREATE-FILE (NAMES 1,2 5,3)
```

which will create a file called *NAMES*, with the DICT section having a *MOD* of 1 and a *SEP* of 2, and with the data section having a *MOD* of 5 and a *SEP* of 3, or

```
CREATE-FILE (DICT PARTONE 5,2)
```

which will create a file called PARTONE, with a DICT section having a *MOD* of 5 and a *SEP* of 2, and without a data section.

On those Pick implementations which allow several data files to share the same dictionary file, the following points apply:

(a) The first dictionary and data section are created in the manner described above:

```
CREATE-FILE (STOCKDICTS 1,1 1,1)
```

if you want both a DICT and a data section, or

```
CREATE-FILE (DICT STOCKDICTS 1,1)
```

if you only want a DICT section.
(b) The second and subsequent data sections are created by means of a command such as:

```
CREATE-FILE (DATA STOCKDICTS,LONDON 5,1)
```

where *STOCKDICTS* is the name of the dictionary (main) file, and
LONDON is the name of the new file for which the data section is to
be established.
(c) In subsequent TCL commands which require the name of the data
file, the file name is represented by the identifier:

`STOCKDICTS,LONDON`

For example, you will use a command such as:

`EDIT STOCKDICTS,LONDON 0001`

to EDIT data item *0001* on sub-file *LONDON* of DICT file
STOCKDICTS, and you will use an Access sentence such as:

`SORT STOCKDICTS,LONDON AGE NAME SEX`

to produce a report on the data items of the same file.

When you are choosing a name for your files, it must not exist when you
are creating the file. For this reason, you cannot have a name such as
LIST, DICT, DATA or OFF, which already exist on your MD. The name
of your file is simply the item-id of the file definition item which is held
on the MD, and like any other item-id it may be up to fifty characters in
length and may contain any characters except the system field separators – attribute marks, value marks and secondary value marks. However, the name should be consistent with the syntax of the Pick TCL
commands, so it cannot contain spaces, and it should not contain
commas, parentheses, apostrophes or quotation marks, otherwise it
may be ambiguous in certain contexts.

On some implementations, the parentheses are not used, and on
others the closing parenthesis may be omitted. Thus the following forms
may be encountered:

```
CREATE-FILE (NAMES 1,2 5,3)
CREATE-FILE (NAMES 1,2 5,3
CREATE-FILE NAMES 1,2 5,3
```

In the present book we shall use the parentheses in the examples, and,
as with other commands, you might care to amend these to match the
situation on your implementation.

The CREATE-FILE verb will establish a new file definition item on
your MD. The first attribute of this item will be D to indicate that it
defines a data area. If you want any special code in this first attribute:

DC to indicate that the file is to hold Basic programs, as discussed in
Section 6.19.
DX to indicate that the file is to be ignored when a file save and file

restore is performed. The file will not exist after such a back-up process. **DY** to indicate that the data on the file are to be ignored when a file save and file restore is performed. The file will be empty after such a back-up process.

You must then use the Editor to change the D to the required code.

5.4.2   CLEAR-FILE verb

This command will clear the entire contents of the file area specified. The format of the command may be:

```
CLEAR-FILE (DICT FILEX)
```

which will clear the entire contents of the dictionary section of the file *FILEX*, leaving only the data-level identifier item remaining, or

```
CLEAR-FILE (DATA PERSONS)
```

which will clear the entire contents of the data section of the file *PERSONS*.

   You must specify (DICT or (DATA, so the form:

```
CLEAR-FILE (PERSONS)
```

will be rejected.

5.4.3   DELETE-FILE verb

This deletes all references to the file on the MD and releases the space currently occupied by the file, returning the frames to the common pool. The format of the command may be:

```
DELETE-FILE (SALESORDERS)
```

which will delete the file *SALESORDERS*, the DICT section and all its data, or

```
DELETE-FILE (DATA SALESORDERS)
```

which will delete the space occupied by the data section of the file but retain the DICT section and its contents.

   A file may be deleted quickly and easily by removing the file definition item from the MD file. This can be done quite simply by means of the Editor or the DELETE Proc:

```
DELETE MD OLDFILE
```

The obvious danger and weakness in this solution lie in the fact that it does not immediately release the space used by the file and its overflow frames. But if a file save and file restore is done soon afterwards, then the space previously occupied by the file will be returned to the common pool.

5.4.4 COPY verb

This allows you to copy one or more items from one file and save them with specified item-ids on the same, or another, file, and can get rather complicated, because you have to specify:

(a) The name of the file *from* which the items are to be copied.
(b) The item-ids of the items which are to be copied.
(c) The name of the destination file *to* which the items are to be copied – if this is omitted, then the source file is assumed.
(d) The item-ids with which the items are to be saved – if these are omitted, then the item-ids of the source items are used.
(e) Whether the original items are to be deleted.
(f) What action is to be taken if the item-ids already exist on the destination file.

As an example, let us take the command:

`COPY SALARY I1 I2 I3`

this will copy items with item-ids *I1*, *I2* and *I3* from file *SALARY*, and copy them to the destination specified in response to the message:

`TO:`

which is displayed by the system. Your response will be one of the following:

`TO:I4 I5 I6` which will copy *I1* to *I4*, *I2* to *I5*, *I3* to *I6*, all on file *SALARY*. The original items *I1*, *I2* and *I3* will be retained on *SALARY*.
`TO:(SALARY I4 I5 I6` this has exactly the same effect as the previous response. The original items *I1*, *I2* and *I3* will be retained on *SALARY*.
`TO:(SALARY2 I4 I5 I6` which will copy *I1* to *I4*, *I2* to *I5*, *I3* to *I6*, all on file *SALARY2*.The original items *I1*, *I2* and *I3* will be retained on *SALARY*.
`TO:(SALARY2` which will copy *I1* to *I1*, *I2* to *I2*, *I3* to *I3*, all on file *SALARY2*. The original items *I1*, *I2* and *I3* will be retained on *SALARY*.

A common – and potentially quite dangerous – mistake is to omit the (before the file name. If your response to the TO: message starts with an open parenthesis, then it is taken to mean that the file name follows. If you omit the open parenthesis, then the system will assume that you are copying back to the same file, and only item-ids follow. For example:

```
COPY SALARY1 I1 I2 I3
TO:(SALARY2 I4 I5 I6
```

is probably what you want to copy from one file to another, but

```
COPY SALARY1 I1 I2 I3
TO:SALARY2 I4 I5 I6
```

will mean that you want to copy the items back to *SALARY1* (since there is no parenthesis before SALARY2), so that it will copy item *I1* on file *SALARY1* to item *SALARY2* on file *SALARY1*, item *I2* on file *SALARY1* to item *I4* on file *SALARY1*, and item *I3* on file *SALARY1* to item *I5* on file *SALARY1*. Not what you wanted!

An error message will be printed if the source items do not exist – and therefore cannot be copied – if the destination items already exist – and therefore cannot be added to the file – or if you try to copy a file definition item with a D in attribute 1. Certain options may be specified on the COPY command to overcome these error conditions. The option O as in the command:

```
COPY INVOICES I1 I2 I3 (O)
```

indicates that the destination items are to be *overwritten* if they already exist. The option D as in the command:

```
COPY INVOICES I1 I2 I3 (D)
```

indicates that the source items are to be *deleted* after a successful copy. You may specify both options:

```
COPY INVOICES I1 I2 I3 (O,D)
```

in which case the destination items will be overwritten if they already exist, *and* the source items will be deleted after a successful copy. Be careful with this. You might copy all the items back onto themselves, and then delete them!

If you use the T option, for example:

```
COPY INVOICES I1 I2 I3 (T)
```

then the items will simply be displayed at the terminal. If you give a null response – that is, just press <RETURN> – at the TO: stage, then the items will be displayed at the terminal and no other action will take place.

If you use the P option, for example:

```
COPY INVOICES I1 I2 I3 (P)
```

then the items will be listed on the printer. In these examples, the system will not prompt the TO: message.

Instead of a list of items, such as *I1*, *I2* and *I3*, you may indicate that *all* the items are to be copied. This is done by putting an asterisk instead of the list of item-ids:

```
COPY INVOICES *
```

If you use the I option, for example:

```
COPY SALARY1 I1 I2 I3 (I)
```

then the system will display the item-ids of all the items as they are copied.

Any logical combination of these options may be specified on the COPY command.

If you wish to copy items from the dictionary of a file, then the COPY command will be of the form:

```
COPY DICT INVOICES I1 I2 I3
```

and if the items are to be copied to the dictionary of a file, then the TO: response will be of the form:

```
TO: (DICT ARCHIVE I4 I5 I6
```

If the COPY processor encounters any items with D as the first attribute, it assumes them to be data definition items and will not copy them to the destination file.

In any of these forms, the item-ids may be enclosed in apostrophes, as shown in Fig. 5.13.

```
COPY SALARY '11' '12' '13'
TO: '14' '15' '16'

COPY SALARY1 '11' '12' '13'
TO: (SALARY2 '14' '15' '16'

COPY DICT INVOICES '11' '12' '13'

COPY INVOICES '11' '12' '13' (D)

COPY INVOICES '11' '12' '13' (O)

COPY INVOICES '11' '12' '13' (O, I, D)

COPY INVOICES '11' '12' '13' (P)

COPY INVOICES '1000' (T)
```

Figure 5.13

5.5   INTERROGATING, SETTING AND CHANGING THE SYSTEM

There is a set of verbs which allows you to inquire about the status of the system or about your own user status. In some cases these are privileged operations available only to the systems programmer account.

DATE-FORMAT sets the format of external dates to the American format *mm/dd/yy*. If the option I is used:

```
DATE-FORMAT (I)
```

then all subsequent external dates will be in the European format *dd/mm/ yy*. This command is often included in a log-on Proc.

DISCIO monitors the system activity for 5 seconds and then displays details of the system usage, as shown in Fig. 5.14.

```
DISCIO OUTPUT

DEVICE    I/O'S PER SECOND    TOTAL I/O'S
  DO           18.77              92
  D1           12.85              63
  D2           15.30              75
  D3           11.83              58
  TOTAL        58.75             288

  READS:       39.5             194
  WRITES:      19.1              94
```

Figure 5.14

DUMP displays the contents of a frame on the screen, as we have seen in Section 2.6. Any non-graphic character will be displayed as a full stop. Options are available: G to display the specified frame and all subsequent linked frames in the group, and X to display the contents of the frame in both character and hexadecimal format.

HUSH suppresses the display of information typed in. Output information is not affected by this action.

NOHUSH reverses the action of the HUSH verb.

LIMITS has the features of WHAT, as described below.

LISTU lists the details of the terminals which are currently logged on to the system. The report shows the time and date when they logged on, their location, and other details as taken from the *ACC* file. Typical output is shown in Fig. 5.15.

PEEK allows one user to *eavesdrop* on the screen input and output of another terminal, displaying the screen image from one terminal on another's screen.

```
LISTU

PORT... PCB-FID NAME.......  LOCATION...........  DATE......  TIME..

000     0500    SYSPROG      SYSTEM CONSOLE       23 JAN 1986 08:30
001     0520    WAGES        ACCOUNTS DEPT        23 JAN 1986 09:07
002     0540    WAGES        JOHN WINDLE          23 JAN 1986 09:35
*005    05A0    PROGS        PROGRAMMERS          23 JAN 1986 07:25
```

Figure 5.15

POVF *print overflow frames* – this displays a list of the disk space which is currently unused and which is available for new files or for overflow from existing files. Typical output is shown in Fig. 5.16. The CLAIM verb converts any linked frames into one contiguous block, if possible. The output is the same as for POVF.

TERM is used for interrogating the characteristics for your terminal, as shown in Fig. 5.17, and these will apply until you log off.

This verb will also re-set the parameters, if the appropriate values are supplied. Some implementations also offer the TERMINAL Proc to re-set the parameters.

```
POVF


   FROM      TO     #FRAMES        FROM      TO     #FRAMES

   63092   LINKED       13
   15077 -  21304     6228       63042 -   63043        2
   64463 -  64463        1       64552 -   64552        1
   64651 -  64651        1       65129 -   65130        2
   65419 -  65419        1       65703 -   65703        1
   65939 -  65939        1       66079 -   66079        1
   66220 -  66220        1       66237 -   66237        1
   66300 -  66300        1       66778 -   66778        1
   66829 -  66829        1       66894 -   66894        1
   67150 -  67150        1       67264 -   67265        2
   67367 -  67367        1       67395 -   67395        1
   68238 -  68238        1       68633 -   68633        1
   68717 -  68717        1       68796 -   68796        1
   69137 -  69981      845       98960 -   98960        1
   99199 -  99199        1       99236 -   99238        3
   99273 -  99277        5       99289 -   99426      138
   99676 - 100394      719      101420 -  153718    52299

   TOTAL NUMBER OF CONTIGUOUS FRAMES   =   60265
   NUMBER OF FRAMES IN THE TEMPORARY SPACE BLOCK =    182
   NUMBER OF FRAMES IN THE TEMPORARY SPACE CHAIN =    860
```

Figure 5.16

```
: TERM

                   TERMINAL  PRINTER
PAGE WIDTH:           79       132
PAGE DEPTH:           23        60
LINE SKIP :            0         0
LF DELAY  :           10
FF DELAY  :           10
BACKSPACE :            8
TERMINAL  :            0
BAUD RATE :         9600
PCI       :           74
```

Figure 5.17

The SET-TERM facility will re-set the standard terminal characteristics which are assigned when a terminal logs on.

TIME displays the current time and date for the system:

```
12 : 30 : 59   17 JAN 1986
```

The current system time may be re-set by the SET-TIME facility, and the current system date may be re-set by the SET-DATE facility.

TIMESLICE displays the length of your current quantum (= timeslice), that is, the maximum length of time for which your processes may run without interruption by the operating system. According to your privileges, you may also interrogate and re-set the timeslices for a specific terminal. The TIMESLICE verb is discussed further in Section 12.4.1.

USER displays the system privileges and the additional workspace which is allocated to your account.

WHAT displays details of the system configuration, as shown in Fig. 5.18. On some systems, this action is performed by the LIMITS verb.

```
WHAT

AB09911           SYSTEM SERIAL NUMBER
256K              OF MEMORY
1279              ABS FRAMES
153719            MAXIMUM FRAME-ID
1280              FID FOR PCB FOR LINE 0
48                PORTS

AVAILABLE DEVICES:

    DISKS:         D0
                   D1

    TAPE(S)        1

    PRINTER(S)     1
```

Figure 5.18

WHERE displays details of the terminals which are currently logged on to the system, showing details of their return-address stack.

This information gives an indication of the work which each terminal is currently carrying out. The report shows the contents of the stack which holds all the routine and sub-routine return addresses for each terminal. You can find details of the meaning of these addresses in the reference manuals for your own system.

WHO displays the port number and the account to which you are currently logged on.

WORKSPACE displays the workspace associated with each terminal.

These operations display any output at the terminal which issued the command. However, as described in Section 5.1.1, where we dealt with TCL options, the P option can be used to direct the output to the printer. For example:

```
POVF (P)

DUMP 12345 (G,X,N)
```

5.6 AFFECTING OTHER TERMINALS

In Section 5.5 we met the PEEK verb which allows you to eavesdrop on another terminal. Now let us see some other verbs which you can use to affect other users' terminals.

If you want to log on to a remote terminal, you can do this with the

```
LOGON
```

verb. The operating system will then ask you for the terminal (or port or channel) number which is to be logged on, and also the name of the account which is to be used. A response such as:

```
3, WAGES
```

will have the same effect as logging on to the *WAGES* account on terminal 3. This is often used in situations where a terminal is failing to respond to data keyed in, and tests whether the channel is functioning properly.

The opposite action, that of logging a remote terminal off, is done by means of the verb:

```
LOGOFF
```

The operating system will then ask which terminal is to be logged off, and will print a confirmatory message at your terminal when this has been done.

The ZAP verb allows you to send a line of input data to another remote terminal which is currently waiting for keyboard input. The format of the command differs according to implementation – indeed, the command is not available on some systems – but you will have to specify the terminal to which the data are to be sent and what the input line is.

These verbs may be privileged operations available only to the *SYSPROG* account.

The LOGTO verb is used to change from one account to another without logging off and logging on again. The account name and password, if any, are specified on the command, exactly as when you log on in the normal manner.

```
LOGTO WAGES,PAUL
```

If this is unsuccessful, then no action is taken and the original account is retained. After a successful change to another account, the original workspace and other account characteristics will be retained.

5.7 PERFORMING ARITHMETIC

A number of TCL verbs are available to perform simple decimal or hexadecimal arithmetic. The calculations use only integer numbers, and the results are displayed directly on the terminal:

ADDD adds together two decimal numbers, and displays the sum:

```
ADDD 10 20
30
```

SUBD subtracts one decimal number from another, and displays the difference:

```
SUBD 10 20
-10
```

MULD multiplies two decimal numbers together, and displays the product:

```
MULD 10 20
200
```

DIVD divides one decimal number by another, and displays the quotient and the remainder:

```
DIVD 100 21
4 16
```

ADDX adds together two hexadecimal numbers, and displays the sum:

```
ADDX A4 CF
173
```

SUBX subtracts one hexadecimal number from another, and displays the product:

```
SUBX A4 CF
FFFFFFFFFFD5
```

MULX multiplies two hexadecimal numbers together, and displays the product:

```
MULX A4 CF
849C
```

DIVX divides one hexadecimal number by another, and displays the quotient and the remainder:

```
DIVX A40 21
C 8C
```

There are also two verbs for performing decimal to hexadecimal conversion, and vice versa:

DTX convers a decimal number to hexadecimal:

```
DTX 1234
4D2
```

XTD converts a hexadecimal number to decimal:

```
XTD CAFE
51966
```

Most implementations offer user exits to perform hexadecimal arithmetic and decimal/hexadecimal conversion within Basic programs and Procs.

5.8 MISCELLANEOUS COMMANDS

There are a number of verbs which do not fall easily into the above categories. Let us have a look at the more useful of these.

5.8.1 MESSAGE verb

The MESSAGE or MSG verb allows you to pass a single-line message to all users, to all users on a specific account or to a specific terminal.

The message will be displayed immediately on all the target terminals which are logged on, interrupting the screen output from any process active on that terminal. The identity of the account from which the message was sent is also displayed with the message.

A typical use of the verb might be when the *SYSPROG* account issues the command:

```
MESSAGE * A FILE SAVE IS DUE TO START
```

or

```
MSG * A FILE SAVE IS DUE TO START
```

either of which will display:

```
09 : 20 : 30  02 JUN 1986  FROM SYSPROG:
A FILE SAVE IS DUE TO START
```

on all terminals which are currently logged on. The message *will not* be displayed on any terminals which log on later. You may send a message to a specific terminal or to a specific account by a command such as:

```
MESSAGE WAGES YOUR FILES ARE NOW AVAILABLE
```

which will sent the message:

```
09 : 30 : 30  02 JUL 1986  FROM SYSPROG:
YOUR FILES ARE NOW AVAILABLE
```

to any users who are currently logged on to the *WAGES* account. If, in this latter example, there are no users logged on to the *WAGES* account, then no action will be taken.

It is recommended that the MESSAGE and MSG verbs be used with restraint, since frivolous messages can be annoying and distracting. Some installations even remove the verb from the users' accounts to avoid abuse.

5.8.2   BLOCK-TERM and BLOCK-PRINT verbs

The BLOCK-TERM and BLOCK-PRINT may possibly be included under this heading. When we discussed the standard files, we saw that the BLOCK-CONVERT file contains a set of prescriptions which enable large block letters to be displayed on the screen or the printer. It is the BLOCK-TERM and BLOCK-PRINT verbs, respectively, which perform this action. The commands are useful for displaying or printing short messages. For example, the command:

```
BLOCK-TERM IN USE
```

will display the message shown in Fig. 5.19 on the screen. You might issue this immediately before invoking a program which runs for some time without showing any signs of life, thus warning others not to interfere.

To print messages on the printer, you might use a BLOCK-PRINT command such as:

```
BLOCK-PRINT ***** INVOICE PROGRAM LISTINGS *****
```

```
IIIIIIIIIII NNNN      NNNN
IIIIIIIIIII NNNNN     NNNN
       IIII    NNNNNN   NNNN
       IIII    NNNNNNN NNNN
       IIII    NNNNNNNNNNNN
       IIII    NNNN NNNNNNN
       IIII    NNNN   NNNNNN
IIIIIIIIIII NNNN     NNNNN
IIIIIIIIIII NNNN      NNNN
```

```
UUUU      UUUU  SSSSSSSSSS   EEEEEEEEEEEE
UUUU      UUUU  SSSSSSSSSSSS EEEEEEEEEEEE
UUUU      UUUU  SSSS         EEEE
UUUU      UUUU  SSSS         EEEEEEEEEE
UUUU      UUUU  SSSSSSSSSSS  EEEEEEEEEE
UUUU      UUUU  SSSSSSSSSSSS EEEE
UUUU      UUUU         SSSS  EEEE
UUUUUUUUUUUU SSSSSSSSSSSS  EEEEEEEEEEEE
  UUUUUUUUUU    SSSSSSSSSS   EEEEEEEEEEEE
```

Figure 5.19

which will produce a five-line message for you to put at the front of your program listings. If you want two or more words to appear on one line, then you should enclose the words in quotes:

BLOCK-PRINT 'DO NOT' TOUCH

The resultant printout is shown in Fig. 5.20.

```
DDDDDDDDDD    OOOOOOOOOO          NNNN      NNNN  OOOOOOOOOO  TTTTTTTTTTTT
DDDDDDDDDD    OOOOOOOOOOOO         NNNNN     NNNN OOOOOOOOOOOO TTTTTTTTTTTT
DDDD    DDDD OOOO    OOOO         NNNNNN  NNNN OOOO    OOOO      TTTT
DDDD    DDDD OOOO    OOOO         NNNNNNN NNNN OOOO    OOOO      TTTT
DDDD    DDDD OOOO    OOOO         NNNNNNNNNNNN OOOO    OOOO      TTTT
DDDD    DDDD OOOO    OOOO         NNNN NNNNNNN OOOO    OOOO      TTTT
DDDDDDDDDD    OOOOOOOOOOOO         NNNN   NNNNN OOOOOOOOOOOO      TTTT
DDDDDDDDDD    OOOOOOOOOO          NNNN      NNNN  OOOOOOOOOO      TTTT
```

```
TTTTTTTTTTTT  OOOOOOOOOO  UUUU      UUUU  CCCCCCCCCC  HHHH      HHHH
TTTTTTTTTTTT  OOOOOOOOOOOO UUUU     UUUU CCCCCCCCCCCC HHHH      HHHH
     TTTT     OOOO    OOOO UUUU     UUUU CCCC    CCCC HHHH      HHHH
     TTTT     OOOO    OOOO UUUU     UUUU CCCC    CCCC HHHHHHHHHHHH
     TTTT     OOOO    OOOO UUUU     UUUU CCCC         HHHHHHHHHHHH
     TTTT     OOOO    OOOO UUUU     UUUU CCCC    CCCC HHHH      HHHH
     TTTT     OOOOOOOOOOOO UUUUUUUUUUUU CCCCCCCCCCCC HHHH      HHHH
     TTTT       OOOOOOOOOO   UUUUUUUUUU   CCCCCCCCCC  HHHH      HHHH
```

Figure 5.20

5.8.3 SLEEP verb

This verb causes the activity at your terminal to sleep for a specific number of seconds. For example:

SLEEP 60

which would sleep for 1 min, or

SLEEP 23 : 00

which would sleep until 23 : 00 hours on the internal clock. When the required period had expired, the terminal would activate once more and continue processing.

This verb is usually embedded within a Proc, such as that shown in Listing 5.1, which might be required to wait until a time when all users are likely to have gone home before proceeding.

If a terminal is sleeping, it may not be used for any other purpose.

```
PQ
HSLEEP 23: 59
P
HRUN MYPROGS END-OF-DAY-ROUTINE
P
HOFF
P
```

Listing 5.1

5.9 UTILITY PROCS

In addition to the standard TCL and Access verbs, there are a number of Procs which are available to all users. These are held on the *PROCLIB* file, and usually include such Procs as:

COMPARE to compare the contents of two items and produce a listing showing any differences.
CP to print the contents of an item or items from a specified file on the printer:

CP STOCK 1234

CT to display an item or items from the specified file on the terminal:

CT STOCK *

DB to invoke the Pick Basic development utility. This provides a simple harness allowing you to perform such activities as EDIT,

COMPILE and RUN on a Basic program by entering simple commands E, C and R.

DELETE to delete an item from a file:

```
DELETE FILEX ITEMA
```

DUMP-FILES to dump a number of files to magnetic tape.

EXCHANGE to switch the item-ids of two items on a file.

LOAD-FILES to load a number of files from magnetic tape.

LISTACC to display the account name of all current users, showing their log-on time, channel number and location.

LISTCONN to display a sorted list of the Access connectives and modifiers in your MD or an optionally specified file.

LISTDICTS to display a sorted list of the contents of all the attribute and synonym definitions in your MD or an optionally specified file.

LISTF4 to display a simple four-column list of the names of all the files on your account.

LISTPROCS to display a sorted list of all the Procs in the *PROCLIB* file or an optionally specified file. If a comment appears as the second line of any Proc, then it will be shown on the display.

LISTQ4 to display a simple four-column list of the names of all the Q-pointers on your account.

PD to print the contents of all the dictionary items on the dictionary of a specified file.

It is quite likely that your implementation will have most of these Procs, and several others besides.

5.10   A TCL PROCESSOR

When you are typing in TCL and Access statements, you will soon realize how easy it is to make a mistake. A frequent question from someone who has just typed in sixty characters of a long sentence – and then noticed a spelling mistake at the beginning of the line is:

'How can I correct that without back-spacing?'

Or the beginner may want to re-issue a sentence which is already displayed on the screen, and asks:

'How can I issue that Access sentence again without typing it?'

The simple answer to both these questions is:

'You can't'.

Pick does not offer screen-editing facilities. Once you have typed in your command it has gone, even though it may still be displayed on the screen.

Realizing this shortcoming, some implementations offer a package, such as the TCL Stacker or the McDonnell Douglas *TCL PLUS* feature, which intercedes between the user and the normal TCL processor. Such a system will store the TCL commands and Access statements and allow the user to inspect the stack of *old* commands, to re-call and re-issue a command over and over again, or to re-call and amend the text of a command before re-issuing it again.

If there is no such package on your implementation, it may well be worth your obtaining or developing one.

5.11   TIPS AND TECHNIQUES – TCL

Since TCL is the primitive working language of many features of the system, there are some situations in which there is no alternative to TCL commands. For example, the creation and deletion of files, attaching and detaching magnetic tape, or handling the spooler.

But its very power means that it can be misused – by intent rather than by accident.

You may decide that a certain verb is too powerful for a particular set of users. In this case, you should force these users to a special account, and then remove from the master dictionary of this account all those verbs which your users are not to have. This is frequently done for such verbs as EDIT, DUMP and MESSAGE. This editing of the master dictionary can also be extended to other areas, such as removing the Q-pointers for important files such as *SYSTEM*.

The principle may even be extended, by amending existing verbs and Procs or by adding new verbs and Procs to the master dictionary, as described in Section 5.1.3.

6

The Basic language

In the earlier chapters we saw how Access allows you to make inquiries about the contents of your files, and to produce reports, assuming that the files exist and that they contain data. However, Access does not allow you to create, amend or delete items held on those files. For these processes, we need to resort to the normal programming languages, or to software such as Update which is offered by Ultimate. The standard Pick operating system offers:

(a) Basic – a version of extended Dartmouth Basic designed to handle the record format associated with Pick. The language is also known as Pick/Basic and Data/Basic.
(b) Proc – a low-level language originally intended to simplify the invocation of a series of TCL commands.
(c) Assembler – this is available on Pick, although it is not offered as a programming medium for users.

In this chapter we look at the Basic programming language. Proc is discussed in Chapter 7. We shall not discuss the Assembler language in the present book.

6.1 LOOKING AT A BASIC PROGRAM

Before we take a detailed look at Pick Basic, let us look at the simple program shown in Listing 6.1. If you've used Basic before, then you'll see many things which are familiar. You'll also see many things which seem different. What does the program do? Well, let us see:

(a) It asks WHAT IS YOUR NAME?
(b) If you enter something like AGNES, then it says "HELLO, AGNES".
(c) It asks HOW MANY NUMBERS SHALL WE PROCESS?
(d) If you enter a number in the range 1, 2, 3, 4, 5, 6, 7, 8, 9 or 10, then it prints the square root, the square and the cube of all the numbers starting at 1 up to the number you specify, and then proceeds to step (f).
(e) If you give any other answer, then it returns you to step (c).
(f) It asks you if you want to process ANY MORE?

```
* SIMPLE DEMONSTRATION PROGRAM
*
55    PRINT
      PRINT "WHAT IS YOUR NAME":
      INPUT NAME
      IF NAME='' OR NAME='END' THEN STOP
      PRINT "HELLO, ":NAME:"!"
20    PRINT
      PRINT "HOW MANY NUMBERS SHALL WE PROCESS":
17    INPUT NUMBERS
      IF NUMBERS='END' THEN STOP
      IF NOT(NUM(NUMBERS)) THEN
21        PRINT
          PRINT 'YOU MUST ENTER A NUMBER 1-9'
          GO 20
      END
      IF NUMBERS<=0 OR NUMBERS>10 THEN GO 21
      PRINT
      PRINT 'SQ.ROOT','NUMBER','SQUARE','CUBE'
      FOR X=1 TO NUMBERS
          NUMBER=X
          SQX=SQRT(X)
          CUBE=X*X*X
          PRINT SQX,NUMBER,X*X,CUBE
      NEXT X
35    PRINT; PRINT "ANY MORE? YES/NO":; INPUT RESP
      IF RESP='YES' THEN GO 20
      IF RESP#'NO' THEN GO 35
      END
```

Listing 6.1

(g) If you answer Y, then it returns to step (c) and repeats the process.

(h) If you answer N, then it stops.

(i) If you give any other answer, then it returns to step (f).

The following points are important:

• The program is made up of a number of separate lines of information – the entire program is held as an item on a Pick file, and each *line* is an attribute of that item.

• Each line of the item is a Basic statement.

• The statements which begin with an asterisk are *comments* and are not executed by the computer:

  `*SIMPLE DEMONSTRATION PROGRAM`

• The final statement must be:

  `END`

• Some statements process information which is held in *variables*. These are recognized by names such as *X* or *NAME*.

```
PRINT X
INPUT NAME
```

- Some pieces of information – *literals* – are enclosed in quotation marks or apostrophes:

```
"HELLO,"
"HOW MANY NUMBERS SHALL WE PROCESS"
'SQ.ROOT', 'NUMBER', 'SQUARE', 'CUBE'
```

- The PRINT statements produce output on the screen:

```
PRINT
PRINT "WHAT IS YOUR NAME":
PRINT SQX, NUMBER, X*X, CUBE
```

- Some statements perform arithmetic calculations:

```
CUBE=X*X*X
SQX=SQRT(X)
```

- Simpler forms of such statements move information from one variable to another:

```
NUMBER=X
```

- The INPUT statement allows you to enter information into the program:

```
INPUT NAME
INPUT NUMBERS
```

- Some statements carry out a test and then take appropriate action:

```
IF NAME=' ' OR NAME= 'END' THEN STOP
IF NUMBERS='END' THEN STOP
IF RESP='YES' THEN GO 20
```

- Some statements have a numeric statement-label at the front:

```
55  PRINT
17  INPUT NUMBERS
```

- You do not need a statement-label on every line.
- The statement-labels need not be in ascending order.

Anyone who is familiar with Basic on other computer systems – including microcomputers – will feel quite at home with Pick Basic, and in this chapter we concentrate upon those points which might surprise or interest the Basic programmer moving to Pick.

Several points raised in this chapter will, however, become clearer if you remember that your Basic program – called the *source* program – is held as an item on a file, and each Basic statement is held as a separate attribute on that item. You will create and change the program by means of the Pick Editor:

```
EDIT MYPROGS PAY001
```

This is why you don't need to use the statement-labels to identify the lines of your program when you change it.

The Pick Basic processor is not interpretive. With an interprctive processor, such as you might find on a microcomputer, the statements are executed and processed one by one. This means that if you have made an error on, say, line 390 of your microcomputer program, this error will only be detected when line 390 is about to be executed.

A Pick Basic program must be *compiled* before it can be executed. You do this by means of the command:

```
BASIC MYPROGS PAY001
```

During this compilation process, the compiler will produce a list of any syntax errors which you might have made in your program. Thus, the following statements would each produce a syntax error message:

```
PRONT "HELLO"
NET=GROSS+
PRINT WHAT IS YOUR NAME:
```

because they contain mistakes. The act of compilation produces a second version of your program – called the *object* program – which is also held as a separate item on the file. If there are any syntax diagnostic errors, then no object program will be produced.

It is the object program which is actually executed – not the Basic source program – and you will execute your program by means of the command:

```
RUN MYPROGS PAY001
```

We shall be taking a further look at the processes of editing, compiling and executing a Basic program later in this chapter.

6.2 VARIABLES AND LITERALS

This is one area in which Pick Basic offers you much more than do other versions of the language. Let us illustrate this by taking a look at a short sequence of statements in another Basic program:

```
FRED=42
BERT="YES"
BERT=FRED+100
```

These statements, like those of many other programming languages, use two types of information: variables such as FRED and BERT, and literals such as 42, 100 and "YES".

In common with other languages, variables are identified by name, and the contents of variables and of literals may be either numeric values, such as 42, 100 and 142, or they may be string values, such as YES. The contents of variables may be changed by the action of the program.

But Pick Basic differs from other languages at this point:

• The variable name may consist of any combination of letters, digits (0 through to 9), full stops and/or dollar signs.
• There is no practical limit to the length of a variable name. The physical limit of 32 768 characters can hardly be considered practical!
• Any variable may contain either a numeric value or a string value, as shown by the examples in which BERT contains a string value "YES" at one place in the program and then a numeric value 142.
   This is an important feature of Pick Basic.
• It is not necessary to use a variable such as BERT£ in order to hold a string value.
• The name of a dimensioned array, as described below, conforms to the same rules, and the various elements of such an array can contain a mixture of string and numeric values.
• The variable name must not conflict with any of the standard Basic reserved words shown in Table 6.1.

Table 6.1

AT	GOSUB	SETTING
CASE	GOTO	STEP
DO	IF	THEN
ELSE	NEXT	TO
END	ON	UNTIL
GO	REPEAT	WHILE

Some valid variable names are shown in Fig. 6.1, and some invalid variable names are shown in Fig. 6.2.

• Most implementations have a CLEAR statement to set all variables to 0.
• If you try to use a variable which has not been assigned a value, then the system will display an error message:

VARIABLE HAS NOT BEEN ASSIGNED A VALUE. ZERO USED!

• A string literal may contain any characters, and must be enclosed in:

apostrophes '
quotation marks ' '
back-slashes \

- A numeric literal may be enclosed in ' or " \ or these may be omitted. It may have an arithmetic sign, or this may be omitted if the value is positive, and it may have a decimal point, or this may be omitted if the value is an integer. Thus, the numeric literals shown in Fig. 6.3 are equivalent.
- Any numeric literal may be used in an arithmetic expression:

```
A=B+"42"
C=100.01 * A * '-32.5'
```

Some valid values are shown in Fig. 6.4, and some invalid values are shown in Fig. 6.5.

A	PRICE£	TAX. TO. DATE
A. .	SUBSCRIPTION. AMOUNT	TOTAL. 1
B£.	TAX	TOTAL1
LOC. 25. A	TAX. . . £	VALUE. IN. £

TOTAL. BALANCE. FOR. THIS. DEPARTMENT. EXCLUDING. LAST. VALUE

Figure 6.1

```
£VALUE
5. TOTAL
DATA FLAG
LOC/25. A
PART-ONE
TAX-TO-DATE
```

Figure 6.2

"+100"	'+100'	+100	\+100. 0\
"+100. 0"	'+100. 0'	+100. 0	\+100\
"100"	'100'	100	\100. 0\
"100. 0"	'100. 0'	100. 0	\100\

Figure 6.3

"-0. 001"	589. 34
"-200"	"ENTER 'END' TO STOP THE PROGRAM"
"23"	"PLEASE INPUT YOUR NAME"
"43. 000"	"Please input your name"
'£60, 000'	'* INPUT YOUR NAME *'
'-100'	'DO YOU WANT TO CONTINUE? (Y/N)'
-100	'WHAT IS YOUR NAME?'
23	

Figure 6.4

```
£60,000
'PLEASE INPUT YOUR NAME"
24A
35,000.00
```

Figure 6.5

6.3 NUMBERS

The numerical range of numbers in Pick may depend upon the hardware, but typically these will be held with an accuracy of up to fifteen digits in the range:

$$-140\ 737\ 488\ 350\ 000 \text{ to } +140\ 737\ 488\ 350\ 000$$

Numbers are normally held with four places of decimals, but you may change this accuracy for any program to none, one, two, three, five or six places of decimals as required. A precision of 0 will ignore all decimal places, giving you the maximum range specified above, and

PRECISION 6

will hold numbers with an accuracy of six places of decimals, in which case the numeric range for your numbers will be:

$$-14\ 073\ 748.350000 \text{ to } +14\ 073\ 748.350000$$

and the smallest value will be

$$0.000001$$

If your program consists of a set of external sub-routines, as discussed in Section 6.18, then the main program and all its sub-routines must have the same *precision*.

You will find that Pick Basic differs from other versions of the language, in that you cannot use the E-notation or D-notation – sometimes called *floating-point notation* – for very large or very small numbers. This means that you cannot specify numbers in forms such as:

```
1E9
1.5E-2
1D9
1.5D-2
```

6.4 DIMENSIONED ARRAYS

All versions of Basic have the facility for declaring arrays:

DIMENSION A(30)

This statement will enable you to store up to thirty separate values, one in each element of the array A. Each element in the array will be identified by the name of the array – A in this example – followed by the subscript showing the position of the element within the array. The subscript is enclosed in parentheses. Thus, the first element will be A(1), the second A(2), and so on up to A(30). These will be used in statements such as:

```
A(7)=42
A(30)=A(9) * 2 + A(8)
PRINT A(1)
```

You may use indirect references for the subscript instead of a number. So, to add up the contents of all thirty elements of this array, you might write:

```
TOTAL=0
FOR X=1 TO 30
   TOTAL=TOTAL+A(X)
NEXT X
```

The main features of Pick Basic dimensioned arrays which might be different from other versions of Basic are:

- The keyword DIMENSION may be abbreviated to DIM:

```
DIMENSION R(20)
DIM B(27)
```

- Array names conform to the standard for other Pick Basic variable names:

```
DIMENSION NAMES(12)
DIMENSION TOTAL.SALES.FIGURES.BY.MONTH(12)
DIMENSION DAYS£(7)
```

- An array may have one or two dimensions:

```
DIMENSION X(30,5)
```

- Several arrays may be declared on one DIMENSION statement:

```
DIMENSION W(4,5), R(8)
```

- All dimensioned arrays must be declared on DIMENSION statements. Some versions of Basic allow you to use references A(1) through to A(10) without previously having defined the array.
- The first element of an array is A(1), and A(0) is invalid, whereas some other versions of Basic would offer A(0), giving thirty-one elements for the above array.
- Non-integer subscripts are truncated to the nearest integer below.
- Subscripts less than 1, and greater than the maximum size of the

array, are invalid and will cause the program execution to terminate with a message:

`ARRAY SUBSCRIPT OUT OF RANGE`

- The MAT statement will allow you to assign values to all the elements of an array. For example:

`MAT W=1`

will assign the value 1 to every element in the array W, and

`MAT W=MAT WSTORE`

will copy the contents of array WSTORE into the array W, element by element. Clearly, care must be taken with the shape and sizes of the arrays.
- There is no MAT INPUT to enter data into an array from the keyboard.
- There is no MAT PRINT to display the contents of an array.
- There are no standard mathematical functions to allow you to perform matrix manipulation.

When we discuss external sub-routines in Section 6.18, we shall see that arrays which are declared on COMMON statements must not be declared again with a DIMENSION statement in the same program.

6.5 DYNAMIC ARRAYS

In addition to these simple dimensioned arrays, the Pick file structure – attributes, values and secondary values – is also offered to the Basic programmer for the manipulation of character strings. Such strings which consist of attributes and/or values and/or secondary values are called *dynamic arrays*. Dynamic – because you can add as many elements as you need, you can move these elements around, and you can delete them; arrays – because each individual element is accessible in a manner very similar to that for dimensioned arrays.

We have already seen that a Basic variable can hold either a numeric value, such as:

`FRED = 32.56`

or a string value, such as:

`FRED = "THE CAT SAT ON THE MAT"`

If a Basic variable contains one or more attribute marks or other system separators, then it can be regarded as being a dynamic array, with each attribute, value or secondary value being accessible individually. For example, the variable FRED might contain:

`SMITH^JONES^WILSON^BROWN`

The concept of dynamic arrays allows us to use this variable in the following contexts:

PRINT FRED<1>   will print the name SMITH.
PRINT FRED<3>   will print the name WILSON.
FRED<2>="FEATHERSTONE"   will change the string to

`SMITH^FEATHERSTONE^WILSON^BROWN`

FRED<5>="MONDAY"   will change this string to

`SMITH^FEATHERSTONE^WILSON^BROWN^MONDAY`

FRED<8>="YES"   will change this string to

`SMITH^FEATHERSTONE^WILSON^BROWN^MONDAY^^^YES`

You can see how the Basic processor inserts sufficient attribute marks to produce null fields up to the new attribute 8 which is to hold the word YES. Such a string can be treated exactly like an ordinary dimensioned array, by using references:

`PRINT FRED<3>`

which is analogous to the form:

`PRINT XXXX(3)`

A dynamic array has a number of advantages over a dimensioned array:

(a) You do not have to declare a dynamic array as such before you use it – a dimensioned array needs a statement such as DIM XXXX(10).
(b) There is no real limit on the number of elements in the array – DIM XXXX(10) only allows you to use XXXX(1) to XXXX(10).
(c) You can remove elements from the dynamic array and close up the gap. Thus:

`DEL FRED<2>`

will change the string to:

`SMITH^WILSON^BROWN^MONDAY^^^YES`

(d) You can insert new elements within the dynamic array:

`INS "WINTER" BEFORE FRED<3>`

will change the string to:

SMITH^WILSON^WINTER^BROWN^MONDAY^^^YES

Let us look a little more closely at the structure of dynamic arrays. You will have realized that, since it may contain the system separator characters, a dynamic array is essentially a Pick item. Like a Pick item each attribute, in turn, may consist of a number of values separated by value marks. Finally, a value may consist of a number of secondary values separated by secondary-value marks. Here are some further examples of valid dynamic arrays:

(a) The dynamic array:

123^456^789]ABC]DEF

comprises the following elements: 123, 456, 789]ABC]DEF are attributes; 789, ABC and DEF are the separate values of attribute 3.

(b) The dynamic array:

1234567890

comprises just one attribute, 1234567890.

(c) The dynamic array:

Q56^3.22]3.56\88\B]C^99

comprises the following: Q56, 3.22]3.56\88\B]C and 99 are attributes; 3.22, 3.56\88\B and C are values of attribute 2; 3.56, 88 and B are secondary values of value 2 of attribute 2.

(d) The dynamic array:

A]]]B]C]D^E]F]G]H^I]J

comprises the following: A]]]B]C]D, E]F]G]H and I]J are attributes; A, null, null, B, C, D, E, F, G, H, I and J are values.

6.6   THE EQUATE STATEMENT

This statement is provided to simplify the programming task and allows you to declare a variable name as being equivalent to another, for example:

EQUATE TARIFF TO RATE

This will allocate both variable names TARIFF and RATE to the same variable. This is a rather doubtful programming practice, but the other uses of the EQUATE statement are more useful.

EQUATE SCREEN TO CHAR(12)

will allow you to use statements such as:

`PRINT SCREEN: 'DEPARTMENTAL REPORT'`

and is more intelligible than the equivalent:

`PRINT CHAR(12): 'DEPARTMENTAL REPORT'`

Similarly, the statement:

`EQUATE POSN TO 10`

is equivalent – in effect – to the statement:

`POSN = 10`

but the EQUATE statement is resolved once and for all at compilation time, whereas the assignment statement is resolved at execution time and thus adds to the program run times. When defined in this manner, the name POSN may be used in contexts such as:

`PRINT @(0,POSN):SPACE(79—POSN):@(0):`

which would have exactly the same effect as:

`PRINT @(0,10):SPACE(69):@(0) :`

the POSN being identical in function to an explicit literal 10. But if it were ever necessary to change the value of POSN, then only the single EQUATE statement need be changed, and after recompilation, all the statements which use POSN would then utilize the new value.

When a variable name has been assigned a constant value, as in this last example, then it is illegal to attempt to change that value. Thus, the sequence:

```
EQUATE POSN TO 10
POSN20
```

would produce an error at compilation time.

One of the most powerful uses of the statement is in conjunction with dimensioned arrays, where a sequence such as:

```
DIMENSION DATAIN(20)
EQUATE NAME TO DATAIN(1), DEPT TO DATAIN(5)
MATREAD DATAIN FROM PERSONNEL.FV, CLOCKNO ELSE GO 10
```

permits the statement:

`PRINT NAME, DEPT`

which is more easily written and maintained than is:

`PRINT DATAIN(1), DATAIN(5)`

If the file layout is ever changed, then, of course, only the EQUATE statement need be changed to accommodate the new field positions.

The keyword EQU may be used instead of EQUATE. The word TO must always be present. The element which precedes the word TO must not be used before the EQUATE statement, and the element following the word TO must be either a literal, a CHAR function or a variable name. Thus, the following statements would be invalid:

```
VAL10
EQU VAL TO VALUE

POSN=SQRT(B)
TITLE=@(0,5)
HEADING='REPORT ':NUMB
```

6.7 STATEMENT FORMAT

Now that we've met some of the entities we shall be dealing with, let us look at the statements which we shall use in Pick Basic. These are similar to those of other versions of Basic, consisting of an optional statement-label followed by the statement. Thus, the following are valid:

```
100 *
    A54
    B50
    GO 50
21  IF A<0 THEN GO 100
```

The following points apply:

(a) Any statement may have a statement-label, but the statement-label need only be present if that statement is the destination of a GO or GOSUB statement.

(b) Statement-labels are not compulsory – this will come as a surprise to anyone fresh from Basic on microcomputers. But when you remember that the statement-labels are used to add and delete the statements of your microcomputer program – because there is no Editor on microcomputers – you will appreciate why they are redundant on Pick.

(c) On some implementations, statement-labels must contain only digits, but others allow alphanumeric labels. For example:

```
GO HERE
```

in which case the destination statement might look like this:

```
HERE: PRINT "RE-ENTER DATA"
```

Note the colon after the label name.

(d) Statement-labels must be unique within the program.
(e) Statement-labels need not be in any specific sequence.
(f) The statement-label must be at the beginning of the line before the Basic statement.
(g) There may be spaces before or after the statement-label.
(h) You must not have a statement-label on its own. There must be a Basic statement following it on the same line, even if it's only a comment, as with statement number 100 in the above sequence.

If required, several statements may be written on one line, and the statements will then be separated by semicolons. For example:

```
100 A=A+1; B=B+2; C=C+3
```

which is the equivalent of the three statements:

```
100 A=A+1
    B=B+2
    C=C+3
```

With certain exceptions which we shall meet later, each Basic statement is normally written on a single line.

6.8 BASIC STATEMENTS

Basic statements may be considered to fall into the following groups:

(a) Control statements which allow you to control the processing sequence of your program:

```
BEGIN CASE    FOR       NULL
CALL          GO        ON
CASE          GOSUB     RETURN
CHAIN         GOTO      STOP
END           IF        SUBROUTINE
END CASE      LOOP
ENTER         NEXT
```

(b) Data declaration statements which you use to define the data which you will be using in your program:

```
COM
COMMON
DATA
DIM
DIMENSION
EQU
EQUATE
PRECISION
```

(c) Data processing statements which you use to manipulate the data:

```
CLEAR
LOCATE
MAT
PROCREAD
PROCWRITE
```

Variable=expression

(d) File processing and dynamic-arrays statements to handle the data which are held on Pick files:

```
CLEAR-FILE    MATREADU      READT       SELECT
DEL           MATWRITE      READU       UNLOCK
DELETE        OPEN          READV       WEOF
INS           READ          READVU      WRITE
LOCK                        RELEASE     WRITET
MATREAD       READNEXT      REWIND      WRITEV
```

Variable = dynamic-array expression
Dynamic-array expression = expression

(e) Input statements which you use to get data into your program:

```
INPUT
INPUTERR
INPUTNULL
INPUTTRAP
MATINPUT
PROMPT
```

(f) Output statements which you use to display or print data from your program:

```
FOOTING       PRINTER CLOSE
HEADING       PRINTER OFF
PAGE          PRINTER ON
PRINT
```

(g) Source program statements which are used to simplify the task of writing your program:

```
!
*
DEBUG
REM
```

(h) Miscellaneous statements which use some of the Pick system features:

BREAK KEY
RQM

6.9   ASSIGNMENT STATEMENTS

One of the simplest – and most important – Basic statements is the assignment statement. This allows you to perform arithmetic and to move information about from literals to variables, and from variables to variables. Here are some assignment statements:

FRED=42   this places the value 42 into the variable FRED.
MARY=FRED   this copies the contents of the variable FRED into the variable MARY – leaving the contents of FRED intact and overwriting whatever was in MARY before.
MARY=MARY+1   this adds the number 1 to the value which is held in the variable MARY and puts the result back into the variable MARY – overwriting the previous value in MARY.

There are three forms of the Basic assignment statement:
$$\text{destination} = \text{arithmetic expression}$$
or
$$\text{destination} = \text{string expression}$$
or
$$\text{destination} = \text{logical expression}$$
where

destination is any valid variable name or element of a dimensioned array or element of a dynamic array, and specifies where the result of evaluating the expression is to go.
arithmetic expression is any combination of:
  Variable names
  Numeric constants
  Numeric literals
  Dimensioned-array references
  Dynamic-array references
  Arithmetic functions
  Arithmetic operators: + / * −
  Parentheses
For example:

```
+&-VALUE=VALUE+1
  VAT=15*PRICE/100
  X=(-B+SQRT(B*B-4*A*C))/(2*A)
  WORDS=COUNT(TRIM(RESPONSE),' ')+1
```

string expression is any combination of:
    Variable names
    String constants
    String literals
    Dimensioned-array references
    Dynamic-array references
    String functions
    Sub-string expressions using [and]
    String operators: CAT :
    Parentheses
For example:

```
A='YES'
RESP="YOUR ANSWER IS '" : ANSWER
INITIAL=NAME[1,1]
MESSAGE=@(0,5):SPACE(60):@(0)
```

logical expression is any combination of:
    Variable names
    Dimensioned-array references
    Dynamic-array references
    Logical functions
    Logical operators: AND OR # < <= < > = > >= EQ GE GT LE LT
    NE
    Parentheses
For example:

```
A=NOT(B)
A=B=C; ** SETS A=1 IF B=C ELSE SETS A=0
OK=TEST1 AND TEST2 AND TEST3
CONTINUE=(TEST1 AND TEST2) OR (TEST2 AND TEST7)
```

Note especially that the statement:

```
A = B = C
```

will not be rejected by the Pick Basic compiler, but will be interpreted as 'If the value of B is equal to the value of C, then set the value of A equal to 1, otherwise set the value of A equal to 0.' If you wish to assign several values at the same time, this can only be achieved by multiple statements, like this:

```
B=C; A=B
```

6.10   STRINGS AND SUB-STRINGS

Pick Basic has a number of statements and functions for processing strings and sub-strings. The following examples illustrate the most important points:

`A=B:C`

which will concatenate the contents of variable B and the contents of variable C and then assign the result to variable A. Literals may also be used:

`A="DEAR MRS ":SURNAME:","`

The colon is the concatenate operator in this context. You may also use the CAT operator:

`A=B CAT C`

`A="DEAR MRS " CAT SURNAME CAT ","`

To extract a sub-string from within a string, you may use the form:

`FIRSTLETTER = WORD[1,1]`

`LASTLETTER = WORD[LEN(WORD),1]`

in which the start position and the length of the sub-string are enclosed in [and]. This facility is similar to the MID£ function which is available in other versions of the language. There are, however, no equivalents of the LEFT£ and RIGHT£ functions. These must be simulated by means of the statements:

`=WORD[1,n]`

and

`WORD[n,9999] or WORD[n,LEN(WORD)]`

respectively.

6.11 FUNCTIONS

As with other versions of Basic, there are a number of standard functions available to you in Pick Basic. These allow you to carry out such tasks as:

(a) Perform mathematical calculations, such as find the square root of a number, or find the sine, cosine or tangent of an angle, or find the logarithm or anti-logarithm of a number. At this point, we might emphasize that Pick is not suitable for scientific processing or sophisticated mathematical calculations.
(b) Position the screen-cursor.
(c) Access the system time and date.

(d) Generate special characters for output.
(e) Generate character strings.
(f) Generate random numbers.
(g) Find the location of one character string within another string.
(h) Remove multiple spaces from a character string.
(i) Process dynamic arrays.
(j) There are also a number of special ICONV and OCONV functions which allow you to perform the sort of data conversions which are offered in Access – internal to external date conversion, inserting decimal points, together with the facilities offered by the user exits.

Pick Basic does not allow you to define functions for your own use. You can only use the standard functions of the language. Table 6.2 shows the functions which are available. Some of these functions will be familiar to you from other versions of Basic, and some of the others are mentioned below. Full details can be found in the *Basic Reference Manual* for your implementation.

Table 6.2

@	DATE	INDEX	OCONV	STR
ABS	DCOUNT	INS	PWR	TAN
ALPHA	DEL	INSERT	REM	TIME
ASCII	DELETE	INT	REPLACE	TIMEDATE
CHAR	EBCDIC	LEN	RND	TRIM
COL1	EXP	LN	SEQ	
COL2	EXTRACT	MOD	SIN	
COS	FIELD	NOT	SPACE	
COUNT	ICONV	NUM	SQRT	

6.11.1   ICONV and OCONV function

The ICONV and OCONV functions of Basic allow you to use all the conversions and correlatives which are available in Access. This is particularly useful when processing data which are held on files in internal format. Look at this example:

```
SECONDS=TIME( )
OUTIME=OCONV(SECONDS,'MT')
```

Here, we use the TIME( ) function to put the internal time into the variable SECONDS. The OCONV function then converts this to the external form using the conversion code MT exactly as in Access dictionary definitions.

Using ICONV:

```
PRINT 'ENTER DATE AS DD/MM/YY: ':
```

```
INPUT DATE
INTDATE=ICONV(DATE,'D2/')
```

will accept a date from the keyboard – let us suppose the user enters

```
01/01/68
```

and this will be converted to the internal format using the conversion code D2/ – putting the value 1 into the variable INTDATE.

The following simple routine shows the use of the two functions to check that the user has entered a valid date in the form:

```
31/12/80
```

and may be adapted to other formats by suitably changing the contents of the variable DCODE:

```
    DCODE='D2/'
10  INPUT DATE
    INTDATE=ICONV(DATE,DCODE)
    EXTDATE=OCONV(DATE,DCODE)
    IF DATE#EXTDATE THEN PRINT 'INVALID'; GO 10
```

Besides the Access conversion and correlative codes, you can also use the user-exits Uefff which we met in Section 4.6.20. An example of these is the McDonnell Douglas user-exit U01A5 which converts all letters to lower case:

```
PRINT 'WHAT IS YOUR NAME':
INPUT NAME
LCNAME=ICONV(NAME,'U01A5')
PRINT LCNAME
```

If you entered FLORENCE or Florence then the above routine will print:

```
florence
```

A useful mnemonic:

ICONV is like the Access INPUT conversion and converts to Internal format,
OCONV is like the Access OUTPUT conversion and converts to Outside (or external) format

although in some cases the effect may be the same.
   Let us have a look at the more important of the other functions.

6.11.2   Functions to handle dynamic arrays

A number of statements and functions are available to process dynamic arrays.

(a) DEL dynamic-array reference
This will delete a single element – attribute or value or secondary value
– and its associated field-separator character:

```
DEL REC<1>
DEL INAREA<1,VAL,SVAL>
DEL OLD.REC<ATTR.NO,VAL.NO,SEC.VAL.NO>
DEL INVOICE<AT,VL,SV>
```

(b) DELETE (expression, attno, valno, sub-valno)
This is an older form of the DEL statement:

```
REC=DELETE(REC,1,0,0)
INAREA=DELETE(INAREA,1,VAL,SVAL)
NEW.REC=DELETE(OLD.REC,ATTR.NO,VAL.NO,SEC.VAL.NO)
```

(c) EXTRACT (expression, attno, valno, sub-valno)
This will extract a specific element – attribute or value or secondary
value – from a dynamic array:

```
NAME=EXTRACT(EMPREC,1,0,0)
THIS.VAL=EXTRACT(INPUT.RECORD,ATTR,VAL,SVAL)
THIS.SVAL=EXTRACT(DARRAY,1,X,Y)
```

The EXTRACT(function is an older version of the simple dynamic-array
assignment statement which we met in Section 6.5. Thus, the above
statements are the equivalents of:

```
NAME=EMPREC<1>
THIS.VAL=INPUT.RECORD<ATT,VAL,SVAL>
THIS.SVAL=DARRAY<1,X,Y>
```

(d) INS expression BEFORE dynamic-array reference
This will insert a new element – attribute or value or secondary value –
into a dynamic array:

```
INS 1000 BEFORE ITEM<3>
INS PRICE BEFORE DARRAY<X,Y>
INS C.VALUE BEFORE INVOICE<AT,VL,SV>
```

(e) INSERT(expression, attno, valno, sub-valno, expression
This is an older form of the INS statement:

```
INP.REC=INSERT(INP.REC,ATTR,VAL,SVAL,NEW.VALUE)
TEMP=INSERT(TEMP,9,0,0,NEW)
Y=INSERT(X,3,2,7,"A321")
Z=INSERT(Z,3,4,23,9)
```

(f) REPLACE(expression, attno, valno, sub-valno, expression)
This will replace a specific element – attribute or value or secondary
value – in a dynamic array:

```
EMPREC=REPLACE(EMPREC,1,0,0,NEWNAME)
INPUT.RECORD=REPLACE(INPUT.RECORD,A,V,SV,NEW.V)
REC1=REPLACE(REC1,X+1,Y+1,Z+1,TOTAL+COUNT)
DYNS=REPLACE(DYNS,-1,0,0,VALUEX)
```

The REPLACE(function is an older version of the simple dynamic-array
assignment statement which we met in Section 6.5. Thus, the above
statements are the equivalents of:

```
EMPREC<1>=NEWNAME
INPUT.RECORD<A,S,V>=NEW.V
REC1 <X+1,Y+1,Z+1>=TOTAL+COUNT
DYNS<-1>=VALUEX
```

In the examples of the REPLACE(and its equivalents above, the use of
−1 to identify the attribute number, will cause the contents of VALUEX
to be appended as the last (new) attribute of the dynamic array DYNS.
Thus, if the dynamic array FRED contains:

```
SMITH^FEATHERSTONE^WILSON^BROWN^MONDAY
```

then either of the statements:

```
FRED<-1>="YES"
```

or

```
FRED=REPLACE(FRED,1,0,0,-1,"YES")
```

will leave the contents of FRED as:

```
SMITH^FEATHERSTONE^WILSON^BROWN^MONDAY^YES
```

(g) LOCATE statement/function
The various implementations offer either a Basic statement, or a Basic
function to locate a specific attribute within a dynamic array. Let us first
look at the statement, and see how we can apply it to sorting data in a
dynamic array. Suppose that the attributes which are held in a dynamic
array called ITEM must be sorted into ascending order of attribute. The
routine shown in Listing 6.2 will accomplish this.

Study this example for a moment. It demonstrates some important
points. Note particularly the insertion of the THIS1 element into the
dynamic array NEW.ITEM only takes place when it is not found in
NEW.ITEM, therefore duplicate values will be ignored. This can be
remedied by changing the routine as shown in Listing 6.3.

```
        NEW. ITEM=''
10    IF ITEM#'' THEN
            THIS1=ITEM<1>
            LOCATE THIS1 IN NEW. ITEM BY 'AL' SETTING POS ELSE
                INS THIS1 BEFORE NEW. ITEM<POS>
            END
            DEL ITEM<1>
            GO 10
      END
      ITEM=NEW. ITEM
```

Listing 6.2

```
        NEW. ITEM=''
10    IF ITEM#'' THEN
            THIS1=ITEM<1>
            LOCATE THIS1 IN NEW. ITEM BY 'AL' SETTING POS ELSE NULL
            INS THIS1 BEFORE NEW. ITEM<POS>
            DEL ITEM<1>
            GO 10
      END
      ITEM=NEW. ITEM
```

Listing 6.3

There is an additional advantage in that the sort may be ordered as ascending or descending, numeric or alpha by only altering the value specified in the BY clause:

AL ascending left-justified. The normal alphanumeric ascending sort.
A is equivalent to AL.
AR ascending right-justified. The normal numeric ascending sort.
DL descending left-justified. The normal alphanumeric descending sort.
D is equivalent to DL.
DR descending right-justified. The normal numeric descending sort.

If the BY sequence clause is omitted, then POS will indicate the end of the dynamic array.

The LOCATE function which is offered on other implementations has the general form:

LOCATE (*value, dynarray, attno, valno, variable; sequence*) **ELSE** . . .

A typical use of the ELSE clause – which action would be taken if the value was not found – might be to insert the value in the correct sequence:

```
LOCATE(THIS1, NEW. ITEM, 1, 0, POS; SEQ) ELSE
    NEW. ITEM=INSERT(NEW. ITEM, ATTNO, SEQ, 0, THIS1)
END
```

Your *Basic Reference Manual* will describe the form which is available on your implementation.

6.11.3 Other Basic functions

Most of the Basic functions are similar in effect to those of other versions of the language. Here we summarize some of the unusual or interesting features of the functions as they are offered on Pick Basic.

CHAR this generates any ASCII character by specifying the integer value of the character. A full list of the Pick character set is shown in the reference manuals for your implementation.

COUNT this counts the number of occurrences of one string within another. Thus,

```
PRINT COUNT('THE CAT SAT ON THE MAT','A')
```

will print the number 3, and the statement:

```
PRINT COUNT(RECORD,CHAR(254))+1
```

will tell you how many attributes there are in the dynamic array RECORD.

DATE this has the form DATE() with null arguments, and returns the internal date.

FIELD this has a form such as:

```
PRINT FIELD('THE CAT SAT ON THE MAT',' ',4)
```

which will regard the string (the first operand) as comprising groups of characters separated by a space (the second operand), and then return the fourth (the third operand) of these groups. Thus, it will print the word ON.

COL1 this has the form COL1() with null arguments, and, after a FIELD function, it returns the position of the group separator preceding the selected string. This will be 12 in the last example, since the word ON begins in position 13.

COL2 this has the form COL2() with null arguments, and, after a FIELD function, it returns the position of the group separator following the selected string. This will be 15 in the last example, since the word ON ends in position 14.

PWR this is the exponential function. The statement

```
PRINT PWR(2,3)
```

will print 2 to the power 3, that is, 8.

RND this returns a random number in the range specified. Thus,

```
PRINT RND(10)
```

will select, and print, a random integer in the range 0–9 inclusive. To bring the number into the required range, 1–10, you might prefer to use:

```
PRINT RND(10)+1
```

SPACE   This generates a string of spaces. For example:

```
GAP=SPACE(80)
```

will place a string of eighty spaces into the variable GAP.
SQRT   this is the normal square-root function.
STR   this generates a string of repeated characters. For example:

```
PRINT STR('0123456789',3)
```

will print the string:

```
012345678901234567890123456789
```

TIME   this has the form TIME() with null arguments, and returns the internal time.
TIMEDATE   this has the form TIMEDATE() with null arguments, and returns a string of the form:

```
12 : 30 : 59  01 JAN 1980
```

TRIM   this removes excess spaces from a string. For example:

```
A='   THE    CAT   SAT ON    THE    MAT   '
PRINT A
```

will display the string:

```
THE CAT SAT ON THE MAT
```

6.12   STATEMENTS FOR KEYBOARD INPUT

Nowadays, we have come to expect our programs to be conversational – asking us for information by displaying a message on the screen, accepting the information as we type it in at the keyboard, and then processing that information. Consequently, almost all programming languages offer statements to allow you to write such programs. Indeed, Basic was one of the earliest languages to allow us to do this easily, and the various compilers offer such statements as INPUT, GET, INKEY and so on.

   The following statements are those which are available for keyboard data input in Pick Basic and compare favourably to other versions of Basic:

INPUT variable
INPUT variable:

INPUT variable,number
INPUT variable,number:
INPUT variable,number_
PROMPT string

Many Pick implementations also offer a further powerful set of statements:

INPUT @(c,r): variable mask
INPUTERR message
INPUTNULL string
INPUTTRAP string GO j,k,l, . . ., m
INPUTTRAP string GOSUB j, k, l, . . ., m

Let us look at the action of these statements.

(a) INPUT variable
This is similar to the INPUT statement found in other versions of the language. For example:

```
INPUT HOURS
```

When this statement is executed, the program will print a question mark and wait for you to enter your data and press <RETURN>. The value which you enter may be either an alphabetic string or a number and will be placed into the variable called HOURS, from where it may be used for further processing.

Unlike some other versions, however, Pick Basic will only allow one variable name to be specified in an INPUT statement. Thus the forms:

```
INPUT NUMBER HOURS
INPUT NUMBER, HOURS
```

would not have the desired effect.

If it is required to accept values for several variables, then several INPUT statements must be used:

```
INPUT NUMBER
INPUT HOURS
```

If messages are to be displayed to prompt the user for the input data, then you must do this by means of PRINT and INPUT statements, in a sequence such as:

```
PRINT 'WHAT IS THE EMPLOYEE NUMBER':
INPUT NUMBER
PRINT 'HOW MANY HOURS DID HE WORK':
INPUT HOURS
```

since Pick Basic does not offer a form such as:

```
INPUT "WHAT IS THE EMPLOYEE NUMBER", NUMBER
```

In these examples, notice the use of a colon after the PRINT statements to hold the cursor in position ready for the INPUT on the same line as the message.

(b) INPUT variable:
The colon after the variable name retains the cursor in position immediately after the last character entered when you have pressed RETURN after entering your input data.

(c) INPUT variable, number
This form can be used to prevent your user entering too much information and possibly upsetting the screen format:

```
INPUT NAME, 7
```

In this case, you are only allowed to enter up to seven characters at the INPUT statement. When you have entered seven characters, the system will assume that you have pressed the <RETURN> key. If you make a typing error at the last character, it will be too late to correct it with the <BACK SPACE> key.

If you enter less than seven characters, then you must press <RETURN> as usual.

The following forms are valid:

```
INPUT XSTRING,1
INPUT CODE,CLENGTH
INPUT VALUE,78:
INPUT ADDRESS,LENADDR:
```

Note the use of the colon in the last two examples to hold the cursor in position *after* the data have been entered. Incidentally, look at the meaning of the Pick Basic statement:

```
INPUT CODE,CLENGTH
```

In some versions of Basic, such a statement will usually mean that two values are to be input – one for the variable CODE and one for the variable CLENGTH.

*(d) INPUT variable, number_*

```
INPUT NAME,30_
```

Like the previous form, this will not allow you to enter more than thirty characters of information at the INPUT statement, but the system will wait for you to press <RETURN>. If you attempt to enter too many characters, then the system will ignore these and the bell on the terminal will sound. However, if you have made a mistake, then you will be able to use the <BACK SPACE> to correct the error before pressing <RETURN>.

If your system is to use any non-standard input devices, such as bar-code reader or telex, then these will feed their data to such INPUT statements.

Data can also be supplied to any INPUT statement by means of DATA statements within the program. In this situation, the combination of DATA and INPUT statements functions exactly like the DATA and READ statements which are available on other versions of Basic. The following are valid examples of the DATA statement:

```
DATA 'STOCK'
DATA 23, "YES", "45"
DATA "'L'"
```

illustrating that there may be several data elements, separated by commas, and string values must be enclosed in quotation marks or apostrophes. We shall meet the DATA statement again in Section 6.21.7.

6.12.1   PROMPT statement

With Pick Basic you may use some other prompt character instead of the question mark, assigning the new prompt character by means of the PROMPT statement:

```
PROMPT ':'
```

in a sequence like this:

```
PROMPT ':'
PRINT 'EMPLOYEE NUMBER':
INPUT NUMBER
PROMPT '?'
PRINT 'HOW MANY HOURS WORKED':
INPUT HOURS
```

When you execute the program the sequence will look like this:

```
EMPLOYEE NUMBER: 1234
HOW MANY HOURS WORKED?42.50
```

You may use any *single* character as the prompt, and you may change this character at any time. You may also have a null prompt character, and this gives a much greater flexibility.

You should note the form of this statement. It is:

```
PROMPT ':'
```

and not:

```
PROMPT = ':'
```

This latter form will merely assign the colon character to a variable called PROMPT without affecting the prompt character.

6.12.2   INPUT @ statement

This is one of a set of statements which offer very powerful facilities for data input on some implementations. Using these statements:

(a) The program will position the cursor before accepting the input data.
(b) The program will display a default value according to a format mask in the field where the data are to be input.
(c) Your user may overwrite the default value, take the default value or enter any of a set of 'special action' codes.
(d) The program will re-display the input value according to the format mask.
(e) The program will display and erase error and other messages at the foot of the screen.

Let us look at an example of this statement:

```
TAX=0
INPUT @(5,5):TAX "R12"
```

This will:

(a) Move the cursor to position (5,5) on the screen.
(b) Display the current contents of the variable TAX – 0 in this example – according to the mask R12, that is right-justified in a field of width 12.
(c) Accept a value for the variable TAX and allow you to type over the displayed value.
(d) Interpret a null response as indicating that the previous contents of TAX – 0 in this example – are to be retained as a *default* value.
(e) Re-display the value which you have entered according to the mask R12.

There are several statements to support the INPUT @ facility:

(a) INPUTERR "message"
This statement controls the displaying and erasing of error messages:

```
INPUTERR "VALUE MUST BE LESS THAN 100"
```

When this statement is encountered it will:

(a) Clear the bottom line of the screen, if there is already an INPUTERR error message there.
(b) Display the text:

```
VALUE MUST BE LESS THAN 100
```

(c) Set an internal system flag to indicate that an error message is present at the foot of the screen, indicating that this is to be cleared prior to subsequent INPUTERR error messages.

There is no implicit error condition associated with this statement, and the INPUTERR statement is executed when it is encountered, exactly like a PRINT statement.

(b) INPUTNULL "character"

Since a null response at an INPUT @ statement will assume the default value, the INPUTNULL statement allows you to specify a character which is to be used to represent a truly null value. For example:

```
INPUTNULL "."
```

This statement is not executed immediately, but must be issued prior to INPUT @ statements to indicate that, if the user enters a response of . to subsequent INPUT @ statements, then this is to be interpreted as null. Any single character may be specified, and this null indicator will stay in operation until changed by a subsequent INPUTNULL statement.

(c) INPUTTRAP "characters"

This statement allows a set of *special action* codes to be established. For example:

```
INPUTTRAP "<>?/#" GO 10,20,30,40,50
```

This statement is not executed immediately, but must be issued prior to INPUT @ statements to indicate that, in this example, a response of < or > or ? or / or # to subsequent INPUT @ statements will cause the system to branch to statements 10, 20, 30, 40 and 50, respectively.

There may be any number of characters and a matching set of destinations, and these INPUTTRAPs will stay in operation until changed by a subsequent INPUTTRAP statement. This is a useful device which allows you to design systems with conventions where:

< means return to the last input stage,

> means skip to the next input stage,
? means display what the user is supposed to enter,
/ means cancel the operation,
means abandon the job

and so on.

The following form is also available:

```
INPUTTRAP "<>?/-" GOSUB 10,20,30,40,50
```

for use in similar circumstances.

6.13   PRINT STATEMENTS

The print output statements in Pick Basic are similar to those which you might have met in other versions of the language, and are designed primarily to display information on the screen at the user's terminal.

The following forms are commonly encountered:

PRINT   to print a blank line.
PRINT TAX   to print the contents of the variable TAX.
PRINT "REPORT 42"   to print the string:

```
REPORT 42
```

PRINT 23.5   to print the numeric value:

```
23.5
```

PRINT 19*34/45   to evaluate the arithmetic expression and print the result:

```
14.3555
```

PRINT 12 : 34 : 56   to concatenate the values and print:

```
123456
```

Notice that Pick Basic uses the *colon* to concatenate strings whereas other versions of the language use a *semicolon*. So the above statement would be written as:

```
PRINT 12;34;56
```

on versions other than Pick Basic, although it would be invalid here. Other examples using the colon are shown below.
PRINT "REPORT ":REPNO   to concatenate the string literal with the value held in the variable REPNO, and print something like:

```
REPORT 100
```

PRINT TAX: to print the value of TAX and then hold the cursor after the last character. Any subsequent PRINT output will then begin at this cursor position.

PRINT 12,34,56   to tabulate the values and print:

```
12                34                56
```

with successive *tab-columns* starting in position 0, 18, 36, 54 of the print line, and so on, each column being eighteen characters wide; similarly:

PRINT "REPORT",REPNO   might produce something like:

```
REPORT            100
```

Pick Basic left-justifies all printed values, irrespective of whether these are numeric values or string values. Thus, a sequence such as:

```
PRINT 'YES'
PRINT 1234.567
PRINT "NO"
PRINT 1
```

will produce the output:

```
YES
1234.567
NO
1
```

Right-justification and other formatting can be achieved by means of format masks in the PRINT statement, as described in the next section.

6.13.1   Printing with a format mask

The *elements* in PRINT statements may consist of a simple value, such as TAX or TEXT or 43 or REPNO, as in:

```
PRINT TAX
PRINT TEXT,43,REPNO
```

or they may comprise a value followed by a *format mask*:

```
PRINT TAX 'R2#########'
```

which will print the contents of the variable TAX according to the format mask R2########, that is right-justified to two decimal places in a field which is nine characters wide. So, if TAX contains the value 123.45, the display will look like this:

```
^^^123.45
```

we use the character in this illustration to indicate a space.

    This form of the Pick Basic PRINT statement is similar to the PRINT USING statement which is offered on other versions of Basic.

230 The Basic language

The format mask is any logical combination of:

R   for right-justification.
L   for left-justification; this is the default assumption.
n   the number of decimal places which are to be shown. If this is omitted, then the actual precision of the value will be used.
£   requesting a £ character to be printed before the first (senior) digit. If this is omitted, then no £ character is used.
,   to insert commas between the thousands. If this is omitted, then no commas are inserted.
a string of # characters to indicate the length of the print field, as in the above example.
#m to indicate a string of *m* # characters. We could have written:

```
PRINT TAX "R2#9"
```

in our example.

Any other characters in the format mask are displayed unchanged.

Figure 6.6 shows some valid examples of this statement. It is this final form which allows *errors* such as:

```
PRINT GROSS NETT
```

to get through the compiler. In this example, the contents of NETT will be interpreted as a format mask and used to display the contents of GROSS. A not uncommon source of error.

These format masks may also be used in assignment statements. For example:

```
PRICE = 2300 "£2,"
```

will put the value:

```
£2,300.00
```

into the variable PRICE.

```
PRINT TAX "R2#3"

PRINT SALARY "£R,2#10"

PRINT 'CURRENT VALUE=': CURR '2#7': ' ENTER NEW VALUE':

PRINT OLD OLDMASK, NEW NEWMASK

MASK='R£,2#10'
PRINT GROSS MASK: DEDUCTIONS MASK: NETT MASK
```

Figure 6.6

6.13.2 Screen formatting

The @ function is used to generate a stream of special characters which – when used in PRINT statements – will position the screen cursor. For example:

```
PRINT @(10,20):TAX
```

will move the cursor to column 10 of line 20, hold it there and then print the contents of the variable TAX. It can be used to advantage in situations such as:

```
PRINT @(0,13):
INPUT TAX
```

which will move the cursor to column 0 of line 13 and then accept the user's input data in that position. The statement:

```
PRINT @(0,20):SPACE(78):@(0):MESSAGE:
```

will clear line 20 of the screen and then, starting in column 0, print the contents of the variable MESSAGE. This illustrates that the @ function may be used anywhere within a PRINT statement.

Note that the row parameter is optional, as in this last example where @(0) moves the cursor to column 0, that is the beginning of the current line. The column parameter must be present, so that a form such as @(,10) is invalid.

Look at a useful application of the function, as illustrated by this section of a program:

```
10    ERRLINE=@(0,20):SPACE(78):@(0)
      :
20    PRINT ERRLINE:"RE-ENTER YOUR NAME":
      :
30    PRINT ERRLINE:RECORD NOT FOUND":
```

Statement 10 places a string of characters into the variable ERRLINE. When we use this string in PRINT statements such as statements 20 and 30, the program will move the cursor to position (0,20), print seventy-eight spaces, thus clearing line 20 of the screen, and then move the cursor back to column 0. These statements, therefore, are identical in effect to:

```
20    PRINT @(0,20):SPACE(78):@(0):"RE-ENTER YOUR
         NAME":
      :
30    PRINT @(0,20):SPACE(78):@(0):"RECORD NOT
         FOUND":
```

although the first version is much shorter, and easier to handle and to use.

The @ function cannot be used for output which is going to the printer.

6.13.3   Headings and footings

Standard Pick headings and footings may be used to control the format and pagination of a report. For example:

```
HEADING "REPORT 42 PAGE 'PL'========='LL'"
```

These statements are identical in format and content to the Access and Runoff headings and footings, and they have the standard option codes:

P   to display the page number.
L   to skip to a new line.
D   to display the date.
T   to display the time and date.

These codes are enclosed in apostrophes, as shown in the example above. Further examples are:

```
HEADING "DATE: 'D' . . . . . . . . PAGE 'P' . . . . . . . .
   'LL'"
FOOTING "'L'————————'L'PAGE 'PP'"
TEXT=TITLE: "'PLL'":UNDERLINE: "'LL'"
HEADING TEXT
```

The operating system will automatically handle the number of lines per page using the screen-depth or page-depth characteristics for your terminal.

The PAGE statement is used when HEADINGs and FOOTINGs are in action and will force a skip to a new page:

```
PAGE
```

The programmer must not use PRINT CHAR(12) to clear the screen when using HEADINGs or FOOTINGs, as this will be regarded as a simple PRINT line and will upset the pagination.

6.13.4   Screen or line printer?

When a Basic program starts to execute, any PRINT statements will send their output to the screen. To direct output to the printer you will use the

```
PRINTER ON
```

statement, then all subsequent PRINT statements will send their output to the printer, or more correctly, to the spooler. We discuss the spooler in Chapter 10.

After you have done this, you may want to switch the PRINT output back to the screen, for example, to ask your users for some more information. You will do this by means of the statement:

PRINTER OFF

When the program execution has finished, then your report (currently being held by the spooler) will be printed as soon as the printer is free.

If you wish to cause your output to be printed *before* the end of your job – you may want to inspect some results before proceeding or you may have a small routine to line up the stationery before you produce your payslips – then you will use the

PRINTER CLOSE

statement. This closes the output file and sends the report to the printer immediately it is free.

If you have a program which is to produce all its output on the printer, you can do this much more simply by executing the program with the command:

RUN MYPROGS ADV003 (P)

The (P) has the effect of issuing a PRINTER ON statement before the program execution starts. In this situation, you will not need PRINTER ON statements in your program. Any PRINTER OFF or PRINTER ON statements will have their normal effect.

In general, all the forms of the PRINT statement which we have discussed – except those using the @ function and certain special print characters – will have the same effect on the terminal screen and on the printer. If your system is to use any non-standard output devices, such as bar-code encoder, plotter or telex, then these will be driven by data sent from such PRINT statements.

6.13.5 Print on

Output may be sent to any number of separate spooler files during the execution of a program. This allows you to generate several reports at the same time, in the same program, and then print them off separately. For example, an account update program might produce separate reports to:

(a) Print the transactions.
(b) Print the customers' statements.

(c) Print the management summary.

(d) Print the name and address labels for the statements.

Each of these might be produced on different stationery. We could achieve this by statements such as:

```
PRINT ON 1 DATE, CODE, VOUCH.NO, AMOUNT
PRINT ON 2 VOUCH.NO, VOUCH.DETAIL, AMOUNT,
   NEW.BALANCE
PRINT ON 3 CODE, NAME, NEW.BALANCE
PRINT ON 4 NAME
PRINT ON 4 STREET
PRINT ON 4 TOWN
```

At the end of job, all the separate spool files will be closed and then output in numerical order, or to separate spooler queues if you have used the SP-ASSIGN verb as described in Section 10.3.

6.13.6 Special display effects

As we have seen, all output to the terminal is produced by means of the PRINT statement, which transmits strings of output to the terminal or to the printer. When sending such strings to the terminal, they may include special characters generated by the CHAR function. The most frequently used of such characters are PRINT CHAR(7) which sounds the audible bell at the terminal, and PRINT CHAR(12) which clears the screen. The other available characters will be shown in the reference manuals for your system.

The CHAR function is also used to produce a range of special screen graphics effects, and to generate data which are to be sent to any non-standard output devices.

In its original form, Pick is virtually devoid of graphics capabilities. If you are looking for the sort of features which you have seen in computer games and video games, then you will be disappointed with Pick. Some implementations do, however, allow the user to down-load software to suitable terminals and allow these to behave more like arcade machines.

The only special screen effects which you can achieve are based upon combinations of one or more of the following:

(a) White characters on a black ground – this is the standard mode.

(b) *Reversed* – black characters on a white ground.

(c) *Faint* – grey characters on a black ground.

(d) *Flashing* – white characters flashing on a black ground.

(e) *Underlined* – white characters with white underline on a black ground.

(f) *Invisible* – non-printed characters on a black ground.

The normal display is:

```
NON-FAINT
NON-REVERSED
NON-FLASHING
NON-UNDERLINED
VISIBLE
```

The various modes are set in operation by displaying – or typing – the mode character, followed by a letter of the alphabet, or other character, as shown in Table 6.3. The combination of mode plus the character appears as a single character on the screen, and whilst this character is on the screen all other displayed information – to the right and below – will appear with the selected mode.

Table 6.3

Character	Bold	Flash	Reversed	Visible	Underlined
Space	Yes	No	No	Yes	No
A	No	No	No	Yes	No
B	Yes	Yes	No	Yes	No
C	No	Yes	No	Yes	No
D	Yes	No	Yes	Yes	No
E	No	No	Yes	Yes	No
F	Yes	Yes	Yes	Yes	No
G	No	Yes	Yes	Yes	No
H	Yes	No	No	No	No
I	No	No	No	No	No
J	Yes	Yes	No	No	No
K	No	Yes	No	No	No
L	Yes	No	Yes	No	No
M	No	No	Yes	No	No
N	Yes	Yes	Yes	No	No
O	No	Yes	Yes	No	No
P	Yes	No	No	Yes	Yes
Q	No	No	No	Yes	Yes
R	Yes	Yes	No	Yes	Yes
S	No	Yes	No	Yes	Yes
T	Yes	No	Yes	Yes	Yes
U	No	No	Yes	Yes	Yes
V	Yes	Yes	Yes	Yes	Yes
W	No	Yes	Yes	Yes	Yes
X	Yes	No	No	No	Yes
Y	No	No	No	No	Yes
Z	Yes	Yes	No	No	Yes

The mode character is hexadecimal 3 and may be represented by any of the following means:

(a) You could enter the character at the keyboard by pressing the <CTRL> and C keys simultaneously.

For example, if you type:

`<CTRL>CBHELLO, MOTHER`

the <CTRL> and the C will generate the mode character, the B will indicate that the flashing mode is to be switched on, and HELLO, MOTHER is the string which will flash.

In fact, everything else following on the screen will flash until the effect is switched off by a sequence such as:

`<CTRL>space`

that is, the mode character followed by a space.

(b) On suitably equipped terminals, the mode character may be generated at the keyboard by pressing the MODE key on the cursor-control pad.

(c) In a Basic program, you could print the CHAR(3) character. For example, the statement:

`PRINT CHAR(3):"BHELLO, MOTHER"`

will display the flashing string HELLO, MOTHER, as above. The statement:

`PRINT CHAR(3):"BHELLO,":CHAR(3):" MOTHER"`

will display the same string with HELLO, flashing and MOTHER non-flashing. The flashing is switched off by means of the mode character and the space before the M of MOTHER.

(d) In a Proc, you could hold the mode character in an O statement. The last Basic example could be achieved in Proc by the statement which would be typed in as:

`O<CTRL>CBHELLO,<CTRL> MOTHER`

The O indicating that this is the Proc output statement, and the <CTRL> and C generating the mode character as before. Using a T statement, we could write:

`T I3,"BHELLO, ",I3," MOTHER"`

Remember that the special modes are switched off by displaying – or typing – the mode character followed by a space.

6.13.7 Printer control

Some of the printers supplied with Pick systems have a form control facility for channel skip and line-feed operations. These functions are obtained by sending a single control character to the printer using the CHAR function in a Basic PRINT statement, or the I element in a Proc L statement. The actual characters which must be transmitted will depend upon your system and the hardware, but the following are typical. Using the function

```
CHAR(128)
```

will skip to channel 1. This is the top-of-form and is identical in effect with CHAR(12). The other channels are obtained by CHAR(129) for channel 2, and so on through to CHAR(139) for channel 12, bottom-of-form.

Using the function

```
CHAR(144)
```

will skip no lines, that is, will overprint the previous line. Subsequent functions have corresponding effects, CHAR(145) will skip one line, CHAR(146) will skip two lines and so on through to CHAR(159) which will skip fifteen lines.

Matrix printers have the facility to produce double height characters. This is achieved by sending the character CHAR(8) at the beginning of the line, like this:

```
PRINT CHAR(8):'WEEKLY SALES REPORT'
```

If any other non-graphic characters are sent to the printer, the results are unpredictable and the device may go off-line or produce anomalous output.

As we mentioned in Section 6.13.4, if your system is to use any non-standard output devices, such as bar-code encoder, plotter or telex, then these will be driven by data generated by the CHAR function and sent from PRINT statements.

6.14 FILE HANDLING

File handling in Basic is done by means of the OPEN, READ, WRITE and DELETE statements. There is no CLOSE statement in Pick Basic. The general sequence for processing a file is otherwise similar to that in other programming languages:

(a) *Open* the file – this checks that the file exists, gets the location of the file on disk, and checks that you have the necessary security (lock codes) to process that file – see the section on opening files below.

In Pick Basic it is possible to process the items on the DATA section and/or the DICT section of one or more data files.

(b) Determine the item-id of the item(s) to be processed – this may be derived by the program, entered conversationally by the user, or extracted from a list of item-ids selected by the program or by the Access processor – as described in Section 4.7 which deals with the processing of lists.

(c) *Read* the item, or an attribute of the item, which is to be processed – see the section on reading items from files below.

(d) Process the item or attribute – see the section on processing file data below.

(e) *Write* the processed item, or attribute, back to the file – see the section on writing items on files below.

Listing 6.4 shows the typical sequence for processing items in Pick Basic. Let us look at these steps in more detail.

```
*     SIMPLE PROGRAM TO UPDATE STOCK FILE
*     OPEN FILE
      OPEN 'STOCK' TO STOCK ELSE; PRINT 'NO STOCK FILE'; STOP
      :
*     ACCEPT PART NUMBER FROM USER
1     PRINT 'ENTER PART-NUMBER TO BE PROCESSED: ':
      INPUT PARTNO
*     READ PART RECORD
      READ PART.REC FROM STOCK, PARTNO ELSE
          IF PARTNO='END' THEN STOP
          IF PARTNO='' THEN GO 1
          PRINT PARTNO: ' NOT ON FILE'
          GO 1
          END
*     PROCESS STOCK ITEM
      :
      PART.REC<5>=LEVEL
      :
*     WRITE AMENDED RECORD
      WRITE PART.REC ON STOCK, PARTNO
      PRINT 'RECORD ':PARTNO: ' UPDATED'
      GO 1
      END
```

Listing 6.4

6.14.1 Opening the files

Before it may be used for reading or writing, each file must be opened by means of the OPEN statement. The general form of the statement is:

OPEN *section, expression* TO *file-variable* ELSE *statement*

Listing 6.5 shows some examples of the OPEN statement. If *section* is 'DICT', as in the first example in Listing 6.5, then the DICT section of the file will be opened for processing. If *section* is either omitted or null, as in the last three examples in Listing 6.5, then the data section of the file will be opened for processing.

```
OPEN 'DICT','PARAMS' TO PARMS ELSE PRINT 'NO PARAMETERS'; GO 50

OPEN "STOCK" TO SFILE ELSE PRINT "CAN'T OPEN STOCK FILE"; STOP

OPEN '','STOCK' TO SFILE ELSE PRINT 'NO STOCK FILE'; STOP

OPEN 'PAYROLL' ELSE PRINT 'NO PAYROLL FILE'; STOP
```

Listing 6.5

Expression specifies the external name of the file, and may be a variable or it may be a literal, as with 'PARAMS', 'STOCK' and 'PAYROLL' in the examples. This name is the same as that which is used when the file is processed by the file-management processors and by Access.

The action of the OPEN statement is:

(a) To check that the file exists, otherwise the ELSE clause will be invoked.
(b) To check that your security is sufficient to access the file; if not then the program execution will terminate with the error message:

    `FILE 'STOCK' IS ACCESS PROTECTED`

(c) To put the base FID, the modulo and separation into the file variable – the variables SFILE and PARMS in the examples.

The statement in the ELSE clause will be executed if the file does not exist. If the OPEN statement is successful, then processing will continue with the statement following the OPEN statement, ignoring the ELSE clause. The ELSE clause may be a multi-line sequence of statements, as described in Section 6.16.2.

If you attempt to READ or WRITE a file which has not been opened, then the program execution will terminate with an error message.

There may be any number of files open and in use at the same time, each file having its own file variable. It will be seen that the use of the file variable is optional, as in the fourth example in Listing 6.5. However, this is bad practice and should not be adopted as it can be particularly confusing – even dangerous – if more than one file is being processed by

240 *The Basic language*

the program. Although the variable used as the file variable may have any name, its contents are only used by the file-handling processor. Any attempt to use the file variable in any other context will result in the program execution terminating with an error condition.

Note that you do not specify whether you are opening the file for reading or for writing.

6.14.2 Reading items from the files

To get data from a file and into your program, there are several forms of the READ statement in Pick Basic, each with its own applications. Each READ statement requires the file variable to identify the file which is being processed, the item-id of the required item, and the destination of the data when it has been read from the file.

(a) MATREAD statement, such as:

```
MATREAD DIMARRY FROM SFILE, '1000' ELSE GO 10
```

reads the item with the item-id 1000, putting each attribute into a separate element of the array DIMARRY. If the item contains more attributes than there are elements in the array, then a message will be displayed at the terminal and the superfluous attributes will be ignored.

(b) MATREADU statement, such as:

```
MATREADU BOOK.REC FROM BOOKFILE, FLIGHTNO ELSE
    STOP
```

is equivalent to the preceding MATREAD statement, except that the entire group to which the item belongs is locked.

(c) READ statement, such as:

```
READ RECORD FROM SFILE, ITEMID ELSE PRINT
    'MISSING'; GO 1
```

reads the item whose item-id is held in the variable ITEMID, putting the contents as a dynamic array into the variable RECORD.

(d) READU statement, such as:

```
READU MREC FROM MASTER, ID ELSE GO 30
READU MREC FROM MASTER, ID LOCKED GO 20 ELSE GO 30
```

is equivalent to the preceding READ statement, except that the entire group to which the item belongs is locked.

(e) READV statement, such as:

```
READV NAME FROM EMP.FILE, '1200', 7 ELSE GO 10
```

reads the single attribute, in this case attribute 7, putting the contents into the variable NAME.

If only one attribute of an item is being processed then it is more efficient to read in that attribute alone, by means of the READV or READVU statements.

(f) READVU statement, such as:

```
READVU FREE FROM BOOKFILE, FLIGHTNO, 23 ELSE GO 2
```

is equivalent to the preceding READV statement, except that the entire group to which the item belongs is locked.

In each of these forms, the ELSE clause will be executed if the item cannot be found on the file, otherwise processing will continue with the statement following the READ statement. The ELSE clause may be a multi-line sequence of statements, as described in Section 6.16.2.

The READU, READVU and MATREADU statements are provided to prevent several users updating the same item at the same time. When one of these statements has been executed, the operating system sets a flag, locking the entire *group* in which the item is held. Subsequent attempts by other users to read any item in that group – and not just the item which locked the group – will detect the flag and wait until the first user issues a WRITE, WRITEV or MATWRITE statement to that group, or until the program terminates.

The various forms of these statements have a *LOCKED* clause whereby you may specify a set of statements to be executed if the group is locked when an attempt is made to read a record in that group:

```
READU SEATS FROM BOOKINGS, "A0123" LOCKED GO 10
  ELSE GO 20
```

You might use such a set of statements to ask your users whether they wish to wait until the locked group becomes free, or whether they wish to abandon the processing in favour of some other action.

Another device which is frequently used in this context is to loop within the READU statement, using the RQM – release quantum – statement to reduce CPU usage whilst you wait. Such a statement might look like this:

```
5  READU SEATS FROM BOOKINGS, "A0123" LOCKED RQM;
   GO 5 ELSE GO 20
```

If an item is retrieved by means of a READU, READVU or MATREADU statement and it is not re-written to the file, then the lock stays in effect until the program execution has terminated.

There are two other statements concerned with group locking:

```
LOCK BOOKFILE, 1234
```

which will lock the group in which item *1234* occurs on the *BOOKFILE* file. This implies that you are about to process this record without reading it; you may, for example, be going to delete it. The other statement:

```
UNLOCK BOOKFILE, 8765
```

will release a group lock which you may have set, without requiring you to write the record back to the file. You may simply have been looking at the record without updating it.

Remember that the lock applies to the *group* in which the item is held and not to the *item* itself.

By careless use of these statements, it is possible for two programs to go into a *deadly embrace* and lock each other out indefinitely! You may have to perform a cold start to recover from such a deadly embrace.

6.14.3 Processing data from the files

Once you have read them in, the data from a file are processed in the same way as any other data, bearing in mind that:

(a) MATREAD & MATREADU – put the attributes into the elements of a dimensioned array, and the elements of the array are processed in the usual manner.
(b) READ & READU – put the entire item, as a dynamic array, into a variable. The statements and functions which are provided for manipulating dynamic arrays were described in Section 6.5.
(c) READV & READVU – put a single attribute into a variable where it is processed in the usual manner.

To illustrate this, let us suppose that our *STOCK* file contains an item with the item-id *1000*, like this:

```
1000^CHAIRS, WOODEN, RED^UK/614^64^50^6125^5875
```

with the first field being the item-id. If we were to read this record in with MATREAD or MATREADU statements:

```
DIM ARRAY(10)
MATREAD ARRAY FROM SFILE, '1000' ELSE STOP
```

then:

```
ARRAY(1) would contain CHAIRS, WOODEN, RED
ARRAY(2) would contain UK/614
ARRAY(3) would contain 64
ARRAY(4) would contain 50
ARRAY(5) would contain 6125
```

`ARRAY(6)` would contain `5875`

and the rest of the array would be set to null.

If we were to use the simple READ or READU statements:

`READ RECORD FROM SFILE, '1000' ELSE STOP`

then the variable RECORD would contain the dynamic array:

`CHAIRS, WOODEN, RED^UK/614^64^50^6125^5875`

and looking at the individual attributes of this dynamic array, we would find that:

`RECORD<1>` would contain `'CHAIRS, WOODEN, RED'`,
`RECORD<2>` would contain `'UK/614'`,
`RECORD<3>` would contain `'64'`,
`RECORD<4>` would contain `'50'`,
`RECORD<5>` would contain `'6125'`,
`RECORD<6>` would contain `'5875'`.

If we were to use the READV or READVU statements:

`READV DESCR FROM SFILE, '1000', 1 ELSE STOP`

then the variable DESCR would contain CHAIRS, WOODEN, RED.

6.14.4   Writing items to the files

There are several forms of the WRITE statement in Pick Basic, each is used according to the format of the data which are being processed, and this may, in turn, be dependent upon the way in which the data were previously READ in:

(a) MATWRITE statement, such as:

`MATWRITE DIMARRY ON SFILE, '1000'`

writes the data to the item-id *1000*, taking each attribute from a separate element of the array DIMARRY. Each element of the array generates one attribute of the item written to the file – the necessary attribute marks being inserted by the operating system – and any trailing null attributes being suppressed.

(b) WRITE statement, such as:

`WRITE RECORD ON SFILE,ITEMID`

writes the data to the file with the item-id ITEMID, taking the contents as a dynamic array from the variable RECORD.

(c) WRITEV statement, such as:

`WRITEV DESCR ON SFILE,ITEMID, 7`

244 The Basic language

takes the contents of the variable DESCR and writes as attribute 7 of the item with the item-id ITEMID. If only one attribute of an item is being processed then it is more efficient to read in that attribute alone, by means of the READV or READVU statements, and then write the updated attribute back by means of the WRITEV statement.

6.14.5 Deleting items from the files

Items which are no longer required can be deleted from a file by means of statements of the form:

DELETE *file-variable, item id*

For example:

```
DELETE STOCK,'1234'
DELETE FILE23,KEY
DELETE XKEY
```

specifying the file variable, if any, and the item-id of the item which is to be deleted from the file.

If it is required to delete all the items from a file, then this can be done by means of the CLEARFILE statement:

```
CLEARFILE STOCK
CLEARFILE
```

specifying the file variable, if any, to which the file has been opened.

6.14.6 Selecting items on the files

As we saw above, the READ statements require an item-id to be specified in order that an item may be read from a file. This implies that the item-id of each item to be processed must be obtained by one of the following methods:

Either you may input the item-id conversationally as the program executes – this is by far the most common method. For example, you may specify a PART.NUMBER or an EMPLOYEE.NUMBER to identify the item to be processed.

Or your program may derive the item-id. For example, if you want to process all the items on a file and the format of the item-ids is known, then a simple loop may be used, as shown in Listing 6.6.

```
*     PROCESS ITEM-IDS 1-3000
      FOR X=1 TO 3000
      READ RECORD FROM FVARIABLE, X ELSE GO 1099
      :
*     PROCESS RECORD
      :
1099 NEXT X
      :
```

Listing 6.6

If you want to process *all* the items on the file, and the item-ids cannot be input or calculated in this manner, then sequential processing of the file may be achieved by either:

(a) Generating a list of all the item-ids on the file, by issuing an Access SELECT or SSELECT verb – or an equivalent GET-LIST or FORM-LIST verb – prior to executing the program. The sequence for this would be something like:

```
SSELECT STOCK BY DESCRIPTION WITH STOCK < "100"
RUN PROGS N99PROG
```

This is the more powerful of the two methods, since the Access processor will select according to any selection criteria specified and sort the items into any required sequence; or:

(b) Using the Basic SELECT statement to generate such a list within the program. For example:

```
SELECT STOCK
```

This will allow you to process *all* the items on the file, and you will have to perform any necessary selection-criteria checks on the records after you have READ them from the file.

When such a list has been produced, the item-ids are retrieved successively from the list by a statement such as:

```
READNEXT RECKEY ELSE GO 100
```

which will place the next item-id from the SELECT list into the variable. Note that this statement does not READ the items from the file. When there are no more item-ids in the list, the ELSE clause will be actioned.

The list of item-ids generated within the program by means of the Basic SELECT statement is slightly different from that generated by the Access SELECT or SSELECT verb, in that the Basic SELECT statement provides access to the next physical item-id on the file each time a READNEXT statement is executed, whereas the Access SELECT and

SSELECT verbs generate the entire list before the execution begins – this means that if the program creates any new items at the same time as using the READNEXT in conjunction with the Basic SELECT statement, then these new items may appear amongst the selected items later in the program, even though they were added to the file *after* the SELECT statement was executed. Another important difference is that the Access SELECT and SSELECT verbs may specify selection criteria, whereas the Basic SELECT statement does not permit this.

Listing 6.7 shows the typical sequence for processing items using the SELECT and READNEXT statements in Pick Basic. The example in Listing 6.8 shows the typical sequence for processing items using the SSELECT verb in a Proc to select the item-ids and then a Basic program to process the items.

```
*
*     SIMPLE PROGRAM TO UPDATE STOCK FILE
*
*     OPEN FILE
*
      OPEN '', 'STOCK' TO STOCK ELSE
           PRINT 'NO STOCK FILE'
           STOP
      END
*
*     SELECT ALL RECORDS ON STOCK FILE
*
      SELECT STOCK
*
*     CONSTANTS
*
          :
*
*     GET PART NUMBERS IN TURN
*
2000 READNEXT PARTNO ELSE PRINT 'END OF JOB'; STOP
*
*     READ PART RECORD
*
      READ PART.REC FROM STOCK, PARTNO ELSE
           PRINT PARTNO: ' SELECTED BUT NOT ON FILE'; GO 2000
      END
*
*     PROCESS STOCK ITEM
*
          :
*
*     WRITE AMENDED RECORD
*
      WRITE PART.REC ON STOCK, PARTNO
      PRINT 'RECORD ':PARTNO: ' UPDATED'
      GO 2000
      END
```

Listing 6.7

```
THE PROC  ...........................................

PQ
C PROC TO SELECT STOCK ITEMS & INVOKE PROGRAM
HSSELECT STOCK WITH LEVEL < "0"
STON
HRUN MYPROGS STOCK99
P

THE PROGRAM  ........................................

*    PROGRAM:   FILE=MYPROGS ITEM=STOCK99
*
*    SIMPLE PROGRAM TO UPDATE STOCK FILE
*
*    OPEN FILE
*
     OPEN '','STOCK' TO STOCK ELSE
          PRINT 'NO STOCK FILE'
          STOP
     END
*
*    CONSTANTS
*
       :
*
*    GET PART NUMBERS IN TURN FROM SSELECT LIST
*
2000 READNEXT PARTNO ELSE PRINT 'END OF JOB'; STOP
*
*    READ PART RECORD
*
     READ PART.REC FROM STOCK, PARTNO ELSE
          PRINT PARTNO:' SELECTED BUT NOT ON FILE'; GO 2000
     END
*
*    PROCESS STOCK ITEM
*
       :
*
*    WRITE AMENDED RECORD
*
     WRITE PART.REC ON STOCK, PARTNO
     PRINT 'RECORD ':PARTNO:' UPDATED'
     GO 2000
     END
```

Listing 6.8

The SELECT statement may have any of a number of forms:

SELECT STOCK

will select all the items on the file which has been opened to file variable STOCK. If no file variable was used when the file was opened, then the SELECT statement will be simply:

SELECT

These forms imply that you are only using one selected file at any time. If you wish, you may process several files simultaneously by means of the statement:

`SELECT STOCK TO STOCKLIST`

The forms of the READNEXT statement are:

`READNEXT KEY ELSE GO 100`

if you are only processing one selected file, or

`READNEXT KEY FROM STOCKLIST ELSE GO 100`

if you have assigned your selected file to the variable STOCKLIST.

6.15   USING MAGNETIC TAPE

Basic has a number of statements which allow you to process magnetic-tape records. The sequence of operations when using the magnetic-tape drive is:

(a) Attach the tape drive by means of the T-ATT command.
(b) Indicate the record size which you will be using – by means of the T-ATT or the T-RDLBL command.
(c) Mount your tape – with a write-permit ring if you are writing data to the tape.
(d) Invoke your Basic program.
(e) Re-wind the tape – by means of the REWIND statement in your program or the TCL T-REW command.
(f) Dismount the tape.
(g) Issue a T-DET command to detach the tape drive, releasing it for other users.

The TCL commands to do this are discussed in Section 10.7. The Basic statements which you will use are READT to read data from the tape:

`READT TRECORD ELSE PRINT 'TAPE NOT ATTACHED'; STOP`

WRITET to write data to the tape:

`WRITET OPUTDATA ELSE GO 10`

REWIND to re-wind the tape:

`REWIND ELSE PRINT 'TAPE NOT ATTACHED'; STOP`

WEOF to write an end-of-file marker on the tape:

`WEOF ELSE GO 400`

You should be completely aware of the format of the tape records when using the READT and WRITET statements.

In all these Basic statements, the ELSE condition will be taken if the tape drive has not been attached prior to running the program. The READT statement will also pass to the ELSE condition if the end-of-file marker is sensed.

6.16 STRUCTURED PROGRAMMING TECHNIQUES IN BASIC

The structured programming capabilities of Pick Basic are similar to those of other versions of the language. If you have used other versions of Basic, the following points may come as some surprise:

- Internal sub-routines are accessed by means of GOSUB and RETURN.
- Internal sub-routines are called via their statement-label. On some implementations, this may be an alphanumeric label.
- Destinations of GO and GOSUB cannot be held in a variable. So a sequence such as:

```
TARGET=1044
GOSUB TARGET
```

would be invalid. But on some implementations, as we saw above, the destination label may be alphanumeric:

```
GOSUB TARGET
```

passing control to a statement such as:

```
TARGET: PRINT 'RECORD NOT FOUND'
```

- When using internal sub-routines, there are no local variables. All variables are global.
- External sub-routines are accessed by means of CALL and RETURN.
- External sub-routines have an alphanumeric name by which they are called:

```
CALL CALC.NEW.BALANCE
```

- When using external sub-routines, parameters may be passed as arguments or via the COMMON area, all other variables are local.
- Nested sub-routines are acceptable.
- Recursive calls are acceptable.
- CASE structures are available.

- Nested CASE structures are acceptable.
- IF . . . THEN . . . statements are available.
- IF . . . THEN . . . ELSE . . . statements are available.
- Multi-line THEN and ELSE clauses are available.
- Nested IF statements are acceptable.
- FOR . . . NEXT loops are available.
- FOR . . . UNTIL . . . NEXT loops are available.
- FOR . . . WHILE . . . NEXT loops are available.
- Nested FOR . . . NEXT loops are acceptable.
- LOOP . . . DO . . . REPEAT loops are available.
- LOOP . . . UNTIL . . . DO . . . REPEAT loops are available.
- LOOP . . . WHILE . . . DO . . . REPEAT loops are available.
- Nested LOOP . . . REPEAT loops are acceptable.
- The processing may jump from within any type of loop and retain all variables and return addresses intact. We shall not discuss here whether this is a bad programming technique.
- ON variable GOSUB . . . are available.
- ON variable GOTO . . . are available.
- RETURN TO . . . may be used with internal sub-routines.
- There are no user-defined functions.
- There are no procedures – such as those which are available in BBC Basic.

In the following sections we shall look at the most important of these features of Pick Basic.

6.16.1   IF statement

The following differences should be noted between the IF statement of Pick Basic and those of other Basic compilers:

(a) There must always be a THEN clause.
(b) The word THEN must be used.
(c) Any valid Basic statement or statements may be used in the THEN clause, not necessarily a GOTO statement.
(d) Multi-line forms of the THEN clause can be used for legibility.
(e) Multi-line forms of the ELSE clause can be used for legibility. These are described below.

The various possible forms are illustrated in Listing 6.9. In these examples, the indentation is optional and is used to make the source program easier to read. You see that a multiple-line clause is much easier to read and to modify than is a single-line statement.

```
IF A=B THEN GO TO 100

IF A=999 THEN STOP

IF TOTAL#0 THEN PRINT TOTAL

IF ANSWER='YES' THEN TOTAL=0; GO 50

IF A=999 THEN GO 42 ELSE GO 56

IF TOTAL=0 THEN PRINT 'FINISHED'; STOP ELSE PRINT TOTAL

IF ANSWER='YES' THEN GO 54 ELSE TOTAL1=0; TOTAL2=1

IF VALUE=INT(VALUE) THEN NULL ELSE GO 55

IF VALUE='' THEN
    PRINT 'NULL VALUE FOUND'
    VAL.STORE(X)=VAL
    ENDMESS=1
    END

IF VALUE='' THEN
    PRINT 'NULL VALUE FOUND'
    VAL.STORE(X)=VAL
    ENDMESS=1
    END ELSE PRINT 'VALUE=':VALUE; VAL.START(X)=VAL

IF VALUE='' THEN
    PRINT 'NULL VALUE FOUND'
    VAL.STORE(X)=VAL
    ENDMESS=1
    END ELSE
        PRINT 'VALUE=':VALUE
        VAL.START(X)=VAL
        END

IF REPLY='NO' THEN TOTAL=0; GO 60 ELSE
    WRITE RECORD ON FILE
    TOTAL1=0; TOTAL2=0
    PRINT MESSAGE
    GO 50
    END

IF A=0 THEN
    GO 50
    END ELSE
        GO 60
        END
```

Listing 6.9

The various relational operators are:

=   meaning *equal to.*
EQ   meaning *equal to.*
>   meaning *greater than.*
GT   meaning *greater than.*

<   meaning *less than.*
LT   meaning *less than.*
meaning *not equal to.*
NE   meaning *not equal to.*
>=   meaning *greater than or equal to.*
GE   meaning *greater than or equal to.*
<=   meaning *less than or equal to.*
LE   meaning *less than or equal to.*

Several such conditions may be linked with AND or OR operators. Thus:

```
IF IX<9999 AND IX>1 AND IX MATCH '4N' THEN GO 400
IF NUMBER<1 OR NUMBER>9 THEN GO 600
```

The relational expression in the IF statement is evaluated to a Boolean value of either:

0   meaning that the expression is *false*, or
1   meaning that the expression is *true.*

This fact means that it is possible to replace the relational expression by an arithmetic expression, and the value of that arithmetic expression will be interpreted in the same way:

FALSE if the value is 0 or non-numeric – non-numeric will generate a run-time error message.

Thus, the statements shown in Listing 6.10 are all acceptable. If the only possible values of SWITCH are 0 or 1, then the last four statements in Listing 6.10 are equivalent, branching to statement number 555 if the value in the variable SWITCH is *true*, or branching to statement number 666 if the value in the variable SWITCH is *false*.

```
IF ANS+VALUE THEN GO 100
IF COUNT(LINE, ' ') THEN PRINT 'LINE CONTAINS SPACES'

IF SWITCH THEN GO 555 ELSE GO 666
IF SWITCH=1 THEN GO 555 ELSE GO 666
IF 1-SWITCH THEN GO 666 ELSE GO 555
IF NOT(SWITCH) THEN GO 666 ELSE GO 555
```

Listing 6.10

Basic also allows you to test a value to see whether it matches a specified pattern. The MATCH operator is used as follows:

IF PT.NUMBER MATCH '4N' THEN GO 100 this will give a match if the value of PT.NUMBER is four numeric digits.

IF CODE MATCH '0A' THEN GO 200 this will give a match if the value of CODE is all alphabetic characters or null.

IF ITEM.ID MATCH "2A'–'3N'–'3N" THEN GO 300 this will give a match if the value of ITEM.ID is of the form:

```
AA-111-111
LM-102-934
```

and so on.

IF EMPNO MATCH '5X' THEN GO 400 this will give a match if the value of EMPNO is five characters long.

The MATCH pattern will include any of the following elements:

(a) nN will test that the value comprises only *n* numeric digits 0–9.
(b) 0N will test that the value comprises only numeric digits 0–9 or if it is null.
(c) nA will test that the value comprises only *n* alphabetic characters A–Z or a–z.
(d) 0A will test that the value comprises only alphabetic characters A–Z or a–z, or if it is null.
(e) nX will test that the value is *n* characters long. The value may consist of any characters.
(f) 0X is not useful.
(g) Any other character string in a pattern string will test for that character string. Such a character string need only be enclosed in quotes if it could be ambiguous:

```
IF ITEM.ID MATCH '2A"–"3N"–"3N' THEN GO 300
IF ITEM.ID MATCH '2A–3N–3N' THEN GO 300
```

(h) The pattern may be enclosed in either single quotes or double quotes, or it may be a variable:

```
IF ITEM.ID MATCH "2A'–'3N'–'3N" THEN GO 300
IF ITEM.ID MATCH '2A"–"3N"–"3N' THEN GO 300

MASK='2A–3N–3N'
IF ITEM.ID MATCH MASK THEN GO 300
```

(i) Any combination of the above patterns may be used.
(j) The word MATCH may be written MATCHES, with the same effect. For example:

```
IF PT.NUMBER MATCHES '4N' THEN GO 100
IF CODE MATCHES '0A' THEN GO 200
IF EMPNO MATCHES '5X' THEN GO 400
```

A non-match may be tested by having a NULL statement in the THEN clause, for example:

```
IF PT.NUMBER MATCH '4N' THEN NULL ELSE GO 100
IF CODE MATCH 'OA' THEN NULL ELSE GO 200
IF ITEM.ID MATCH "2A'-'3N'-'3N" THEN NULL ELSE GO
   300
IF EMPNO MATCH '5X' THEN NULL ELSE GO 400
```

or, more neatly, by using the NOT function:

```
IF NOT(PT.NUMBER MATCH '4N') THEN GO 100
IF NOT(CODE MATCH 'OA') THEN GO 200
IF NOT(ITEM.ID MATCH "2A'-'3N'-'3N") THEN GO 300
IF NOT(EMPNO MATCH '5X') THEN GO 400
```

For a purely numeric test, you could also use the NUM function:

```
IF NUM(MYCODE) THEN GO 40
```

which will pass control to statement number 40 if the variable MYCODE has any numeric value such as 10 or 10.5 or 0.01 or -10.222.

The points about the logical expression in the IF statement also apply to those in the CASE statement described below.

6.16.2   ELSE clause

Since the OPEN, READ, READT, REWIND and certain other Basic statements have ELSE conditions in the event of the action of the statement failing, the above comments on the multi-line IF statement also apply; some examples are shown in Listing 6.11. As before, the indentation is merely for clarity.

6.16.3   ON . . . statement

This statement offers a parallel to the *computed* GO TO which you may know from other programming languages. For example:

```
ON TAX GO TO 100,30,55,66
```

where the value of TAX, rounded to the nearest integer below, is tested. If the value is 1, then a branch is taken to statement 100, if the value is 2, then a branch is taken to statement 30, and so on. If the value of TAX is, say, 5, as in this example, then an error message will be displayed:

```
BRANCH INDEX OF 5 EXCEED NUMBER OF STATEMENT-LABELS
BRANCH TAKEN TO LAST STATEMENT-LABEL
```

and the program execution will continue. If the value of TAX is less than 1, then an error message will be displayed:

```
OPEN 'STOCK' TO STOCKID ELSE GO 350

READT RECORD ELSE PRINT 'TAPE NOT READY'; STOP

OPEN 'DICT',FILE TO FID ELSE
     IF FILE='END' THEN STOP
     PRINT FILE: ' CANNOT BE FOUND'
     GO 60
     END

REWIND ELSE
     GO 350
     END

OPEN FILE TO FID ELSE
     PRINT "NO FILE ":FILE; STOP
     END

READ DETAIL FROM STOCKID, '1234' ELSE GO 45

READ RECORD FROM FID, ITEMID ELSE FLAG=1; GO 122

READ RECORD FROM FID, ITEMID ELSE
     IF ITEMID='END' THEN STOP
     PRINT ITEMID: ' IS A NEW RECORD'
     RECORD=''
     END

READ DETAIL FROM STOCKID, '1234' ELSE
     GO 45
     END

READ RECORD FROM FID, ITEMID ELSE
     FLAG=1; GO 122
     END
```

Listing 6.11

```
BRANCH INDEX OF 0 IS ILLEGAL
BRANCH TAKEN TO FIRST STATEMENT-LABEL
```

and the program execution will continue.

There is a corresponding GOSUB statement:

```
ON TAX GOSUB 5,67,32
```

Listing 6.12 shows some valid examples of this statement.

```
ON CODE+1 GOTO 1,2,3,4,5
ON SEQ(OPTION)-64 GOTO 98,78,76,56,54,34,32,12,98,98
ON IVAL GOTO 1,1,2,2,3,3,4,4
ON CODE+1 GOSUB 1,2,3,4,5
ON SEQ(OPTION)-64 GOSUB 98,78,76,56,54,34,32,12,98,98
ON IVAL GOSUB 1,1,2,2,3,3,4,4
```

Listing 6.12

6.16.4 CASE structure

Pick Basic offers a powerful CASE structure to allow you to test for any of a number of conditions. Look at the sequence of IF statements shown in Listing 6.13. We can write this, and similar sequences, much more efficiently and more conveniently as a CASE statement, as shown in Listing 6.14. The CASE statement provides conditional selection of a sequence of statements. The general form of the CASE statement is shown in Fig. 6.7.

```
1    PRINT "WHAT IS YOUR CHOICE? Y / N / A / X: ":
     INPUT REPLY
     IF REPLY='Y' THEN GO 100
     IF REPLY='N' THEN GO 200
     IF REPLY='A' THEN GO 300
     IF REPLY='X' THEN STOP
     GO 1
```

Listing 6.13

```
1    PRINT "WHAT IS YOUR CHOICE? Y / N / A / X: ":
     INPUT REPLY
     BEGIN CASE
           CASE REPLY='Y'
                 GO 100
           CASE REPLY='N'
                 GO 200
           CASE REPLY='A'
                 GO 300
           CASE REPLY='X'
                 STOP
           CASE 1
                 GO 1
     END CASE
```

Listing 6.14

```
                    BEGIN CASE
                        CASE expression
                                statement(s)
                        CASE expression
                                statements(s)
                            :
                            :
                            :
                        END CASE
```

Figure 6.7

When the BEGIN CASE statement is encountered during execution, the first CASE expression is evaluated and if the logical value of this expression is true, then the statement or sequence of statements that immediately follows the CASE statement is executed, and, when this has been done, control passes to the statement following the END CASE statement. If the first expression is false, then it is ignored and the second CASE expression is evaluated. If the logical value of this expression is true, then the statement or sequence of statements that immediately follows the CASE statement is executed, and, when this has been done, control passes to the statement following the END CASE statement, and so on. In this way each CASE statement is tested and the first TRUE one is processed, and all others are ignored.

```
BEGIN CASE
     CASE A < 5
          PRINT 'VALUE IS LESS THAN 5'
     CASE A < 10
          PRINT 'VALUE IS GREATER THAN OR EQUAL TO 5 AND LESS THAN 10'
     CASE 1
          PRINT 'VALUE IS GREATER THAN OR EQUAL TO 10'
END CASE
PRINT 'VALUE TESTED OK'
```

Listing 6.15

Consider the example shown in Listing 6.15. Let us suppose that A has a value of 3, then the first PRINT statement will be executed, and the printed output will be:

VALUE IS LESS THAN 5
VALUE TESTED OK

Notice that although the value of A also satisfies the second CASE statement $(A < 10)$ the execution of the previous CASE statement $(A < 5)$ is carried out first and then execution passes directly out of the CASE sequence to the statement following the END CASE.

If A has a value of 7, then the second PRINT statement will be executed, and the printed output will be:

VALUE IS GREATER THAN OR EQUAL TO 5 AND LESS THAN 10
VALUE TESTED OK

If A has a value of 10 or greater, then the third PRINT statement will be executed, and the printed output will be:

VALUE IS GREATER THAN OR EQUAL TO 10
VALUE TESTED OK

The CASE 1 statement is a catch-all facility, which will satisfy any conditions not met by the preceding CASE expressions.

There may be several conditions in the CASE expression. For example, the following are all valid CASE expressions:

CASE A=B and C=D

```
CASE (X<O AND Y<O) OR (X>O AND Y>O)
CASE V AND W
CASE N MATCH '1NON' OR N MATCH 'ON.ON'
```

The statements may be written on the same line as the CASE expression, as shown in Listing 6.16. The CASE expression is followed by a semicolon.

```
BEGIN CASE
     CASE REPLY='Y'; GO 100
     CASE REPLY='N'; GO 200
     CASE REPLY='A'; GO 300
     CASE REPLY='X'; STOP
     CASE 1; GO 1
END CASE
```

Listing 6.16

CASE statements may be nested, as shown by the example in Listing 6.17. Great care must be taken with the BEGIN CASE and END CASE statements, since the compiler diagnostics are not particularly explicit when errors are encountered in CASE statements.

```
BEGIN CASE
     CASE A=1
          BEGIN CASE
               CASE B<A; GO 110
               CASE B=O; GO 210
               CASE B>A; GO 310
          END CASE
     CASE A=2
          BEGIN CASE
               CASE B<A; GO 120
               CASE B=A; GO 220
               CASE B>A; GO 320
          END CASE
     CASE A=3
          BEGIN CASE
               CASE B<A; GO 130
               CASE B=A; GO 230
               CASE B>A; GO 330
          END CASE
     CASE 1
          BEGIN CASE
               CASE B<A; GO 140
               CASE B=A; GO 240
               CASE B>A; GO 340
          END CASE
END CASE
```

Listing 6.17

6.17   LOOP STRUCTURES

A loop is a section of a program which is written in such a way that it will execute over and over again, until a certain condition is satisfied. Basic has a number of statements which are designed to simplify the common task of writing a loop, the most familiar of which are the FOR and NEXT statements:

```
TOTAL=0
FOR A=12 TO 20
    TOTAL=TOTAL+A
NEXT A
PRINT TOTAL
```

The Pick Basic version has all the standard features:

- A STEP clause.
- Variables for the initial value, for the terminal value or for the STEP value.
- The values may be specified as a literal or as an arithmetic expression.
- The values may be integer or fractional numbers.
- An omitted STEP value is assumed to be +1.
- Ascending and descending movement with positive or negative STEP values.
- There must be a variable on the NEXT statement.
- You may have loops within loops, provided that the various loops have different counters.

    Loops may be nested to any number of levels, and a nested loop must be completely contained within the range of the outer loop, that is, the ranges of the loops must not cross.
- You must never change the value of the counter inside the loop.
- It is possible, though potentially dangerous, to jump into or out of a loop.
- Intersecting loops are invalid.

Unlike many other versions, the terminal value in the TO clause of the FOR statement is evaluated at each iteration, so that a loop such as:

```
FOR X=1 TO X+1
    IF RECORD<X>=' ' THEN GO 20
    PRINT RECORD<X>
NEXT X
20  *
```

is quite aceptable, with the value of X increasing until the RECORD<X>='' condition is satisfied.

The WHILE and UNTIL clauses of the extended FOR statement are discussed in the next section.

6.17.1   Extended FOR structure – WHILE and UNTIL

The WHILE and UNTIL clauses allow you to devise more powerful FOR loops. For example:

```
FOR A=1 TO 20 UNTIL SALES(A)=''
    PRINT A,SALES(A)
NEXT A
```

will repeat until A reaches a value of 20 or until the value of SALES(A) equals null, whichever is attained sooner.

```
STRING=''
FOR B=1 TO 10 UNTIL STRING='*****'
    STRING=STRING: '*'
NEXT B
```

will execute five times, an '*' being added to the variable STRING until it reaches '*****'.

```
A=20
FOR J=1 TO 10 WHILE A<25
    A=A+1
    PRINT J,A
NEXT J
```

will execute five times, printing:

```
1          21
2          22
3          23
4          24
5          25
```

because variable A reaches a value of 25 before variable J reaches a value of 10.

```
A=0
FOR J=1 TO 10 WHILE A<25
    A=A+1
    PRINT J,A
NEXT J
```

which will execute ten times because variable J reaches a value of 10 before variable A reaches a value of 25.

6.17.2 LOOP structure

Even more powerful program loops may be constructed by means of the LOOP statement. For example:

```
LOOP PRINT A UNTIL A=4 DO A=A+1; PRINT A REPEAT
LOOP UNTIL NUMB=5 DO FACT=FACT*NUMB;
    NUMB=NUMB+1 REPEAT
```

The execution of a LOOP statement proceeds as follows:

(a) Any statements following LOOP will be executed.
(b) The *condition* is evaluated.
(c) One of the following is then performed depending upon the form used:

> If the WHILE form is used:
> (i) If the condition evaluates to true, then any statements following DO will be executed and program control will loop back to the beginning of the loop at step (a).
> (ii) If the condition evaluates to false, then the LOOP will be terminated and program control will proceed with the next sequential statement following REPEAT.

> If the UNTIL form is used:
> (i) If the condition evaluates to false, then any statements following DO will be executed and program control will loop back to the beginning of the loop at step (a).
> (ii) If the condition evaluates to true, then the LOOP will be terminated and program control will proceed with the next sequential statement following REPEAT.

Let us look at a few more examples to illustrate these points:

```
LOOP UNTIL A=4 DO A=A+1; PRINT A REPEAT
```

assuming that the initial value of variable A is 0, this statement will execute four times, printing the sequential values of A from 1 through 4.

```
LOOP VAL=VAL-10 WHILE VAL>40 DO PRINT VAL REPEAT
```

assuming that the initial value of variable VAL is 100, this statement will execute five times, printing the values from 90 down through 50 in increments of −10.

```
CNTR=0
LOOP
    PRINT CNTR
```

```
        CNTR=CNTR+1
WHILE CNTR<4 DO REPEAT
```

this will execute four times printing sequential values from 0 through 3.

```
INCR=6
LOOP INCR=INCR−1 WHILE INCR DO
        PRINT INCR
REPEAT
```

this will execute five times printing the values of variable INCR in the order 5, 4, 3, 2 and 1.

```
XVAL=6
LOOP PRINT XVAL WHILE XVAL DO
        XVAL=XVAL−1 REPEAT
```

this will execute seven times, printing the values of variable XVAL in the order 6, 5, 4, 3, 2, 1 and 0.

As these examples show, the statement may be spread over several lines and indented for clarity. Incidentally, a statement such as:

```
LOOP
    PRINT XVAL
WHILE
    XVAL
DO
    XVAL=XVAL−1
REPEAT
```

is invalid. The WHILE *condition* DO element must be on the same line.

6.18   SUB-ROUTINES

In Pick Basic, as in most other programming languages, a sub-routine allows you to arrange for the same sequence of statements to be accessed from several places within your program. There are two types of sub-routine in Pick Basic:

(a) Internal sub-routines – these are held within the program in which they are used and compiled as a part of that program. These are exactly the same as internal sub-routines on other versions of the language, and must be called by an explicit statement number.

```
GOSUB 300
```

returning to the main program by means of the

```
RETURN
```

statement. You *cannot* call internal sub-routines by means of a statement number held in a variable:

```
TARGET=300
GOSUB TARGET
```

as is possible on some versions of Basic.
(b) External sub-routines – these are written, held, compiled and catalogued as separate (sub)routines and may be used from any program. These are called by the explicit program name:

```
CALL CALC.ROUTINE
```

You may call an external sub-routine by means of a program name held in a variable:

```
TARGET='CALC.ROUTINE'
CALL @TARGET
```

Let us have a look at the external sub-routines.

An external sub-routine is one which is written, held, compiled and catalogued separately from the main calling program or programs which call it, and for this reason an external routine can be used by one or more programs on your account. This makes it easier to use a routine which you may need in several programs. For example:

(a) A routine to perform a particular calculation, such as VAT.
(b) A check-digit routine.
(c) An input-validation routine.

Both the calling program and the called sub-routine must be catalogued, and both must have the same arithmetic precision.

A particularly attractive feature of catalogued programs and sub-routines is that they are created, compiled and catalogued individually, and you can change, re-compile and re-catalogue a sub-routine without having to re-compile and re-catalogue the entire set of programs in which it is used. The CALL, SUBROUTINE and RETURN statements allow you to define and access external sub-routines.

The simplest form of the CALL statement is:

```
CALL PRINT.ROUTINE
```

which transfers control to the external sub-routine called PRINT. ROUTINE. If data are to be passed to the sub-routine, then this will be specified in an argument list, like this:

```
CALL VAT(A,B,C)
```

which will pass control to the external sub-routine called VAT and take the contents of the three variables A, B and C with it, or:

```
CALL VAT(PRICE,15,TOTAL)
```

which will pass control to the external sub-routine called VAT taking the contents of the variable PRICE, the literal 15 and the variable TOTAL.

As these examples show, the arguments in the CALL statement may be variables or literals. Care should be taken to ensure that literals are not used for any parameters which are altered in the SUBROUTINE – as with the third parameter in the examples here.

The external sub-routine is like an ordinary Basic program, except that it must begin with a SUBROUTINE statement. It may contain any Basic statements, including calls to internal and external sub-routines. It will contain a RETURN statement to pass control back to the calling program. Since the sub-routine is an independent unit, it will be terminated by an END statement just like any other Basic program.

The SUBROUTINE statement will have one of the forms:

```
SUBROUTINE PRINT.ROUTINE
```

or, if data are to be passed between the calling program and the sub-routine:

```
SUBROUTINE VAT(X,Y,Z)
```

Any argument lists in corresponding CALL and SUBROUTINE statements must contain the same number of parameters. When control is passed to the sub-routine, a one-to-one correspondence is set up between the parameters in the CALL statement and those in the SUBROUTINE statement. If the number of parameters does not match, then an error message will be printed and the debugger will be entered.

Since the various programs and their sub-routines are compiled separately, there is complete independence between variable names or labels in the calling program and the sub-routine. In the example below, the variable A in the calling program is quite different from the variable A in the VAT sub-routine.

The following small sub-routine takes three parameters from the calling program, regards the first as a price, the second as a VAT rate, and performs the VAT calculation putting the result into the third parameter. It then returns control to the calling program:

```
SUBROUTINE VAT(X,Y,Z)
A=Y/100
Z=X*A
RETURN
END
```

We should create this sub-routine as an item VAT – the same name as that on the SUBROUTINE statement – on any of our program files. We should then compile and catalogue it, as described below. Then, whenever we wish to perform the VAT calculation, we will call the sub-routine:

```
CALL VAT(A,15,P)
```

or

```
CALL VAT(PRICE,RATE,TOTAL)
```

If the sub-routine processes a dimensioned array, then you will pass this across in CALL and SUBROUTINE statements, like this:

```
CALL MOVE(MAT NAMES, MAT TARGET)
SUBROUTINE MOVE(MAT A, MAT B)

CALL SUBR1(MAT NN, PARM, NUMBER)
SUBROUTINE SUBR1(MAT A, DATAX, NUMB)
```

Such arrays must appear on DIMENSION statements in both the calling program and the sub-routine.

The actual array dimensions may be different, as long as the total number of elements match. The values in the arrays are passed across in row major order, as illustrated by the routines in Fig. 6.8. If X in the

```
Calling program            External subroutine
===============            ===================

DIM X(10),Y(10)            SUBROUTINE MOVE (MAT A, MAT B)
X(2)=7                     DIM A (5,2), B(10)
CALL MOVE (MAT X,MAT Y)    PRINT A(1,2)
END                        RETURN
                           END
```

Figure 6.8

calling program contains the values shown in Fig. 6.9, then A in the called sub-routine will contain the values shown in Fig. 6.10.

A much easier way to pass data between a program and its sub-routines is by means of the COMMON statement. Let us suppose that our main program includes the statement:

```
COMMON NAME, AGE, ADDRESS(5), TOTAL
```

This will identify the first eight variables in the common storage area by the names NAME, AGE, ADDRESS(1), ADDRESS(2), ADDRESS(3), ADDRESS(4), ADDRESS(5) and TOTAL, respectively, within the main program. This common area is held in a region separate from that used

```
: : : : : : : : : : :
: 1 : 7 : 3 : 4 : 5 : 6 : 2 : 8 : 9 : 10 :
: : : : : : : : : : :
```

Figure 6.9

```
                    COL 1 :  COL 2
                   . . . . . . : . . . . . .
                   :      :        :
         ROW 1 :   1    :   7    :
                   . . . . . . : . . . . . .
                   :      :        :
         ROW 2 :   3    :   4    :
                   . . . . . . : . . . . . .
                   :      :        :
         ROW 3 :   5    :   6    :
                   . . . . . . : . . . . . .
                   :      :        :
         ROW 4 :   2    :   8    :
                   . . . . . . : . . . . . .
                   :      :        :
         ROW 5 :   9    :  10    :
                   . . . . . . : . . . . . .
```

Figure 6.10

for the other variables used by the program and the sub-routines. If one
of the external sub-routines contains a statement:

`COMMON EMP, YEARS, ST, DIST, TOWN, COUNTY, CODE, ACC`

this will identify the first eight variables in the common storage area by
the names EMP, YEARS, ST, DIST, TOWN, COUNTY, CODE and
ACC. A one-to-one correspondence will be set up, matching NAME in
the main program with EMP in the sub-routine, AGE with YEARS, and
so on. You can see how important it is to get the variable names in the
correct order.

Now, when control is passed to the sub-routine by a statement such
as:

`CALL SUBR55`

it will not be necessary to pass the data values across, since these are
already in the common area. The sub-routine will begin with a simple
statement:

`SUBROUTINE SUBR55`

If the data are organized in this manner, the transfer between the calling
program and the sub-routine is much quicker than with an argument
list.

You may use COMMON statements and argument lists at the same
time, if necessary.

6.19   DEVELOPING A PROGRAM

A Basic program is held as a single item on a file and is processed in the same way as any other data item. Each statement line in the program is held as a separate attribute in the item, values and secondary values being meaningless in this context.

The source program is created, maintained and edited by the standard Pick Editor:

EDIT MYPROGS CALCO1

If you want to print a copy of your Basic source program, then you may use either of the commands:

COPY MYPROGS CALCO1 (T)

or

CT MYPROGS CALCO1

to display the program on the terminal screen, and

COPY MYPROGS CALCO1 (P)

or

CP MYPROGS CALCO1

to print the program on the printer. You may also produce a program listing as you compile the program, as we shall see.

The program is compiled by means of the TCL verb:

BASIC MYPROGS CALCO1

There are several options available with this verb. Full details will be found in your *Basic Reference Manual*, but the following are of particular interest:

E   produces the object program in a compacted form without end-of-line indicators at the end of each statement line. This reduces the physical size of the object program.
L   produces a listing of the source program as it is compiled.
M   produces a map of the compiled program, showing the variables used, the statement-labels used, and their addresses, together with an indication of how the source statements are spread over frames of the object program. This option also generates the symbol table which is used by the *symbolic debugger* as we shall see in Section 6.20.
P   sends any printed output, including diagnostic error messages and the source program listing, to the printer.

These options are specified in parentheses on the Basic command:

```
BASIC MYPROGS CALC01 (E,M,L,P)
```

The compiler will check the syntax of the source program and report any errors. If no errors are detected, then the object program will be produced and saved. If errors are detected, then no further action will be taken.

The destination of the object program depends upon the Pick implementation being used. On the earlier systems, the source and object programs were held on the same file and with the same item-id prefixed by a pound sign/dollar sign. Thus:

```
BASIC MYPROGS CALC01
```

will generate an object program on the file *MYPROGS* with the item-id *£CALC01*. On later implementations, the program file has a DICT section and a separate data section, with the source programs being held on the data section. The compiler will then place the object program and the symbol table on the DICT section of the file. The file definition item for such a file is, of course, held on the MD and must have DC instead of D for the first attribute.

A number of programs on the same file may be compiled by a single command:

```
BASIC MYPROGS UPD001 UPD023 (P,L)
```

and a select list or a saved list may be used to specify the items to be processed, as in a sequence such as:

```
SSELECT MYPROGS >= UPD000" AND <= "UPD030"
BASIC MYPROGS (E)
```

On some implementations, the verb

```
COMPILE
```

is available as an alternative to the BASIC verb shown here.

The command:

```
PRINT-HEADER MYPROGS CALC01
```

will tell you when the program was last compiled.

We have written and compiled our Basic program, and now we want to execute it. In the simplest case, a Basic program is executed by means of the command:

```
RUN MYPROGS CALC01
```

There are several options available with this verb. Full details will be found in your *Basic Reference Manual*, but the following are of particular interest:

P has the effect of issuing a PRINTER ON statement at the start of the program execution.

D invokes the symbolic debugger at the start of the program execution. This is discussed further below.

S suppresses the display of any program error messages.

I indicates that the contents of program variables are not to be initia-lized, but are to retain any values which they held from the last Basic program which was executed. We discuss this further in Sections 6.21.7 and 6.21.8 when we deal with passing control to TCL and to Procs.

These options are specified in parentheses on the RUN command:

```
RUN MYPROGS CALCO1 (S,P)
```

If you catalogue your program, which you need to do if it uses external sub-routines as described below, then it – the calling program – will be invoked as if it were a TCL verb by means of the command:

```
CALCO1
```

The catalogued program may also be invoked with the options shown for the RUN verb. So you might use the command:

```
CALCO1 (S,P)
```

We have already met the concept of external sub-routines. If a program is to use external sub-routines, then the calling program and all the external sub-routines which it uses must be *catalogued*. The act of cata-loguing essentially makes the catalogued item accessible to all users. It achieves this by creating a *core image* version of your object program. This form is much quicker to *load* than would be the object program held as an item on a file. An entry is made in your MD pointing to that object program, so that you have effectively created your own verb. On some implementations, the catalogue process also places a pointer to this core-image form on the *POINTER-FILE*, from where it is accessible to all users.

The sequence of development for such an external sub-routine or a program which uses external sub-routines is:

(a) Create and edit the program/sub-routine in the usual manner.
(b) Compile the program/sub-routine.
(c) Catalogue the program/sub-routine. This is done by a verb of the form:

```
CATALOG MYPROGS MYMAINP
```

which will assume the existence of an object version of the program *MYMAINP* on the file *MYPROGS*, and then catalogue this.

(d) Execute the main calling program. You must execute a catalogued program as if it were a verb, typing

`MYMAINP`

at TCL level. If you were to execute the calling program by means of the statement:

`RUN MYPROGS MYMAINP`

then there will be problems when the CALL statements were encountered, and the execution will terminate with an error message telling you that the

`CALLING PROGRAM MUST BE CATALOGUED`

When you are cataloguing a program, remember that the name of the program will be placed on the MD, so you cannot use program names such as LIST, COUNT, OFF and the like. For the same reason, you cannot catalogue two programs with the same name – *CALC*, for example. Even though the programs may be on different files, they will both be catalogued on the MD with the same name, and one will overwrite the previous one.

The command:

`PRINT-CATALOG MYPROGS MYMAINP`

will tell you when the program was last catalogued. You can remove a catalogued program by means of one of the commands:

`DELETE-CATALOG MYMAINP`

or

`DECATALOG MYMAINP`

according to which Pick implementation you are using.

6.20   THE SYMBOLIC DEBUGGER

The symbolic debugger is a powerful program development tool for Basic programmers, allowing you to follow the execution path taken through the program, to halt the processing at specific points or under specific conditions, to inspect the contents of the program variables, to change the contents of the program variables, and to direct the processing to a specific statement. You may invoke the symbolic debugger during the execution of a Basic program by hitting the <BREAK KEY>, by including the DEBUG statement within your source program, or accidentally, as a result of a program execution error. However it is invoked, the symbolic debugger displays something like:

```
*I20
*
```

showing that processing was interrupted at line 20 of the Basic program, and that you are now in the symbolic debugger.

Before we look at the symbolic debugger, there are two entities which you must be aware of – the *symbol table* and the *break table*.

In order to use the full features of the symbolic debugger which allow you to identify each variable by name, the program should be compiled with the M option in order to produce the program symbol table:

```
BASIC MYPROGS CALC001 (M)
```

The symbol table is a list of the names of all the variables and their locations within the program. In this example the symbol table is held on the file *MYPROGS* under the name **CALC001*. If you have not produced the symbol table in this way, then you cannot use those facilities of the symbolic debugger which allow you to inspect and change the contents of variables.

The break table is a list held by the symbolic debugger, and contains the names of up to six variables which are to be displayed each time the program execution is interrupted, and a set of up to four conditions, the satisfaction of any one of which will invoke an interruption in the processing. By means of commands given to the symbolic debugger, you will specify the variables and the break conditions – if any – which are to go into the break table.

Whenever the symbolic debugger displays the asterisk, you may issue any of these commands:

END this will terminate the execution of the program – this is exactly the same as for the *interactive debugger*.

END followed by <RETURN> will pass to TCL level.

END followed by <LINE FEED> will pass to TCL level, or to the calling Proc if the Basic program was executed from a Proc.

/variable this will display the contents of the variable, and allow you to change it. Thus, if you enter:

```
/EMPNAME
```

the symbolic debugger might respond with:

```
SMITH=
```

showing that the string SMITH is currently held in the variable EMP-NAME. If you wish to change the value held in the variable, then you will enter the new value followed by <RETURN>.

If you press <RETURN> without entering any new value, then the contents of EMPNAME will be left unchanged. If you enter any other value, then this new value will overwrite the value SMITH.

If a single element of a dimensioned array is to be specified, then this should be entered as:

```
/RA(36)
```

If, in this situation, you were to enter:

```
/RA
```

then the symbolic debugger will display and accept new values for all the elements in the array.

If you enter the form:

```
/*
```

then the current contents of all variables will be displayed.

Bcondition this will add a break condition to the break table. Typical examples are:

B£=30 which will cause a break immediately *before* the execution of line number 30 of the program.

BX>100 which will cause a break when the variable X reaches a value greater than 100.

BX=5&Y=32 which will cause a break when the variable X has a value of 5 and variable Y has a value of 32.

D this will display the current contents of the break table.

En this will cause the symbolic debugger to break after executing *n* statements:

E1 will invoke a break after every statement is executed.

E will cancel any previous En specification.

G this will cause the execution to continue to the next break point.

Gn this will transfer the execution to line number *n*.

Whenever a line number is specified in a debug command, it is the program line number and not the Basic statement number. Thus:

```
G1
```

will go to the start of the program and not to the statement labelled 1. The contents of all variables in the program will remain as they were at the break point.

Kn this will kill break condition number *n* by removing it from the break table, and is the reverse of Bcondition command.

OFF this will log you off the system – this is exactly the same as for the *interactive debugger*.

P this is an *on/off* switch suppressing or continuing printed output from the program – this is exactly the same as for the *interactive debugger*.

Tvariable this will add a variable to the break table, causing that variable name and its contents to be displayed at every break point.

Uvariable this will remove a variable from the break table.

<LINE FEED> this will cause the execution to continue to the next break point, exactly like the G command.

<RETURN> this will have no effect.

The symbolic debugger displays the following messages:

*Bc n when a break occurs as a result of satisfying break condition number *c*.

*E1 when a break occurs as a result of initiating execution and interrupt by means of the

```
RUN fffff iiiii (D)
```

command.

*En when a break occurs as a result of an En command.

*In when a break occurs as a result of a program execution error.

+ after a successful Tvariable or Bcondition command indicating that the entry has been added to the break table.

− after a successful Uvariable or Kn command indicating that the entry has been removed from the break table.

 # > PROGRAM LENGTH if you issue a Gn command in which *n* is greater than the number of lines in the program.

CMND? if you enter an invalid debug command.

SYM NOT FND after a Tvariable command of which the variable cannot be found in the symbol table.

TBL FULL after a Tvariable or Bcondition command if the break table is full.

UNASGN VAR if you attempt to use the /variable command to change the value of a variable which has not yet been assigned a value.

In all cases, *n* is the number of the line at which the break occurred and which is *about to be executed*.

6.21   TIPS AND TECHNIQUES – BASIC

One of the most useful tips for solving many of the questions concerning Basic, and many other aspects of Pick, is:

'If in doubt, write a small program to try it out.'

If you want to test the action of a specific statement, then you will find it very easy to write a small program to display the contents of a set of variables, perform the statement in question and then display the set of variables again to verify the action of the statement.

If you have a large program which is not behaving as it should, then isolate the problem area and use it in a smaller program. This is invariably simpler than trying to unravel the action of the statement within the large program by means of the symbolic debugger.

6.21.1   To save space – compressed source code

There is an additional facility which allows the programmer to hold source programs in a compressed form. Any string of three or more spaces or of three or more asterisks will be replaced by a three-character code:

c x n

where *c* is the escape character (hexadecimal 10) showing that a compressed string follows, *x* is the character which has been replaced, space or *, and *n* is the hexadecimal count of the number of characters replaced.

Thus, a statement such as:

100^^^^^^^^^^PRINT^"*****^HEADING^*************"

where ^ represents a space, will be compressed to:

100.^xPRINT^".*y^HEADING^.*z"

where . represents the escape character and *x*, *y* and *z* represent the hexadecimal equivalents of the counts 10, 5 and 13, respectively. The 48 characters of the original statement are here reduced to 29 in the compressed form.

In this situation, the program is edited by the command:

EEDIT PROGS N99PROG

or

EED PROGS N99PROG

The Editor and the EEDITOR commands are identical and the source statements are displayed in their expanded form.

A compressed source program is compiled by means of the command:

EBASIC PROGS N99PROG

and is expanded by means of the command:

ECOPY PROGS N99PROG (O)

which has the usual COPY options. This same verb will be used to produce a printer listing of the source program:

```
ECOPY PROGS N99PROG (P)
```

Some Pick implementations offer a feature whereby a frequently used set of Basic statements may be saved on a file, say as item *XRTN* on the file *MYPROGS*. Then, by means of a statement such as

```
$INSERT MYPROGS XRTN
```

or

```
£INCLUDE MYPROGS XRTN
```

this set of statements will be incorporated during compilation.

6.21.2   To simulate sequential access – Basic

Since each Pick item is accessed directly by means of its item-id, this means that in order to access all the items on a file we have to know all their item-ids. This can be achieved in a number of ways.

If we know the format of the item-ids and these can be created by a Basic program or a Proc, then the items can be read directly. A sequence such as that shown in Listing 6.18 will allow you to process all the items with item-ids in the range 1000–2000.

```
     FOR KEY=1000 TO 2000
          READ RECORD FROM FILEVAR, KEY ELSE GO 100
*    PROCESS THE RECORD HERE
:
:
100  NEXT X
```

Listing 6.18

```
     OPEN 'STOCK' TO FILEVAR ELSE STOP 'NO STOCK FILE'
     SELECT FILE
10   READNEXT KEY ELSE STOP
     READ RECORD FROM FILEVAR, KEY ELSE GO 10
*    PROCESS THE RECORD HERE
:

     GO 10
```

Listing 6.19

If the item-ids cannot be derived by program, then other means must be used. Within a Basic program, the SELECT and READNEXT statements can be used to retrieve the item-ids of all the items on a file.

In the sequence shown in Listing 6.19, the items will be retrieved in the order in which they are encountered on the file. There is no SSELECT statement in Basic. If it is required to process the items in a specific sequence, then the item-ids must be sorted into the required sequence before processing, as shown in Listing 6.20.

```
     OPEN 'STOCK' TO FILEVAR ELSE STOP 'NO STOCK FILE'
     SELECT FILEVAR
10   READNEXT KEY ELSE GO 20
*    SORT KEYS INTO ORDER HERE AND STORE IN 'LIST'
:
     GO 10
20   * PROCESS KEYS
     FOR K=1 TO KEYNO
     KEY=LIST<K>
     READ RECORD FROM FILEVAR, KEY ELSE GO 29
*      PROCESS RECORD HERE
:
29   NEXT K
```

Listing 6.20

6.21.3   To build internal lists – dynamic arrays

The sequence in Listing 6.21 shows how a set of data may be incorporated into a dynamic array. In this example, the variable DYNARR is to be used as a dynamic array and is initialized to null. The contents of VALUE are appended to the end of the array by any of the statements:

```
DYNARR=DYNARR:CHAR(254):VALUE
  DYNARR=REPLACE(DYNARR,-1,0,0,VALUE)
  DYNARR<-1>=VALUE
```

```
     DYNARR=''
10   PRINT "ENTER VALUE":; INPUT VALUE
     IF VALUE='END' THEN GO 20
     DYNARR=DYNARR:CHAR(254):VALUE
     GO 10
20   * PROCESS THE LIST IN DYNARR
```

Listing 6.21

6.21.4   To build a sorted list – dynamic arrays

If you want to sort the entries into sequence as you add them to the list, then the LOCATE statement will do this quite elegantly, as shown in

```
      DYNARR=''
10    PRINT "ENTER VALUE":; INPUT VALUE
      IF VALUE='END' THEN GO 20
      LOCATE VALUE IN DYNARR BY "A" SETTING POSN ELSE
          DYNARR=INSERT(DYNARR,POSN,0,0,VALUE)
      END
      GO 10
20    * PROCESS THE LIST IN DYNARR
```

Listing 6.22

Listing 6.22. The entries are added to the list in ascending order, as specified by the parameter A in the LOCATE statement, and duplicate values are ignored. If duplicate values were to be retained, then the sequence could be changed to that shown in Listing 6.23.

```
      DYNARR=''
10    PRINT "ENTER VALUE":; INPUT VALUE
      IF VALUE='END' THEN GO 20
      LOCATE VALUE IN DYNARR BY "A" SETTING POSN ELSE NULL
      DYNARR=INSERT(DYNARR,POSN,0,0,VALUE)
      GO 10
20    * PROCESS THE LIST IN DYNARR
```

Listing 6.23

6.21.5 To sort item-ids added to a dynamic array

In the previous example, you type in the data which are to be added to the list. The entries to be added could equally well be item-ids derived from a SELECT and READNEXT sequence like that shown in Listing 6.24.

```
      DYNARR=''
      OPEN 'STOCK' TO STOCKID ELSE STOP
      SELECT STOCKID
10    READNEXT ITEMID ELSE GO 20
      LOCATE ITEMID IN DYNARR BY "A" SETTING POSN ELSE
          DYNARR=INSERT(DYNARR,POSN,0,0,ITEMID)
      END
      GO 10
20    * PROCESS THE LIST IN DYNARR
```

Listing 6.24

6.21.6 To use a list held in a dynamic array

When the dynamic array has been built in any of the ways suggested above, the respective elements of the array may be processed in turn by any of the sequences shown in Listing 6.25. If, however, there may be null values in the dynamic array, this method will fail and could be replaced by a sequence such as that shown in Listing 6.26. This solution uses the fact that the attribute mark, character 254, is the element separator in a dynamic array. An alternative solution is shown in Listing 6.27.

This last solution will run more slowly than the previous sequence, since the deletion of elements in a dynamic array is a time-consuming operation. However, it might be used in a situation where the size of the dynamic array was to be kept to a minimum.

```
     FOR X=1 TO X+1 UNTIL EXTRACT(DYNARR,X,0,0)=''
          VALUE=EXTRACT(DYNARR,X,0,0)
*    PROCESS VALUE HERE
*
     NEXT X
```

Listing 6.25

```
     NO. OF. ITEMS=COUNT(DYNARR,CHAR(254))+1
     FOR X=1 TO NO. OF. ITEMS
          VALUE=EXTRACT(DYNARR,X,0,0)
*    PROCESS VALUE HERE
*
     NEXT X
```

Listing 6.26

```
10   IF DYNARR#'' THEN
          VALUE=EXTRACT(DYNARR,X,0,0)
          DYNARR=DELETE(DYNARR,X,0,0)
*    PROCESS VALUE HERE
*
          GO 10
     END
```

Listing 6.27

6.21.7   To invoke TCL commands – 1

You can pass control from a Basic program to a Proc or TCL operation by means of a Basic statement such as:

CHAIN "PROC322 1234 1000 STOCK"

which will invoke the Proc PROC322 and put the four parameters

```
PROC322 1234 1000 STOCK
```

into the Proc input buffer, just as if they had been typed in at TCL level.
▸They may be picked up from the input buffer in the normal manner.
PROC322 will, of course, be held on the master dictionary.

A TCL command could be invoked in a similar manner by statements
such as:

```
CHAIN "CREATE-FILE (STOCK132 1,2 3,4"
CHAIN "SORT ":FILEN:" LPTR"
```

where FILEN is a Basic variable containing the name of the file to be
processed by the Access sentence.

The CHAIN statement will issue the command exactly as if it had been
typed in at TCL level, and the DATA statement may be used to supply
any necessary input data to the chained command. In this context, it has
exactly the same action as the Proc *stack*, and is used to advantage in a
sequence such as that shown in Listing 6.28.

```
        OPEN 'STOCK' TO FILEVAR ELSE STOP 'NO STOCK FILE'
10      READNEXT KEY ELSE
            IF COUNTER#0 THEN STOP
            DATA "RUN PROGS PROGA"
            CHAIN "SSELECT STOCK BY DESCRIPTION"
        END
        COUNTER=COUNTER+1
        READ RECORD FROM FILEVAR, KEY ELSE GO 10
*       PROCESS RECORD HERE
:
:
        GO 10
```

Listing 6.28

The action of this sequence is:

(a) The program is assumed to be held on the file *PROGS* under the
item-id *PROGA*.
(b) When the program is invoked initially, the READNEXT statement
will fail since no SELECT list is available.
(c) The ELSE clause tests to see if any items have been processed yet, if
so then the program execution stops; if no items have been processed and the value in COUNTER is 0, then the Access sentence:

```
SSELECT STOCK BY DESCRIPTION
```

is invoked after the TCL verb:

```
RUN PROGS PROGA
```

has been put into the data stack.

(d) The SSELECT sentence will then be processed and after selecting the items this program will again be executed by the RUN verb in the DATA stack.

(e) This time, there will be a SELECT list available and the READNEXT and processing sequence will be executed normally.

(f) In this situation, the SSELECT sentence may have any valid Access format.

After a CHAIN statement has been issued and executed, the processing does not return to the Basic program. If you wish to return to the Basic program, then you must use the EXECUTE statement which is available on some implementations.

Listing 6.29 shows how we could re-write the above sequence using the EXECUTE statement instead of the CHAIN and DATA statements. The TCL statement of Open Architecture Pick has the same effect as the EXECUTE statement.

```
       OPEN 'STOCK' TO FILEVAR ELSE STOP 'NO STOCK FILE'
10     READNEXT KEY ELSE
           IF COUNTER#0 THEN STOP
           EXECUTE "SSELECT STOCK BY DESCRIPTION"
           GO 10
       END
       COUNTER=COUNTER+1
       READ RECORD FROM FILEVAR, KEY ELSE GO 10
*      PROCESS RECORD HERE
:
:
       GO 10
```

Listing 6.29

6.21.8   To invoke TCL commands – 2

Let us now look at an extension of the method described in the previous section. This allows you to return to a specific point within your Basic program, rather than starting again at the beginning. It is particularly useful on implementations which do not have the EXECUTE statement, and involves the following logical steps:

(a) Run the Basic program.

(b) Use the CHAIN statement to pass control to a Proc containing the TCL commands or Access statements, after setting a flag for use on return to the Basic program.

(c) Process the Proc and its TCL commands and Access sentences.

And, still within the Proc:

(d) Re-run the original Basic program, preserving the original contents of the variables.

(e) Test the flag to determine where the processing is to be resumed.

These steps are shown in the Basic program and the Proc in Listing 6.30, which would be invoked by the command:

```
RUN MYPROGS BP004 (S)
```

and the above logical steps would be taken.

```
PROGRAM -- MYPROGS BP004 -------------------------------------

     COMMON FLAG
     IF FLAG=1234 THEN GO 1000
     *
     * ALL INITIAL PROCESSING HERE
     *
     * VALUES WHICH ARE TO BE USED LATER ARE STORED IN
     * THE COMMON VARIABLES
     *
     :
     :
     FLAG=1234
     CHAIN 'PROC630'
     *
1000 * BACK IN PROGRAM
     *
     * AND CONTINUE PROCESSING
     :
     :
     END

PROC -- PROC630 HELD ON MD -----------------------------------

PQ
C
C DO ALL PROC PROCESSING AND TCL COMMANDS HERE
C
C THEN RETURN TO BASIC PROGRAM
C
:
:
HRUN MYPROGS BP004 (I)
P
```

Listing 6.30

When the Basic program is re-run from the Proc, the I option on the command:

```
RUN MYPROGS BP004 (I)
```

will cause all the *common* variables in the program to retain their original values. Execution of the program will, of course, start at the first statement, so we test the flag and take a branch to the point following the CHAIN statement. The same flag could be used to pass control to any of a number of external Procs and would hold a unique value to return it to the appropriate place in the Basic program on return from one of these Procs.

Since the flag will be tested on the very first execution of the program, we use the S option to suppress the error message which would be generated when the flag variable had not been assigned a value.

7
The Proc language

The Proc language is essentially concerned with saving and using Access sentences and TCL commands. Let us suppose that Joe down in the Stores needs to produce a report on his stock files. He could do this by means of the Access sentence:

```
SORT STOCK NAME LOCATION QUANTITY MINIMUM LPTR
```

Every time Joe wanted to produce his Stock Report, he would have to type in this sentence. You could make his life easier and eliminate much of the typing by creating a Proc:

```
PQ
HSORT STOCK NAME LOCATION QUANTITY MINIMUM LPTR
P
```

The PQ on the first line identifies this as a Proc. The second line begins with an H and builds a string of characters representing the Access sentence which we want. The P on the third line tells the processor to process the Access sentence which we have created. Before you ask, the H stands for Hollerith, the pioneer of character and data representation on computer systems!

Using the Editor:

```
EDIT MD JOE
```

you could create this Proc on your MD. Then, whenever Joe wants to produce his report, he need only type in the command:

```
JOE
```

exactly as if it were a TCL verb. The Proc will then be called into action and Joe's report will appear just as if he had typed in the full Access sentence.

For a more powerful example, let us suppose that you have a system which performs the following operations:

(a) Establish a temporary work file.
(b) Execute a program which incorporates all the items on the

ORDERS.INWARD file with those on the ORDER.IN.PROGRESS file, and creates control records on the work file. This program might also create dictionary definition items on the TEMP.WORK file.

(c) List the control records held on the work file.

(d) Delete the work file.

(e) Log off.

All these operations could be performed by a sequence of TCL commands and Access statements in a Proc, as shown in Listing 7.1. When the Proc is invoked, it will process each of the operations in turn.

```
PQ
HCREATE-FILE (TEMP.WORK 1,1 19,1
P
HRUN PROGS NEW.ORDERS
P
HSORT TEMP.WORK CUSTOMER DATE BALANCE
P
HDELETE-FILE (TEMP.WORK
P
HOFF
P
```

Listing 7.1

You might save this Proc on your MD with a name such as ADD.ORDERS and then type this name whenever you wish to invoke the Proc:

ADD.ORDERS

and the five operations will proceed without any intervention from the user. In this way, you are really extending the range of Pick facilities and building your own vocabulary.

7.1   THE PROC BUFFERS

Proc does not have *variables* in the same sense as other programming languages. The fundamental entities involved when writing Procs are the *buffers*. The *input* buffer holds the TCL command which invoked the Proc, and the *output* buffer is where your Proc will generate a TCL command and from which this TCL command will be passed to the TCL processor for execution.

There are two output buffers: the *primary output buffer* – which contains the TCL command, as described above – and the *secondary output buffer*, or *stack* – which is used to hold data which may be required to feed the process invoked by the command in the primary output buffer.

Uses of the stack are described in Section 7.10.3. To a certain extent, the input buffer can be considered as a work area into which data are input from the keyboard, stored, moved and manipulated.

The Proc processor considers these buffers to be dynamic arrays, and notes which parameter (attribute) of each buffer is being processed by having *pointers* to point to the current parameter. Certain Proc statements move these pointers, whilst other statements do not.

When data go into the buffer as the Proc is invoked, all spaces are converted to attribute marks, and when data are passed from the output buffer to the TCL processor, all attribute marks are converted to spaces. Thus, if we type the command:

```
SORTFILE T STOCK 1000 2000
```

to invoke the Proc *SORTFILE* which is shown in Listing 7.7, the input buffer actually contains:

```
SORTFILE^T^STOCK^1000^2000
```

and, if we build the output buffer to look like this:

```
SORT^STOCK^>="1000"^AND <="2000"
```

then this will be passed as:

```
SORT STOCK >="1000" AND <="2000"
```

for processing by the P command.

7.1.1   Moving data into the buffers

As the above Procs illustrate, data are moved into the output buffer by statements such as:

```
HSORT
```

which places the word SORT into the output buffer, or

```
A
```

which copies the current parameter from the input buffer into the current parameter of the output buffer, and then advances the pointers to both buffers, or the statement

```
A3
```

which copies the third parameter of the input buffer into the current parameter of the output buffer and advances the pointers. A form such as:

```
A"5
```

will set the input buffer pointer to 5, then copy the fifth parameter of the input buffer into the current parameter of the output buffer and enclose the value in quotation marks, and then advance the pointers.

To move data into the input buffer, you will use the form:

```
IHSORT
```

which places the word SORT at the end of the input buffer, or in the current buffer position.

If you want to move the word SORT to a specific parameter in the input buffer, say parameter 1, then you will use the statement S1 to position the current input buffer pointer, like this:

```
S1
IHSORT
```

If there are several words on an H or IH statement, then these will be placed in *successive* parameters of the destination buffer. Thus, if the input buffer originally looked like this:

```
THE^CAT^SAT^ON^THE^MAT
```

and we issued the statements:

```
S2
IH1 2 3 4
```

then the input buffer will look like this:

```
THE^1^2^3^4^SAT^ON^THE^MAT
```

the four values 1, 2, 3 and 4 being inserted into the position occupied by parameter 2, and creating new parameters in the input buffer. The IBH statement allows us to move the spaces as well, so that the statements:

```
S3
IBHAAA BBB CCC
```

will now produce:

```
THE^1^AAA BBB CCC^3^4^SAT^ON^THE^MAT
```

The S statement moves the input buffer pointer to the position specified *or* to the end of the input buffer, whichever is encountered first. Thus, if we were now to issue the statements:

```
S11
IHXXX
```

the S11 parameter will only move the pointer to the end of the buffer, so that our input buffer will now contain:

```
THE^1^AAA BBB CCC^3^4^SAT^ON^THE^MAT^XXX
```

Later Pick implementations allow you to refer directly to these buffers and their parameters. The input buffer is known as % and the output buffer as #. Each individual parameter is identified by a reference of the form %2 = the second parameter of the input buffer, %7 the seventh parameter of the input buffer, #3 the third parameter of the output buffer, and so on. These implementations also allow you to move data and literals between these buffers by statements such as:

MV #1 "SORT" to move the word SORT into the output buffer.
MV #2 %3 to move the third parameter of the input buffer into the second parameter of the output buffer.

This is much easier to use, and more powerful, than the H, IH and A statements.

7.2 LOOKING AT PROC

One of the advantages of interactive computing such as that offered by Pick, is the *try it and see* approach. If you are in doubt about the effect of any command or statement, it is a simple matter to write a small routine to test it. This same approach is useful when writing a program or a Proc. By writing a small Proc with a few statements, it is possible to enhance this gradually until it eventually does all you need.

Let us demonstrate this with a small Proc which lists our *STOCK* file. We would use the Editor to create this Proc, let us call it *SORTFILE*, and hold it on the MD. The first version might look like that shown in Listing 7.2.

```
PQ
HSORT STOCK
P
```

Listing 7.2

To execute this Proc we simply type in the name:

```
SORTFILE
```

and this will generate and then issue the Access sentence:

```
SORT STOCK
```

Let us now change this Proc so that we ask the user to specify the name of the file to be processed, instead of using the *STOCK* file every time. This Proc is shown in Listing 7.3.

This version will be invoked as before, but will now ask the user for

```
PQ
HSORT
O
OWHAT IS THE NAME OF THE FILE+
IP?
IF A = END X
A
P
```

Listing 7.3

the name of the file. If the user types the name *PERSONNEL* when asked, then the Proc will generate the Access sentence:

SORT PERSONNEL

An alternative version uses the S2 statement to put the user's answer into the second parameter of the input buffer, where it is then referred to as A2. This version may be easier to follow, as shown in Listing 7.4.

```
PQ
HSORT
O
OWHAT IS THE NAME OF THE FILE+
S2
IP?
IF A2 = END X
A2
P
```

Listing 7.4

Let us extend the Proc further so that it asks the user whether the report is to be displayed on the screen or printed on the printer, as

```
PQ
HSORT
O
OWHAT IS THE NAME OF THE FILE+
S2
IP?
IF A2 = END X
A2
1 O
OOUTPUT TO THE SCREEN OR THE PRINTER? S / P+
S3
IP?
IF A3 = END X
IF A3 = S G 3
IF A3 # P G 1
H LPTR
3 P
```

Listing 7.5

shown in Listing 7.5. If our user gives the file name INVOICES in response to the first message, and the destination P to the second message, then the Proc will generate the Access sentence:

SORT INVOICES LPTR

We can extend this further to ask the user for the range of item-ids which are to be included in the report, as shown in Listing 7.6. If our user gives the responses, STOCK, P, 1000 and 2000 to the four requests from our Proc, then this will generate the Access sentence:

SORT STOCK LPTR >= "1000" AND <= "2000"

The statements A"4 and A"5 enclose the parameters in quotation marks as they move them to the output buffer.

```
PQ
C
C PROC INVOKED BY COMMAND SORTFILE
C
C DATA IS ENTERED CONVERSATIONALLY:
C
C NAME OF FILE
C OUTPUT DEVICE = S / P
C START OF ITEM-ID RANGE
C END OF ITEM-ID RANGE
C
HSORT
O
OWHAT IS THE NAME OF THE FILE+
S2
IP?
IF A2 = END X
A2
1 O
OOUTPUT TO THE SCREEN OR THE PRINTER? S / P+
S3
IP?
IF A3 = END X
IF A3 = S G 3
IF A3 # P G 1
H LPTR
3 O
OSTART OF RANGE+
S4
IP=
O
OEND OF RANGE+
S5
IP=
H >=
A"4
H AND <=
A"5
P
```

Listing 7.6

It is usual to hold such large Procs on a separate file, rather than on the MD. So we might copy this Proc – exactly as it is here – and save it as item *SORTFILE* on the file *MYPROCS*. The item on the MD will now look like this:

```
PQ
(MYPROCS SORTFILE
```

or, since the Proc on the MD has the same item-id as the Proc held on the *MYPROCS* file, we could write this more simply as:

```
PQ
(MYPROCS)
```

and the Proc will be invoked exactly as before, but the Proc on the MD would pass control to the Proc held on the file *MYPROCS* with the item-id *SORTFILE*.

If we wish to enable our users to type in all the parameters as they invoke the Proc, like this:

```
SORTFILE STOCK P 1000 2000
```

then we could further change the Proc to the version shown in Listing 7.7.

```
PQ
C
C PROC INVOKED BY:   SORTFILE file device start end
C
C NO DATA VALIDATION IS PERFORMED
C
HSORT
A2
IF A3 # S H LPTR
H >=
A"4
H AND <=
A"5
P
```

Listing 7.7

This is about as far as most people go with Procs, using them to issue a stream of TCL commands.

From the original use illustrated in the above examples, Proc has been extended until, on some implementations, it is a complete programming language with facilities for:

• Data input from the terminal keyboard during execution.
• Printing messages and results on the terminal screen.

- Printing messages and results on the printer on some implementations.
- Data input and output from data files on some implementations.
- Data processing – moving data around within the Proc.
- Arithmetic processing on integer values.
- Logical operations – comparison of values.
- Program control by means of IF and GOTO statements.
- Data conversion using the conversions and correlatives used by Access.
- Internal sub-routines.
- External sub-routines.

Procs also allow you to:

- Issue any command which can be issued at TCL, including those which invoke Basic programs and other processes and supply them with data, Access sentences or TCL verbs.
- Lock operations invoked from the Proc, thus preventing several users performing the same operation simultaneously.
- Use special and standard user exits for such utilities as date and time retrieval.

Procs do not allow you to do some of the things which other languages do. Arithmetic is limited to simple addition, subtraction, division and multiplication, and this only with integer quantities. You cannot process magnetic-tape files directly in Proc. However, you can invoke a Basic program from your Proc to perform any of these actions. The actual facilities offered will vary according to the implementation.

Let us have a look at some of the Proc statements.

Table 7.1

+	F-WRITE	IF E	P	STOFF
−	F;	IF S	PH	STON
A	FB	IFN	PL	T
B	FBU	IH	PP	TR
BO	G	IN	PW	U
C	GO	IP	PX	Uxxxx
D	GO B	IS	RI	X
F	GO F	IT	RO	[ ] n
F-CLEAR	GOSUB	L	RSUB	[file item]
F-DELETE	H	MARK	RTN	( ) n
F-FREE	IBH	MV	S	(file item)
F-OPEN	IBN	MVA	SP	
F-READ	IBP	MVD	SS	
F-UREAD	IF	O	ST	

7.3   THE PROC STATEMENTS

Table 7.1 above shows the Proc statements which you might encounter on your implementation. We shall have a look at the most important of these statements. A full description is given in the *Proc Reference Manual* for your implementation.

7.3.1   Proc input statements

Let us take a look at some of the Proc input statements. The form which we used above:

```
IP?
```

will display the prompt character ?, then accept a response from the user, and then place this response in the current parameter of the primary input buffer.

If you enter several words – separated by spaces – at such an input, then each word will be regarded as a separate parameter of the buffer. Thus, if the input buffer originally contained:

```
AAA^BBB^CCC^DDDD^EEEE E ^FFF
```

and you entered:

```
EVELYN SMITH
```

in response to the sequence:

```
S2
IP?
```

then the input buffer would contain:

```
AAA^EVELYN^SMITH^CCC^DDDD^EEEEE^FFF
```

However, if we had used the sequence:

```
S2
IBP?
```

instead of the IP, then the blank would be inserted, and the input buffer would contain:

```
AAA^EVELYN SMITH^CCC^DDDD^EEEEE^FFF
```

The IP statement, then, inputs data into the primary input buffer. There are two further input statements: IS to input data into the secondary input buffer and IN to input data into whichever is active of the primary or the secondary input buffers. You may specify any single prompt character – we used ? in the above examples. There are two statements to switch on (or, activate) one of the two input buffers: SS to set the secondary buffer as active, and SP to set the primary buffer as active.

Those implementations which permit direct addressing of the buffer parameters also offer forms such as:

```
IN%2
IBN#3
IBN&2.1
```

allowing you to input data into other than the input buffer.

7.3.2   Proc output statements

We have already seen how the O statement can be used to display messages on the screen:

```
OFINISHED
OWHAT IS THE NAME OF THE FILE+
```

If the statement ends with a + sign, then the cursor will be held in position after displaying the message.

To display a parameter of the input buffer, you may use a statement of the form:

```
D2
```

which will display parameter 2 of the input buffer. This, too, may be followed by a + sign, so that a sequence such as:

```
OTHE VALUE OF PARAMETER 2 IS "+
D2+
O"
```

might display a message such as:

```
THE VALUE OF PARAMETER 2 IS "EVELYN"
```

The simple statement:

```
D
```

will display the current parameter of the active input buffer, and the statement:

```
DO
```

will display the entire contents of the active input buffer, attribute marks and all.

More flexible output to the terminal is performed by the Proc T statement:

```
T element{,element}{,element}  . . .
```

where *element* is one of the following:

"text" is the character string which is to be displayed. This must be enclosed in quotation marks.

(c,r) indicates that the cursor is to be positioned at column *c* on line *r*. Either *c* or *r* may be direct or indirect buffer references.

(c) indicates that the cursor is to be moved to column *c* of the current line. *c* may be a direct or indirect buffer reference.

(,r) indicates that the cursor is to be moved to line *r* in the current column. This form is not allowed on some implementations where only the *(c,r)* format may be used.

(−n) some implementations offer special screen effects codes:

(−1) clears the screen.
(−2) positions the cursor *home*.
(−3) clears the rest of the screen.
(−4) clears the rest of the current line.
(−5) switches the blinking display on.
(−6) switches the blinking display off.
(−7) switches screen-protect on.
(−8) switches screen-protect off.
(−9) moves the cursor back one column
(−10) moves the cursor up one row.

+ this, when used as the last element in a statement, holds the cursor in the current position, thus allowing later displayed output to be appended to the current line. Certain implementations do not have this + element, and in such cases the cursor is always held after executing a T statement.

B rings the terminal bell.

C clears the screen.

D causes a delay before continuing.

I*i* converts the integer value *i* to its equivalent ASCII character. The parameter *i* must have a value in the range 0–255 inclusive.

L loops back the last T marker in this statement. The loop will be carried out three times, and then the output operation will continue with the element following the L element.

S*r* displays *r* spaces.

T marks the beginning of a loop which will be terminated by an L statement.

U moves the cursor up one line.

X*x* converts the hexadecimal value *x* to its equivalent ASCII character. The parameter *x* must have a value in the range 00–FF inclusive.

Other elements are available on some implementations:

r is a direct or indirect buffer reference and causes the contents of that buffer to be displayed.

r:output: indicates that the contents of direct or indirect buffer reference *r* are to be displayed subject to the Access output conversion applied before displaying. For example %10:MD2:

r;input; indicates that the contents of direct or indirect buffer reference *r* are to be displayed subject to the Access input conversion applied before displaying. For example %7;D;

A long T statement may be continued onto several lines, if necessary, by ending each incomplete line with a comma. The continuation lines do not begin with a T, as illustrated in Listing 7.8.

```
T C, (15, 0), "CODE VETTING", B, (5, 5), "ENTER YOUR USER CODE:  ", +
IN

T C, "***** DAILY UPDATE RUN ***** DATED ***** ", %3

T C, (15, 15), "END OF JOB"

T (5, 1), "NUMBER: ", S60, (13), &1. O,
(7, 3), "NAME: ", S60, (13), &1. 1,
(4, 5), "ADDRESS: ", S60, (13), &1. 2

T C, "NAME ", T, "======== ", L, "DATE"
```

Listing 7.8

Those implementations which offer output direct to the printer, or the spooler, perform this by means of the L statement. The general format of this statement is:

L *element*{,*element*}{,*element*} . . .

where *element* is one of the following:

"text" is the character string which is to be printed.

(c) indicates that the next element is to be printed in column *c*. *c* may be a direct or indirect buffer reference.

+ inhibits carriage-return/line-feed at the end of the L statement, thus *holding* the printer in position for later printed output.

C closes the print file and dumps accumulated printout.

E ejects to the top of the page.

n indicates that 'n' blank lines are to be skipped.

The elements *r*, *r:output:* and *r;input;* may also be available, as described above.

As with the T statement described above, an L statement may be continued onto several statement lines, by ending each line with a comma if it is to be continued. The continuation lines do not begin with an L, as illustrated in Listing 7.9.

```
L  HDR, T, (25), "PAGE ", P
L  (4), "NAME: ", %1, (25), "NUMBER: ", &1. O
L  E
L  "DATE  JOINED: ", &5. 7: D2:
L  E, "END OF JOB"

L  (10), "TIME:   ", %7: MT: ,
(10), "DATE:   ", %8: D2/: ,
(20), "NAME: ", (10), &3. 2
```

Listing 7.9

The LN statement forces subsequent L output to the terminal, such as might be required for debugging purposes. There are no other elements in this statement.

Headings and pagination are controlled by the L HDR statement which has the general form:

L **HDR**, *element*{,*element*}{,*element*} . . .

and this is used to specify a heading which is to be used at the top of all subsequent pages.

The elements used in the statement may be any of:

"text" see above.

(c) see above.

P prints the current page number. This element may only be used in an L HDR statement.

T prints the current time and date. This element may only be used in an L HDR statement.

Z zeros the current page number in a heading. This element may only be used in an L HDR statement.

The elements *r*, *r:output:* and *r;input;* may also be available, as described above.

Listing 7.9 shows some examples of the various L statements.

7.4 ARITHMETIC IN PROC

There are two statements for performing simple integer addition and subtraction:

+105

will add 105 to the current parameter in the input buffer, and

-27

will subtract 27 from the current parameter in the input buffer.

A statement of the form S2 is normally used to position the buffer pointers at the parameter on which the arithmetic is to be performed. This can be used for simple loop control, as in the sequence shown in Listing 7.10. In this Proc the S2 statement points to the second parameter in the input buffer, the IH0 statement moves 0 to that parameter of the input buffer, and the subsequent + and A2 (attribute) references also relate to that same parameter.

```
PQ
S2
IH0
10 C PROCESS GOES HERE
  :
  :
S2
+1
IF A2 # 30 G 10
C CONTINUE WITH PROC
  :
```

Listing 7.10

Advanced implementations offer greater scope for the arithmetic operations by including Access-type F; statements such as:

```
F;%1;10;*;?%3
```

which will multiply the contents of the first parameter of the input buffer by 10, and place the result in the third parameter of the input buffer, or

```
F;%1;%3;*;%7;+;?#5
```

which will multiply together the first and third parameters of the input buffer, add the contents of the seventh parameter to this, and then place the result in the fifth parameter of the output buffer, or

```
F;%1;%2;/;?P
```

which will divide the contents of the first parameter of the input buffer by the contents of the second parameter of the input buffer, and then place the result in the current parameter of the input buffer. Incidentally, subtraction and division operate differently from those of Access.

7.5 USER EXITS AND PROC

For more powerful processing, Proc offers user exits. These are routines designed to perform any special processing which is otherwise not available within the standard Pick system. Despite their name, these routines are usually supplied by the manufacturer rather than you, the user. For example, there may be user exits to:

- Convert all alphabetic characters in a text string to lower case or to capitals.
- Get the current account name.
- Get the current date.
- Get the current time.
- Get the current screen width.
- Get the current terminal number.
- Get the system serial number.
- Pad a numeric field with leading zeros.
- Perform file processing.
- Position the screen cursor prior to printing.
- Remove a specific character from a text string.
- Remove non-alphanumeric characters from a text string.
- Scan a string replacing all occurrences of one character with another character.
- Strip leading zeros from a numeric field.

These routines are available in other areas of the Pick system; as conversions and correlatives in Access as described in Section 4.6.20, with the ICONV and OCONV functions in Basic as described in Section 6.11.1, and within Procs.

```
PQ
S2
U01AD
STOCK 1000 1 P
XCANNOT FIND REQUIRED ITEM
OPRODUCT DESCRIPTION IS '+
D2+
O'
```

Listing 7.11

As an example of a user exit, Listing 7.11 shows a Proc which uses the McDonnell Douglas user exit U01AD to perform file processing. In this particular case, the line following the U01AD line contains or is expected to contain the file name, the item-id, the attribute which is to be read and a code indicating the destination of the data read in. The next line is the action to be taken if the item cannot be found.

Some of the advanced implementations offer comprehensive file-handling statements:

```
F-OPEN 1 STOCK
F-READ 1 1000
F-WRITE 1
F-DELETE 1
F-CLEAR 1
```

These will be described in the appropriate Proc reference manuals.

7.6   STRUCTURED PROGRAMMING TECHNIQUES IN PROC

The structured programming capabilities of Pick Proc include the following features:

- The statement MARK, GO B and GO F can be used instead of statement labels.
- Internal sub-routines = GOSUB and return statement.
- Internal sub-routines may only be called via their numeric statement label

  ```
  GOSUB 1044
  ```

- When using internal and/or external sub-routines, there are no local variables, all variables are the global buffers.
- External sub-routines = [file item] and return statement.
- External sub-routines are identified by the alphanumeric item-id of the item in which they are held

  ```
  [MYPROCS CALC]
  ```

- Nested sub-routines.
- Recursive calls.
- IF . . . and IFN . . . statements.
- The IF statement may have a multi-statement (THEN) clause.
- Nested IF statements

  ```
  IF A1 = YES IF A2 = YES IF A3 = NO GO 100
  ```

- According to the implementation, RTN n and RSUB n may be used to return to the statement which is *n* statements after the calling statement.

Let us have a closer look at some of these structures.

7.6.1   Control statements in Proc

The following statements are used to control the sequence of execution in a Proc, and are similar to those of other programming languages:

GO 10 will pass control to statement 10, that is, to the statement with the label 10.

IF A = 11 GO 20 will pass control to statement 20 if the current parameter of the input buffer is 11.

IF A4 = END XDONE will test the contents of the fourth parameter of the input buffer, and if this is the three letters END, then the Proc will print the message DONE and terminate.

IF A2 = (4N) GO 30 will pass control to statement 30 if the contents of input buffer parameter 2 is four numeric digits. The pattern matching in Proc is similar to that described in Section 6.16.1 for Basic.

IF A5 = Y]YE]YES GO 40 will pass control to statement 40 if input buffer parameter 5 is either Y, YE or YES.

IF A9 = 10]20]30 GO 1]76]92 will inspect the contents of input buffer parameter 9 and pass control to statement 1 if the contents are 10, to statement 76 if the contents are 20, and so on.

All the above comparisons regard the various parameters as simple character strings, *scanning from left to right*. But if we use one of the operators < or > this could produce undesirable effects. For example, if the first parameter of the input buffer contained the value 100 when the statement:

```
IF A1 < 99 GO 10
```

then because of the left-to-right comparison, the value 100 will be considered to be less than 99. This can be overcome by a sequence such as:

```
S1
+100000
IF A1 < 100099 GO 10
```

Some implementations have a numeric IF statement for such situations:

```
IFN A1 < 99 GO 10
```

which does a numeric comparison, and will have the desired effect.
   Some of these forms are not available on all implementations.

7.6.2   MARK, GO B and GO F

The MARK statement sets a control pointer at that position within the Proc. Any subsequent GO B – GO Back – statement will then return to the last physical control pointer.

   The GO F – GO Forward – statement will cause the processing to jump forward to the next physical MARK statement.

These present obvious problems when you are attempting to debug a Proc, and it is recommended that they be used sparingly.

7.6.3 Sub-routines

Internal sub-routines are called by the GOSUB statement:

```
GOSUB 123
```

with the return being accomplished by the RSUB statement.

Some implementations achieve this by modifying the standard call to an external sub-routine statement, for example:

```
[] 123
```

with the return being accomplished by the RTN statement, or by the X statement.

External sub-routines may be called by a statement of the form:

```
[PFILE ITEM99]
```

to pass control to the Proc held as item *ITEM99* on the file *PFILE*. In the called Proc, according to the implementation, an RTN or X statement will return control to the calling Proc.

The statement:

```
(STANDP PRINTA)
```

will pass control to the Proc held as item *PRINTA* on the file *STANDP*, and will not return to the calling program. This is a chaining operation.

7.6.4 Processing the output buffer

We have seen how a TCL command or an Access sentence can be constructed in the Proc output buffer. The command in the output buffer is then executed by means of the P statement.

The following forms are available:

P the simplest form, will process the contents of the output buffer without any of the special actions described below.
PH indicates that no terminal displayed output connected with the execution of that statement will be produced. This includes warning and error messages, as well as program printed output.

This option is used to suppress the system output from such TCL operations as CREATE-FILE, where your users may not be interested in the information which the process displays:

```
HCREATE-FILE (@@DUMMY.WORK.FILE 1,1 19,1
PH
```

PLn indicates that lock number n is to be set by the first user of this Proc, and any attempts to access this Proc by another user will be prevented until the execution invoked by the PLn statement has terminated.

The number n may be any integer 0–63, inclusive. These locks should not be confused with the file-group locks which we met earlier. They are quite arbitrary system locks, and unless they are used with care, they could produce deadly embraces.

PP indicates that the contents of the output buffer are to be displayed at the terminal before execution. When this happens, the user may enter N to abandon the Proc, or S to suppress the processing of the output buffer and continue with the Proc. Any other response will cause the processing of the output buffer to continue.

PW indicates that the contents of the output buffer are to be displayed at the terminal before execution. When this statement is offered, then the PP command does not wait for user intervention before processing.

PX suppresses return to the Proc when the processing has completed.

When execution has terminated, control returns to the Proc statement immediately following the just-executed P statement, except in the case of a PX statement. After processing, the stack will be turned off and both output buffers will be cleared.

7.7   MAINTAINING A PROC

Like Basic programs, Procs are created and maintained by the standard Editor:

```
EDIT MD SORTFILE
```

or

```
EDIT MYPROCS SORTFILE
```

If you want to look at your Proc, you may use either of the commands:

```
COPY MYPROCS SORTFILE (T)
```

or

```
CT MYPROCS SORTFILE
```

to display the Proc on the terminal screen, and

```
COPY MYPROCS SORTFILE (P)
```

or

```
CP MYPROCS SORTFILE
```

to print the Proc on the printer.

The Proc is, of course, executed simply by typing the name of the Proc as it is held on the MD:

```
SORTFILE
```

The language has a few statements which are useful for debugging purposes when developing a Proc. You may use the D, PP or PW statements, as we have already seen, and you may also use the TR statement. The statement:

```
TR ON
```

will activate the trace routine, displaying each statement before it is executed, allowing you to follow the path taken through the Proc, and the statement:

```
TR OFF
```

will switch off the trace routine.

On some implementations, the Proc may be compiled. The act of compilation removes all comments and statement-labels, and resolves the destination of any GO statements as an actual frame address, thereby producing a physically smaller Proc which executes more quickly than its uncompiled counterpart. Such compilation is achieved by means of the command:

```
PQ-COMPILE MYPROCS SORTFILE
```

which will check the syntax of the Proc which is held as item *SORTFILE* on the file *MYPROCS*, and if there are no errors, will produce a compiled version of that Proc. The compiled version is held by the same name, *SORTFILE*, on a separate file specified by the user in response to the PQ-COMPILE message:

```
DESTINATION FILE:
```

Listing 7.12 shows the compiled equivalent of the Proc shown in Listing 7.6. In this particular example, the compiled Proc was 156 bytes smaller than the original version.

```
        Compiled version of the PROC shown in LISTING 7.6
PQ
HSORT
O
OWHAT IS THE NAME OF THE FILE+
S2
IP?
IF A2 = END X
A2
O
```

```
OOUTPUT TO THE SCREEN OR THE PRINTER? S / P+
S3
IP?
IF A3 = END X
IF A3 = S 0019
IF A3 # P FF9E
H LPTR
O
OSTART OF RANGE+
S4
IP=
O
OEND OF RANGE+
S5
IP=
H >=
A"4
H AND <=
A"5
P
```

Listing 7.12

7.8   ADVANTAGES OF PROCS

Proc is a way of simplifying the use of set routines and standard pieces of processing by, effectively, establishing a new vocabulary within the TCL repertoire. Thus, if Doris in Accounts or Fred down in Progress Chasing want to produce standard reports or make standard inquiries, they may do this by means of Access, as we have seen elsewhere, or the analyst may establish the necessary commands on the master dictionary to produce a user-friendly repertoire of commands, such as DORIS1 to produce the outstanding orders, DORIS2 to list the unpaid accounts, FRED1 to list the late deliveries, and so on.

Proc is an interpretive processor, that is, the statements are processed as they are encountered, unlike Basic which has to be compiled first. This means that Proc is quicker to invoke. However, as with any interpretive processor, any syntax errors will only be detected when the erroneous statement is encountered for execution.

7.9   DISADVANTAGES OF PROCS

If you wish to do more than simply generate Access sentences and TCL commands, you will realize that Proc is not an easy language to write. The statements themselves are almost at Assembler language level. The buffers are the only means of storing data during execution, and their use requires more than a little practice. This is true even on the most advanced implementations, where, for example, the statement to move a string ABCD into the first element of the input buffer might be:

```
MV %1 "ABCD"
```

A programmer or analyst who is concerned with processing which is more sophisticated than simply invoking TCL commands, should consider invoking a Basic program.

On those implementations which offer the EXECUTE or TCL statements in Basic, allowing your programs to issue TCL commands and Access statements and then continue processing the Basic Program, *the use of Procs will become negligible or even obsolete.*

7.10   TIPS AND TECHNIQUES – PROCS

Since a Proc is used at TCL level, it must be held on the master dictionary. As the number of Procs increases, so the master dictionary can become large and cumbersome, thus rendering the seeking and processing of any TCL command a slow operation. To overcome this, you should hold your Procs on a separate file with only a simple pointer on the master dictionary. Thus, if the actual statements for Proc *DORIS1* are held on the file *MYPROCS*, then these may be invoked via a simple Proc comprising only:

```
PQ
(MYPROCS DORIS1)
```

or, more simply,

```
PQ
(MYPROCS)
```

which will be held on the master dictionary with the item-id *DORIS1*. You will then invoke the Proc by typing:

```
DORIS1
```

at TCL level.

7.10.1   To simulate sequential access – Proc

In those implementations which offer file processing and a PQ-SELECT facility in Proc, sequential access can be achieved much more simply in Procs then in Basic. The sequence shown in Listing 7.13 illustrates this.

The SSELECT sentence may have any valid Access format, and generates the select list. This solution then uses the PQ-SELECT verb to place the contents of the select list into a Proc select register – register 1 in this case. The successive elements are picked up from this register and placed into parameter 1 of the input buffer by means of the statement:

```
MV %1 !1
```

```
F-CLEAR 1
F-OPEN 1 STOCK
XNO STOCK FILE
HSSELECT STOCK BY DESCRIPTION
STON
HPQ-SELECT 1
P
10 MV %1 !1
IF # %1 G 20
F-READ 1 %1
GO 10
C PROCESS RECORD HERE
:
GO 10
20 CONTINUE
```

Listing 7.13

The end of the list is tested by the statement:

```
IF # %1 G 20
```

this means *if there are no data in the first parameter of the input buffer, then go to statement number 20*, and this will, therefore, pass control to statement 20 when the selected list has been exhausted.

There are five such select registers, !1 through to !5, and each use of the !1 identifier removes the top element from the register. Once a select list has been placed in one of these registers, the list may be re-initialized to start at the first element again by means of a sequence such as:

```
HPQ-RESELECT 1
P
```

without issuing the SELECT sentence again.

7.10.2   To suppress Proc messages

When you are creating files, copying items or, indeed, when performing any TCL operation which generates a message at the terminal, you may inhibit the message by using the

```
PH
```

statement to Hush the messages, instead of the usual P statement, as described in Section 7.6.4.

This is recommended when, for example, your Proc creates a work file. The actual nature and location of the work file is of no consequence to your users, and the ordinary CREATE-FILE verb displays messages showing the FID, *MOD* and *SEP* of the file. By using PH like this:

```
PQ
HCREATE-FILE (@@DUMMY.WORK.FILE 1,1 19,1)
PH
```

the output messages will not be displayed, thus rendering the Proc less mysterious to the non-technical user.

7.10.3 To use the stack

The stack is another name for the second of the two output buffers. It is used to hold data which are to feed the process which is invoked by the command held in the primary output buffer.

It can be used with the Editor, as shown in Listing 7.14, which deletes the item *ITEMY* from the file *FILEX*. It can also be used to COPY items to another file, as shown in Listing 7.15, or it can be used to generate and save a selected list, as shown in Listing 7.16.

```
PQ
HED FILEX ITEMY
STON
HFD
P
```

Listing 7.14

```
PQ
HCOPY STOCK *
STON
H(STOCK2
P
```

Listing 7.15

```
PQ
HSSELECT STOCK BY COLOUR
STON
HSAVE LIST STOCK99
P
```

Listing 7.16

If several parameters are to be passed to a Basic program, then this may be done by a sequence such as that in Listing 7.17 which will pass across parameter 2 of the input buffer, and the word YES, and parameter 7 of the input buffer to feed three INPUT statements in the Basic program *P030*. The < character sent by the H< statement has the effect of a carriage-return after each of the various parameters.

```
PQ
HRUN MYPROGS P030
STON
A2
H<
HYES<
A7
H<
P
```

Listing 7.17

The < character must be at the end of the Proc H statement, so we could *not* use:

H<YES<

in place of the two statements:

H<
HYES<

in this last sequence.

Further use of the stack to pass data to a Basic program is illustrated in the following section.

7.10.4   To link a Proc to a program

The concept of modular programming or structured programming is widely accepted as one which improves the speed and efficiency of writing and maintaining a computer system. An entire task may be divided into a number of smaller units. The work may then be allocated to a number of programmers, each unit being written, developed and tested individually, before being linked together in a final test.

Pick lends itself ideally to such a structure, and as a systems analyst, you should remember that:

(a) Data may be passed quite easily between the various modules.
(b) The various modules may be written in any of Basic or Proc in order to take best advantage of the facilities offered by the two languages.
(c) The Proc modules may invoke any TCL statements. Simple activities such as creating a work file, clearing the contents of a file and deleting an old file may be performed quite simply.
(d) The Proc modules may invoke Access statements. Access reports can be easily produced instead of writing – and maintaining – elaborate report programs.

Here, we look at the ways in which the programmer can pass control between Basic programs and Procs, and we also see how data can be carried across during such transfers.

Program to program linkage was covered in Section 6.18 when we looked at external sub-routines in Basic, and Proc to Proc linkage in Section 7.6.3 when we looked at external sub-routines in Proc.

A program is invoked from a Proc in the same way that it would be invoked at TCL. That is:

```
RUN MYPROGS PROG182
```

when the program is held as item *PROG182* on the file *MYPROGS*. The relevant section of the Proc might be:

```
HRUN MYPROGS PROG182
P
```

When the program has been catalogued with the name PROG189, you will invoke the program simply by its name:

```
PROG189
```

The relevant section of the Proc might look like this:

```
HPROG189
P
```

How are the data passed across?

Data may be passed to the Basic program as conversational data which are to be read from the Proc stack by means of INPUT statements within the program. In the example shown in Listing 7.18, the four data values

```
PQ
HRUN MYPROGS PROG182
STON
H1234<
HSMITH<
H01/02/59<
HNO<
P
```

Listing 7.18

1234, SMITH, 01/02/59 and NO will be read into the program *PROG182* by the first four INPUT statements, for example:

```
INPUT CLOCKNO
INPUT NAME
INPUT EXTERNAL.DATE
INPUT OPTION
```

To pass control from a Basic program to a Proc, you can use the simple CHAIN statement which is discussed in Section 6.21.7.

Some implementations offer a pair of statements which allow a Basic program to handle the data in the Proc input buffer. These are:

```
PROCREAD FRED ELSE . . .
```

which will retrieve the Proc input buffer as a dynamic array and place it into the variable FRED. The ELSE condition is taken if the program has not been invoked from a Proc. The dynamic array can then be manipulated as necessary, and the result placed back into the Proc input buffer by the statement:

```
PROCWRITE FRED
```

before terminating the program – by means of the STOP or END statement – and returning to the Proc.

7.10.5 Complex processing in Proc

We have seen that the processing powers of Proc can be limited to keyboard input, simple arithmetic, displayed or printed output, and invoking TCL commands. For more powerful operations such as file and record handling, or complex arithmetic, you should pass control to a Basic program. A typical sequence can be seen in Listing 7.19 which shows a Proc called *PROC1*, which passes control to a Basic program – *PROGRAMA* – and this, in turn, passes control to a further Proc *PROC2*.

```
THE PROC --- PROC1 ---------------------------------------

PQ
HRUN MYPROGS PROGRAMA
STON
A2
H<
A3
H<
A4
P

THE PROGRAM --- PROGRAMA --------------------------------

INPUT PARM2;  ** FROM PROC
INPUT PARM3;  ** FROM PROC
INPUT PARM4;  ** FROM PROC
*
* PERFORM CALCULATION / PROCESSING
* AND PUTS RESULTS INTO RESULT1, RESULT2 ETC
*
CHAIN 'PROC2 ':RESULT1:' ':RESULT2
END

THE PROC --- PROC2 ---------------------------------------

PQ
C A2 CONTAINS RESULT1 FROM PROGRAMA
C A3 CONTAINS RESULT2 FROM PROGRAMA
C
C PROC PROCESSING FOLLOWS
:
```

Listing 7.19

8
Runoff

For many years, computers have been used to process data in the form of numbers, bank balances, sales figures, salaries and so on. But only within the last few years has the concept of *word-processing* come to the fore. Nowadays, most large offices have dedicated word-processing equipment, and most users of microcomputers are familiar with the concepts of Wordstar and other proprietary packages.

Runoff is the text-processing system offered on the Pick operating system and a standard part of Pick software. Like standard word-processing systems, Runoff is designed to allow you to produce and print documents, such as:

(a) Manuals,
(b) Specifications,
(c) Standard letters,
(d) Any document which may have to go through several stages of alteration and amendment,
(e) Any document which will be required – with or without changes – over and over again,
(f) Any documents which are composed of one or more standard paragraphs or sections,

and will enable you to type the text of your document into the machine, and then:

(a) File a document for use later.
(b) Display a document in the required format on the screen.
(c) Print a document in the required format on the line printer.
(d) Make changes to any part or parts of the text of a document – by inserting, correcting and deleting parts of the text, as required.
(e) Make changes to the format and layout of a document – by changing the page depth, line length, paragraphing, headings and so on.
(f) Incorporate part or parts of other documents already held on the system.

The features of Runoff – and remember that the system was conceived in the 1960s – have long since been overtaken by newer word-processing systems, and for this reason we shall use the term *text processing* to distinguish the primitive features of Runoff from the advanced facilities offered by more sophisticated word-processing systems. If you have used any of the modern packages, then you will soon realize how far word processing has come in recent years. Let us see what Runoff can do.

8.1 LOOKING AT RUNOFF

The simplest way to use Runoff is to create an item holding the text which you want to print. You will use the Editor to create an item looking something like that shown in Listing 8.1. As you can see, this item contains only lines of text, and these lines can be as long or as short as we like with any number of spaces between the words.

```
This is the ANNUAL REPORT of the HARLINGTON DAHLIA SOCIETY AND
CHRYSANTHEMUM GROWERS' GUILD.
 in the report, we shall review the year's progress
and look forward to the Society's plans for next
year.     we shall also        present     the membership figures.
these figures have been audited by Mrs Whiteley.
```

Listing 8.1

Let us suppose that we have saved this piece of text as the item *MEETING* on a file called *REPORTS*. Then to display this report, we should type the command:

```
RUNOFF REPORTS MEETING
```

or, to print the report, we should type the command:

```
RUNOFF REPORTS MEETING (P)
```

The printed report is shown in Fig. 8.1. Notice how the Runoff processor re-organizes the lines as it prints them, padding them out to the correct length by inserting extra spaces between the words. You may also have

```
        This  is  the  ANNUAL REPORT  of the  HARLINGTON DAHLIA
SOCIETY AND CHRYSANTHEMUM GROWERS' GUILD.

        In  the  report, we shall review the year's progress and
look forward to the Society's plans for next year.   We shall
also present the   membership  figures.    These   figures have
been audited by Mrs Whiteley.
```

Figure 8.1

noticed that where we put a space at the beginning of a line in the input item, the Runoff processor takes this to mean that we want to start a new paragraph. In the printed document, the first line of each paragraph is indented by five spaces.

If we use the .NOJUSTIFY command, then we can stop the processor padding the lines to the correct length, and the command

```
.PARAGRAPH 0
```

will stop the indentation on the first line of each paragraph. If we use these two commands, then our item will look like that shown in Listing 8.2, and the printed document as that shown in Fig. 8.2. The Runoff commands begin with a full stop at the start of the line, and they are on separate lines, away from the text of the document.

```
. NOJUSTIFY. PARAGRAPH 0
 this is the ANNUAL REPORT of the HARLINGTON DAHLIA SOCIETY AND
CHRYSANTHEMUM GROWERS' GUILD.
 in the report, we shall review the year's progress
and look forward to the Society's plans for next
year.      we shall also      present      the membership figures.
these figures have been audited by Mrs Whiteley.
```

Listing 8.2

```
This is the ANNUAL REPORT of the HARLINGTON DAHLIA SOCIETY
AND CHRYSANTHEMUM GROWERS' GUILD.

In the report, we shall review the year's progress and look
forward to the Society's plans for next year.  We shall also
present the membership figures.  These figures have been
audited by Mrs Whiteley.
```

Figure 8.2

So far so good. But what if we want to include a table of information in our text? How can we get Runoff to leave the information exactly as we type it in? The NOFILL command – meaning *do not fill up the printed lines to the full line length* – will do this for us. Then we use the FILL command to switch the filling action on again. We use these commands in the item shown in Listing 8.3. The resultant document is shown in Fig. 8.3.

Let us add a few more lines of text – the items on the agenda – and indent them. We can use the command:

```
.INDENT MARGIN 5
```

to shift the margin five places to the right, and then use the command:

```
.INDENT MARGIN −5
```

to shift it back again. This is shown in the item in Listing 8.4, and the resultant printed document shown in Fig. 8.4.

```
. NOJUSTIFY. PARAGRAPH 0
 this is the ANNUAL REPORT of the HARLINGTON DAHLIA SOCIETY AND
CHRYSANTHEMUM GROWERS' GUILD.
 in the report, we shall review the year's progress
and look forward to the Society's plans for next
year.      we shall also      present      the membership figures.
. NOFILL

                 LAST YEAR           THIS YEAR

HDS members         132                 401
CGG members         391                 423
                 =========           =========
TOTAL               523                 624

Subs             £1046               £1872
. FILL
 these figures have been audited by Mrs Whiteley.
```

Listing 8.3

```
This is the ANNUAL REPORT of the HARLINGTON DAHLIA SOCIETY
AND CHRYSANTHEMUM GROWERS' GUILD.

In the report, we shall review the year's progress and look
forward to the Society's plans for next year.  We shall also
present the membership figures.

                 LAST YEAR           THIS YEAR

HDS members         132                 401
CGG members         391                 423
                 =========           =========
TOTAL               523                 624

Subs             £1046               £1872

These figures have been audited by Mrs Whiteley.
```

Figure 8.3

```
. NOJUSTIFY. PARAGRAPH 0
 this is the ANNUAL REPORT of the HARLINGTON DAHLIA SOCIETY AND
CHRYSANTHEMUM GROWERS' GUILD.
 in the report, we shall review the year's progress
and look forward to the Society's plans for next
year.      we shall also      present    the membership figures.
. NOFILL

                LAST YEAR            THIS YEAR

HDS members         132                  401
CGG members         391                  423
                =========            =========
TOTAL               523                  624

Subs              £1046                £1872
. FILL
 these figures have been audited by Mrs Whiteley.
 other items on the agenda are:
. INDENT MARGIN 5
 1) the Exhibition and Flower Show for next year.
 we must choose the venue by the end of next month.
 2) is the annual competition to be continued
or will it be coupled with
the Upper Soddington Fair?
 Mr Smarte to report to the committee.
. INDENT MARGIN -5
   Any other business
```

Listing 8.4

```
    This is the ANNUAL REPORT of the HARLINGTON DAHLIA SOCIETY
    AND CHRYSANTHEMUM GROWERS' GUILD.

    In the report, we shall review the year's progress and look
    forward to the Society's plans for next year.   We shall also
    present the membership figures.

                LAST YEAR            THIS YEAR
    HDS members     132                  401
    CGG members     391                  423
                =========            =========                .
    TOTAL           523                  624

    Subs          £1046                £1872

    These figures have been audited by Mrs Whiteley.

    Other items on the agenda are:

            1) The Exhibition and Flower Show for next year.

        We must choose the venue by the end of next month.

            2) Is the annual competition to be continued or will it
        be coupled with the Upper Soddington Fair?

        Mr Smarte to report to the committee.

    Any other business
```

Figure 8.4

```
. NOJUSTIFY. PARAGRAPH 0
 this is the ANNUAL REPORT of the HARLINGTON DAHLIA SOCIETY AND
CHRYSANTHEMUM GROWERS' GUILD.
 in the report, we shall review the year's progress
and look forward to the Society's plans for next
year.        we shall also        present      the membership figures.
. NOFILL

                    LAST YEAR              THIS YEAR

HDS members             132                   401
CGG members             391                   423
                    =========              =========
TOTAL                   523                   624

Subs                  £1046                  £1872
. FILL
 these figures have been audited by Mrs Whiteley.
 other items on the agenda are:
. INDENT MARGIN 5
. INDENT -3
 1) the Exhibition and Flower Show for next year.
 we must choose the venue by the end of next month.
. INDENT -3
 2) is the annual competition to be continued
or will it be coupled with
the Upper Soddington Fair?
 Mr Smarte to report to the committee.
. INDENT MARGIN -5
 any other business
```

Listing 8.5

This is the ANNUAL REPORT of the HARLINGTON DAHLIA SOCIETY
AND CHRYSANTHEMUM GROWERS' GUILD.

In the report, we shall review the year's progress and look
forward to the Society's plans for next year.   We shall also
present the membership figures.

                    LAST YEAR   THIS YEAR

HDS members   132   401
CGG members   391   423
                    =========   =========
TOTAL   523   624

Subs   £1046   £1872

These figures have been audited by Mrs Whiteley.

Other items on the agenda are:

   1) The Exhibition and Flower Show for next year.

      We must choose the venue by the end of next month.
   2) Is the annual competition to be continued or will it be
      coupled with the Upper Soddington Fair?

      Mr Smarte to report to the committee.

Any other business

Figure 8.5

If we use the command:

`.INDENT -3`

as shown in Listing 8.5, this will indent the very next line by −3 spaces, causing the numbers to *stick out* to the left, as shown in Fig. 8.5.

Let us just review the commands which we have used:

```
.FILL              .F
.INDENT            .I
.INDENT MARGIN     .IM
.NOFILL            .NF
.NOJUSTIFY         .NJ
.PARAGRAPH         .P
```

These commands, and the abbreviated forms shown alongside, are enough to let you do a lot of text processing. If you want to do other, more sophisticated things, then you should have a look at Section 8.3 where we discuss some of the other Runoff commands.

There is one final Runoff command that we might look at here. This is the SET TABS command which will allow us to enter the table of information a little more easily. We use the command:

`.SET TABS 17,25,35,43`

to set *tabulator stops* in columns 17, 25, 35 and 43 – just like the tab stops of an ordinary typewriter – and then use the special character < to shift the following text across to start on the next tabulator stop, and the character > to shift the text across to end on the next tabulator stop. We switch the tabulator stops off with the SET TABS 0 command when we have finished. This is shown in Listing 8.6. Notice that, in this final example, we have used the abbreviated forms of the Runoff commands, and we have also put several commands on one line. The resultant document is shown in Fig. 8.6.

```
. NOJUSTIFY. PARAGRAPH 0
 this is the ANNUAL REPORT of the HARLINGTON DAHLIA SOCIETY AND
CHRYSANTHEMUM GROWERS' GUILD.
 in the report, we shall review the year's progress
and look forward to the Society's plans for next
year.       we shall also        present        the membership figures.
. NF. SET TABS 17,25,35,43

<LAST YEAR<THIS YEAR

HDS members>>132>>401
CGG members>>391>>423
<=========<=========
TOTAL>>523>>624
```

```
Subs>>£1046>>£1872
. F. SET TABS 0
 these figures have been audited by Mrs Whiteley.
 other items on the agenda are:
. IM 5
. I -3
 1) the Exhibition and Flower Show for next year.
 we must choose the venue by the end of next month.
. I -3
 2) is the annual competition to be continued
 or will it be coupled with
 the Upper Soddington Fair?
 Mr Smarte to report to the committee.
. IM -5
 any other business
```

Listing 8.6

```
This is the ANNUAL REPORT of the HARLINGTON DAHLIA SOCIETY
AND CHRYSANTHEMUM GROWERS' GUILD.

In the report, we shall review the year's progress and look
forward to the Society's plans for next year.   We shall also
present the membership figures.

                     LAST YEAR           THIS YEAR

HDS members             132                 401
CGG members             391                 423
                     =========           =========
TOTAL                   523                 624

Subs                  £1046               £1872

These figures have been audited by Mrs Whiteley.

Other items on the agenda are:

   1) The Exhibition and Flower Show for next year.

      We must choose the venue by the end of next month.

   2) Is the annual competition to be continued or will it be
      coupled with the Upper Soddington Fair?

      Mr Smarte to report to the committee.

Any other business
```

Figure 8.6

8.2   USING RUNOFF

The main processes which are involved when you use the Runoff system are creating the document, displaying or printing the document, correcting the document, and finally deleting the document when it is no longer needed. The main emphasis in this cycle is on the correct and print stages. Let us look at these more closely.

8.2.1 Creating and changing a Runoff document

The text of a document – or a part of a document – is held as an item on a file, and is created, maintained and filed away by means of the standard Editor:

```
EDIT MYDOCS CONTRACT85
```

specifying the name of the file and the item which you are processing.

You will remember that the Editor is a very simple – but powerful – way of changing an item. If you have used those sophisticated word-processing systems – such as Jet and Textpro – which reformat the text and the document on the screen, then you will find the Editor somewhat naive by comparison.

The Editor, of course, doesn't concern itself with the content of the item which you are editing, nor whether you are entering a personnel record, a Basic program, a Runoff command or a piece of text, and you have the full range of Editor commands at your disposal.

When you are typing Runoff commands, you should remember the following points:

- All Runoff commands begin with a full stop.
- The full stop must begin in column 1.
- Runoff is sensitive about the format of its commands. You must spell the keywords correctly and specify any parameters in the correct format.
- Some of the Runoff commands may be abbreviated: NF for NOFILL, IM for INDENT MARGIN and so on, as shown in Table 8.1 on p. 323.
- The Runoff commands are not shown when the final document is printed. They merely give instructions about the *format* of the document.
- There may be several Runoff commands on each command line, in which case the commands will follow each other with no space between. For example:

```
.IM 5
.NF
.SK
```

may be entered on one line as:

```
.IM 5.NF.SK.
```

and when you are typing in the text lines, you should remember the following points:

- The text may consist of any combination of capital letters, lower-case letters, numbers and the special characters discussed below.
- The text is always held exactly as you type it in. Runoff does not re-format or re-organize your text – neither on the screen nor on the item which you are creating and saving on file.
- The first character of a text line must not be a full stop, otherwise it will be interpreted as a Runoff command.
- The text may be entered in lines of any length – in order to make it easier to edit and change the text, it is preferable to keep lines as short as possible.
- There may be any number of blank spaces between the words and at the end of a line, although this is wasteful of space and unnecessary.
- A new paragraph is indicated by the Runoff PARAGRAPH com-mand, by a blank line or by putting one or more spaces before the first letter of the line – this is the simplest method.
- For reasons of ease and efficiency when manipulating the text, it is preferable to start each new sentence on a new line.

If you wish to incorporate all, or just a part, of another document which already exists on file, then you may use the Editor command:

`ME999/DOC34/`

to copy the document into your current document and then change it as you wish. If you wish to incorporate an entire document unchanged, a standard clause, for example, then you can use the Runoff command:

`.READ STANDARDTEXT CLAUSE45`

and Runoff will read in the required piece of text when you print your document. The latter method is recommended, because, if *CLAUSE45* is ever changed, all documents which use that clause will also change when they are next printed.

8.2.2 Printing a Runoff document

The Runoff verb allows you to print the contents of an item containing your text. Any Runoff commands in the item will be interpreted by the Runoff processor to determine the shape and form of the final document.

`RUNOFF MYTEXT DOC233`

which will display the document on the screen. When a Runoff document is being displayed on the terminal screen, the system will pause at the end of each page, and you must then press <RETURN> to continue with the next page. If required, the process can be abandoned at this stage by pressing the <CONTROL> X character, or the <CONTROL> E character on some implementations, instead of <RETURN>.

If you want to print the document on the printer, then you will use the form:

```
RUNOFF MYTEXT DOC233 (P)
```

The P option directs the document to the spooler. The Runoff reference manual will give details of the other options and their effects.

If you wish to combine several separate sections to produce a single document, then you can do this most easily by specifying them on the Runoff command:

```
RUNOFF CONTRACTS PARA1 PARA2B PARA3 PARA4C (P)
```

which is much simpler than having READ commands within the documents. The effect of this sequence would be exactly the same as having a single item – let us call this *WORKDOC* – which contains the commands:

```
.READ CONTRACTS PARA1
.READ CONTRACTS PARA2B
.READ CONTRACTS PARA3
.READ CONTRACTS PARA4C
```

and then issuing the command:

```
RUNOFF CONTRACTS WORKDOC (P)
```

In both these cases, the effect of any Runoff commands will carry over into the following document. One useful difference is that, if item PARA2B is missing, then the first Runoff command will simply ignore the missing item, whereas the command:

```
.READ CONTRACTS PARA2B
```

will abort the production of the remainder of the document in the second case.

A select list or a saved list may also be used to specify the items to be processed, as in a sequence such as:

```
SSELECT CONTRACTS = "[SALES]" AND = "[JBC]"
RUNOFF CONTRACTS (P)
```

A document produced by means of Runoff will, of course, look like any other computer printout. For high-quality output, other devices such as letter-quality terminal printers, are available. It is also possible to Runoff your document to a magnetic tape and use this as input for phototype-setting equipment to produce top-quality documents.

If you simply want to inspect a copy of the raw text and Runoff commands which make up the item, then you may use either of the commands:

```
COPY MYTEXT DOC233 (T)
```

or

```
CT MYTEXT DOC233
```

to display the item on the terminal screen, and

```
COPY MYTEXT DOC233 (P)
```

or

```
CP MYTEXT DOC233
```

to print the item on the printer.

8.2.3   Deleting a Runoff document

Your old documents are deleted by means of the Editor, or by means of the TCL command:

```
DELETE file item
```

In practice, you will find that your old documents are rarely deleted. Instead, a process of cannibalization and evolution takes place whereby one document serves as precedent and source for later documents.

8.3   RUNOFF COMMANDS

Table 8.1 shows the commands which are available in Runoff. The forms in parentheses are acceptable abbreviations for the keywords. Remember that each command is preceded by a full stop, and several commands may be included on one line. Thus, the following four sequences are equivalent:

```
.IM 5
.NF
.SK 5

.IM 5.NF.SK 5

.INDENT MARGIN 5.NOFILL.SKIP 5

.IM 5.NOFILL.SKIP 5
```

Table 8.1

*	NOCAPITALIZE SENTENCES (NCS)
BEGIN PAGE (BP)	NOFILL (NF)
BOX	NOJUSTIFY (NJ)
BREAK (B)	NOPAGING
CAPITALIZE SENTENCES (CS)	NOPARAGRAPH
CENTER (C)	PAGE NUMBER
CHAIN	PAPER LENGTH
CHAPTER	PARAGRAPH (P)
CONTENTS	PRINT
CRT	PRINT INDEX
FILL (F)	READ
FOOTING	READNEXT
HEADING	RESET MARGIN (RM)
HILITE	SAVE INDEX
INDENT (I)	SECTION
INDENT MARGIN (IM)	SET SECTION
INDEX	SET TABS
INPUT	SKIP (SK)
JUSTIFY (J)	SPACE (SP)
LEFT MARGIN	SPACING
LINE LENGTH	STANDARD
LOWER CASE (LC)	TEST PAGE
LPTR	UPPER CASE (UC)

We have already met some Runoff commands, so let us have a further look at the action of some of the more common commands. Full details are given in the *Runoff Reference Manual* for your implementation.

8.3.1 * Text

This allows you to put comments in your document. The text is ignored by the Runoff system and does not appear in the final printed document. For example:

```
* PUT NEW SALES FIGURES HERE LATER
```

8.3.2 BEGIN PAGE

This causes a skip to a new page. The processor will space to the foot of the page and print the page footing, if there is one. It then skips to a new page. The page number is incremented by 1 and the page heading, if there is one, is printed.

8.3.3   CAPITALIZE SENTENCES

This is a default command, and specifies that the first letter of a new sentence is to be capitalized. This is illustrated in the text shown in Listing 8.1. The sentences were entered in lower-case letters, but the resultant document has capital letters at the start of each sentence. The action is cancelled by the NOCAPITALIZE SENTENCES command.

8.3.4   CENTER

This causes the text on the next (single) line to be printed in the centre of the page, and is effective in FILL or NOFILL mode. If you wish to centre a number of lines, then each line must be preceded by a C command, as shown in Listing 8.7. The output from this sequence is shown in Fig. 8.7. Notice the American spelling of the word CENTER.

```
. SK. C
*********************************
. SK. C
JOHN SMITH AND CO LTD
. SK. C
ANNUAL REPORT
. SK. C
YEAR ENDING 31 MARCH 1985
. SK. C
*********************************
```

Listing 8.7

```
*********************************

        JOHN SMITH AND CO LTD

          ANNUAL REPORT

     YEAR ENDING 31 MARCH 1985

*********************************
```

Figure 8.7

8.3.5   FILL

This is possibly the most useful feature of Runoff, and causes all sub-sequent text lines to be re-formatted when the document is printed, so that they fill the page width. Excess spaces between words in the input text are reduced to single spaces, and lines which are longer than the page width are truncated and the superfluous words are carried on to the next line.

If the JUSTIFY action is in effect, then extra spaces are inserted between the words in the output text so that the lines are of the required LINE LENGTH.

The filling action is cancelled by the NOFILL command, as we saw in Section 8.1 where we displayed tabular information within our document.

8.3.6 HEADING AND FOOTING

The HEADING command is used to specify a heading which is to appear at the top of every page, and the FOOTING command is used to specify a footing which is to be printed at the foot of every page. The contents of the heading or footing are specified on the line immediately following the HEADING or FOOTING command.

Certain characters have special significance when enclosed in single apostrophes within a FOOTING or HEADING command:

T prints the time and the date in the format:

10:30:59 01 JAN 1987

D prints the current date in the format:

01 JAN 1987

L skips to a new line within the heading.
P prints the current page number, left-justified.
PP prints the current page number, right-justified within a field of four spaces.

These are exactly the same as for headings and footings in Access and Basic. The sequence shown in Listing 8.8, for example, will produce the footing as shown in Fig. 8.8. Note that the footing must be written on a

```
.FOOTING
ANNUAL REPORT: PAGE NUMBER 'PL'PRODUCED:   'D'
```

Listing 8.8

```
ANNUAL REPORT: PAGE NUMBER 1
PRODUCED: 01 JAN 1987
```

Figure 8.8

single line, although the use of the L parameter means that several output lines may be represented by this footing specification.

8.3.7   INDENT n

This indents the next line by the specified number of spaces. If you specify a negative identation, such as:

`.INDENT -3`

as we did in Section 8.1, then the next line will overhang to the left.

8.3.8   INDENT MARGIN n

This causes the left margin to be moved the specified number of places to the right of the current setting. If the shift is negative, then the margin is moved to the left on the current setting. This shift is relative to the current setting as was illustrated in the text used in Section 8.1, where we used the commands:

`.INDENT MARGIN 5`

and

`.INDENT MARGIN -5`

to move the paragraphs dealing with the agenda.

8.3.9   INDEX 'text'

This causes an entry to appear in the Runoff index, and this index will be printed when a PRINT INDEX command is encountered. The index will show the text of the index entry followed by the page number(s) on which the entry was printed. The following examples illustrate the use of this command:

.INDEX 'BUDGET'   and   .INDEX BUDGET will cause the single entry BUDGET to appear in the index.
.INDEX BUDGET PLANS FORECAST will cause the three entries BUDGET and PLANS and FORECAST to appear in the index.
.INDEX 'BUDGET PLANS' will cause the single entry BUDGET PLANS to appear in the index.

8.3.10   JUSTIFY

This puts Runoff into JUSTIFY mode, causing the filled text lines to be padded with random spaces between the words so that the right-hand edge of the paragraphs is even, as shown in Fig. 8.1. This action is cancelled by the NOJUSTIFY command.

8.3.11 LINE LENGTH n

This re-sets the maximum number of characters per line. If you have not issued this command, then default values will be taken from the terminal characteristics, as described in Section 5.5 where we discussed the TERM command. The value specified for the line length is absolute, each command overriding the effect of any previous such command.

8.3.12 PARAGRAPH n

This causes any blank line, or line beginning with a space, to be considered as the start of a new paragraph. The simple command:

.P

has the same effect as the BREAK command. But with a numeric parameter, such as:

.P 5

it causes the first line of all subsequent paragraphs to be indented by five spaces; the second and subsequent lines of the paragraph will not be indented.

This is illustrated by the example shown in Listing 8.9 which uses the PARAGRAPH command in conjunction with the INDENT MARGIN command. The resultant document is shown in Fig. 8.9.

8.3.13 PAGE NUMBER n

This sets the page number used in HEADING and FOOTING to the number specified.

8.3.14 PAPER LENGTH n

This re-sets the maximum number of lines per page. If you have not issued this command, then default values will be taken from the terminal characteristics, as described in Section 5.5 where we discuss the TERM command. The value specified for the paper-length is absolute, each command overriding the effect of any previous such command.

8.3.15 READ {DICT} {fffff} iiiii

This causes the contents of item *iiiii* on file *fffff* to be incorporated into the text at this point. If the file name is omitted, then the name of the

```
. NJ
 the important points to note are as follows:
. IM 5
. P -3
 1) the rate will be dependent upon the demands
 2) any special changes must be discussed with Head Office before
they may be considered
 3) all special changes will be notified to management.
. P 0
 this must be done in writing to the following members of staff:
. IM 5
. P -2
 * the chief accountant
 * the head of sales
 * the head of marketing
 * all regional sales and marketing staff. only
those within a distance of 40 miles of the customer concerned need
be notified.
 * the accounts clerks
. IM -5
. P -3
 4) the changes will become effective one month from the date
of such communications
. IM -5. P 0
 this note will be observed by
all members of staff concerned with such changes.
```

Listing 8.9

```
        The important points to note are as follows:

    1) The rate will be dependent upon the demands

    2) Any special changes must be discussed with Head Office
       before they may be considered

    3) All special changes will be notified to management.

       This must be done in writing to the following members
       of staff:

           * The chief accountant

           * The head of sales

           * The head of marketing

           * All regional sales and marketing staff.  Only
             those within a distance of 40 miles of the
             customer concerned need be notified.

           * The accounts clerks

    4) The changes will become effective one month from the
       date of such communications

 This note will be observed by all members of staff concerned
 with such changes.
```

Figure 8.9

current file, or the name of the file on the last READ or CHAIN statement, will be used. The following are acceptable forms of this command:

```
.READ DICT ALLDOCS ITEMA
.READ FILEN DOC32
.READ CONTRACTS 5
.READ PARA5
```

8.3.16 SECTION n text

This allows you to specify section headings, the number indicating the level of section heading. The level may be any of 1, 2, 3, 4 or 5. A number greater than 5 will be taken as 5. Section numbering is carried out automatically, each CHAPTER command incrementing the first section level by 1, and each SECTION command incrementing the appropriate section level by 1. The section number is printed in the form:

```
1.2.3.4.5
```

The text shown on the SECTION command will be used as the heading for that section, and will appear in the Table of Contents which is generated if a CONTENTS command is subsequently issued. Listing 8.10 shows a simple document which contains SECTION commands. Fig. 8.10 shows the document as it would appear and the Table of Contents.

```
. SECTION 1 AAAAAAAAAAAAAAAAA
 TEXT for section A
. SECTION 2 BBBBBBBBBBBBBBBBBB
 TEXT for section B
. SECTION 2 CCCCCCCCCCCCCCCCC
 TEXT for section C
. SECTION 3 DDDDDDDDDDDDDDDDD
 TEXT for section D
. SECTION 1 EEEEEEEEEEEEEEEEE
 TEXT for section E
. SECTION 2 FFFFFFFFFFFFFFFFF
 TEXT for section F
. SECTION 3 GGGGGGGGGGGGGGGGG
 TEXT for section G
. CONTENTS
```

Listing 8.10

1 AAAAAAAAAAAAAAAAA

     TEXT for section A

1. 1 BBBBBBBBBBBBBBBBB

     TEXT for section B

1. 2 CCCCCCCCCCCCCCCCC

     TEXT for section C

1. 2. 1 DDDDDDDDDDDDDDDDD

     TEXT for section D

2 EEEEEEEEEEEEEEEEE

     TEXT for section E

2. 1 FFFFFFFFFFFFFFFFF

     TEXT for section F

2. 1. 1 GGGGGGGGGGGGGGGGG

     TEXT for section G

-------------- SKIP TO A NEW PAGE AT THIS POINT ------------
                    TABLE OF CONTENTS

Figure 8.10

8.3.17 SKIP n and SPACE n

The SKIP command causes a skip of the specified number of blank lines. If the printing is near the foot of the page and there is insufficient space for the required SKIP, then the command has the same effect as the BP command.

If it is essential that a space of, say, fifteen lines is to be left – you may want to insert a diagram or an illustration later – then you should use the command:

```
.SPACE 15
```

which will ensure that a gap of at least fifteen spaces is left at that point in the document.

8.3.18 STANDARD

We have seen that it is possible to print a Runoff document without the use of any commands. This is because there are certain default commands assumed whenever Runoff is invoked. If you have issued any Runoff commands and then want to return to these defaults, then you may use the STANDARD command to achieve this.

The command re-sets the standard settings:

```
CAPITALIZE SENTENCES
FILL
INDENT MARGIN 0
JUSTIFY
LEFT MARGIN 0
LINE LENGTH – taken from terminal characteristics
PAPER LENGTH – taken from terminal characteristics
PARAGRAPH 5
```

8.4 RUNOFF CONTROL CHARACTERS

There are certain characters, or combinations of characters, which have special significance to Runoff. If any of these characters is encountered within the text of a document, then the character itself will not be printed and certain actions will be taken. These control characters allow you to:

(a) Print a character string in CAPITALS.
(b) Print a character string in lower case.
(c) Underline a character string. This is used for headings and titles.
(d) Print a character string in **boldface**. This is achieved by overprinting the relevant part of the line.

(e) Shift character strings to start or end at the next TAB STOP.

The Runoff control characters are as follows:

∧ prints the *following letter only* in *capitals*.

\ prints the *following letter only* in *lower case,* and is useful for overriding the normal capitalization of the first letter of a sentence/paragraph.

∧∧ puts Runoff *in* the *capitalization* mode, producing all subsequent output in that mode.

\\ takes Runoff *out* of the *capitalization* mode.

& *underlines* the *following character only.* This is particularly important and means that an ampersand must be preceded by the underscore character if it is to appear in the text. Thus, text which is to appear as:

JOHN SMITH & CO LIMITED

must be entered as:

JOHN SMITH _& CO LIMITED

If it were entered simply as:

JOHN SMITH & CO LIMITED

then it would be printed as:

JOHN SMITH _CO LIMITED

on the printer. On the screen terminal, however, it would appear (after a subliminal flash of the true text) as:

—

because underlining is achieved by first printing the actual line, and then overprinting a line of spaces with _ characters in the required position.

The choice of & as a control character in a text-processing system is a little unexpected.

&∧ puts Runoff *in* the *underline* mode, producing all subsequent output in that mode.

&\ takes Runoff *out* of the *underline* mode.

@∧ puts Runoff *in* the *boldface* mode, producing all subsequent output in that mode.

@\ takes Runoff *out* of the *boldface* mode.

< if tabulator stops have been set by means of the SET TABS commands, then the < character shifts the next word to start at the next available tabulator stop. If there is no SET TABS command in effect, then this character ceases to be a special control character and is printed without any special effect.

> shifts the next word to finish at the next available tabulator stop, if these have been set by the SET TABS commands.

_ prints the *following character* exactly as it is, and will be used if you want to print one of the above 'reserved' control characters, as illustrated with the use of & above.

These characters will appear amongst the text of your document.

If you have a matrix printer, some implementations have a special control character which will allow you to print a line in *large (double-width) letters* or even to print a line of characters sideways.

The effect of some of these characters is illustrated by the item shown in Listing 8.11, and the resultant document shown in Fig. 8.11.

```
. NJ
. C. SK
&^ANNUAL REPORT OF MESSRS JOHN BROWN _& CO LTD&\
 The last year has been one of the most important
in the Company's
history. we have had several new ventures:
. IM 3. P -3
 \a) The formation of ^^JB _& C management services\\ in the
^southern ^region, and
 \b) the merger of JBC(S) and JBC(N) to form JBC(U)
. IM -3. P 5
 we shall discuss these later in this report, together with the
plans for the coming year.
```

Listing 8.11

```
        ANNUAL REPORT OF MESSRS JOHN BROWN & CO LTD

        The last year has been one of the most important in the
Company's history.   We have had several new ventures:

a)  The formation of  JB & C MANAGEMENT SERVICES  in the
    Southern Region, and

b)  the merger of  JBC(S) and  JBC(N) to form  JBC(U)

        We shall discuss these later in this report, together
with the plans for the coming year.
```

Figure 8.11

8.5 ADVANTAGES OF RUNOFF

If it is used carefully, Runoff offers you most of the features of any text-processing system. The text of the present book was prepared using

Runoff, and used most of the techniques which you will need in your text-processing activities:

(a) Justification of the text.
(b) Pagination and page-numbering.
(c) Indentation and text formatting.
(d) Chapter and section numbering.
(e) Table of contents.
(f) Indexing.
(g) Combining several individual documents to form the whole. Each section is held as a separate item.

Since Runoff uses simple Pick items, and each document or part of a document may be held as a separate item, it fits in comfortably and quite compatibly with all other areas of Pick. Many of the examples and lists used in this book were composed by taking them from other files, such as the MD, and copying them into the file holding the text of the book.

This compatibility means that it is relatively easy to write small programs to make up for what Runoff lacks, particularly in such areas as:

(a) Splitting a document into its separate sections and sub-sections, and saving each section as a separate item. This makes better utilization of the disk space and speeds up the access time when reading the documents.
(b) Combining several small documents into one, and saving these as a single document. This simplifies the task of making several parts of a document uniform.
(c) Re-formatting the document by breaking the text into units of lines of text down into smaller lengths to render them more easily manageable with the Pick Editor.
(d) Checking the syntax of Runoff commands.
(e) Scanning a number of documents for the occurrences of specific character strings. The Pick Editor, of course, allows this only within a single document.

8.6 DISADVANTAGES OF RUNOFF

By comparison with many of the latest word-processing systems, Runoff has many drawbacks and shortcomings:

(a) All text must be created and maintained by the standard Pick Editor. This requires each user to become familiar with the Editor commands.
(b) There are no facilities for graphics, diagrams or illustrations.

(c) There are no simple ways to input foreign languages.

(d) Technical and scientific formulae are difficult to handle.

(e) Special typefaces and founts cannot be incorporated into the text.

(f) The Runoff commands must be entered explicitly.

(g) You must keep control over the commands which you use. Too many INDENT MARGIN commands, for example, will result in a very narrow, or even non-existent, page width.

Clearly, then, Runoff is not suitable for the casual or the non-technical user. Indeed, the ability to store and print text is the most that many people make of Runoff, typing in their text exactly as they want it to appear – or more accurately, making do with the text they have typed in.

It is because of these shortcomings that, on some implementations of Pick, the features of Runoff are enhanced by the simplified input, output and editing features offered by the commercial packages Jet and Superjet or by the McDonnell Douglas Textpro package.

8.7   USING RUNOFF IN PROCS

Runoff – or its more sophisticated relatives Jet, Superjet and Textpro – are not used as widely as they should be. Even when producing large specifications and reports, many analysts still use the typist, Tipp-Ex and the photocopier to produce their printed material. You should consider Runoff – or its relatives – for any textual matter, even for simple memos. If a document has to undergo major revision, then the stronger is the case for using a text-processing system. For this reason, it is worth teaching members of the clerical and secretarial staff to use the text-processing powers of Runoff – despite the disadvantages which we have just enumerated.

Let us now see how Runoff may be used for purposes other than printing documents.

You can use Runoff within your Procs to simplify the production of menus and other screen displays. Listing 8.12 shows a simple Proc which invokes Runoff to display a menu, and then uses Proc statements to accept the user's response and proceed accordingly. The format of the *MENUA* item which holds the menu is shown in Listing 8.13, and the appearance of the menu on the screen is shown in Fig. 8.12.

This technique has several advantages:

(a) The actual menu text can be easily incorporated into the program documentation. It is for this reason that the final Runoff command:

```
.F.SET TABS 0.IM -5.SK
```

is included in the above examples.

```
PQ
C GENERAL FILE PROCESSING HARNESS
10 HRUNOFF MYTEXT MENUA
P
O                 OPTION+
11 IN
IF A = 1 (MYPROCS PN1)
IF A = 2 (MYPROCS PN2)
IF A = 3 (MYPROCS PN3)
IF A = 4 (MYPROCS PN4)
IF A = 5 (MYPROCS PN5)
IF A = 6 (MYPROCS PN6)
IF A = END X
OINVALID OPTION.    TRY AGAIN+
G 11
```

Listing 8.12

```
. C
*** GENERAL FILE UPDATE UTILITY ***
. NF. SK 3. SET TABS 15. IM 5
1<CHANGE TO NEW FILE
2<ADD ITEMS TO FILE
3<INSPECT ITEMS ON FILE
4<DELETE ITEMS ON FILE
5<CHANGE TO NEW ITEM
6<COPY ITEMS TO ANOTHER FILE
END<TERMINATE ACTIVITY
. F. SET TABS 0. IM -5. SK
```

Listing 8.13

```
            *** GENERAL FILE UPDATE UTILITY ***


        1               CHANGE TO NEW FILE
        2               ADD ITEMS TO FILE
        3               INSPECT ITEMS ON FILE
        4               DELETE ITEMS ON FILE
        5               CHANGE TO NEW ITEM
        6               COPY ITEMS TO ANOTHER FILE
        END             TERMINATE ACTIVITY
```

Figure 8.12

(b) Time, effort and space can be reduced by using the Runoff tabulation facilities, as in the above example.
(c) The effective size of the Proc is reduced and simplified for maintenance purposes.
(d) The Runoff menu can be modified more easily than the corresponding Proc O and T statements.

Runoff can also be used for displaying user instructions, prior to starting a program, in a simple Proc such as:

```
PQ
HRUNOFF MYTEXT MSG001
P
HRUN MYPROGS ANALYSIS
P
```

which uses the items MSG001 shown in Listing 8.14.

For these reasons, it is worthwhile looking at Runoff and the text-processing aspects of Pick and considering their use when designing Pick application systems.

```
. * THESE ARE THE INSTRUCTIONS FOR THE ANALYSIS PROGRAM
. HEADING
'D'           ***** MYPROGS ANALYSIS PROGRAM *****
 this is the analysis program.
 Before you start the program, you should have
the latest ledger sheets.
. FOOTING
'L'PRESS RETURN WHEN YOU ARE READY TO START
```

Listing 8.14

8.8 JET

Before we leave this topic, let us have a brief look at the advantages of word-processing packages such as Jet over the simple features of Runoff.

The most attractive attribute of Jet is that it is screen-oriented. Whenever a piece of text is corrected or re-organized, the new appearance of the text is displayed immediately on the screen – what you see is what you get! The screen cursor is controlled from the keyboard and moves through the text of your document, skipping from word to word, from sentence to sentence, or from paragraph to paragraph. The position of the cursor determines where your corrections and changes are to be made.

Quite simply, Jet is user-friendly, offering inquiry and help facilities, displaying a status line with prompts and messages, and providing *ruler* lines specifying the format, margins and tabulator settings for your text.

Jet is used in two principal modes: JET-IN to create, change and correct your text:

```
JET-IN TEXTS CHAPTER1
```

```
JET-IN TEXTS CHAPTER5 CHAPTER7
```

and JET-OUT to display the final text on the screen or to print it on the printer:

```
JET-OUT TEXTS CHAPTER1
```

```
JET-OUT TEXTS CHAPTER1 (P)
```

The documents are held on a normal Pick file, called *TEXTS* in these examples, and the format of the items is controlled by Jet.

There is also the JET-EDIT facility which is a separate routine offering a means of creating and maintaining Procs, Basic programs, dictionary definition items and other information – even Runoff documents – in a way which is much simpler than the standard Pick Editor:

```
JET-EDIT MYPROGS CALCRTN
```

8.8.1 JET-IN

JET-IN allows you to create, correct and change your Jet documents. In addition to the textual material, your Jet document also contains command lines which are similar to the Runoff commands which we saw earlier:

```
\bp
\footing
\heading
\justify
\page width
\read TEXTS CHAPTER1.1
```

and ruler lines to specify the format of the text.

(a) Entering text

When you begin to process a new document, JET-IN automatically accepts the text for the document. Subsequently, you may change the text and input additional text by moving the cursor to the required position within the document and then using the keys:

I to insert a new piece of text, starting at the current cursor position.

L to insert a new line after the current line.

R to replace – character for character – starting at the current cursor position.

W to replace the word at the current cursor position.

In each case, the screen image of the document is modified as the new text is entered, and the activity is terminated by pressing the escape – ESC – key.

When you are in the I, L, R or W states, the keys on the keyboard have their normal meaning to input the text for your document. When you are not inputting text – that is, when you are outside the I, L, R and W states – the keys on the keyboard have a special significance in invoking the Jet editing functions and in cursor positioning.

(b) Cursor positioning

In order to identify the part of your document which is to be changed, you will move the cursor to the required position before entering the I, L, R or W states. The following keys move the cursor:

T moves the cursor to the top left-hand corner of your document.

B moves the cursor to the bottom – the end – of your document.

<RETURN> moves the cursor back to the beginning of the current line.

^ moves the cursor to the end of the current line.

6 advances the cursor to the following character.

4 moves the cursor back to the previous character.

9 advances the cursor to the start of the following word.

7 moves the cursor back to the start of the previous word.

1 advances the cursor to the start of the following sentence.

3 moves the cursor back to the start of the previous sentence.

} advances the cursor to the start of the following paragraph.

{ moves the cursor back to the start of the previous paragraph.

The choice of these keys is based upon the layout of the numeric key-pad:

7	8	9
4	5	6
1	2	3

The S – search – function will locate the cursor at a specific word, and the G – go to – function will move the cursor to a specific line within the document.

(c) Function keys

Still outside the I, L, R and W states, the keys of the keyboard have a special significance for editing, deleting, replacing, moving, inserting and saving the text of your document. The most commonly used of these keys are:

? display a list describing the action of all the function keys.
D delete the current character.
E edit the ruler.
K delete the current line.
M merge text from this or another document.
O display the document starting at the current line.
] cut – save a section of the text for use later.
P paste – recover a previously cut section of text.
Q delete the current word.
V switch the VIEW on and off. When VIEW is on, all command lines and rulers are displayed.
Y delete the current sentence starting at the cursor position.
Z transpose the current character and the following character.
! change all words in the current line from capitals to lower case, or vice versa.
* change all letters in the current word from capitals to lower case, or vice versa.
: change the current letter from capitals to lower case, or vice versa.

When you are satisfied with your document, you will save it by means of Jet functions which are similar to those of the Editor:

FI file the document and leave the Jet processor.
FS file the document and remain within the Jet processor.
FD delete the document and leave the Jet processor.
FX abandon the current document – rather like the EX command of the Editor.
FK abandon the current document and all subsequent documents – rather like the EXK command of the Editor.

(d) Control keys

The special effects, such as underlining, which Runoff achieves so laboriously by means of special characters within the text, are obtained with Jet by using the CTRL key as you type in your text. The control keys are:

CTRL-B to switch boldface printing on.
CTRL-D to switch boldface printing off.
CTRL-V to underline words and blanks.
CTRL-W to underline words, but not blanks.
CTRL-X to switch underlining off.

Jet, of course, implements the appropriate effects as it displays the text on the screen during entry.

(e) Rulers

Rulers are used to specify the format of your document, and look something like this:

L	>	A	A	C	Z	R

The characters within the ruler are :

L setting the position of the left-hand margin.
R setting the right-hand margin.
> allowing data to be right-justified to this position.
< allowing data to be left-justified at this position.
·   allowing numeric data to be aligned around the decimal point in this position.
A setting the tabulation stop.
C setting the centre tab stop.
Z setting the start of the hyphenation zone. When text is being entered, and a word extends outside the zone specified by the Z and R characters, Jet will indicate that this word must be hyphenated.

Rulers are created and changed by means of the E function, and there may be any number of rulers within a document, each one remaining in operation until replaced by a subsequent ruler.

(f) Spelling check

The U function is used to switch the spelling-check feature on and off. When this feature is active, as each word is entered, Jet will check the presence of the word in a file called *WORDS*. If the word cannot be found in this dictionary, the Jet will ask:

`word spelled correctly?`

and, according to your response, will allow you to correct the word, accept the word or add it to the dictionary for future reference.

The | function will invoke a check of the spelling of all the words in an existing document.

(g) Incorporating data into a document

Jet offers simple facilities for incorporating data from the keyboard, and from other Pick files, into a document as it is being printed with JET-OUT. This is achieved by entering one of the control commands:

```
~INPUT
~INSERT
~READNEXT
```

within the text of your document. For example, if the text contained the line:

```
Thank you for your inquiry of ~INSERT and I enclose
```

then JET-OUT would require the user to enter a value at the keyboard, and this value would be inserted at the appropriate place within the printed document, to produce something like this:

```
Thank you for your inquiry of 1st January and I
enclose
```

The Jet command line:

```
\prompt
```

could be used to display a message when demanding the data from the keyboard operator.

The ~INSERT command might appear in your document like this:

```
Your balance is currently ~INSERT CUSTOMER BALANCE
and we
```

and JET-OUT would read the field, as defined by the Access definition *BALANCE*, from the *CUSTOMER* file, and incorporate this into the printed document. The item-ids of the records to be processed are derived from a selected list generated prior to issuing the JET-OUT command.

The ~READNEXT command has a similar effect, except that the data are taken as successive elements from a previously selected list.

8.8.2   JET-OUT

JET-OUT has a number of possible options, the simplest of which is P:

```
JET-OUT TEXTS CHAPTER10 (P)
```

JET-OUT MANUALS PART1 PART2 PART4 (P)

which will direct the document to the printer. The most interesting of the other options are:

L to print line numbers on the document. This is useful when editing a draft document.

Q to indicate that a letter-quality printer is to be used.

S to request proportional spacing instead of random blanks between words when justifying right-hand margins. This is only applicable with letter-quality printers.

The Jet reference literature contains full details of the other options.

9
Security

When you are introducing any computer system, be it a new operating system or a new application, you will inevitably be asked *'What about security?'* What about security? Do you mean:

Stopping people logging on to the system?
Finding out who is logged on to the system?
Finding out who has logged on to the system?
Controlling the work which users carry out?
Stopping users looking at the files?
Finding out who has been doing what?
Stopping users changing the contents of the files?
Finding out who has been changing the files?
Preventing simultaneous updates?
Finding out what changes are made to the files?
Controlling the changes made to the files?
Discovering whether data have been lost or corrupted?
Recovering in case data are lost or corrupted?
Recovering in case the machine goes down?

The question may have implied any – or all – of these. Some of these problems are not specific to Pick. Some of the solutions are.

9.1   STOPPING PEOPLE LOGGING ON THE SYSTEM

The Pick database is divided into accounts. Each account has its own account name and it is this name which is entered at log-on time in order to identify the user. In your company, the computer may be used by both the Sales Department and the Payroll Department, and the files and programs for these two departments would be quite separate, therefore we should expect to have separate accounts for Sales and Payroll.

To afford an extra level of security when logging on to your account, you may also specify a password which is to be entered at log on. Let us suppose that the Payroll Department want their account to be called *WAGES*, and that they want this *WAGES* account to have the password

PAUL. When they, or anyone else, log on to the *WAGES* account, the sequence would look like this:

```
LOGON PLEASE: WAGES,PAUL
```

This is correct, so the computer will accept the user and proceed to do the work required on the *WAGES* account.

If the user enters only the account name:

```
LOGON PLEASE: WAGES
```

then the operating system will demand:

```
PASSWORD:
```

and the user must enter the correct password:

```
PASSWORD: PAUL
```

In this second sequence, most implementations will render the password invisible as it is typed in. So two keys are necessary to get into the Pick operating system. If the account name is wrong, then the system will display:

```
USER ID INCORRECT
LOGON PLEASE:
```

and the user will have to start again. If the password is wrong, then the system will display:

```
PASSWORD INCORRECT
LOGON PLEASE:
```

and the user will have to start again.

There are a few important points to remember about the password:

(a) The password is held as attribute 7 of your account definition item on the *SYSTEM* file. On some implementations the password is held in a coded, non-legible, form, and is changed by a special utility program.
(b) There can only be one password for each account at any one time. The account may, of course, have synonyms with their own password.
(c) The password can be changed whenever you wish and will apply for all users who subsequently log on to that account.
(d) The password is only used when you log on to the account, and it does not affect file security or any other aspect of the Pick security.

9.2   FINDING OUT WHO IS LOGGED ON TO THE SYSTEM

In a large installation with many terminals at many sites and in many places, there is often a need to know who is logged on to the system. You might even want to know what they are doing. The following TCL verbs can help you to do this:

WHO 7 tells you the name of the account which is logged on to terminal number 7.

WHO tells you the name of the account which is logged on this terminal.

WHERE tells you which terminals are logged on, and displays the contents of the return address stack to show what work they are doing. The correspondence between the ABS return address and the process which is being carried out will be shown in the reference manuals for your implementation.

LISTU displays a list of the terminals which are currently logged on, showing their location and when they logged on. This information is taken from the *ACC* file, as described in Section 2.11.1.

CHARGES 8 displays the logging information for terminal number 8, showing the time at which it was logged on, how long it has been logged on, the amount of processing used, and so on, exactly as displayed in the log-off message.

CHARGES displays the logging information for this terminal.

PEEK 9 echoes the actual screen which is currently displayed at terminal number 9.

If there are any unauthorized users, these may be forced off the system by means of the

```
LOGOFF
```

verb. This will ask you for the number of the terminal which is to be logged off. It will then interrupt any processing at that terminal, as if the <BREAK> key had been pressed, and then log the user off.

9.3   FINDING OUT WHO HAS LOGGED ON TO THE SYSTEM

We have already mentioned that whenever a user logs off the system, the operating system displays a message showing the date and time when the user logged on, the date and time when the user logged off, the time for which the user was connected, the amount of CPU time which the user used, and the amount of disk activity which the user's processing demanded. This information is also logged on the *ACC* file if there is a U in attribute 9 of the account definition item for the account, and a report on the information on the ACC file can be produced by Access sentences such as:

```
LIST ACC LPTR
```

We know that the operating system will reject you if you get either the account name wrong or the password wrong, but Pick does not record – or report – any invalid attempts to log on to the system, whether these were accidental failures or fraudulent. Application systems have been developed which get around this by having – as a part of the log-on Proc for each account – a standard routine which demands a further second-ary password from the user. This routine logs the following information on a file:

(a) The name of the account which was used.
(b) The date and time when the user tried to log on.
(c) The terminal which was used.
(d) The secondary password which was entered. Each person could have their own secondary password.
(e) Whether or not the secondary password was accepted.
(f) How many attempts were made before the would-be user was rejected by the system.

During the checking of this secondary password, the <BREAK> key was disabled to prevent users breaking out of the vetting program and thus getting to TCL unhindered.

9.4   FINDING OUT WHO HAS BEEN DOING WHAT

A process and transaction logging system is the best way of finding out what your users have been doing whilst they were logged on to the Pick system. Pick does not have such a recording system, but packages are available to record on a file – or on magnetic tape – the activities of all users who log on to the system – or you could devise your own. The information which might be logged could include:

(a) The user-identification – the account name.
(b) The time and date of log on.
(c) The programs which were used.
(d) The time at which each program was used.
(e) The identity and location of the terminal which was used.
(f) The names of the files which were handled.
(g) The time at which the files were used.
(h) The item-ids of the items which were used.
(i) The time at which the item was accessed.
(j) The appearance of the item before the change.
(k) The appearance of the item after the change.

The overheads on time in performing these routines, and those on space in holding the information, mean that most installations implement only one or two of these features. Thus, if you were handling large amounts of data and it would be inconvenient to have your database return to the state at the last file save, then you might choose to have the transaction logging features to record, on magnetic tape, all changes made to your files. Then, in the event of loss of data, you could recover by using the information logged on the tape to regenerate your files. Furthermore, reports on this information may be produced periodically, or on request, and these may aid in detecting the persons responsible for data corruption.

9.5   STOPPING USERS LOOKING AT FILES

The most effective way of preventing users looking at files is by means of the lock codes which we discussed in Section 3.2.

There will always be people who regard any security measures as a personal challenge, and Pick does not offer much resistance to these people. You can, however, make their task a little harder by:

(a) Using lock codes extensively.
(b) Removing the Q-pointer to the SYSTEM file from all MDs.
(c) Including special characters in your lock codes. For example, ABC is much easier to spot and reproduce than is:

<CTRL> A <CTRL> B <CTRL> C

(d) Regularly using a simple Basic program which re-sets the lock codes on your files *and also on your entry on the SYSTEM file* to randomly selected strings.

Apart from these measures, there are other ways in which you can protect your data by rendering the data on your files illegible. Sensitive data may be encrypted (or encoded) whenever there is a possibility that an unauthorized user may gain access to it. This measure is often adopted for highly sensitive data which are to be accessed from remote terminals as a countermeasure to such risks as wire-tapping. The data would be encoded when they are keyed into the system, and then decoded on output. Clearly, precautions need to be taken to restrict access to the algorithm which performs the encoding and decoding operation. The simplest expedient would be to remove the source code of the relevant algorithms and programs from the machine.

9.5.1   Account synonyms

A synonym account is a means whereby the owner of a Pick account may allow the account to be used by a different name. Thus permitting

various sub-sets of your users to access all or any sub-set of the programs and data files as the main account. For example, the *wages*
account could have synonyms of *timekeeper* and *paymaster*, one to process
the clock-cards and attendance information, and the other to calculate
the wages and salaries. It would be possible to log on to any of the three
accounts – *wages, timekeeper* or *paymaster* – and all three would access the
same files. But you could give each one different lock codes, for example, so that *timekeeper* could not actually look at the employees' salaries.

The synonym account will normally have a different password, lock
codes and privileges from those of the main account, and it may also
invoke a different log-on Proc. In fact, the three are, to all intents and
purposes, separate accounts, except that they all have the same master
dictionary.

9.6   CONTROLLING THE WORK WHICH USERS CARRY OUT –
LOG-ON PROCS

When you log on to your account – let us suppose that the account name
is WAGES – then after validating your account name and password, and
before passing you to TCL level, the operating system will scan your MD
for a Proc called *WAGES*. If there is no such Proc, then you are set to
TCL level. If there is a Proc called *WAGES*, however, then this Proc will
be invoked. Such a Proc must have the same name as the account, that
is, *WAGES* in this illustration, and is known as a log-on Proc.

You will design and create your own log-on Procs, and you will decide
what the Proc is to do. For example, the log-on Proc may ask for extra
user-identification like the secondary password which we looked at in
Section 9.3, or it may display an important message to users of that
account.

More importantly, however, the log-on Proc may call up a standard
program and confine the users to this program, guiding them, prompt-
ing them, controlling them, and restricting the activities which they
perform. This means that your users need not know about TCL commands or how to invoke a Proc or a program – your program takes over
immediately they have logged on. Such a routine is shown below.

As you know, if the users press the <BREAK> key, then they may
interrupt the processing and get back to TCL level. But you can prevent
this, so that any attempt to break out in this way will return the user to
the initial log-on Proc. If you organize your processing in this way, it is
called a closed system

The advantage of a closed system is that the user can be prevented
from accessing any part of the database for which he or she does not
have the necessary authorization, no matter how technically competent

he or she is to do so. All user operations are controlled and monitored by applications programs and the user is never allowed to use the facilities available at a lower TCL level.

Let us see how this can be done. Your master account WAGES, might be defined like this on the *SYSTEM* file:

```
        item-id:  WAGES
   attribute  1:  D
   attribute  2:  599034
   attribute  3:  37
   attribute  4:  1
   attribute  5:  . . . ]ABC
   attribute  6:  QP@ZM
   attribute  7:
   attribute  8:  SYS2(80)
   attribute  9:  L
   attribute 10:  10
```

Let us suppose that you wish to create a synonym account which is to be part of a closed system. Then you will use the Editor to create the following synonym account definition on the *SYSTEM* file:

```
        item-id:  PAYROLL
   attribute  1:  Q
   attribute  2:  WAGES
   attribute  3:
   attribute  4:
   attribute  5:  ABC
   attribute  6:
   attribute  7:
   attribute  8:  SYS1(30)
   attribute  9:  R
   attribute 10:  10
```

This synonym definition will allow a user to log on to the *PAYROLL* account. You will notice that the *PAYROLL* account has different lock codes in attributes 5 and 6, different system privileges and workspace in attribute 8, and – most importantly – has:

R

in attribute 9. It is this R in attribute 9 which prevents your user from breaking out of the log-on Proc.

The log-on Proc on the MD for the *PAYROLL* account will look like this:

item-id:	PAYROLL
attribute 1:	PQ
attribute 2:	HRUN PAYROLL MASTER.MENU
attribute 3:	P
attribute 4:	HOFF
attribute 5:	P

Obviously, when you are doing maintenance and other work on the account, you do not wish to be restricted to the closed system. For such work, you will log on to the master *WAGES* account. This will have a different – or no – log-on Proc.

9.6.1   Restricted menus

A user, or a group of users, is often only required to perform a limited number of well-defined operations on the computer. For example, data preparation staff may be allowed to input new orders, take on new product details, and amend prices and product details. But they may not be allowed to change stock levels or delete product details. The data-preparation supervisor, however, will probably be allowed to change stock levels and delete product details. In such cases, it is good practice to offer a menu of operations to the user immediately he or she logs on. Different users will, of course, be allowed to perform different operations – the data-preparation supervisor will have greater scope than the data-preparation staff – so it is necessary to be able to identify the user at log-on time in order to select the correct menu.

The user (or the user-group) may be identified by the account name or by some extra identification solicited by the log-on Proc. Having identified the user, the relevant menu is displayed on the screen and the user is asked to choose an operation from the list shown. This arrangement is attractive in that the user is not aware of the operations which he or she may not perform.

Alternatively, though cosmetically less attractive, the same menu may be shown to all users but restrictions placed on the options which users may choose. In this environment, the user may choose a particular option from the menu offered but then have this choice rejected with an appropriate message indicating insufficient authorization to perform that operation. This method has some advantages in programming ease and flexibility, but it has the serious disadvantage that it may act as a challenge and a taunt to the user to overcome the restrictions which are openly displayed.

Restricted menus are particularly powerful when linked to log-on Procs.

9.6.2   Program security

A program is held on a file in exactly the same way as a piece of data, and is therefore subject to the same lock-code security as data files.

You may write your own special security checks into a program. Thus, a program might ask the user to enter a special code-word before being allowed to use the program. This code-word may be changed regularly, or derived in a way known only to authorized users. If this is done, it is best *not* to hold the code-word as a literal. For example, if you had used the statements shown in Listing 9.1, then it would be very easy for someone to inspect the object program and locate or amend the literal 12345.

A better sequence might be that shown in Listing 9.2. This method can also be applied to prevent copies of your programs being taken and used on other machines. Most implementations have a user exit which returns the serial number of the system. If this were used, then the programmer could arrange to log the user off – or worse – if he or she tried to use a pirate copy. On the McDonnell Douglas implementation, such a system would look like that shown in Listing 9.3, and would only allow this program to be used on the system which has the serial number 12345. The previous comments on encoding the number 12345 apply here.

```
INPUT CODE
IF CODE#12345 THEN CHAIN 'OFF'
```

Listing 9.1

```
PASSWORD=''
FOR X=1 TO 5
PASSWORD=PASSWORD: X
NEXT X
IF CODE#PASSWORD THEN CHAIN 'OFF'
```

Listing 9.2

```
SHOULD=12345
REALLY=OCONV(0, 'U10DD')
IF REALLY#SHOULD THEN CHAIN 'OFF'
```

Listing 9.3

With a little thought, the programmer will be able to design even more devious ways of protecting his or her programs, and of retaliating for any abuse. Your programs can also be further protected if you remember that the Basic source program is only needed for compilation. After that, it may be removed from the system. If you are selling a program to another party, then you need only pass on the object version of your system. Similarly, the object program may be removed from the system if you are going to use the catalogued version.

9.7   STOPPING USERS CHANGING THE CONTENTS OF FILES

All those involved with the design and establishment of a database will consult with the technical staff and management to decide which files are to be accessible to which groups of users. We have seen the way in which the *L/RET* and *L/UPD* lock codes can be used to restrict access to files. The technical staff will provide management with a list of all files in the database and their contents. Management will then decide which user groups may read from or write to each of the files. For example, let us suppose that the personnel system contains the following files:

(a) *SALARIES* file containing salaries figures for staff.
(b) *PERSONNEL* file containing personal details such as name, age, address, etc.
(c) *CONFIDENTIAL* file containing initial interview analysis, review details, complaints, etc.
(d) *PROGRAMS* file containing personnel system programs.

Then we might allocate read or write access as shown in Table 9.1

Table 9.1

Files	Salaries Read	Salaries Write	Personnel Read	Personnel Write	Confidential Read	Confidential Write	Programs Read	Programs Write
Management	Yes	Yes	Yes	Yes	Yes	Yes	Yes	No
Technical	Yes	Yes	Yes	Yes	Yes	Yes	Yes	Yes
Accounts	Yes	No	No	No	No	No	Yes	No
Data entry	No	Yes	No	No	No	No	Yes	No

Lock codes may then be allocated to files and account synonyms to give the required pattern of authorization, and the operating system will check that the lock codes match. It is the analyst's responsibility to establish the correct lock codes for both files and accounts, and to ensure that they match correctly.

9.7.1 Preventing simultaneous file updates

When files are being updated from several terminals it is possible that two terminals may simultaneously wish to update the same item. This is a possible cause of error and may be prevented by applying group locks when updating from Basic programs. For this purpose, the following Basic statements are available:

```
READU
READVU
MATREADU
RELEASE
```

as discussed in Section 6.14.2.

9.8 DISCOVERING WHETHER DATA HAVE BEEN LOST OR CORRUPTED

A file statistics report may and should be produced after each file save. This will list the accounts which have been saved and give statistics for each file on each account. The statistics report should be scrutinized immediately for group format errors and the appropriate action taken if any are discovered.

The CHECK-SUM command enables the user to generate a hash-total for any attribute or attributes on a file. This may be used to see whether the file has undergone changes since the last CHECK-SUM was obtained. This is a useful method of detecting corruption of constant files including program and Proc files. A periodic CHECK-SUM on operational program files will quickly detect any changes to the files.

9.9 RECOVERING IN CASE DATA ARE LOST OR CORRUPTED

All Pick users must realize the importance of producing regular back-up copies of the system and its files. This is done by copying the contents of all files to magnetic tape and then restoring and re-organizing the files from this copy. If this is done thoroughly and frequently, then the consequences of accidental or intentional loss of data can be minimized.

There are several ways in which data may be lost or corrupted: a file or an item may be deleted by accident or unintentionally, or a group format error may occur. A group format error – GFE – is an inconsistency in the database which renders the data on all or part of a specific file inaccessible to Access and the other file-handling processors. It may occur due to someone upsetting the file definition information for the file, or – more rarely – it may be due to a machine error.

If back-up copies of the file are available, then they should be used to recover the corrupted data. If this cannot be done, then the FIX-FILE-ERRORS verb is available at TCL level.

9.10 RECOVERING IN CASE THE MACHINE GOES DOWN

After a machine failure or a system re-start, the processing continues, if possible, from the point at which it was interrupted. If this is successful, then no data will be lost and processing will resume from the point at which it stopped. Otherwise it will be necessary to try further recovery methods, as you will find in the operations manuals for your implementation.

(a) Try a warm start.
(b) If a warm start doesn't work then try a cold start.
(c) If a cold start doesn't work then try to reload the ABS section of disk from a magnetic-tape copy.
(d) If this ABS load doesn't work then call an engineer.

If program re-start facilities are required, within the usual batch meaning of the expression, then you must handle this in the same way as on a batch computer, taking your own check-points and writing your programs so that they are able to pick up and recover the processing from the last such check-point.

9.11 TIPS AND TECHNIQUES – SECURITY

You will find other tips and techniques in the relevant sections of Chapter 2 dealing with files, Chapter 3 dealing with accounts and Chapter 11 dealing with system management.

9.11.1 To switch the BREAK key on/off

The <BREAK> key is the final solution to programs and systems which have run riot – an unending loop, a 1000-page listing which you asked for by mistake. All these can be terminated by hitting the <BREAK> key and typing END or OFF, as is discussed in Section 12.8 where we deal with the interactive debugger.

However, there are occasions when you want to stop the user doing this. There are two reasons why the <BREAK> key should sometimes be disabled.

(a) When a program needs to update several files, the <BREAK> key may be disabled while the updating is taking place. Otherwise, some records may have been updated whilst others have not. There are two Basic verbs for this purpose:

```
BREAK-KEY-ON
BREAK-KEY-OFF
```

Within a Proc, you may invoke the corresponding TCL verbs:

```
DISABLE-BREAK-KEY
ENABLE-BREAK-KEY
```

(b) It is often desirable to prevent the user from reaching TCL level and the facilities which are available at that level. As we saw in Section 9.6 when we were dealing with log-on Procs and closed systems, your users could be offered a menu of operations as soon as they log on and only allowed to perform the operations offered in that menu. Normally they could press the <BREAK> key to exit from the menu and reach TCL level but this may be prevented by suitably altering the account definition item in the SYSTEM file.

10
The spooler

Within the Pick software, there are two important components: the monitor, which controls access to the central processor, the main memory, and disk storage; and the spooler, which controls access to the magnetic tape unit and the printer.

There is not much that you can do concerning the monitor. It is something of a *black box* which you have to accept. The spooler, however, is rather more tangible, so let us look at what it does.

We should, perhaps, say at the start that it is the spooler which varies most from one implementation of Pick to another. There are several points which apply generally, and these are incorporated into the general discussion here. All changes which have been made in the various versions render the spooler easier to use, or add more facilities.

The Pick spooler performs the same function as any spooler, except that *it is only used on program output*:

(a) It allows the output – this may be from a Basic program or one of your Access reports – which you have directed to the printer or magnetic tape, and holds this output on a disk file until the job has finished.
(b) At the end of a job, the output stored on the disk file is sent to the required device under the control of the spooler.
(c) Generally, your programs cannot access the spooler's files directly.

Such a system is clearly necessary in the Pick environment where dozens of users may all be producing reports at the same time.

10.1 SPOOL FILES AND SPOOL QUEUES

All output which is sent to the spooler is stored on one of a series of spool files, one report per file. Each file is identified by a sequence number 1, 2, 3 and so on. The actual limit depends upon your implementation. The first line of your output opens a spool file, and the file is closed at the end of the job of if you force it – as with the Basic PRINTER CLOSE statement.

Each file holds one report, and frames are added to the spool-file space automatically as the report builds up, and released as the output is dumped to the device. The FID and status of each file are held in the *spool queue*. There may be several spool queues, each identified by number or by name, and the queues are accessible to all users. The default queue is known as queue 0 or the STANDARD queue and is assigned to the system printer. All the jobs sent to the standard queue will be submitted for printing as soon as they are complete and the printer is free.

You may, if you wish, assign your output to a queue other than the standard queue. By doing this, your spool file will be held after the processing is complete, and you may then:

(a) Inspect it – to check the results before printing.
(b) Delete it – the results may be wrong.
(c) Move it to the standard queue – from where it will be output to the printer.
(d) Change the number of copies.
(e) Hold the job for printing overnight.
(f) Hold the job until you have had a chance to load and line-up the special stationery onto the printer.

If you need to do any of these, then you must become aware of the spooler.

The standard queue is normally assigned to the printer, but other queues can be assigned to the printer, to the magnetic-tape drive, or even to a terminal (port). If your system has several printers and several tape drives, then these can be controlled quite easily with the spooler.

10.2   THE DE-SPOOLING PROCESS

The de-spooler process takes your output – stored on disk – and sends it to the output device – this may be to the printer for printing or to the magnetic-tape drive. This process periodically examines the spool queue to see if there is a closed file needing output. If there is such a closed spool file, then the process attaches the printer and begins to output the report. When the report has been completely output, the process detaches the printer and deletes the spool file from the spool queue and releases the disk space used to hold the output.

The spooler process is started automatically when the system is re-started, such as that following a machine or power failure, and has its own workspace and its own routines, quite independently of the rest of the system.

10.3 SPOOLER ASSIGNMENT

The normal situation has been described above, printed output going into the spooler, onto a queue and then out to the printer. Most users can work quite innocent of the spooler – sending their Access reports and Basic program output into the system and out onto the printer. If we need to use the spooler, then we must use the spooler verbs.

The first verb allows us to assign our jobs to a queue other than the standard:

SP-ASSIGN options

This alters the spool procedure *for that user*, according to the options which you specify; these options apply until you issue another SP-ASSIGN or until you log off.

Typically, the SP-ASSIGN verb has such options as:

n   a number specifies how many copies you want to print.

= q   assigns your job to the queue named here instead of the standard queue.

S   suppresses the output, that is, it does not output the job to the printer. You might do this if you were just testing a program.

T   sends the job to the tape drive.

H   holds the file after it has been printed. You may want to print another copy later or you may want to inspect the output before printing.

I   requests instant printing, and causes de-spooling before the spool file is closed; as each frame of output is filled, it is sent to the device.

N   requests no spooling and causes direct output from the user's process instead of via the spooler, and *attaches* the device for use by your terminal alone, thus excluding all other users. The spool queue, the spool files and the spooler process are not involved at all.

Rn   is used with the Basic PRINT ON statement, and allows you to associate a specific spool queue with a specific document stream from your program.

You may have any valid combination of these options.

When your process begins to send output to the spooler and a spool file is opened, these options are stored in the spool queue so that the spooler process knows how to dispose of the file when it has been closed.

10.4 SP-EDIT

If you have asked that your output be assigned to a special spool queue, or if you have assigned it to the standard queue with the H option, then this output will be retained after output.

The files on the spool queues may be inspected by means of the SP-EDIT verb. This allows you to:

(a) Display parts of the file on your screen.
(b) Scan through the file to locate specific strings.
(c) Use a part of the file to align the stationery on the printer.
(d) Submit the file for output.
(e) Delete the file.

For security reasons, it is not possible to change a file which is held on the spooler – so it is not a true EDIT facility – otherwise you might have people amending their pay cheque! As we have already mentioned, it is not possible to access the spool files in your Basic programs. Some implementations, however, do offer a facility to unload a spool file and save it in Runoff format on an ordinary Pick file.

10.5   SP-TAPEOUT

The SP-TAPEOUT verb reads data from magnetic tape and outputs them according to the current SP-ASSIGN options. It is normally used in situations where the tape holds a spool file which was previously written to tape using the T option of SP-ASSIGN, and will accept any valid combination of the options shown for the SP-ASSIGN verb.

10.6   DEVICE ATTACHMENT

In Chapter 1 we saw that the standard Pick system has only one printer and one magnetic-tape device, but there may be many users. Any terminal can gain exclusive access to either of these devices by *attaching* the device. The TCL verbs which perform this are:

T-ATT to attach the tape unit.
P-ATT to attach the printer.

Once you have attached a device in this way, no one else will be able to use that device until you have released it by means of:

T-DET to detach the tape unit.
P-DET to detach the printer.

The U option can be used to detach the device from whichever terminal is using it:

```
T-DET (U)
P-DET (U)
```

Attaching the printer for your own use clearly has *anti-social* implications in a large installation, but you might have to do this if you were generating a report which would occupy too much disk space if it were to be held on a spooler queue in the normal way. This could be achieved with a sequence like this:

```
P-ATT
SP-ASSIGN N
RUN MYPROGS LONG.REP
SP-ASSIGN
P-DET
```

In this case, each line would be printed immediately it had been generated by the program LONG.REP.

If your system has several printers or several magnetic-tape drives, then you must specify an identifying unit number on these commands.

10.7   VERBS FOR USE WITH MAGNETIC TAPE

When you use the magnetic-tape drive, you will go through the following sequence of operations:

(a) Attach the tape drive.
(b) Indicate the record size which you will be using.
(c) Carry out your processing.
(d) Re-wind the tape.
(e) Detach the tape drive.

The repertoire of TCL and other commands allows you to do all of these.

Like any other magnetic tapes, those generated and used by Pick consist of a set of files separated by end-of-file markers. Each file consists of a set of records separated by end-of-record markers.

Let us look at the commands which you will use to manipulate your magnetic tapes:

• To attach the tape drive and indicate the record size, you will use the command:

```
T-ATT n
```

where *n* indicates the number of bytes in your record. Typical commands might be:

```
T-ATT
```

which will assume a record size of 512 bytes, the default value:

```
T-ATT 100
T-ATT 8192
```

If the tape drive is already attached to another terminal, then you will not be able to attach it or use it on another terminal.

You cannot perform any magnetic-tape operations until you have attached the tape drive with the T-ATT command.

- If you are reading in data from the tape, you may pick up the record size from the tape by issuing the command:

```
T-RDLBL
```

after you have attached the tape drive.

This command reads the tape label which the operating system writes to your output tape.

- Having attached the tape drive, you can perform any of the other tape-processing operations.
- To display the contents of the tape on your screen, you could use the command:

```
T-READ
```

and the display will continue until the end-of-file marker is reached. You can interrupt the process by hitting the <BREAK> key and typing END.

- To position the tape at the end of the current file, you will use the command:

```
T-FWD
```

- The command:

```
T-CHK
```

will cause the system to read through the current file – without displaying the records. It is designed to check a file for the presence of tape write-errors.

- To go back to the start of the previous file on the magnetic tape, you will use the command:

```
T-BCK
```

- To re-wind the tape to the very beginning, you will use the command:

```
T-REW
```

- The command:

```
T-WEOF
```

will write an end-of-file marker to the tape.

- The command:

```
T-WTLBL
```

will write a label showing the date and time, and the record size.
- Finally, you will detach the magnetic-tape drive by means of the command:

```
T-DET
```

To write data to your tapes and read them back, you can use either a Basic program or Access verbs. The Basic statements are:

```
READT variable ELSE statement
WRITET expression ELSE statement
WEOF ELSE statement
REWIND ELSE statement
```

as described in Section 6.15.
   The Access verbs are:

```
REFORMAT
SREFORMAT

T-DUMP
T-LOAD
```

The last two Access verbs are particularly useful for saving small amounts of data – single items or single files – and much simpler to handle than the longer file-save or account-save processes.

10.8   VERBS FOR CONTROLLING THE SPOOLER PROCESS

There are certain other verbs which are used to control the spooler and its output, and these will be more or less powerful according to your implementation:

SP-KILL this command can be used to cancel the output of the spool file which is currently being output by the spooler process.
SP-STOP this command can be used to stop the spooler process. It will take effect immediately after completion of the file output which is currently being performed.
   This verb is usually used when it is desired to output a line at a time (N option of SP-ASSIGN), but the spooler process is retaining the peripheral which you require (tape and/or printer).
   When the spooler process finishes outputting a file, and it finds that someone has done an SP-STOP, it detaches the printer and/or tape and stops. At this point, you can output a line at a time in the usual way, then detach the printer and/or tape and then re-start the spooler.
SP-RESUME this command re-starts the spooler process if it has stopped. It may have stopped either because of an SP-STOP (see above)

or because of an incident occurring when outputting to the tape unit, such as parity error, tape not ready or end of tape.

SP-SKIP This command stores a parameter within the spooler process, which specifies up to nine page ejects to be output to the printer on completion of printing by the spooler process. The parameter thus stored remains effective until the next SP-SKIP or cold start.

Note that the page ejects will only occur just before the printer is detached; they will not occur when one print-out is completed and the next print-out is already waiting in a spool file.

Obviously, this parameter will not affect line-at-a-time output.

SP-STATUS this command is the means of inquiring about the status of the spooler, and it tells us:

(a) What the spooler process is doing, that is, whether it is not active, outputting a closed file, or waiting for the printer to become detached.

(b) Which line the printer is attached to, if any.

(c) The status of the printer, that is, whether it is off-line, printing, or ready but inactive – in which case there is no message. Off-line printing.

(d) Which line the tape unit is attached to, if any.

SP-CHECK this command scans the spool queue, looking for files with the H option, and displays the result of its search.

Finally, there is one very important verb:

STARTSPOOLER or   **RESTARTSPOOLER** which will be required if, for any reason, the spooler has been corrupted. The operation will kill any jobs currently on the queues. This action is normally performed after a system re-start or after a cold start.

11
System management

The Pick system is designed to be used with a minimum of effort. For this reason, most Pick installations – even the large ones – do not have dedicated operators. It is not uncommon for a system to be left running day and night, without many of the conventional maintenance duties required on other systems.

The day-to-day running of the system is usually performed as one of the duties of the DP manager, the technical manager, the senior programmer or other member of the programming team. The actual work and who does the work generally depend upon the organization of the user's company. The operations tasks can be broken down according to the frequency with which you will need to perform them:

(a) Trouble-shooting tasks – handling problems such as disk head-crashes.
(b) Daily tasks – performing file saves, checking to see if the printer ribbon needs renewing.
(c) Weekly tasks – performing the complete file-save and file-restore operation.
(d) Periodic maintenance – essentially a service or preventive maintenance by the manufacturer.

To these, we might add such system or application tasks as the librarian, database administrator or data manager, who records what data items are held where, and the systems programmer, who is responsible for developing and publicizing standards and techniques for the organization.

Let us have a look at these in a bit more detail, and see how you might tackle these in your company.

We shall see that there are a number of routine and trouble-shooting tasks to be performed on a Pick system. Many of these are hardware dependent and will not, therefore, be described in detail. The reference manuals for your implementation and equipment will give complete details of the switches, knobs and keys which must be switched, turned and pressed.

There is one general observation which could be made at this point, however. Since Pick does not demand a dedicated operations staff, there is much to be said for the simplification of the routine tasks to be performed. This is particularly true where these tasks are to be carried out by the last one to leave, or by whoever is standing nearest to the machine at 5:30. Even a relatively simple process such as a file-save usually demands the user for information about the block size to be used, what tape label is to be assigned, and so on. The simpler you can make this, the better it will be for anyone to use. With this and similar processes, you should endeavour to modify the standard Procs and programs so that they make the standard assumptions and are thereby more simple to use.

11.1 SOME DEFINITIONS

Because certain terms and expressions are used with different connotations on different systems, you are reminded of the meaning of the following in the context of the Pick operating system. These and other important Pick terms are summarized in the Glossary at the end of the book.

RE-START the system may need to be re-started for any of a number of reasons.

A warm start may be necessary if the system stops functioning, without any apparent reason. After the warm start, the processing will continue as if there had been no interruption.

In order to recover from complete system failure, or after closing the system down for a time, a cold start should be performed.

ACCOUNT SAVE the dumping of the entire contents of the files of a specific account as formatted records on a magnetic tape – this produces an account-save tape.

ACCOUNT RESTORE the copying of the entire contents of the files of a specific account back onto the system from a file-save or account-save magnetic tape. When an account restore is performed, the files of the account are physically re-organized and re-located so that they occupy contiguous areas of the high disk space, and dead space and odd frames left after deleting files will not be recorded by the account-save operation and will be closed up.

BINARY SAVE the dumping of the entire contents of the system as a series of unformatted records to magnetic tape – essentially just a disk image dump. This produces a binary-save tape. This is also known as an unformatted file save. This and the corresponding binary-restore feature are not offered on some Pick implementations.

BINARY RESTORE the copying of the entire contents of the files of a specific account back onto the system from a binary-save magnetic tape – unlike the account restore, this does not re-organize the disk space.

This and the corresponding binary-save feature are not offered on some Pick implementations.

FILE SAVE the dumping of the entire contents of the system to magnetic tape – this produces a file-save tape. This is also known as a formatted file save.

FILE RESTORE the copying of the entire contents of the system from a file-save tape back onto the system. When a file restore is performed, the files of all accounts are physically re-organized and re-located so that they occupy contiguous areas of the high disk space, and dead space and odd frames left after deleting items will not be recorded by the file-save operation and will be closed up.

ITEM RESTORE the copying of one or more items on a specific file back to the system from a file-save or account-save magnetic tape. The item(s) to be restored may come from any file on any account, and may be restored to any file on any account.

SELECTIVE RESTORE is another name for item restore.

T-DUMP the data or dictionary section of a single file may be dumped to magnetic tape – item by item – by means of this Access verb. It is inefficient in comparison with the above routines, and is normally used for one-off security copies. The contents of several files may be dumped to a single magnetic tape by means of a sequence of T-DUMP sentences.

T-LOAD the items saved on magnetic tape by means of the T-DUMP command may be copied back onto disk by this operation.

ABS LOAD if the system software which is held in the ABS – absolute – storage has become corrupted for any reason, then this may be recovered by performing an ABS load from any file-save or account-save tape.

Table 11.1 shows the ways in which these facilities are used to save and retrieve a single item, an entire file, an account and the entire system.

Table 11.1

	To save	To recover
An item	T-DUMP file "item"	T-LOAD file from T-DUMP Selective restore from account save or file save
A file	T-DUMP file	T-LOAD file from T-DUMP Selective restore from account save or file save
An account	Account SAVE	Account restore from account save or file save
The system	File save Binary save	File restore from file save Binary restore from binary save

11.2   TROUBLE-SHOOTING TASKS

Things go wrong in the best-regulated families, and Pick is no exception:

(a) Data may be lost accidentally.
(b) Group format errors may be encountered.
(c) The disk space may be filled, or there may simply be a shortage of free space. Here are some solutions:
   (i) Try dumping a few large files to tape and then delete the files.
   (ii) Try dumping a few accounts to tape and then delete the accounts.
   (iii) Try performing a file save and then a file restore.
(d) Disk errors may be encountered. These are revealed when the system displays one or more ampersands on a user's terminal:

&&&&&&&&

This means that the system has tried unsuccessfully to read a section of the disk – usually one ampersand means ten unsuccessful attempts. The system will not proceed until the read has been completed successfully, so the end of the ampersands means the end of the problem. If you get screens full of ampersands then the manufacturer or the service engineer should be called in without delay.

Since such disk errors are associated with a specific part of the disk, they do not affect all users and they do not show on every terminal.

(e) There may be mechanical failure of the hardware. The manufacturer or the service engineer should be called in without delay.

11.3   DAILY TASKS

A daily routine should be established to produce the routine reports and to ensure that the computer area is kept clean, and that all the equipment is working properly:

(a) List the accounting information:

```
LIST ACC LPTR
```

and then clear the data section of the file:

```
CLEAR-FILE (DATA ACC
```

(b) Is the air-conditioning and the temperature/humidity recording equipment performing satisfactorily?
(c) Tidy the computer area and clear up any waste paper around the printer.

(d) If you can log on to the system, this is usually sufficient a test to see if the disks are working properly.
(e) Is the printer ribbon satisfactory?
(f) Is there sufficient stationery in the printer? Is a new box of paper available for use?
(g) The printer can be tested by a simple:

BLOCK-PRINT THIS IS OK

Most manufacturers have a more elaborate test to verify the performance of the features of the printer: character density; character alignment; line feed and carriage control.
(h) Clear away any unused write-rings around the magnetic-tape unit.
(i) Are all the magnetic tapes filed away correctly?
(j) Most manufacturers have tests to verify the performance of the features of the magnetic-tape unit.

The file-save/file-restore operation and the related duties are described in the next section.

11.4 WEEKLY TASKS

The most important task – the file-save/file-restore operation – should be performed as frequently as possible. The following points should be borne in mind when performing the file save:

(a) Have a carefully controlled archiving file for the file-save tapes. A 28-day cycle is adequate for most purposes. One installation which I know has the following tape-retention pattern for file-save tapes:
   (i) Daily tapes are retained for 28 days.
   (ii) Weekly (= Friday) tapes are retained for 1 year.
   This pattern requires eighty magnetic tapes.
(b) Perform the task overnight – if there are other users on the system during a file save, their response times will suffer and any work which they do *after* their files have been saved may be lost.
(c) If you must perform other tasks whilst users are logged on, then you must ensure that they are informed of the fact. They may wish to make a quick copy of any files which they changed whilst the file save was running, and then restore their files from these quick copied.
(d) Request a file-statistics report. This report shows a vast amount of information about the files which were saved:
   (i) The number of items on each file.
   (ii) The size of each file.
   (iii) Details of the overflow of the groups in each file – the figures

here will indicate whether the shape of a particular file should be re-defined.
(iv) Whether there were any group format errors on the file – this will highlight any such errors which were not detected by the user.
This information is essential to ensure good system usage.

When the file-save operation has been completed, the tape should be filed safely. Many installations lodge a copy with a bank or other secure place.

The following points should be borne in mind when performing the file restore:

(a) Perform the task overnight – if there are other users on the system during a file restore, their response times will suffer and any work which they do *after* their files have been restored may be lost.
(b) If you must perform other tasks whilst users are logged on, then you must ensure that they are informed of the fact. They may wish to make a quick copy of any files which they changed whilst the file restore was running, and then restore their files from these quick copies.

Another installation which I know, has written a simple Proc which performs the following tasks when it is set running around 16:30 each day:

(a) A simple program is invoked to select the correct tape for today's file save, and a message is displayed instructing the operator to mount the tape.
    If the tape is not available, then the operator can indicate this and alternative tapes will be suggested.
(b) The program then updates the tape-library information to show the status of the tape.
(c) The Proc invokes a simple Basic program which writes a number of test records to the magnetic tape and then reads these back.
    If there are any read/write errors, then the program terminates with a message asking for a new magnetic tape.
(d) The Proc sleeps until there are no active users on the system, or until all terminals (except its own) have been inactive for 10 mins.
(e) The file save is set in operation.
(f) The file-statistics file is scanned, and if there are any files with group format errors, the process terminates with a suitable message.
(g) If there are no group format errors, then the system re-winds the tape and performs a file restore and the users arrive next morning to a newly organized set of files.

This method assumes, amongst other things, that your system can be saved on one magnetic tape – some large installations require several reels – and that your users do not work overnight. If this is not the case, then you could modify the sequence accordingly.

Many of the operational aspects associated with the Pick operating system are frequently handled by the user's own housekeeping routines. However, it is important that you are able to perform these operations at their lowest level and without such utilities.

11.5   THE FILE SAVE

The sequence of events which takes place during the file-save operation is as follows:

(a) The *cold-start* section of the magnetic tape will be dumped to tape. This section will be used in the event of a cold start after a complete system failure, or when re-starting after the system has been closed down for some time.

(b) The ABS – absolute frames – section of the system will be dumped to tape. This section records the contents of the ABS frames. This is the group of frames which hold the system software and other routines supplied by the manufacturer.

The saving of the cold start and ABS sections is optional, and need only be done from time to time.

(c) The routine then dumps all the system files and the users' files to tape. This is done in the following manner:

 (i) The contents of the SYSTEM file are dumped to tape, and as this is being done, the routine produces a list of all the accounts on the system. This list contains the names of the accounts in the order in which they are encountered on the SYSTEM file.

 (ii) Using this list of the accounts on the system, the routine then processes each account in turn.

For each account on the system:

 (iii) The contents of the master dictionary are dumped to tape, and as this is being done, the routine produces a list of all the files on that account. This list contains the names of the files in the order in which they are encountered on the master dictionary of the account. Q-pointers and DX file-definition items will not be included in this list.

 (iv) Using this list of files on the account, the routine then processes each file in turn.

For each file on the account:

(v) The routine dumps the contents of the dictionary section to tape, and as this is being done, the routine produces a list of all the file-definition items on that dictionary. This list contains the names of the file-definition items in the order in which they are encountered on the dictionary of that file. DY file-definition items will not be included in this list.

(vi) Using this list of data-level identifiers on the dictionary, the routine then processes each data-level identifier in turn.

For each data-level identifier on the file dictionary:

(vii) The routine dumps the contents of the data section to tape.

Step (vii) is repeated for each data-level identifier on the file dictionary (remember that some implementations only allow a single data-level identifier, as we saw in Fig. 2.1), steps (v) to (vii) are repeated for each file on the account, and steps (iii) to (vii) are repeated for each account on the system.

This is illustrated in Fig. 11.1 which shows the sequence in which the files are dumped to tape:

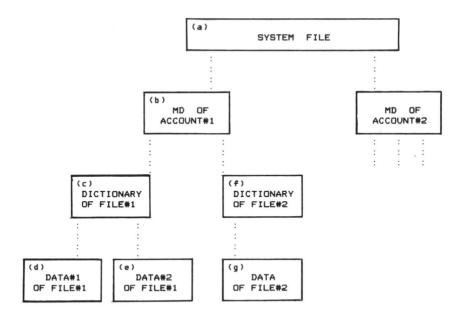

Figure 11.1

(a) the contents of the *SYSTEM* file;
(b) the contents of the master dictionary of the first account encoun-
     tered as (a) was dumped;
(c) the contents of the dictionary section of the first file encountered as
     (b) was dumped;
(d) the contents of the first data section encountered as (c) was dumped;
(e) the contents of the second data section encountered as (c) was
     dumped;
(f) the contents of the dictionary section of the second file encountered
     as (b) was dumped;
(g) the contents of the first (and only) data section encountered as (f)
     was dumped.

This process continues, dumping to tape all the files on each account, for
all accounts on the system.

As these various steps are carried out, the information about the
accounts and their files are stored on the file statistics file *STAT-FILE*.
This file holds details of each file on the system, including the *MOD*, the
SEP, the number of items, the maximum and minimum number of items
per group, the number of frames, the degree to which the groups of the
file are full or overflowing, and the number of group format errors on
the file. This file should be listed after each file save operation, and the
listing retained for reference. The contents of this listing should be
reviewed from time to time to ensure that the files have the most
suitable *MOD* and *SEP*.

11.6   LIBRARIAN OR DATABASE ADMINISTRATOR

Many of the important figures about the files and their sizes can be
obtained from the file-statistics report produced during the file-save
operation.

You should, however, remember that TCL and Access are available to
all Pick users, and a particularly convenient area to which they can be
applied is in producing (up to the minute) reports and analyses relating
to:

(a) The files which are held on each account – look at the MD for each
     account.
(b) The dictionary items which are held for each file – look at the DICT
     for each file on the account.

The TCL and Access facilities which are relevant in this context are:

(a) ISTAT file.

(b) COUNT file.
(c) LIST DICT file.

The danger is that the librarian might be tempted to produce too many reports. But if he or she remembers that these reports can be displayed at any time – rather than printing them off and filing them away – he or she will be encouraged to make better use of the on-line nature of Pick.

11.7   SYSTEMS PROGRAMMER

SYSPROG is an important account on all Pick machines. From SYSPROG it is possible to access a number of important and essential system files, including the most important of all files: *SYSTEM*.

The *SYSTEM* file contains the passwords, privileges and lock codes of all accounts and synonyms on the machine. It is therefore essential to security that access to the SYSPROG account should be limited by giving it a password and making the password known only to a few essential and responsible users.

SYSPROG is also the only account which is able to perform certain privileged operations:

(a) A range of facilities to save, verify and re-load data.
(b) File saves and file restores.
(c) Create accounts.
(d) Delete accounts.
(e) Various security facilities.

It should be remembered that the Pick system does not afford any special privileges to any user. The power of the SYSPROG account only exists because of the verbs which are available on that account and no other.

11.8   RE-CHARGING FOR USAGE

The *ACC* file records the log-on and log-off information on all accounts which have a U in attribute 9 of their account definition item. You will recall this from our discussion of the *SYSTEM* file.

The charges for a session are displayed when a user logs off. The current charges for a session may be displayed at any time by means of the verb:

CHARGES

For the situation in which one account is doing work which is to be re-charged to another account, the CHARGES-TO verb may be used to force the charges for a particular session to another account.

The information which is held on the ACC file can be listed by means of an Access sentence such as:

```
LIST ACC LPTR
```

as shown in Fig. 11.2, and this can then be used as a basis for re-charging for computer resources used by the departments of a company.

After producing this report, the data section of the file should be cleared by the command:

```
CLEAR-FILE (DATA ACC
```

The manner in which this information is converted into money depends upon your own particular installation, and how you wish to recoup your costs. A typical basis is to make a charge for the number of minutes of connect-time, and another charge for the number of charge units.

11.9 FILE ARCHIVES

When data have reached the end of their useful life, the user may often elect to archive the data and remove them from the system. This may be a single record which has been processed, or it may be an entire file at the year-end.

In the simplest case, off-line file archiving can be achieved by T-DUMPing the appropriate records or files to magnetic tape, and subsequently reinstating them by T-LOADs. Any file archiving system which demands facilities beyond those of the standard Pick operating system, must be done by the users' own application system.

Frequently, such solutions are simply harnesses for the standard facilities allowing the user to specify which file is to be saved, dumping the file to off-line storage, and then later allowing the file to be recovered. In addition, the surrounding application system must provide some means for indexing and locating the archived files, and this is often linked to a tape library system. When several files are to be retained on a single magnetic tape, the application system will also have facilities for adding data to the end of existing files on the tape and for producing an index of contents for the reel.

If you have sufficient disk space on your machine, then there is, of course, no reason why the files should not be archived on-line, that is, by copying the data from one file to another. In this case, the indexing and retrieval of the archived data is simplified.

11.10 TO ENSURE SYSPROG SECURITY

We have stressed the power of the *SYSPROG* account in terms of what

ACC	DATE. . . . . . LOGGED ON	TIME. . . . . . LOGGED ON	CONNECT. TIME	CHRGE UNITS	DISK. . . READS	TOTAL. . . CONNECT TIME	TOTAL. UNITS	TOTAL DISC READS
WAGES	09 SEP 85	10:08:50	00:00:04	118	16	32:42:	5177935	17593259
		10:09:18	00:00:07	177	20			
		10:09:50	32:42:	17793222	593223			
PROGS	23 SEP 85	12:42:36	00:11:24	6182	128	555:02:2 2	84796	3178
		12:54:29	00:01:01	945	100			
		12:38:51	00:23:22	17714	396			
		12:29:30	00:33:05	18306	604			
		12:33:25	00:29:12	15126	459			
		12:55:51	00:06:58	1922	97			
		13:02:56	00:00:04	197	3			
		14:02:57	00:01:12	900	62			
	31 AUG 85	14:14:58	00:01:30	822	81			
		14:23:55	552:02:48	2367	279			
	23 SEP 85	14:27:02	00:00:34	284	14			
		14:28:50	00:01:05	940	138			
		14:24:47	00:13:18	9044	446			
		14:30:10	00:09:18	4343	110			
		14:38:18	00:01:43	1670	51			
		14:28:02	00:12:00	2112	61			
		14:06:16	00:33:48	1922	149			
SYSPROG	23 SEP 85	13:07:20	00:00:16	1145	134	02:27:21	517521	12746
		11:44:34	01:34	44208981	4802			
		13:35:44	00:52	21307395	7810			

3 ITEMS LISTED.

Figure 11.2

verbs are available on its MD. This power can only be preserved if the MD and access to the SYSPROG account are maintained.

- Access to the account can be maintained by changing the password regularly – be sure to communicate the changes to all authorised users.
- A log on Proc should also be added. This would immediately log the users off if they did not satisfy certain criteria, such as:

  Which terminal is being used? The Proc could test whether the *SYSPROG* account is being used from a designated terminal or not. Can the user provide a further password? The Proc would ask for one or more special codes to be entered.

  Whilst this Proc/program is running, the <BREAK> key should be disabled to prevent the user dropping to TCL unhindered.
- Access to the files can be maintained by setting *L/RET* and *L/UPD* lock codes on all files on the account.

12
System features

In this chapter we shall take a brief look at some of the internal features of the operating system. The information presented here is only of interest to the technical user or systems programmer, and can be ignored by readers who are less technically motivated. The range of facilities and the details can be found in the reference manuals for your implementation.

12.1 MAIN MEMORY

Each Pick system has a specific amount of core memory available, and the size of the main memory for the system may be interrogated by means of the WHAT verb. Since Pick is a multi-user system, this memory is allocated to users by the Pick monitor on an *as-needed* basis. The monitor is the only item of software which is permanently resident in the main memory.

As information is required for processing, the frames holding that information are copied from the disk into the memory area. Whenever any user requires any information from the disk – this may be a frame of the program which is required for execution or an item which is to be read for processing – then the monitor checks a 'table of memory contents' to see if the (copy of the) required frame is already in the memory. If the required information *is* present in the memory, then your process is directed to the *memory copy* of the frame holding that information. When the same frame is used simultaneously by several users, then they will all process the same *memory copy* of that frame. If the required information is *not* present in the memory, then the monitor looks around the memory to find the least-used frame – that is the frame which has been unused for the longest period of time – and then writes this copy back to the disk – if a *write-required* indicator shows that the contents of this frame have been altered – and copies the new frame which you need into the memory, overwriting the old information in that part of the memory. When the situation arises in which a frame has to be swapped in this way, it is known as a *frame fault*.

Since some Pick systems may have a very large memory, there may be considerable loss of data if the system were suddenly to fail. Such losses can be minimized by demanding that frames be written back to the disk, not only when they are to be overwritten, but after, say, two hundred actions have been performed on a frame. This is done by the SET-WRITE verb on some implementations. If the SET-WRITE verb assigns too small a value, then much time will be wasted writing each frame to the disk after only a few activations. If too large a value is assigned, then there is a possibility of losing more data in the event of the system failing.

12.2 VIRTUAL MEMORY USAGE

The Pick operating system utilizes the available disk storage space by associating it with the actual core memory space, thus constituting a virtual memory system, with the operating system copying data from a disk into the memory for processing, and back, as required. In this section, we look at the usage of the various parts of this virtual storage, and the logical structure of the disk storage as shown in Fig. 12.1.

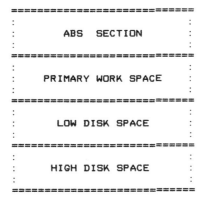

Figure 12.1

The first group of frames is called the ABS – absolute – section and is reserved exclusively for use by the operating system. The size of the ABS area can be interrogated by means of the WHAT or LIMITS verb. On later implementations, such as Open Architecture, the ABS frames are held on a Pick file, rather than in specific frames.

Immediately after the ABS section comes the *primary workspace*. Within this area, there is one thirty-two-frame block area reserved for each port on the system, whether the port is active or not. This block comprises the following:

(a) The process control block – PCB – one frame defining the state of that port at any instant. The data relating to each port includes the accumulators, the address registers, the arithmetic condition flags and the sub-routine return address stack. The location of the PCB of port 0 can be displayed by means of the WHAT verb, and the PCBs of the other ports can be calculated from this figure.
(b) The Proc work area.
(c) The Basic debugger work area.
(d) The system debugger work area.
(e) Six frames for each of three logical work areas called, symbolically, HS, IS and OS.

Initially, each port is assigned a set of eighteen contiguous frames for the HS, IS and OS workspaces. If a larger workspace is required, when you are processing large data records, for example, then you will demand that by means of the

SYS2(10)

entry of the SYSTEM log-on entry for each account. The (10) parameter requests that, when users of this account log on, they be allocated ten frames for each workspace, instead of the standard six.

The additional workspace, twelve frames in this example, is taken from the *low disk space* area which follows immediately after the primary workspace. The HS, IS and OS workspaces are always contiguous, and the additional HS, IS and OS workspaces are also always contiguous. Details of workspace allocation can be seen by means of the WORK-SPACE verb.

The remaining space in memory is called *high disk space* and is used for:

(a) Work areas for the system processors such as SORT and the spooler.
(b) Users' files.
(c) Standard files, including the standard files such as *SYSTEM*, *ERRMSG* and so on.

The amount of available disk space can be interrogated by means of the POVF verb, which displays a table showing the FIDs of unused frames, as described in Section 5.5.

When a new file is created, the system searches the high disk area for a contiguous block of frames large enough to accommodate the file. If there is insufficient space, then the process is abandoned and a message displayed.

When a file is deleted, the disk space is returned to the common pool of frames. The main (primary) space of the file is returned to the pool of contiguous frames, and any individual frames which were linked to the main file space to accommodate file overflow, will be attached to a chain of linked frames. The CLAIM verb can be used to convert any such linked frames – which are not available for use when creating a new file – into contiguous space, which can be used for new files.

If any process fails to find sufficient space in the high disk area, then it attempts to find space in the low disk area.

12.3   FRAME ADDRESSING CONVENTIONS

In user terms, all data are identified as items on a file. Data are read and written in this way by the Editor, the file processors and Basic programs. The operating system, however, identifies data by the FID of the appropriate frame and the position of the data within that frame.

If one of the system's processes is interrupted, or fails, then the operating system may display the address at which the interruption occurred. For example:

!123.45

means that the process was interrupted at the instruction which lies at byte 69 (= hexadecimal 45) in frame 123.

The only occasion on which you will need to address specific addresses is when you are using the interactive debugger. You will do this by specifying the FID of the frame to be considered and the displacement (distance from the start of the frame) of the byte to be processed.

12.4   PRIORITY AND TIMESLICE

Within the Pick operating system, no account has priority over any other account. The *SYSPROG* – systems programmer – account is only *special* in so far as it has privileged verbs, such as CREATE-ACCOUNT and DELETE-ACCOUNT, on its MD, whilst other accounts do not have these verbs.

When several users are processing, they are all treated with equal respect by the various Pick processors. The only preference which is afforded is by means of the timeslicing feature. The timeslice is the maximum length of time for which a port, or terminal, has control of the central processing unit. The monitor holds details of the timeslice allocated to each terminal.

The TIMESLICE verb is available to control this, and will, if your system privileges permit, allow you to display and change the values for the timeslice on any terminal. These are discussed below. By giving a terminal a large timeslice, the processes on that terminal will have longer control of the central processor to the detriment of processes on other terminals.

When a user starts to carry out a process, the identity of that user is placed in a queue of processes which are waiting for activation. To determine which terminal is to be activated next, the monitor scans the queue from top to bottom. If a terminal cannot be activated, as would happen with such events as:

(a) the process is waiting for a frame of information to come in from disk, a frame fault,
(b) the process is sleeping,

then the monitor ignores that terminal and scans the next entry in the queue.

When the monitor finds a terminal which *can* be activated, then that terminal is given control of the CPU until:

(a) It uses up its timeslice.
(b) It requires data input from the keyboard.
(c) The terminal output buffer is full.
(d) It suffers a frame fault, that is, when it references a frame which is not in the main memory.
(e) It de-activates itself, as with the Basic RQM statement.
(f) It references a frame which is being processed by another resource.

After a cold start, all terminals have a timeslice of 10 ms.

12.4.1   TIMESLICE verb

The general form of this verb is:

```
TIMESLICE (t) m
```

and this will assign a timeslice of *m* milliseconds to terminal number *t*, and then display a message to confirm this.

The following are valid forms:

TIMESLICE will display the timeslice for the current terminal, that is, the terminal issuing the command. The system will display a message such as:

```
TIMESLICE FOR LINE 27 EQUALS 10 MILLISECONDS
```

TIMESLICE 30 will set the current terminal's timeslice to 30 ms.
TIMESLICE (5) will display the timeslice for terminal number 5.

TIMESLICE (7) 50 will set the timeslice for terminal number 7 to 50 ms – thereby giving it a high processing priority.
TIMESLICE (A) will display the timeslice for *all* terminals.
TIMESLICE (A) 10 will set the timeslice for *all* terminals to 10 ms.

A timeslice can be any length in the range 1–1023 ms and, once set, the timeslice remains in effect until re-set by another TIMESLICE command.

Note particularly that the timeslice applies to a terminal and not to an account.

On some implementations, the timeslice cannot be changed.

12.5   FILE READING AND WRITING

Whenever you read a record from a file, the frame (or frames) which will be affected by such a read operation are copied into memory in the way described above, and the monitor records their identities in its table of contents, showing which frames are *held* in memory.

If the record is updated and written back to the file, then a *write-required* flag is associated with the frame to indicate that its new contents must be written back to disk when the frame's life expires. The frames are not physically copied back to disk until their life in the main memory *expires* by their becoming least-used. If you, or any other users, require to read the new *disk* record whilst that record is still in the main memory, then you will be directed to the main-memory version of the record.

Note that this method of handling physical read/write operations can result in loss of data if the system is not properly flushed before switching off the machine.

12.6   FRAME FAULTS

A frame fault is not an error condition in the accepted sense of the term, but it is the Pick term for the situation which arises when:

(a) You are processing,

and

(b) Your processing needs more information from the disk – this may be a data record, or a segment of your program,

and

(c) The frame holding that information is not held in the memory.

Whilst the operating system reads in the necessary frame, a *frame fault* is said to occur and your processing will be suspended until the required frame has been read in.

Do not confuse a *frame fault* with the more serious *group format error*.

12.7 FIRMWARE

Most Pick implementations hold the operating system as a collection of software, but some of the larger versions utilize firmware. This comprises many frequently used processes, such as terminal input and output, the virtual memory processor, the item-id hashing algorithm, the Access processor and the Basic compiler, which are held as microcode programs on integrated circuits. These integrated circuits are mounted on firmware boards and invoked in the same way as – but much faster than – a program would be called into operation.

12.8 INTERACTIVE DEBUGGER

You have already seen how you can interrupt any operation by pressing the <BREAK> key on the terminal keyboard. If you interrupt a Basic program whilst it is executing, then you will get a display something like:

```
*I40
*
```

showing that you are in the Basic symbolic debugger, and have interrupted the program at line 40.

If you interrupt any other process, you will get a display something like:

```
I 123.45
!
```

showing that the process has stopped at the instruction at byte 45 (hexadecimal 45 = decimal 69) of frame number 123, and you are in the *interactive* debugger.

With either debugger, you may type:

END<RETURN> to terminate the processing and return to TCL.
<**LINE FEED**> to continue the processing, if possible.
OFF<RETURN> to log off.

Let us look at some of the other commands which you can enter when the system displays the prompt:

```
!
```

! <LINE FEED> this causes the processing to continue from the point of interrupt (if possible). It is identical to the G command below.

! <RETURN> in general, <RETURN> after any of the DEBUG commands shown below will process the command but stay in the DEBUG mode.

! **P** this switches the terminal print output function on or off.

! **END**<RETURN> this terminates the current action and returns the processing to TCL.

! **END**<LINE FEED> this terminates the current activity and returns the processing to the calling Proc, if any.

! **OFF** this terminates the current activity and logs the account off the system.

! **G** this causes the processing to continue from the point of interrupt (if possible). It is identical to the <LINE FEED> response above.

The above commands are available to any user with SYS0 or higher privileges. The following commands are only available to users with SYS2 privileges.

! **A** this displays the address at which the execution was interrupted.

! **L***f* this displays the link fields of frame *f*. For example:

`!L12345<RETURN> 7 :  12346 12344 :  2`

indicating that there are seven next contiguous frames at forward link 12346, and two previous contiguous frames at backward link 12344.

! **G***aaaa* this causes the processing to continue from address *aaaa*, where *aaaa* is the address format shown below.

12.8.1 Caaaa;wwww – Iaaaa;wwww – Xaaaa;wwww

This causes the system to display the contents of the disk area specified by the user, and allows him or her to amend the data held at the frame address *aaaa*, where *aaaa* is the address format and *wwww* is the window which is to be displayed, as shown below:

Caaaa;wwww displays the information in character format.
Iaaaa;wwww displays the information in integer format.
Xaaaa;wwww displays the information in hexadecimal format.

In each case, the debugger will display the current contents of the specified window of the frame in the required format, and then invite the user to enter the new contents of that window. For example:

`!C12345;20<RETURN> . . . .=`

A response of <RETURN> will leave the frame unchanged. If the contents of the frame are to be changed, then the new data must be entered in the format shown below.

12.8.2   ADDRESS = FID and DISPLACEMENT

Each byte in the virtual memory is identified by an address consisting of a *FID* (frame identifier) and a *displacement*:

(a) The *FID* is the frame identifier of the frame containing the byte.
(b) The *displacement* is the number of bytes to be skipped (from the start of the frame) to reach the required byte. The displacement must represent a value in the range 0–512 inclusive.

The FID and/or displacement may be given in either decimal or hexadecimal. The general forms of an address are shown below, where *f* represents the FID value, and *d* represents the displacement value:

f,d specifies that the FID is given in decimal, and the displacement is given in decimal – this is the most commonly used form of this specification.
f.d specifies that the FID is given in decimal, and the displacement is given in hexadecimal.
.f,d specifies that the FID is given in hexadecimal, and the displacement is given in decimal.
.f.d specifies that the FID is given in hexadecimal, and the displacement is given in hexadecimal.
.d specifies that the displacement is given in hexadecimal.
,d specifies that the displacement is given in decimal.

12.8.3   WINDOW = DISPLACEMENT and SIZE

The *window* specifies the number of bytes to be displayed, and consists of an optional *displacement* and a specification of the *size* of the window:

(a) The *displacement* is the number of bytes by which the *address* is to be *moved back* – this has a negative effect, in that a value of *w* indicates that the window is to begin *w* bytes before the address specified by *f* and *d*. If the displacement is omitted, then a value of 0 is used.
(b) The *size* is the number of bytes to be displayed. If the size is omitted, then a value of 4 is used.

The displacement and/or the size may be given in either decimal or hexadecimal. The general forms of a window are shown below, where *w* represents the displacement, and *s* represents the size of the window.

;s specifies that the size is given in decimal – this is the most commonly used form of this specification.

;.s specifies that the size is given in hexadecimal.

;,s specifies that the size is given in decimal – this is equivalent to *; s.*

;w,s specifies that the displacement is given in decimal, and the size is given in decimal.

;w.s specifies that the displacement is given in decimal, and the size is given in hexadecimal.

;.w,s specifies that the displacement is given in hexadecimal, and the size is given in decimal.

;.w.s specifies that the displacement is given in hexadecimal, and the size is given in hexadecimal.

12.8.4 Replacement data

The data entered by the user in response to a prompt such as:

`!C12345;20<RETURN> . . . . =`

will be used to replace the data in the window, in this case 4 bytes.
The replacement data may be any of the following:

= **<RETURN>** this will leave the data unchanged and return to the ! prompt.

= **<LINE FEED>** this will leave the data in the current window unchanged and then pass on to display the data in the next window.

= **<CTRL>N** this will leave the data in the current window unchanged and then pass on to the next window, displaying the address and the data there.

= **<CTRL>P** this will leave the data in the current window unchanged and then pass on to the previous window, displaying the address and the data there.

= **'cccc<RETURN>** this will replace the data in the current window by the characters *cccc*.

= **n<RETURN>** this will replace the data in the current window by the integer value *n*.

= **.xxxxxx<RETURN>** this will replace the data in the current window by the hexadecimal data *xxxxxx*. There must be an even number of hexadecimal digits.

12.9 PROCESSING WITHOUT A TERMINAL

When you are carrying out any processing – be it a long Access report, an update program or whatever – your terminal will be locked out until the process has finished and control returns to TCL. This can be inconvenient.

Some implementations, including Open Architecture Pick, allow you – when you are in the midst of a process – to press the ESCAPE key and issue a TCL statement. The prompt at this stage will be:

::

to indicate the level at which you are processing, instead of the single colon. This second process may, in turn, be interrupted and a further operation invoked. The processing may be nested up to nine levels in this manner. When each process has completed, the previous process will be resumed.

Open Architecture and other implementations offer a terminal-independent process handler which allows you to log on to a remote terminal and invoke a process there, thus releasing your own terminal for other work. When this phantom processor is called up, it asks for information including:

(a) The name and password of the account which is to be used.
(b) The terminal or line number which is to be logged on. If that terminal is already in use, then the process will fail. You may ask the operating system to choose any free terminal.

   In fact, there does not have to be a physical terminal in existence on that line. For that reason, the system is sometimes known as the *phantom processor*.
(c) The stream of commands which is to be invoked.
(d) Whether the terminal output is to be displayed on the remote terminal (if the terminal is actually switched on), or whether the output is to be sent to the spooler.

When the processor has been invoked, your own terminal will be released for other work, and the system will then log on to the appropriate terminal, process the commands in the job-stream and then log off. Such a facility is particularly useful for producing long reports, for generating select lists and saved lists based upon large files, for background processing and for batch applications.

12.10 GROUP FORMAT ERRORS

Group format errors – GFEs – are detected by the operating system when the 4-byte hexadecimal item-length count is corrupt or is incompatible with actual data within the item, or when there is incompatibility in the forward and backward link control information in a group of frames.

Their presence is shown by a message of the form:

```
*GROUP FORMAT ERROR 30475
```

showing that there is a GFE in frame 30475. Such a message will be displayed if you attempt to use the Editor, Access or any other system utility on a group which contains a GFE.

On some implementations, the detection of a GFE will automatically invoke a GFE handler which will offer the user the options of ignoring the error, entering the system debugger, or fixing the error. The last of these will invariably result in the loss of some data from the group concerned.

On implementations such as those of McDonnell Douglas, the FIX-FILE-ERRORS facility is provided to assist users in recovering from GFEs. In many cases, this is the only way of recovering data which would be lost or inaccessible by means of the standard Pick processors. Any recovered items, or data records, are deleted from the original file and saved on the file called *TSYM* which you must create on your own account.

To fix a GFE you should follow these steps:

(a) Create a DICT level file called *TSYM*:

```
CREATE-FILE (DICT TSYM 17, 1
```

The size of the file is arbitrary.

If the file already exists, then you can use this after clearing any previous data:

```
CLEAR-FILE (DICT TSYM
```

(b) Type the command:

```
FIX-FILE-ERRORS ffffff
```

where *ffffff* is the name of the file on which GFEs were detected. The FIX-FILE-ERRORS operation will scan through your file *ffffff* and transfer to the TSYM file any data which have GFEs.

(c) Edit the items on TSYM so that they reflect – as accurately as possible – the correct format of the items as they were on your file *ffffff*.

This will require knowledge of the data item format.

(d) Copy the items back to the original file *ffffff* and at the same time allocate the required item-ids:

```
COPY TSYM H30475 2H30475 3H30475 (D)
TO(ffffff A002 B006 F009
```

The following points should be borne in mind when using the FIX-FILE-ERRORS verb:

(a) If the FIX-FILE-ERRORS routine encounters the system separator segment mark (hexadecimal FF) in the attributes of an item, then it will generate an error message of the form:

`+SM AT fid,dd`

showing the position of the offending character (as a displacement *dd* from the beginning of frame *fid*), and the erroneous items will be amended and returned to the original file, the offending character being replaced by the character hex(5F), and no item will be placed on *TSYM*. A segment mark, or any other non-hex character, in the item byte count will, however, generate an item on *TSYM*.

(b) The item recovered as a result of a non-hex character in the item byte count will necessarily lose much of its data.

(c) The FIX-FILE-ERRORS operation overwrites all the items on the DICT of the file *TSYM*, including the data-level identifier, and you should understand how to re-create the TSYM file when necessary. For this reason, the facility should not be used again – by any user on the same account – before the results of a previous FIX-FILE-ERRORS have been recovered, and the *TSYM* file cleared or deleted.

(d) Before FIX-FILE-ERRORS is used you should investigate and understand the nature of the GFE. If there is another method of reconstructing the data which is 100% reliable then this should be used.

(e) Patching of frames, for any reason, is not recommended. It is undertaken at your risk.

(f) Before using FIX-FILE-ERRORS you should ensure that *TSYM* is empty and that no other user will be handling FIX-FILE-ERRORS at the same time.

(g) Because the operating system is unable to interpret the data correctly – otherwise there would not be a GFE – the data which are left on *TSYM* are in a very raw state, and include the 4-byte hexadecimal item-length field *and* the item-id of the original items.

The FIX-FILE-ERRORS operation should only be utilized by experienced users and then with great care, and for this reason it is recommended that you follow the above sequence very carefully.

Appendix 1
A Pick glossary

- In this appendix we define some of the terms which you will encounter in the present book and elsewhere in the Pick literature.

ABS FRAMES: The system software which is held in the ABS – absolute – area of disk storage. If this area has become corrupted for any reason, then it may be recovered by performing an ABS load from a file-save or account-save magnetic tape.

ACCESS: The Pick database retrieval language which is used to make inquiries and produce reports on the items held on your files. You will establish a set of dictionary definition items to instruct the Access processor how the various attributes of the data items of your files are to be interpreted. Some implementations use other names, such as English.

ACCOUNT: A working environment based around a collection of files which are available to all users of that account.

ACCOUNT DEFINITION ITEM: The item on the system file which holds the password, the location of the MD, the lock codes, the system privileges, the additional workspace requirements and the logging indicator for each account.

ACCOUNT RESTORE: The copying of the entire contents of the files of a specific account back onto the system from a file-save or an account-save magnetic tape.

ACCOUNT SAVE: The dumping of the entire contents of the files of a specific account on a magnetic tape. This produces an account-save tape.

ADDITIONAL WORKSPACE: Any additional disk storage space which is to be allocated to an account in order to allow the users to process large programs or large data items. The required additional workspace is specified in the account definition item for the account. Normal workspace comprises three sets of six frames each.

ATTRIBUTE: The Pick equivalent to the term field which is used in other areas of data processing. An item may comprise one or more attributes, each attribute may comprise one or more values, and each value may comprise one or more secondary values.

ATTRIBUTE MARK: The system character (hexadecimal 254) which separates the individual attributes in an item.

BASIC: The high-level Pick programming language.

BINARY RESTORE: The copying of the entire contents of the system from a binary-save magnetic tape back onto the system. Unlike the account restore, this does not re-organize the disk space. Binary save and binary restore are not offered on some Pick implementations.

BINARY SAVE: The dumping of the entire contents of the system to magnetic tape. Essentially, this is just a disk-dump, and produces a binary-save tape. It is also known as an unformatted file save. Binary save and binary restore are not offered on some Pick implementations.

CATALOGUE: The action of saving a compiled Basic program in a loadable core-image form. This makes the loading and execution of such programs much faster. External sub-routines and programs which use external sub-routines must be catalogued.

CLOSED SYSTEM: A working environment in which the user is retained under the control of an application program, without ever being allowed to use the TCL language.

COLD START: A cold start should be performed in order to recover from complete system failure, or after closing the system down for a time.

COMPILE: To convert a set of Basic statements into an executable object program. The compiler also diagnoses any syntax errors in the Basic program.

DATA-LEVEL IDENTIFIER: An item on the dictionary section of a file which specifies the location and shape of the data section of the file.

DATA SECTION: That section of a file which contains the true data of the file. The dictionary definitions which Access uses to interpret the file are held on the dictionary section.

DATE: An internal calendar allows the date to be handled internally as an integer number, with 31st December 1967 as day 0. Dates before that have negative values. This internal date can be stored and retrieved, and Access, Basic and Runoff have facilities to convert it to external forms such as 29 JUL 1987 and 29/07/87.

DEFINITION: May refer to a file definition or a dictionary definition item.

DICT: *See* Dictionary.

DICTIONARY: That section of a file which contains definitions which Access uses to interpret and display the attributes of the items which are held on the data section.

DICTIONARY DEFINITION: An item on the dictionary section of a file which enables Access to interpret and display the data held on the data section of the file.

DL/ID: *See* Data-level identifier.

FIELD: *See* Attribute.

FIELD SEPARATOR: One of the characters which Pick uses as a data delimiter. They are the segment mark (character 255), attribute mark (character 254), value mark (character 253) and secondary-value mark (character 252).

FILE: A collection of items. This is the standard usage of the term within data processing.

FILE DEFINITION: An item on the master dictionary which defines a file, showing its location and its shape.

FILE RESTORE: The copying of the entire contents of the system from a file-save tape back onto the system.

FILE SAVE: The dumping of the entire contents of the system to magnetic tape. This produces a file-save tape, and is also known as a formatted file save.

FRAME: The basic unit of storage on the Pick system. This is 512 bytes in size, of which 500 are available for data, the remaining 12 bytes being used to show the linkage between frames. Some implementations have a 2048-byte frame, with 2000 bytes available for data.

ITEM: Item is the Pick equivalent to the term record which is used in other areas of data processing. A file is made up of one or more items. Each item may comprise one or more attributes, each attribute may comprise one or more values, and each value may comprise one or more secondary values. Each item is identified by its unique item-id.

ITEM-ID: This is the Pick equivalent to the record key in other areas of data processing. Each item on a file is uniquely identified by its item-id.

ITEM RESTORE: The copying to one or more items of a specific file from a file-save or account-save magnetic tape. This is another name for selective restore. The item(s) to be restored may come from any file on any account, and may be restored to any file on any account.

LOCK CODE: The information held in attributes 5 and 6 of file definitions and account definitions which enables read or write activities on those files to be restricted.

LOG ON and LOG OFF: The action of identifying yourself to the Pick operating system by typing in your account name. If your account name and password are correct, then you will be allowed to use the system. Log off is the action of terminating your use of the Pick system.

LOG-ON PROC: If the master dictionary for an account contains a Proc with the same name as the account itself, then this Proc will be invoked whenever a user logs on to that account. This enables closed systems to be implemented.

M/DICT: *See* Master dictionary.

MASTER DICTIONARY: The main file of every account which holds all the TCL verbs, Procs and file definitions for that account. It is also known as the MD and M/DICT.

MD: *See* Master dictionary.

PASSWORD: An optional piece of information to be specified in addition to the account name in order to log on to an account.

PROC: The low-level Pick programming language. A sequence of statements in the Proc language is also called a Proc, just as a sequence of statements in the Basic language is called a program.

PROGRAM: A sequence of statements in the Basic language is called a program.

Q-POINTER: An item on the master dictionary which enables that account to access a file on another account.

RECORD: *See* Item.

RECORD KEY: *See* Item-id.

RE-START: The system may need to be re-started for any of a number of reasons. This may be done by a warm start or cold start.

RUNOFF: The Pick text-processing package.

SECONDARY VALUE: A value may comprise one or more secondary values.

SECONDARY-VALUE MARK: The system character (hexadecimal 252) which separates the individual secondary values in an item.

SELECTIVE RESTORE: This is another name for item restore.

SYNONYM: An alternative name by which an account may be used. Such synonym accounts normally have privileges or lock codes different to those on the main account.

SYSTEM FILE: The file which holds all the account definition items for the accounts which are available on your Pick machine.

SYSTEM PRIVILEGES: That part of the account definition item which specifies which of the system's special features the users of an account may invoke.

T-DUMP: The data or dictionary section of a file may be dumped to magnetic tape – item by item – by means of this command. It is inefficient in comparison with the file-save and account-save routines, and is normally used for one-off security copies.

T-LOAD: The items saved on magnetic tape by means of the T-DUMP command may be copied back onto disk by this operation.

TCL: The Pick terminal control language: a primitive command language which you will use to tell the operating system what work you want to do. At TCL level, you may type in any verb, Proc or Access sentence.

TIME: An internal clock allows the time to be handled internally as an integer number, with midnight as time 0 and the clock incrementing in units of one second. This internal time can be stored and retrieved, and Access, Basic and Runoff have facilities to convert it to external forms such as 11 : 30 : 59 and 11 : 30 AM.

TIMESLICE: The maximum length of time for which a user is allowed to process. This is normally 10 ms, and after that time, the user's processing is interrupted and another user is allowed to process. Under certain conditions, the user's processing may be terminated before his or her timeslice has expired. The timeslice is also known as the quantum.

VALUE: An attribute may comprise one or more values, and each value may comprise one or more secondary values.

VALUE MARK: The system character (hexadecimal 253) which separates the individual values in an item.

VERB: Any of the repertoire of TCL commands which are provided to operate the Pick system.

WARM START: It may be necessary to re-start the system if it stops functioning, for any reason. After the warm start, the processing will continue as if there had been no interruption. If a warm start does not succeed, then a cold start must be performed.

WORKSPACE: *See* Additional workspace.

Appendix 2
The Pick system –
an application user guide

We have seen that Pick is an excellent tool for non-technical users. Nevertheless, when you have written a system for your users, you still have to tell them how to use it. This appendix is offered to these ends.

A2.1 USING THE COMPUTER

When you are using a Pick system, you will almost certainly be provided with a *user manual* which will answer questions such as:

(a) What information am I expected to enter?
(b) What does the information look like?
(c) Where do I get the information from?
(d) How do I switch the computer terminal on?
(e) How do I use the computer system?
(f) What happens if I make a mistake?
(g) Can I correct a mistake?
(h) What do I do with the forms when I've processed them?
(i) What do I do when I've done all my work?
(j) How do I switch the computer terminal off?

However, the following general points should be observed when using a Pick system.

A2.2 BEFORE YOU START

Before you begin, let us have a look at the computer terminal which you'll be using:

(a) The *screen* is the place where the computer displays your results. When you type in, the computer will also display what you are typing. Make sure that you can see the screen properly without straining your eyes or your neck.

(b) The *keyboard* is the means by which you type information into the computer. Later on we'll see what to do if you make a mistake.

The rest of the computer – the printer, the magnetic tapes and the disks – need not concern you just yet.

(a) Make a note of where the *on* switch is on the computer terminal which you will be using, and ensure that the terminal is *on* before you start.
(b) Make a note of the *log-on* code which you must use, and enter this when the computer asks you to:

LOGON PLEASE:

(c) You might also need a password. Make a note of this too.

A2.3   USING THE SYSTEM

If you have never used a computer terminal keyboard before, then you probably think that you'll never get the hang of it. But you will!
   Let us have a look at some of these keys:

(a) The digits 0, 1, 2, 3, 4, 5, 6, 7, 8 and 9 may be entered either with the keys along the top row of the keyboard, or with the special key-pad which you may have on the right of the keyboard.
(b) The keyboard is used exactly like a standard typewriter keyboard.
(c) The space is entered by pressing the long space-bar at the bottom of the keyboard.
(d) Always press the RETURN key to indicate the end of a piece of data.
(e) The SHIFT key is required to enter certain special characters, as with a standard typewriter.
(f) The only coloured keys which you will use are:
    (i) RETURN – to send your information to the computer.
    (ii) BACK SPACE – to correct a typing error.
    (iii) SHIFT – to type the special characters.
(g) In almost every case, the screen will display the information which you type in.
(h) You must distinguish carefully between certain characters, such as:
    (i) The letter I and the number 1.
    (ii) The letter O and the number 0.
    (iii) The letter T and the numbers 1 and 7.
    (iv) The letter Z and the number 2.
    (v) The number 7 and the number 1.

This is particularly important when you are typing information which is taken from hand-written documents.

A2.4   CORRECTING MISTAKES

(a) If you notice a mistake, then use the BACK SPACE key to erase the incorrect characters and then re-type the correct characters *before* you press the RETURN key.

(b) If you notice a mistake *after* you have pressed the RETURN key, then the possible course of action is:

  (i) The computer system may detect your error and ask you to re-enter it correctly:

    (1) The contents of a field may be invalid, for example:

        `30 XANUARY 1984`

    (2) The customer number may not exist.

    (3) A date may be invalid, for example:

        `30 FEB 1984`

    in which case you should re-enter the line.

  (ii) The computer system may accept your data:

    (1) You may have entered an address as

        `34 HIGH ST`

    instead of

        `43 HIGH ST`

and the computer may not have any way of knowing that 34 is incorrect.

(2) You may have entered customer number

    `0123`

    instead of

    `9123`

    and both may be acceptable.

(3) You may have entered:

    `20 MARCH`

    instead of

    `21 MARCH`

    In this case, you should make a note of the mistake and correct it later.

(c) If your keyboard has a separate pad of keys on the right, then you must only use the numbers 0, 1, 2, 3, 4, 5, 6, 7, 8, 9 and the full stop, unless you are told otherwise.

A2.5   WHEN YOU HAVE FINISHED

(a) Type the full stop (.) to terminate your processing.

(b) If the computer system responds with a question mark in the top left-hand corner of the screen, then you should type

`OFF`

followed by the RETURN key.

(c) If the computer system responds with a colon (:), then you should type

`OFF`

followed by the RETURN key; this will disconnect you from the computer.

(d) If the computer responds with an asterisk (*), then you should type

`OFF`

followed by the RETURN key; this will disconnect you from the computer.

(e) If the computer responds with an exclamation mark (!), then you should type

`OFF`

followed by the RETURN key; this will disconnect you from the computer.

(f) When the computer asks you to

`LOGON PLEASE:`

then you may enter your *log-on* code and start your work again, or you may switch the terminal on/off switch to *off*.

Index